VOYAGES
IN ENGLISH
GRAMMAR AND WRITING

Patricia Healey, I.H.M.
B.A., Immaculata University
M.A., Temple University
20 years teaching; 20 years in administration

Irene Kervick, I.H.M.
B.A., Immaculata University
M.A., Villanova University
46 years teaching

Anne B. McGuire, I.H.M.
B.A., Immaculata University
M.A., Villanova University
M.A., Immaculata University
*16 years teaching; 14 years as elementary
principal; 10 years staff development*

Adrienne Saybolt, I.H.M.
B.A., Immaculata University
Pennsylvania State Board of Education,
professional certification
M.A., St. John's University
40 years teaching

LOYOLAPRESS.

Loyola Press has made every effort to locate the copyright holders for the cited works used in this publication and to make full acknowledgment for their use. In the case of any omissions, the publisher will be pleased to make suitable acknowledgments in future editions. Continued on page 567.

Cover Design: Think Book Works   Cover Artist: Pablo Bernasconi
Interior Design: Kathryn Seckman Kirsch/Maggie Hong/Loyola Press
Art Director: Judine O'Shea/Loyola Press
Editor: Jennon Bell/Loyola Press

ISBN-13: 978-0-8294-2840-7
ISBN-10: 0-8294-2840-2

LOYOLA PRESS.
3441 N. Ashland Avenue
Chicago, Illinois 60657
(800) 621-1008
www.loyolapress.com

Webcrafters / Madison, WI, USA / 10-09 / 1st Printing

Contents

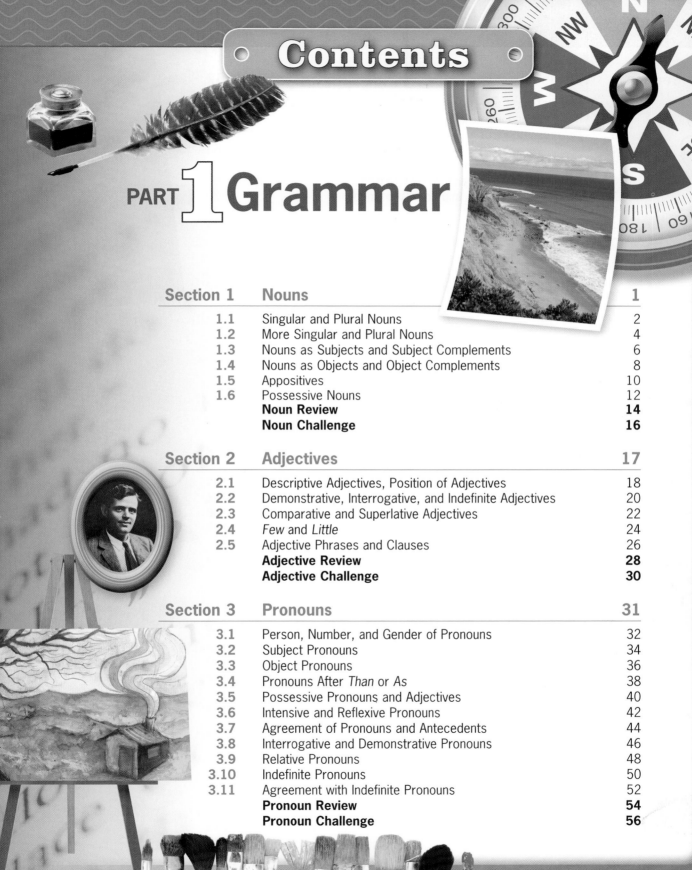

PART 1 Grammar

PART 2 Written and Oral Communication

I'd definitely like to take a few more persuasive writing classes.

SECTION ONE

Nouns

1.1 Singular and Plural Nouns

A **noun** is a name word. A **singular noun** names one person, place, thing, or idea. A **plural noun** names more than one person, place, thing, or idea.

Add -s to most nouns to form the plurals.

SINGULAR	PLURAL		SINGULAR	PLURAL
artifact	artifacts		minute	minutes

Add -es to form the plural of a noun ending in s, x, z, ch, or sh.

SINGULAR	PLURAL		SINGULAR	PLURAL
guess	guesses		crash	crashes

Form the plural of a noun ending in y preceded by a vowel by adding -s.

SINGULAR	PLURAL		SINGULAR	PLURAL
monkey	monkeys		birthday	birthdays

Form the plural of a noun ending in y preceded by a consonant by changing the y to i and adding -es.

SINGULAR	PLURAL		SINGULAR	PLURAL
baby	babies		victory	victories

Some plural nouns are not formed by adding -s or -es. Check a dictionary for the correct plural form.

SINGULAR	PLURAL		SINGULAR	PLURAL
ox	oxen		goose	geese
oasis	oases		medium	media

The plural forms of some nouns are the same as the singular forms.

SINGULAR	PLURAL		SINGULAR	PLURAL
series	series		corps	corps
sheep	sheep		Portuguese	Portuguese

EXERCISE 1 Some of the nouns in the list below are singular, and some are plural. Use a dictionary to help you write the correct singular or plural form of each one.

1. ranch
2. barrel
3. bus
4. taxis
5. berries
6. journeys
7. colony
8. fisherman
9. party
10. lilies
11. crises
12. buzz
13. datum
14. thesis
15. larva
16. women

EXERCISE 2 Complete each sentence with the plural form of the noun or nouns in parentheses.

1. Adults always tell _____ (child) to eat their fruits and vegetables.
2. A lot of the food we buy and put on our _____ (dish) is changing.
3. Every day there are new _____ (discovery) in genetic engineering.
4. Genetic engineering is the science of changing organisms by making changes in their _____ (gene).
5. It can produce changes in _____ (species).
6. For example, it can make tomatoes that are redder and look more attractive in supermarket _____ (display).
7. In the future there may be _____ (peach) that are resistant to frost.
8. Scientists also hope to produce _____ (potato) that are resistant to disease.
9. But nothing tastes as good as the _____ (berry, pea, and tomato) that you can grow yourself.
10. We grow more vegetables than we can eat, so we sell the rest at _____ (farmer's market) around the state.

APPLY IT NOW

Look up each singular noun in a dictionary and write the plural form. Then use either the singular or plural form in a sentence.

1. princess
2. inquiry
3. species
4. buffalo
5. church
6. chimney
7. process
8. appendix
9. flurry

1.2 More Singular and Plural Nouns

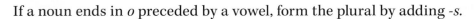

If a noun ends in *o* preceded by a vowel, form the plural by adding *-s*.

SINGULAR	PLURAL		SINGULAR	PLURAL
studio	studios		stereo	stereos

If a noun ends in *o* preceded by a consonant, form the plural by adding *-es*. There are exceptions to this rule. Always check a dictionary.

SINGULAR	PLURAL		SINGULAR	PLURAL
tomato	tomatoes		hero	heroes
EXCEPTIONS			*EXCEPTIONS*	
piano	pianos		kimono	kimonos
zero	zeros or zeroes		cello	cellos

For most nouns ending in *f* or *fe*, form the plurals by adding *-s*. For some nouns, however, you must change the *f* or *fe* to *ves*. Always check a dictionary.

SINGULAR	PLURAL		SINGULAR	PLURAL
roof	roofs		loaf	loaves

Form the plurals of most compound nouns by adding *-s*.

SINGULAR	PLURAL		SINGULAR	PLURAL
disc drive	disc drives		fireplace	fireplaces
cover-up	cover-ups		drive-in	drive-ins

Form the plurals of some compound nouns by adding *-s* to the principal words or by making the principal word plural. Always check a dictionary.

SINGULAR	PLURAL		SINGULAR	PLURAL
brother-in-law	brothers-in-law		man-of-war	men-of-war

Form the plurals of compounds ending in *ful* by adding *-s*.

SINGULAR	PLURAL		SINGULAR	PLURAL
handful	handfuls		spoonful	spoonfuls

Some nouns are used only in the plural form.

clothes   **pliers**   **jeans**

Some nouns are plural in form but singular in meaning and use.

politics   **measles**   **news**

EXERCISE 1 Write the plural of each noun. Check a dictionary if you are not sure of a plural form.

1. lady
2. suffix
3. trespasser
4. radio
5. dispatch

6. sister-in-law
7. jockey
8. eyetooth
9. chimney
10. burro

11. mumps
12. shelf
13. alumnus
14. fox
15. cargo

16. sketch
17. fish
18. hoof
19. mouse
20. cactus

EXERCISE 2 Write these words in two columns, one column with singular forms and the other with plural forms. Some words will go into both columns. Check a dictionary if necessary.

zoos	Balinese	oases	species
potatoes	cod	data	larva
corps	crisis	trout	swine
salmon	miracles	men	series
children	victories	woman	strata
taxes	vertebrae	goose	radius
deer	Inuit	grouse	treasure

APPLY IT NOW

You and your friends are planning a camping trip. Create a list of supplies that you will need for the whole group. Use both singular and plural nouns.

With an adult, search online for camping necessities.

Tech Tip

1.3 Nouns as Subjects and Subject Complements

A noun can be used as the subject of a sentence. The **subject** tells what or who the sentence is about.

In this sentence the noun *wars* is the subject.

> *Wars* **have occurred throughout human history.**

A noun or pronoun that renames or identifies the subject is a **subject complement.** A subject complement follows a linking verb such as *be* and its various forms *(am, is, are, was, were)*, *become*, and *remain*.

In this sentence *World War II* is the subject and *conflict* is the subject complement.

> *World War II* **was a major** *conflict* **of the 20th century.**

What are the subject and the subject complement in this sentence?

> **Winston Churchill became the prime minister of England for the first time in 1940.**

To find the subject, ask yourself *who* or *what* the sentence is about *(Winston Churchill).* Then see if there is a linking verb. If so, ask *Is the linking verb followed by a noun that renames the subject?* That noun is the subject complement *(prime minister).*

EXERCISE 1 Name the subject of each sentence. Name the subject complements if there are any.

1. Winston Churchill's role in World War II was crucial.
2. His most important contribution was to give the British people hope.
3. German planes were bombing London primarily by night.
4. Great Britain needed aid during the war.
5. President Franklin D. Roosevelt convinced the United States to help Britain.
6. Churchill was a brilliant orator and a source of strength.
7. His six-volume publication *The Second World War* earned Churchill the Nobel Prize for literature.
8. Churchill was also an officer in the British army, a historian, and an artist.
9. London is a city that has seen its share of wars.

EXERCISE 2 Identify the subject of each sentence. Then name the subject complement if there is one.

1. The United Kingdom includes England, Scotland, Wales, and Northern Ireland.
2. Great Britain is only England, Wales, and Scotland.
3. The British monarch remains a symbol of the nation.
4. The reigning monarch has little real power.
5. The real ruler of Britain is Parliament.
6. Parliament is the legislature, similar to the U.S. Congress.
7. Cricket has been a popular British sport.
8. Baseball had its origins in cricket.
9. Shepherd's pie is a popular British food.
10. Its main ingredients are beef and potatoes.
11. Tea with milk and sugar is a popular hot beverage with most Britons.
12. The favorite British sport football is called soccer in America.
13. The Welsh prefer rugby.

EXERCISE 3 Complete each sentence. Then tell whether you added a subject or a subject complement.

1. My favorite place around here is _____.
2. _____ is a spot that is just beautiful.
3. My favorite food has always been _____.
4. A food I liked when I was younger was _____.
5. _____ remains a popular sport with people my age.
6. _____ became my favorite kind of music.
7. London is a _____ that history buffs love to visit.
8. Old English sheepdogs are _____ that are considered highly intelligent.

APPLY IT NOW

Write five sentences, each one using a subject complement and telling about something you either enjoy or do not enjoy. Use the verbs *become* and *remain* in two of the sentences.

1.4 Nouns as Objects and Object Complements

A noun can be used as a direct object. The **direct object** answers the question *whom* or *what* after the verb. In this sentence the direct object is *center*. It answers the question *What did the community open?*

The community opened a neighborhood *center*.

A noun can be used as an indirect object. An **indirect object** tells *to whom* or *for whom*, or *to what* or *for what*, an action is done. In this sentence the indirect object is *children*. It answers the question *To whom does the center offer classes?*

The center offers *children* **classes.**

A noun can be the **object of a preposition** when it follows a preposition such as *in, into, on, to, by, for, from, with,* or *without*. In this sentence *ceramics* is the object of the preposition *in*. It answers the question *What did I take a class in?*

I took a class in *ceramics* **there.**

A noun can be an object complement. Just as a subject complement renames the subject, an **object complement** renames the direct object. In this sentence *pot* is the direct object. The noun *masterpiece* is an object complement that renames *pot*.

I called my first ceramic pot a *masterpiece*.

Some common verbs that take object complements are *appoint, call, consider, choose, elect, make,* and *name*.

EXERCISE 1 Name the direct object in each sentence.

1. Some high school students take art classes every Saturday.
2. Some students use the computer in art class.
3. Students draw pictures on the computer.
4. The students are planning an art show.
5. They will invite their parents.
6. Hopefully, the show will raise money for supplies.
7. Professional artists in our community often make donations too.

Name the indirect object in each sentence.

8. Mrs. Simpson, the coordinator of the center, sends schools fliers with information on the center's courses.

9. The center offers students classes on Saturdays.

10. Many teachers give the center their time voluntarily.

11. Local artists give students special instruction once in a while.

Name the object of a preposition in each sentence.

12. Mr. Susick organized a field trip for the art students.

13. The exhibition including works by famous photographers was fascinating.

14. An image of a quiet lake was my favorite photo.

15. The picture showed water evaporating in the sunlight.

Name the object complement in each sentence.

16. Everyone declared the field trip an enjoyable experience.

17. To express our thanks, we appointed Ed spokesperson.

18. The class considers Mr. Susick a good teacher.

19. He makes history an exciting topic.

EXERCISE 2 Tell whether each underlined noun is a direct object, an indirect object, an object of a preposition, or an object complement.

1. My family attended an <u>exhibit</u> on <u>life</u> in the 1600s.

2. I gave my <u>parents</u> the <u>trip</u> to the exhibit as a present.

3. We were first to arrive at the <u>exhibit</u> that day.

4. We saw life-sized <u>mannequins</u> in period <u>costumes</u>.

5. Mannequins of the 1920s wore shiny dance <u>outfits</u>.

6. We considered the <u>exhibit</u> a real learning <u>experience</u>.

APPLY IT NOW

Write five sentences about an extracurricular activity that you have enjoyed. Use at least one direct object, one indirect object, and one object of a preposition in your sentences. Label the direct objects, indirect objects, and objects of prepositions.

Post sentences on your class blog for peer review.

1.5 Appositives

An **appositive** is a word that follows a noun and helps identify it. An appositive names the same person, place, thing, or idea as the noun it explains. An **appositive phrase** is an appositive and its modifiers.

In the first sentence below, *writer* is the appositive in the appositive phrase *a 19th-century writer* that explains the noun *Louisa May Alcott.* The appositive is set off by commas because it is **nonrestrictive,** which means the appositive is not crucial to understanding the sentence. In the second sentence below, the noun *Little Women* is an appositive that explains the noun *novel.* Here the appositive is not set off by commas because it is **restrictive.** The appositive is necessary in order to know which novel is meant.

Louisa May Alcott

Louisa May Alcott, a 19th-century writer, produced many novels.
Her most popular work is the novel *Little Women*.

In the first example below, the appositive is not set off by commas because the writer's name is necessary in order to know which 19th-century writer is meant. The appositive in the second sentence is set off by commas because it is nonrestrictive. It is not necessary for the meaning of the sentence.

The 19th-century writer Louisa May Alcott produced many novels.
***Little Women*, a novel by Louisa May Alcott, is her most popular work.**

In the first example below, the appositive *Abigail* is nonrestrictive—Alcott had only one mother. In the second example, the appositive *Elizabeth* is restrictive because it is necessary in order to know which of Alcott's three sisters is meant.

Alcott's mother, *Abigail*, encouraged Louisa in her writing.
Alcott's sister *Elizabeth* was probably the model for Beth.

EXERCISE 1 Identify the appositive in each sentence. Then tell which noun the appositive explains.

1. Louisa May Alcott, a famous American writer, was born in Germantown, Pennsylvania, in 1832.

2. She spent most of her youth in Concord, a town near Boston.

3. She was the daughter of the teacher Bronson Alcott.

4. Louisa, a good student, was educated at home.

5. Her family was poor but had contact with the famous American intellectuals Ralph Waldo Emerson, Nathaniel Hawthorne, and Henry David Thoreau.

6. She eventually became editor of the children's magazine, *Merry Museum.*

7. My home state, Pennsylvania, was home to many famous people.

EXERCISE 2 Identify the appositive in each sentence and decide whether it is restrictive or nonrestrictive. Correct the sentences with nonrestrictive appositives by adding commas where necessary.

1. The Marches the characters in *Little Women* are based on Louisa May Alcott's family.

2. The character Jo was based on Louisa herself.

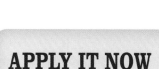

Henry David Thoreau

3. The novel a tale of the trials and hardships of four sisters follows them as they grow up.

4. The novel takes place during the Civil War the conflict between the North and South.

5. The book an early example of realistic fiction for children supports family values.

6. My sister Kendall wants to write books like Alcott's and my baby sister Bette will illustrate them.

7. I also have four sisters Kendall Bette Margaret and Alden just like Alcott's character.

8. We grew up in Connecticut a northern state.

9. Connecticut part of New England was also involved in the Civil War.

APPLY IT NOW

Write a paragraph about a novel or movie with which you are familiar. Summarize it, using both types of appositives to explain any nouns in your paragraph. Label each appositive as restrictive or nonrestrictive. Be sure to use appropriate punctuation.

Tech Tip With an adult, search for reviews online.

1.6 Possessive Nouns

A **possessive noun** expresses possession, or ownership. The sign of the possessive is usually *'s*.

To form the singular possessive, add *-'s* to the singular form of the noun.

boy	boy's	Tommy	Tommy's

To form the possessive of plural nouns ending in *s*, add the apostrophe only. If the plural form of a noun does not end in *s*, add *-'s*.

students	students'	women	women's
teachers	teachers'	children	children's

The singular possessive of a proper name ending in *s* is usually formed by adding *-'s*.

Alexis	Alexis's	Mrs. Hess	Mrs. Hess's

To form the plural possessive of a proper noun, first form the plural of the noun and then add an apostrophe.

Jones	Joneses'	Adams	Adamses'

The possessive of compound nouns is formed by adding *-'s* to the end of the term.

editor in chief	editor in chief's
mothers-in-law	mothers-in-law's

If two or more nouns are used together to indicate separate possession—that is, each person owns something independently— *-'s* is used after each noun.

J. K. *Rowling's* and Shel *Silverstein's* writings provide wonderful entertainment.

If two or more nouns are used together to indicate joint possession—that is, to show that one thing is owned together— *-'s* is used after the last noun only.

Terri and Shari's garden is beautiful.

EXERCISE 1 Complete each sentence, using the singular possessive or plural possessive form of the noun in parentheses.

1. On Sunday mornings our _____ (city) park department holds "green markets."

2. At a local park, space is cleared, and many _____ (farmer) products are displayed in booths.

3. The _____ (seller) products are all fresh from their farms and look very tempting.

4. Many _____ (customer) arms are soon filled with packages and bags containing vegetables and fruits.

5. My _____ (family) visit to the green market last week was a great success.

6. One _____ (woman) stand displayed homemade jam.

7. We couldn't resist, and we bought several jars of _____ (Mrs. Prentiss) blackberry jam.

8. Her prize blackberry _____ (bush) fruit is so sweet, it needs no sugar.

9. Her whole family helps her each year; it is all of the _____ (Prentiss) hard work that makes their jam the best.

EXERCISE 2 Based on the information given for each item, write your own sentence that indicates either separate or joint ownership.

1. Finn and Meg have a roadside stand. It features vegetables.

2. Mary has a garden plot. Anna has her own garden plot. These garden plots produce herbs.

3. Michael and Fiona grow sunflowers together. Their sunflowers have won prizes.

4. Lilly sells flowers. Fran also sells flowers. Their stands are at the mall.

5. Richard and Les each have farm stands. The farm stands are very profitable.

6. Claude planted a strawberry patch. His little sister Pilar helps him water it. Their strawberries are juicy and sweet.

7. Pip grows wonderful tomatoes. Eli grows tasty mangos. They make good salsa with their harvests.

APPLY IT NOW

Write five sentences about achievements of family, friends, or others that you admire. Use both single and plural possessive nouns in your sentences. Include at least one sentence that indicates separate or joint possession accurately.

Noun Review

1.1 Complete the sentences with the plural form of the nouns in parentheses.

1. ___ (People) in both our ___ (family) have unique ___ (hobby).
2. My twin ___ (cousin) are ___ (member) of the youth and adult ballet ___ (corps).
3. Monique answers e-mail ___ (query) about homework.
4. My little sister raises ___ (mouse) for the pet store.
5. David is an artist who works in several (medium).
6. My mother raises ___ (tomato) in the garden.
7. Every autumn, flocks of Canadian ___ (goose) fly south.
8. Every morning the bakery bakes hundreds of ___ (loaf) of bread.

Write the plural of each noun.

9. ox
10. crisis
11. half
12. inquiry
13. colony
14. matrix
15. life

1.2 Write the plural of each noun.

16. boat
17. fox
18. radio
19. potato
20. zero
21. maid of honor
22. spoonful
23. deer
24. drive-in

1.3 Identify the subject of each sentence. Then name the subject and the subject complement if there is one.

25. Newfoundland is a province in Canada.
26. This province is an island off the east coast of Canada.
27. The island has miles of jagged coastline.
28. Newfoundlands, huge black dogs, originated there.
29. Brave animals such as Newfoundlands are the subjects of some fables and dramatic novels.
30. The Newfoundland is courageous yet gentle.
31. These dogs are both amazing water-rescuers and wonderful companions.

1.4 Tell whether each underlined word is a direct object, an indirect object, an object of a preposition, or an object complement.

32. Many experts recommend music <u>lessons</u> for <u>children</u>.
33. Our local arts center sends <u>parents</u> the <u>information</u> about music <u>instruction</u> in <u>September</u>.
34. I have studied the <u>flute</u> for 10 <u>years</u>.
35. I called my first <u>lesson</u> a <u>disaster</u>.

36. I consider <u>Mr. Ramos</u> a good <u>teacher</u>.

37. He offers <u>students</u> the <u>chance</u> to learn different kinds of music.

38. I love <u>jazz</u> more than any other type of music.

39. I especially love Miles Davis's masterpiece called "<u>Kind of Blue</u>."

Use the following words in sentences as the part of speech indicated in parentheses.

40. leaves (direct object)

41. friends (indirect object)

42. jacket (object of a preposition)

43. experience (object complement)

1.5 **Identify the appositive in each sentence. Correct the sentences with nonrestrictive appositives by adding commas where necessary.**

44. Harriet Tubman a slave born on a plantation in Maryland led other slaves to freedom on the Underground Railroad.

45. The slave and preacher Nat Turner led a revolt and became a hero to Tubman.

46. Tubman's mother Harriet Greene worked as a slave for the Brodas family.

47. Over many years Harriet traveled the Underground Railroad a series of safe houses for slaves.

48. The Underground Railroad involved the efforts of many "conductors" individuals responsible for moving fugitives from one safe house to the next.

Identify the appositive in each sentence as restrictive or nonrestrictive.

49. Nellie, the horse with the black mane, is very difficult to ride.

50. Louise is a descendant of the writer Oscar Wilde.

51. Steven King's book *It* is about a scary clown.

52. J.K. Rowling, the author of the Harry Potter series, hails from England.

53. George Washington, a great army general during the Revolution, led his troops across the Delaware in the dead of winter.

1.6 **Write the possessive form of each noun.**

54. neighbors

55. teens

56. mothers-to-be

57. principals

58. Father Jess

59. woman

60. boys

61. the Davises

62. separate possession: music of Bach and of Mozart

63. joint possession: cars of Mom and Dad

64. separate possession: reports of Darnell and Melissa

Go to www.voyagesinenglish.com for more activities.

Noun Challenge

EXERCISE 1 Read the selection and then answer the questions.

1. A painting by the celebrated American artist James McNeill Whistler hangs in the Louvre. 2. *An Arrangement in Gray and Black* is the imposing title of this portrait, but to the millions who know and love it, the likeness is best known as *Whistler's Mother*. 3. At first the picture brought the artist little recognition. 4. Many years later, however, it was the opinion of more than one committee of critics that this picture alone would have made Whistler a true master. 5. For connoisseurs of art, the beauty of this painting lies in the perfect placement of objects and the harmony achieved through its many tones of gray. 6. Its appeal to the heart of the ordinary person rests in the noble traits of motherhood that Whistler has captured and enshrined forever on canvas.

1. What is the subject of sentence 1?
2. Name an appositive in sentence 1 and identify it as either restrictive or nonrestrictive.
3. Name a possessive noun in sentence 2.
4. What is the subject complement in sentence 2?
5. Identify the object of a preposition in sentence 2.
6. What are the direct object and the indirect object in sentence 3?
7. Name the object complement in sentence 4.
8. Identify the objects of the prepositions in sentence 4.
9. What is the singular form of the word *connoisseurs,* used in sentence 5?
10. Which nouns in sentence 6 are objects of prepositions?

EXERCISE 2 Read the following and respond.

Musicians, like painters, have unique artistic styles. Their music is often categorized in a genre such as rock, jazz, classical, or hip-hop. Write a paragraph identifying one of your favorite musicians or bands and why. Do you like the vocals or the instruments? Do you enjoy the lyrics? Explain, using at least one each of the following:

1. a direct object or an indirect object
2. a subject complement or an object complement
3. an object of a preposition
4. a possessive noun
5. and an appositive

Adjectives

2.1 Descriptive Adjectives, Position of Adjectives

A descriptive adjective describes a noun's or pronoun's number, color, size, type, or other qualities. An adjective usually goes before the word it describes. However, adjectives may also directly follow nouns. In this sentence the adjectives *thick* and *hot* describe the noun *ashes*.

> **Ashes, *thick* and *hot*, rained down on Pompeii.**

In this sentence the adjectives *eminent* and *Roman* describe the noun *writer*.

> **An *eminent Roman* writer described the disaster.**

An adjective acts as a **subject complement** when it follows a linking verb and describes the subject. Linking verbs include the different tenses of the verbs *be, become, taste, sound, feel, look, remain, appear,* and *seem*. In this sentence *fearful* describes the subject *people*.

> **People were *fearful* because of the disaster.**

An adjective can also act as an **object complement** when it follows a direct object and describes it. In these sentences *fearful* describes the direct object *people*, and *happy* describes *brother*.

> **The disaster left people *fearful*.**
> **Our new puppy made my brother very *happy*.**

EXERCISE 1 Name the descriptive adjectives in each sentence.

1. Pompeii was an Italian city that was destroyed by a volcanic eruption in AD 79.
2. The sudden eruption of Mount Vesuvius was a surprise to the residents of ancient Pompeii.
3. Wealthy Romans built palatial villas in the bustling town.
4. Before the huge eruption, trees and gardens covered the mountain's gentle slopes.
5. Powerful forces, however, were building within the peaceful mountain, causing extreme pressure.
6. Archaeological digs unearthed startling evidence that the unfortunate people were stopped in their tracks.
7. The excavated town reveals a moment of daily Roman life frozen in time.

EXERCISE 2 In each sentence identify the nouns modified by the italicized adjectives. Then tell whether each adjective comes before the noun or after the noun, and identify if it is used as a subject complement or as an object complement.

1. In AD 79, on August 24, the *entire* top of Mount Vesuvius blew off.
2. A cloud, *huge* and *threatening*, formed over the mountain.
3. The day became *dark* as night.
4. The volcano spewed out rock, *black* but *hot*, and *poisonous* gas.
5. A *thick* blanket of ash, *fine* pumice stone, and other debris covered Pompeii to a depth of 20 feet.
6. Survivors called the scene *infernal*.
7. The city remained *buried* for centuries.
8. The volcano proved *deadly* again in 1631, when it buried a new city.
9. Discovery of old Pompeii beneath the new city's ruins left rescuers *speechless*.

EXERCISE 3 Use the following descriptive adjectives in sentences of your own.

1. historic
2. noisy
3. energetic
4. magnificent
5. mysterious
6. sparkling
7. crowded
8. Japanese
9. sincere
10. excited
11. thoughtful
12. colorful

Use an appropriate descriptive adjective with each noun.

13. ocean
14. skyline
15. painting
16. movie
17. idea
18. shirt
19. shoes
20. music
21. mail
22. hawk
23. beach
24. statue

APPLY IT NOW

Think of an amazing event that you've experienced. Brainstorm a list of adjectives to describe what you saw, heard, and felt. Then write a paragraph describing it. Include adjectives before and after the words they modify, two subject complements, and two object complements.

Grammar in Action. Identify the subject complements in the first paragraph of the p. 223 excerpt.

2.2 Demonstrative, Interrogative, and Indefinite Adjectives

Demonstrative adjectives point out definite people, places, things, or ideas. The demonstrative adjectives are *this, that, these,* and *those.*

DEMONSTRATIVE ADJECTIVES

This **glass is half full.**
Those **glasses need to be washed.**

Interrogative adjectives are used in questions. The interrogative adjectives are *what, which,* and *whose. Which* is usually used to ask about one or more of a specific set of items.

INTERROGATIVE ADJECTIVES

What **equipment do you need?**
Which **bat is mine?**
Whose **uniform is this?**

Indefinite adjectives refer to any or all of a group. Indefinite adjectives include *all, another, any, both, each, either, few, many, more, most, much, neither, other, several,* and *some.* Note that *another, each, every, either,* and *neither* are always singular.

INDEFINITE ADJECTIVES

Each **student receives a progress report once a week.** (singular)
Every **student should write a thank-you note.** (singular)
Neither **friend was at home when I called.** (singular)
Few **students are chosen for this honor.** (plural)
I am thankful for the *many* **gifts I have received.** (plural)

EXERCISE 1 Tell whether each italicized adjective is demonstrative, interrogative, or indefinite.

1. *This* vase holds a beautiful arrangement of summer flowers.
2. *What* flowers are these?
3. *Whose* flower arrangement is this?
4. The placement of *each* blossom is perfect.
5. *Both* arrangements in this room have a variety of colorful flowers.

6. *That* vase holds a bouquet of herbs.

7. *Some* herbs are said to have healing powers.

8. With its tiny blue blossoms, *this* rosemary is decorative as well.

9. Adding *several* large sprigs of rosemary to bathwater is thought to help sprains and pulled muscles.

10. Lavender also has *many* uses in healing.

11. Aloe is *another* plant used for healing.

12. *Each* fleshy leaf contains fluid that takes the sting out of sunburn.

13. *This* plant can also be used to treat acne.

EXERCISE 2 Complete each sentence with an adjective of the type indicated in parentheses.

1. Long before there were pills, _____ people used herbs and other plants to treat illnesses. (indefinite)

2. _____ herbs did they use? (interrogative)

3. _____ herbs included rosemary, sage, and lavender. (demonstrative)

4. _____ advice do you seek when you are sick? (interrogative)

5. Why do you value _____ advice? (demonstrative)

6. Although _____ doctors prescribe herbs to treat illnesses today, a great _____ have proven to be effective treatments. (indefinite)

7. It is important to be careful with _____ treatments, because the improper application of _____ treatment can be dangerous. (indefinite)

8. _____ rule is very important to follow: never mix _____ pills or medicinal herbs without a doctor's approval. (demonstrative, indefinite)

9. _____ consequences are there for mixing treatments? (interrogative)

10. _____ different herb and pill contains different chemicals. (indefinite)

11. _____ chemicals, when combined, can have _____ unexpected effects. (demonstrative, indefinite)

12. _____ cold medications, when mixed with _____ cold medications or herbs, can have life-threatening side-effects. (indefinite, indefinite)

Tech Tip Post your results on your class blog or wiki.

2.3 Comparative and Superlative Adjectives

Most adjectives have three degrees of comparison: positive, comparative, and superlative. The **positive** degree of an adjective shows a quality of a noun. The **comparative** degree is used to compare two items or two sets of items. This form is often followed by *than*. The **superlative** degree is used to compare three or more items.

For adjectives of one syllable and some adjectives of two syllables (including those ending in *y*), the comparative degree is formed by adding *-er* to the positive form, and the superlative degree is formed by adding *-est* to the positive form.

POSITIVE	COMPARATIVE	SUPERLATIVE
warm	warmer	warmest
sunny	sunnier	sunniest
fine	finer	finest
hot	hotter	hottest

For adjectives of three or more syllables and many adjectives of two syllables, the comparative degree is formed by using *more* or *less* with the positive form, and the superlative degree is formed by using *most* or *least* with the positive form.

POSITIVE	COMPARATIVE	SUPERLATIVE
important	more important	most important
extreme	more extreme	most extreme
thoughtful	less thoughtful	least thoughtful
resistant	less resistant	least resistant

Certain adjectives have irregular comparisons.

POSITIVE	COMPARATIVE	SUPERLATIVE
good	better	best
bad	worse	worst
many	more	most
little	less	least

Some adjectives, such as *dead, perfect,* and *eternal* cannot be compared. If you are uncertain about comparatives and superlatives, always check a dictionary.

EXERCISE 1 Complete each sentence with the comparative or superlative form of the adjective in parentheses.

1. Alaska's coastline is _____ (long) than that of all the other states combined.

2. The _____ (old) rock in the world, 3.8 billion years old, was found in Minnesota.

3. The pueblos at Taos, New Mexico, are in _____ (good) condition than any other pueblos in the United States.

4. Some people consider the stalagmites and stalactites in Lechuguilla Cave in the Carlsbad Caverns of Kentucky the _____ (beautiful) in the world.

5. Mammoth Cave, also in Kentucky, has a _____ (extensive) cave system than the Carlsbad Caverns do.

6. Although Rhode Island is the _____ (small) U.S. state, it has some of the _____ (many) beautiful beaches in New England.

EXERCISE 2 Rewrite each sentence to correct errors in comparison. Not every sentence requires rewriting.

1. In my opinion Maryland is the pleasantest state.

2. I think that the weather there is more temperate than it is in any other Middle Atlantic state.

3. Summer heat and humidity are no worser than they are in many other places I could name.

4. Night skies over Chesapeake Bay are at their brilliantest in winter, when the air is cold and clear.

5. The seafood in Maryland is more better and fresher than in other places, and crab cakes are the deliciousest seafood dish.

6. The southern states make the bestest southern fried chicken.

7. I think Alabama has the tastest cooking of them all.

APPLY IT NOW

What do you think are the best aspects of a place where you would like to visit? Write six sentences to convince someone else that your choice is a great place. Use positive, comparative, and superlative forms of adjectives in your writing. Consult a dictionary as needed.

 Tech Tip With an adult, search online for images of these places.

2.4 *Few and Little*

Concrete nouns name things that you can see, touch, or count. They can be made plural because they can be counted: *chair, screwdriver, hat, river.* **Abstract nouns** name things that generally cannot be seen, touched, or counted. They express qualities or conditions: *life, patience, happiness, disgust.* They generally cannot be made plural. For some nouns you can use either *less* or *fewer* depending on the noun's usage in the sentence.

Use the adjectives *few, fewer,* and *fewest* to compare concrete nouns that can be counted. Note that the noun *errors* is in the plural form.

USING: *FEW, FEWER, FEWEST*

Anthony's report contained *few* errors.
Cynthia's report contained *fewer* errors than Anthony's did.
Jackie's report contained the *fewest* errors of all.

Use the adjectives *little, less,* and *least* to compare abstract nouns by quantity. They are used for nouns that cannot be counted, such as *love, maturity,* or *sleep.* Note that the nouns *motivation* and *effort* are singular.

USING: *LITTLE, LESS, LEAST*

Anthony showed only a *little* motivation for writing his report.
Lydia put even *less* effort into her report than Anthony did.
Of all the students, Debbie showed the *least* motivation or effort.

EXERCISE 1 Place these words in two columns, one with concrete nouns and the other with abstract nouns.

penny	strength	oxygen	sadness
jewelry	newspaper	justice	chemistry
patriotism	gold	quality	bottle
scenery	weather	hammer	milk
mountain	thunder	belief	necklace
sandwich	tennis	apple	confidence
knowledge	safety	leadership	work

EXERCISE 2 Tell whether the noun being compared in each sentence is abstract or concrete. Then choose the correct word to complete the sentence.

1. Our school's "garage sale" attracted (fewer less) people this year than it did last year.
2. I think there was (fewer less) publicity for the auction this year.
3. I saw (fewer less) bands in the parade this July 4th.
4. People had (fewer less) enthusiasm for the rodeo this year.
5. We definitely collected (fewer less) vegetables to sell at the market.
6. I have (fewer less) jewelry than my older sister.
7. My father has (fewer less) talent in the kitchen than my grandmother.
8. An athlete has to master (fewer less) skills in diving than in gymnastics, but both are very difficult sports.
9. After riding the carousel, Molly had the (fewest littlest) tickets left for the carnival.
10. Fish cannot live in some parts of the ocean because pollution has left too (few little) oxygen in the water.

EXERCISE 3 Complete each sentence with *fewer* or *less.*

1. All of us had _____ time to work on the class yearbook this year than we had last year.
2. All of us had _____ homework last year.
3. Some of us had _____ after-school activities last year too.
4. Generally, we had many _____ hours to work on the yearbook this year.
5. We also got _____ help from faculty advisors.
6. As a result, there were _____ errors in last year's yearbook.
7. Also, there are _____ pages in this year's book.
8. There is _____ material on school activities and _____ photos.
9. There is also _____ space for seniors' comments and quotes, although _____ seniors are likely to complain.
10. Everyone is _____ enthusiastic about this year's yearbook, and we will print _____.

APPLY IT NOW

Write five sentences about a change in your life over the past year—something you now spend less time doing. Use any forms of *few* or *less* in your sentences at least three times each.

Tech Tip Post your work on the class blog or wiki for peer review.

2.5 Adjective Phrases and Clauses

A **prepositional phrase** is made up of a preposition, the object of the preposition, and any modifiers. A prepositional phrase can be used as an adjective. Prepositions that begin adjective phrases include *with, to, in, at, of, under,* and *over.* In this sentence the prepositional phrase *in bright colors* modifies the noun *shirts.* It is an **adjective phrase.**

> Shirts *in bright colors* are often worn by people in warm climates.

A **clause** is a group of words that has a subject and a predicate. A dependent clause does not express a complete thought. Some dependent clauses are **adjective clauses.** They describe nouns. In this sentence *which has many rich cultural traditions* is a dependent clause. The dependent adjective clause modifies *Hawaii.*

> Hawaii, *which has many rich cultural traditions*, is both a beautiful and an interesting place to visit.

A **restrictive adjective clause** is necessary to the meaning of a sentence. A **nonrestrictive clause** is not necessary to the meaning. Nonrestrictive clauses are set off with commas. Adjective clauses are introduced by *who, whom, whose, that, which, where,* and *when.* As a general rule, the relative pronoun *that* is used in restrictive clauses and *which* in nonrestrictive ones. Note that proper nouns are usually followed by nonrestrictive clauses.

> The shirt *that I bought* has red flowers on a white background. (restrictive—necessary in order to know which shirt)
>
> Maui, *which is one of the Hawaiian Islands*, is a popular tourist destination. (nonrestrictive—not necessary in order to identify the specific island)

EXERCISE 1 Identify the adjective phrases and name the words they modify.

1. Our trip to Hawaii was a great success.
2. When we left Boston, the temperature at Logan Airport was freezing.
3. When we landed, we felt the warmth of the Hawaiian sunshine.
4. Dad quickly shed his coat with the heavy lining.
5. We saw people in short-sleeved shirts.

EXERCISE 2 In each sentence identify the adjective clause and name the noun it modifies. Then tell whether the clause is restrictive or nonrestrictive.

1. Hawaiian shirts, which are colorful shirts with short sleeves, are a popular clothing item in many places today.

2. The shirts were first manufactured commercially in Hawaii in 1936 by Ellery J. Chun, who named them Aloha shirts.

3. An ancestor of the Aloha shirt was the "thousand-mile shirt," which was a sturdy garment worn by missionaries.

4. The Hawaiians, who up to that time had not worn Western-style garments, supposedly added patterns and color to the shirts.

5. Early shirts were of tapa cloth, which Hawaiians produced from the bark of the paper mulberry plant.

6. Patterns were taken from native flowers and other vegetation that grew on the islands.

7. The fabric that became popular for the shirts was rayon because it was easier to dye than natural fibers.

8. The 1950s was the period that Hawaiian shirts became popular throughout the United States.

9. At the time, celebrities such as Frank Sinatra and Elvis Presley wore them in movies, and then fans who wanted to imitate these stars began to wear them also.

10. Hawaiians say that Hawaii is the only place that authentic Aloha shirts can ever be produced.

11. I have a Hawaiian shirt that I got when I visited Maui.

12. Maui, which is a Hawaiian island with a fertile valley between two volcanoes, is also called the "Valley Island."

APPLY IT NOW

For each word below, write a sentence containing an adjective clause modifying it.

homework	park
gift	mouse
holiday	toys
television	Ohio
man	

Grammar in Action. Find the adjective phrases in the p. 222 excerpt.

Adjectives • 27

Adjective Review

2.1 Name the descriptive adjectives in each sentence. Identify adjectives used as subject complements or object complements.

1. Seven different shapes make up an ancient Chinese puzzle called a tangram.
2. Rearranging the seven pieces is difficult for some people.
3. The seemingly simple puzzle leaves many frustrated.
4. A description of a finite set of patterns called a convex is highly complicated.
5. Some players find the puzzle addictive.
6. Sudoku is a logical puzzle invented by an American architect.
7. It became popular in Japan first, however, which is why it has a Japanese name.
8. Suduko is a symbol-based puzzle that entertains subway commuters everywhere.
9. Sudoko keeps my sister occupied whenever we travel long distances.

2.2 Identify each underlined adjective as demonstrative, interrogative, or indefinite.

10. Every ninth grader has to write a research paper.
11. Which topic have you chosen?
12. I've read several sample papers in the library.
13. Those students certainly did extensive research.
14. Each paper receives a grade for content and a grade for writing.
15. Whose computer will you be using?
16. Neither machine was working last week.
17. What department do we need to contact to have them fixed?.
18. Those computers crash several times a week.
19. I worry that I will lose my work each time I use them, so I save my files every half hour.
20. Neither Jesse nor Suzanne are in the habit of saving their work.

2.3 Identify the following words as positive, comparative, or superlative.

21. brighter
22. most generous
23. extensive
24. shady
25. most difficult
26. less extreme
27. least tolerant
28. hyper

Write the positive, comparative, and superlative forms of each word.

29. delicate
30. healthy
31. extreme
32. eternal
33. red
34. little

35. wise

36. fanciful

37. hot

38. common

39. much

40. far

2.4 **Identify each noun as concrete or abstract. Then complete each sentence with the correct form of *few* or *little*.**

41. _____ people can resist the aroma that comes from a bakery.

42. I have _____ resolve than Ali when we see the sweet treats.

43. I try to make _____ trips down Main Street so I can avoid temptation.

44. It only takes a _____ time to take an alternate route.

45. Greater diligence results in _____ mistakes.

46. Of all my teachers, she gives the _____ homework but the most quizzes.

47. Isabella had the _____ subjects to study, but the most amount of work.

2.5 **Identify each adjective phrase and adjective clause and tell the words they modify. Then add commas where necessary.**

48. Our research trip to the Field Museum was a huge success.

49. We wanted to get firsthand information about the *T. rex* Sue whose skeleton is the largest and most complete ever discovered.

50. *T. rex* which is a species of dinosaur weighed five to seven tons.

51. The museum storyteller told us a story that was fascinating.

52. It was about a dinosaur in the water, and it was much bigger than the ones on land.

Identify the following groups of words as either adjective phrases or adjective clauses, then use them in sentences.

53. on the floor

54. which is blue

55. on your left

56. by the river

57. who is a student

58. which sits by the door

59. beside Miguel

60. that we built

61. under the bridge

62. whom are ill

63. who got the job

For the sentences that you wrote in the preceding exercise, change three nonrestrictive clauses to restrictive clauses, OR three restrictive clauses to nonrestrictive clauses. Rewrite the sentences as necessary.

 Go to www.voyagesinenglish.com for more activities.

Adjective Challenge

EXERCISE 1 Read the selection and then answer the questions.

1. Suppose birds became extinct. 2. We can appreciate the negative consequences of such an event when we consider the many ways that birds help us. 3. The destruction of harmful insects, which is perhaps birds' most important function, makes farmers' tasks easier. 4. Further, some birds help keep weeds under control by eating their seeds, while many larger birds prevent mice and rats from becoming really bad pests. 5. You can see why we consider birds essential in our ecosystem. 6. They are among our greatest benefactors. 7. Every action that we can take now to save our bird population will pay off in the future.

1. What is the subject complement in sentence 1?
2. Find an adjective clause in sentence 2. What noun does it modify? Is it restrictive or nonrestrictive? What is the relative pronoun?
3. Name the superlative form of an adjective in sentence 3. What are its positive and comparative forms?
4. What is the object complement in sentence 3? What is its degree of comparison?
5. Find an adjective clause in sentence 3. What noun does it modify? Is it restrictive or nonrestrictive? What is the relative pronoun?
6. Name two indefinite adjectives in sentence 4. What noun does each one modify?
7. Give the degrees of comparison for the adjective *bad* in sentence 4.
8. What is the object complement in sentence 5?
9. Name the superlative form of an adjective used in sentence 6. What are its positive and comparative forms?
10. Name the indefinite adjective in sentence 7.

EXERCISE 2 Descriptive imagery in poems require adjectives. Write a descriptive poem in which you use the following:

1. a demonstrative, an interrogative, or an indefinite adjective
2. an adjective clause
3. a comparative or a superlative adjective

Pronouns

3.1 Person, Number, and Gender of Pronouns

A **pronoun** is a word used in place of a noun. **Personal pronouns** are one kind of pronoun. Look at this chart.

PERSONAL PRONOUNS	SINGULAR	PLURAL
FIRST PERSON (SPEAKER)	I	we
	me	us
SECOND PERSON (SPOKEN TO)	you	you
	you	you
THIRD PERSON (SPOKEN OF)	he, she, it	they
	him, her, it	them

Personal pronouns change form depending on **person**—whether they refer to the one who is speaking, is spoken to, or is spoken of.

Personal pronouns also may have different forms depending on **number**—whether they refer to one person or thing (singular) or to more than one person or thing (plural).

Third person singular personal pronouns also change form depending on the **gender** (feminine, masculine, or neuter) of the **antecedent,** the word the pronoun refers to.

Can you identify the type (person, number, and gender) of the pronouns in these sentences?

I **am taking computer science as an elective.**

Frank hasn't decided on an elective yet, but *he* **is thinking of taking band.**

In the first sentence, *I* is a first person singular pronoun. In the second sentence, *he* is third person singular and masculine. It agrees with its antecedent *Frank*.

Pronouns allow writers to avoid the constant repetition of nouns and make their writing sound more natural.

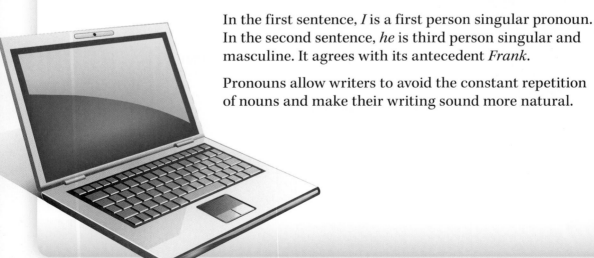

EXERCISE 1 Identify the pronouns in each sentence. For each pronoun, tell the person, number, and, if appropriate, gender.

1. Recently I discovered short stories by Jack London.
2. People know him from the novels he wrote about Alaska.
3. One of those stories, "To Build a Fire," is the first story that I will recommend to you.
4. It is about a man traveling through Alaska.
5. He does not understand what cold can do.
6. He hikes through the snow with a dog.
7. As they traveled through the terrible cold, the dog began to mistrust the man.
8. I felt I was with that man, watching him.
9. Beverly says she felt the same way I did.
10. I read that *White Fang* is also set in Alaska.
11. Those novels sound interesting to me.
12. The librarians say they will put the books on reserve.

Jack London

EXERCISE 2 Complete each sentence with a pronoun. Use the directions in parentheses.

1. This year _____ will have a chance to choose some classes ourselves. (first person, plural)
2. Our teachers created the courses, and _____ call these *electives*. (third person, plural)
3. _____ am trying to decide between art and keyboarding. (first person, singular)
4. My mom wants me to take keyboarding, so I'll probably take _____. (third person, singular, neuter)
5. What will _____ take? (second person, singular)
6. Maybe _____ will be in the same class. (first person, plural)

EXERCISE 3 Change the following nouns to appropriate pronouns.

1. Jorge and Jack
2. you and your family
3. me and the dog
4. our teacher

APPLY IT NOW

Write a paragraph about a short story that you have read. Your purpose is to convince a friend either to read or not to read it. In your finished paragraph, underline all the personal pronouns and circle their antecedents.

3.2 Subject Pronouns

A **subject pronoun** can be the subject or subject complement in a sentence. The subject pronouns are *I, we, you, he, she, it,* and *they.*

> **I watched the movie twice.** (subject)
>
> **The actor who won the award was he.** (subject complement)

One common error is not using a subject pronoun when it is part of a compound subject or complement. How would you edit these sentences?

> **Cynthia and me went to the movies.**
>
> **The students attending the play were her and Gregory.**

You are correct if you changed *me* to *I* in the first sentence. The pronoun is part of a compound subject, so the subject form of the pronoun is needed.

You are also correct if you changed *her* to *she* in the second sentence. It is part of a compound subject complement: *she and Gregory* rename the subject—*students.*

EXERCISE 1 Choose the correct pronoun to complete each sentence.

1. My friends and (me I) watch old movies together.
2. (Us We) usually meet at Elisa's house.
3. (She Her) and Peter provide refreshments.
4. (They Them) often have juice and soda.
5. Jane and (I me) usually bring popcorn to pop.
6. David knows a lot about old films, and the ones who usually choose the films are Elisa and (he him).
7. Sometimes (we us) vote on the film to see the next time.
8. David and (she her) suggested *The Sound of Music.*
9. Kevin and (he him) had never seen the film.
10. It was (they them) who really wanted to see the film.
11. But (us we) all enjoyed it.
12. Next week, (she her) will choose the movie with us.
13. (Us We) decided to pick another musical that we all enjoy.
14. (He Him) is a terrible singer, so we are hoping that he won't sing along!

EXERCISE 2 In each sentence use the correct pronoun for the underlined words. Tell whether the pronoun is a subject or a subject complement.

1. My <u>friends and I</u> planned to see *The Sound of Music*, and _____ saw it together yesterday.

2. The <u>movie</u> won an Oscar, and _____ is considered a classic.

3. The main character in the film is <u>Maria</u>. _____ is in a convent at the beginning of the movie.

4. Maria gets a job taking care of <u>children</u>. _____ seem well behaved, but they are quite mischievous with Maria.

5. _____ are called the <u>von Trapp family</u>.

6. Their <u>father</u> is a widower, and _____ was strict with them.

7. <u>Captain von Trapp</u> was a military officer, and it was _____ that the Germans wanted for their own military.

8. <u>Nancy</u> likes sentimental movies, and the person who was crying at the end was _____.

9. <u>Elaine and I</u> knew the words of the songs, and it was _____ who sang along during the film.

10. The <u>von Trapp family</u> now live in Stowe, Vermont, where _____ settled after their daring escape.

11. At the lodge, <u>guests</u> can join the family in sing-alongs, and _____ can enjoy its beautiful mountain views.

12. <u>Guests</u> can also learn maple sugaring, or _____ can ski all day and night.

Scene from *The Sound of Music*

EXERCISE 3 Rewrite the sentences so that the use of subject pronouns is correct. Not all the sentences have errors.

1. *The Sound of Music* was based on a real-life story of a woman. She was Maria von Trapp.

2. It was her who wrote the book on which the musical was based.

3. Her and her family were well-known singers.

4. Her husband and her were from Austria.

5. Him and her met when she was caring for one of his children.

6. They escaped from Austria by hiking over the Alps.

7. Their children and them traveled around the world.

APPLY IT NOW

Write the plot of a movie you like and give your reaction to the film. After you have finished, check that you have used subject pronouns correctly, especially in compound subjects.

Tech Tip Post your review online.

3.3 Object Pronouns

An **object pronoun** can be used as the object of a verb or a preposition. The object pronouns are *me, us, you, him, her, it,* and *them.*

> **Abraham Lincoln was the president during the Civil War. The nation elected *him* in 1860.** (direct object, answers *who? what?*)
>
> **Lincoln liked to entertain people, and he often told *them* amusing stories.** (indirect object, answers *to whom? to what?*)
>
> **"With malice toward none, with charity for all" was written by *him*.** (object of a preposition)

One of the sentences below shows a common error in object pronoun usage. Which sentence is correct?

> **The Gettysburg Address was memorized by Kristi and I.**
> **The Gettysburg Address was memorized by Kristi and me.**

If you chose the second sentence, you are correct. The object pronoun *me* should be used as the object of the preposition. It is part of the compound object *Kristi and me.*

EXERCISE 1 Identify the object pronouns. Tell whether each is a direct object, an indirect object, or an object of a preposition.

1. Mrs. Urbanski read us the Gettysburg Address.
2. She gave a fine dramatic reading of it.
3. She explained the speech's importance to us.
4. A cemetery was being established at Gettysburg, and Lincoln and others were dedicating it.
5. The Civil War ended two years after he delivered it.
6. Many soldiers had died at the site, and the cemetery honored them.
7. Lincoln was asked to speak, and the event became an occasion for him to explain the reasons for the war.
8. Historians say that the address was important; to them the words defined the nation as one people dedicated to one principle—equality.
9. The address was important to Americans; the speech gave them a reaffirmation of the basic beliefs of liberty and equality.
10. Some people call it one of the greatest speeches in American history.

Lincoln delivering the
Gettysburg Address

EXERCISE 2 Complete each sentence with a pronoun. Then tell whether the word you added is a direct object, an indirect object, or an object of a preposition.

1. Lincoln was not the first speaker. Edward Everett, the orator who spoke before _____, addressed the crowd for two hours.

2. As Everett spoke, people gave _____ polite attention.

3. Lincoln's speech was completed in a few minutes, but even today we are moved by _____.

4. Lincoln believed that those who died in battle had consecrated the ground, and he gave _____ credit for their sacrifice.

5. Many people present were expecting a long speech from Lincoln; he must have disappointed _____.

6. A few people in the crowd must have realized that Lincoln had given _____ something memorable.

Abraham Lincoln

EXERCISE 3 Rewrite the sentences so that the use of object pronouns is correct. Not all sentences have errors.

1. Lincoln is one of the most honored presidents; perhaps Americans admire George Washington and he the most.

2. Perhaps the most famous speech in the history of the country was given by him.

3. We learned that speeches were given at Gettysburg by both Edward Everett and he.

4. Mrs. Urbanski called on Susan and I for a dramatic reading of the speech.

5. Our reading was listened to attentively by she and the class.

EXERCISE 4 Write the correct form of the personal pronoun indicated in parentheses.

1. Lincoln's speech was presented to the class by both (third person singular feminine) and (first person singular).

2. For the original speech in 1863, it is estimated that over 15,000 people came to listen to (third person singular masculine).

3. After the students listened to the speech, we helped (third person plural) repeat it.

4. We agreed that Lincoln made the nation a better place for both (second person singular) and me.

APPLY IT NOW

Write a brief paragraph about an imaginary encounter with someone you admire. After you have finished, find and underline all the object pronouns in your writing. Remember that you should use pronouns in your writing to avoid repetition and make your writing sound more natural.

3.4 Pronouns After *Than* or *As*

The words *than* or *as* are used in comparisons. Often these conjunctions join two clauses.

> **Jacob is as good a singer *as* she is.**
> **Teachers choose him for solos more often *than* they choose her.**

Sometimes, however, part of the second clause is omitted. You may need to add the missing parts mentally to determine whether to use a subject pronoun or an object pronoun after *than* and *as*.

Study these examples. The words that can be omitted from the clauses are in brackets.

> **Emily is a better dancer than *she* [is a good dancer].**
> **Emily's dancing impressed me more than [it impressed] *them*.**

In the first sentence, the pronoun after *than* is the subject of the clause. So the correct pronoun is *she*—a subject pronoun. In the second sentence, the pronoun after *than* is the direct object of the verb *impressed*. So the correct pronoun is *them*—an object pronoun.

In sentences where either a subject or an object pronoun could be correct, it is important to express the comparison completely to avoid confusion.

> **I've known Jacob longer than she [has known Jacob].**
> **I've known Jacob longer than [I've known] her.**

As you come across sentences with *than* and *as,* remember to supply missing words mentally to check for correct pronoun usage.

EXERCISE 1 Identify the word to which the underlined pronoun is compared in each sentence.

1. The theater interests Rosa more than <u>me</u>.
2. Gordon has taken more dancing lessons than <u>she</u>.
3. Janice is a more experienced actress than <u>she</u>.
4. Ian has been in more plays than <u>I</u>.
5. Our drama teacher has chosen Diana for bigger parts than <u>her</u>.
6. Being onstage scares me more than <u>him</u>.
7. Will is as good a dancer as <u>he</u>.
8. The drama teacher has helped Lewis more than <u>him</u>.
9. Alicia memorizes lines faster than <u>they</u>.
10. Brian has tutored Lydia more than <u>her</u>.

EXERCISE 2 Choose the correct pronoun to complete each sentence.

1. Everyone is as excited about the drama club's new musical as (I me).
2. Elena has sold more tickets than (she her).
3. Elena's a good salesperson, so the drama teacher has given her more tickets to sell than (they them).
4. I have passed out more fliers to friends than (they them).
5. Carol knew her lines. During rehearsal, the teacher had to give Edward more help with lines than (she her).
6. Edward's singing impressed me as much as (she her). We had never heard him sing as well.
7. No one is as talented at singing and dancing as (she her).
8. The ending of the play surprised me as much as (they them)—there was a big gasp from the audience.
9. The play was as entertaining to me as it was to (she her).
10. No one worked harder than the drama coach, and no one was more pleased about the success of the play than (he him).

EXERCISE 3 Choose the correct pronoun to complete each sentence. Then tell the word or words that have been omitted from each sentence.

1. Evelyn walks more quickly than (she her).
2. Dustin sings better than (I me).
3. Sasha swims as fast as (he him).
4. That band is as good as (we us).
5. Juan is older than (I me).
6. I hope to be as proficient as (she her).
7. Ben finished his homework before (I me).
8. She prepares her work better than (I me)
9. Darnell is not so witty as (he him).
10. Antonio climbs as well as (she her).
11. He drove no faster than (we us).
12. Sarita skied down a steeper trail than (she her).
13. I arrived at the movies before (he him).
14. Ed recognized the star sooner than (she her).
15. Our sprinters are faster than (they them).

APPLY IT NOW

Write seven sentences in which you compare skills of famous athletes and entertainers. Use *than* and *as* followed by personal pronouns.

3.5 Possessive Pronouns and Adjectives

Possessive pronouns show possession, or ownership. They take the place of possessive nouns.

> **The paints are** *Jerome's.* (possessive noun)
> **The paints are** *his.* (possessive pronoun)

Possessive pronouns change in form to indicate person, number, and gender. Make sure possessive pronouns agree with their antecedents. Be careful of the spelling. Unlike possessive nouns, possessive pronouns do not contain apostrophes. Study the chart.

POSSESSIVE PRONOUNS	SINGULAR	PLURAL
FIRST PERSON	mine	ours
SECOND PERSON	yours	yours
THIRD PERSON	his, hers, its	theirs

Possessive pronouns have the same roles in sentences as nouns do.

> *Hers* **is the large painting.** (subject)
> **That sculpture is** *his.* (subject complement)
> **Have you seen** *mine*? (direct object)

Words similar to possessive pronouns are possessive adjectives. The possessive adjectives are *my, our, your, his, her, its,* and *their*. Possessive pronouns stand alone. **Possessive adjectives** always precede the nouns they modify.

POSSESSIVE PRONOUNS	POSSESSIVE ADJECTIVES
Mine is on that wall.	*My* painting is on that wall.
Hers is beautiful.	*Her* ceramic pot is beautiful.

EXERCISE 1 Identify the possessive pronoun or possessive adjective in each sentence. Identify the noun each possessive adjective modifies.

1. The art department was organizing its annual art show.
2. Entrants could submit watercolors, ceramics, sculptures, and so on; the choice of medium was theirs.
3. Even our teachers could enter the show.

EXERCISE 2 Complete the sentences with possessive pronouns. The pronoun should refer to the underlined antecedent.

1. Raphael likes to work with clay. That clay sculpture of a basketball player shooting a basket must be _____.

2. I know Jill submitted an acrylic piece. Do you think that the picture with the big colorful fruit is _____?

3. Did you decide to do a collage? Is the collage with pictures from magazines _____?

4. Yolanda and Michael decided to work together. I think the sculpture made from old bicycle wheels is _____.

5. Lila does wonderfully detailed pencil drawings. I'm sure that drawing of a cactus is _____.

EXERCISE 3 Rewrite the sentences so that the use of possessive pronouns and possessive adjectives is correct.

1. A panel of students and teachers is judging the prizewinners. That difficult decision is their's.

2. Everyone was impressed by Jill's painting. So no one was surprised when the top prize became hers'.

3. The eighth-grade teacher's pencil portrait of hers mother earned her a special prize.

4. The pieces of artwork from the show now hang throughout the school. Ours' are in the library.

EXERCISE 4 Complete the sentences with appropriate possessive pronouns.

1. That blue sweater is not _____.

2. Take _____ but leave _____.

3. _____ is not as warm as _____.

4. The book is _____ but that is _____.

5. Mr. Rodriguez sold _____.

6. _____ ran away.

7. The umbrella with the purple stripes is _____.

8. Someone stole _____.

9. _____ was left on the beach.

APPLY IT NOW

Imagine that you took your brother's or sister's books to school and your brother or sister took yours. In 10 sentences, explain how this happened. Use at least three possessive pronouns to keep your writing from becoming repetitive.

3.6 Intensive and Reflexive Pronouns

Intensive pronouns and reflexive pronouns end in *self* or *selves*.

An **intensive pronoun** is used to emphasize a preceding noun or pronoun.

> I *myself* **researched family vacation spots on the Internet.**
> **My mother** *herself* **was surprised at all the information I found.**

A **reflexive pronoun** is usually the object of a verb or a preposition. The reflexive pronoun refers back to the subject of the clause or sentence.

> **I enjoyed** *myself* **at the cabin.** (direct object)
> **They cooked** *themselves* **meals over an outdoor grill.** (indirect object)
> **My mother packed the car by** *herself*. (object of a preposition)

The chart shows forms of intensive and reflexive pronouns. These pronouns should agree with their antecedents in person, number, and gender.

INTENSIVE AND REFLEXIVE PRONOUNS	SINGULAR	PLURAL
FIRST PERSON	myself	ourselves
SECOND PERSON	yourself	yourselves
THIRD PERSON	himself herself itself	themselves

Note that *hisself* and *theirselves* are not good usage. What words from the chart would you use instead of those words? You are correct if you said *himself* and *themselves*.

It is also incorrect to use forms with *self* instead of subject and object pronouns.

> **Edward and I** (*not* myself) **don't know how to swim.**
> **The meal was made by Hans and me.** (*not* myself)

> **Grandpa and you** (*not* yourself) **are great pals.**
> **Grandpa relies on Maya and you.** (*not* yourself)

EXERCISE 1 Identify the intensive or reflexive pronoun in each sentence. Then identify its antecedent.

1. My parents decided on our vacation plans for this year themselves—with the help of my cousins' family.

2. As we prepared ourselves for the vacation, we wondered how we would get along with our cousins for a month.

3. I packed my suitcase myself, but I knew I had forgotten something.

4. My father drove most of the way to the lake himself.

5. The lake itself was beautiful, though the mountains were rather barren.

EXERCISE 2 Complete each sentence with an intensive or a reflexive pronoun. The pronoun should refer to the underlined antecedent.

1. We treated _____ to the rental of a sailboat.

2. My older sister proved _____ to be a good skipper.

3. I _____ learned a little about handling the boat.

4. Our parents _____ informed us about safety rules.

EXERCISE 3 Complete each sentence with an intensive or a reflexive pronoun. Then identify its antecedent.

1. Maya blamed _____ for the misunderstanding.

2. Josh cut _____ on a piece of the broken ketchup bottle.

3. Every woman must answer for _____.

4. The firefighters _____ could not find the source of the smoke.

5. Levi _____ had been hiking in the forest that afternoon.

6. You _____ heard the judge's verdict.

7. The fugitives hid _____ from the sheriff.

8. We _____ were responsible for the broken window.

9. Kim's turtle hid _____ behind a pile of stuffed animals.

10. You and your classmates disagreed among _____.

11. I _____ made the birdhouse.

12. Louis XIV called _____ the Sun King.

APPLY IT NOW

Describe a project you have undertaken that proved to be more than you had expected. Use two intensive and reflexive pronouns in your description.

 Tech Tip Post your description on a class blog or wiki.

3.7 Agreement of Pronouns and Antecedents

The word to which a pronoun refers is called its antecedent. Pronouns agree with their antecedents in person, number, and gender. You need to make sure you use the correct person, number, and gender when you replace a noun or a pronoun with another pronoun.

> *Lloyd Alexander* **wrote** *Time Cat*, **and** *he* **has written several other fantasy books.**

The antecedent of the subject pronoun *he* is *Lloyd Alexander,* so the third person singular masculine form is used.

In the following, what is the antecedent of *he*? of *her*?

> **Lloyd Alexander wrote about Vesper Holly. He places her in exciting and dangerous situations.**

You are correct if you answered *Lloyd Alexander* for the antecedent of *he*. The subject pronoun *he* is third person singular masculine. The antecedent of *her* is *Vesper Holly*. The object pronoun *her* is third person singular feminine to agree with its antecedent.

Mark Twain

EXERCISE 1 Identify the pronoun or pronouns that refer to each underlined antecedent.

1. <u>Readers</u> are interested in time travel, and many books on this topic will appeal to them.

2. Mark Twain is probably best known for his books set near the <u>Mississippi</u>, but he also wrote books set far from it—in other times and places.

3. Twain's <u>novel</u> *A Connecticut Yankee in King Arthur's Court* is set in the year AD 528, and it is, in fact, a time-travel book.

4. <u>Hank Morgan</u>, the main character, travels to the past, where he uses his knowledge of 19th-century technology to get himself a good life and even a place at the Round Table itself.

5. <u>Twain</u> uses the book to critique the society of his time, and yet he makes readers laugh at the humorous situations that befall the main character.

EXERCISE 2 Identify the antecedent for each underlined pronoun. Then tell the person, number, and, as appropriate, gender of that antecedent.

1. I have a book to recommend, a favorite of <u>mine</u>.
2. The book is about time travel, and <u>it</u> entertains from start to finish.
3. The title is *Time Cat,* and the title <u>itself</u> describes the content.
4. Gareth, a cat who lives in the present, has the ability to travel into the past, where <u>he</u> has adventures at different times in history.
5. Gareth takes his master, Jason, with <u>him</u>.
6. Gareth and Jason travel to nine different times and places, and <u>they</u> experience everyday life in each.
7. The adventures they have are so much fun that I forgot I was actually learning from <u>them</u>.

EXERCISE 3 Complete each sentence with the appropriate pronoun. Make sure your choice agrees with its antecedent in person, number, and, where appropriate, gender.

1. Ms. Chaplin, our social studies teacher, has made an assignment that, _____ said, is completely different from her usual ones.
2. We are to write a story, and _____ is to be set in a time and place we've learned about in class.
3. She _____ will do the assignment along with us.
4. I've spoken to some students, and _____ told me that they plan to do a lot of research.
5. Some students have chosen their periods, and I've chosen _____—the colonial period in America.

EXERCISE 4 Complete each sentence with a possessive pronoun that agrees with its antecedent.

1. Brian has finished _____ dinner and is now clearing the table.
2. Janet is going to the movies, and Phillip is going with _____.
3. The clean-up crew finished early because one of the teams helped _____.
4. We could not take any of the kittens into _____ home until the vet had checked them.

APPLY IT NOW

Imagine you have received the assignment described in Exercise 3. Describe the period in history that you would use as your setting and tell why you chose it. Underline all the pronouns and circle their antecedents.

Grammar in Action. Identify pronoun antecedents in the last paragraph of the p. 261 excerpt.

3.8 Interrogative and Demonstrative Pronouns

Interrogative pronouns are used to ask questions. The interrogative pronouns are *who, whom, whose, which,* and *what.*

Who refers to persons. It is often the subject of a question.

> **Who visited New York?** (subject)

Whom refers to persons. It is the object of a verb or a preposition.

> **Whom did you visit there?** (direct object)
> **With whom did you go on the trip?** (object of a preposition)

Whose is used when asking about possession. *Which* is used when asking about a group or class. *What* is used for asking about things and seeking information.

> **Whose are those photos of New York?**
> **Which of the other states would you like to visit?**
> **What did you take with you on your trip?**

What is the error in the sentence below?

> **Who did you show your photos to?**

The interrogative pronoun must be in the object form because it is the object of the preposition *to.* Therefore, *whom* is the correct choice.

The **demonstrative pronouns** point out a particular person, place, or thing. They are *this, that, these,* and *those.*

> **This is a picture of a historic skyscraper.** (near)
> **That is a picture of my grandmother with whom I stayed.** (far)
> **These are some souvenirs I bought.** (near)
> **Those are presents for you.** (far)

EXERCISE 1 Complete each question with an interrogative pronoun.

1. _____ has ever visited Arizona?
2. _____ are some of the sights you can see there?
3. _____ of the cities did you visit?
4. _____ of the Native American nations have lived in Arizona?
5. _____ were the various types of Native American dwellings?

6. _____ was instrumental in preserving the ancient ruins?

7. By _____ was the area ruled in the 1600s?

8. From _____ was the area of Arizona purchased for the United States?

9. _____ are some famous Arizonians?

10. _____ is the best time of the year to visit Arizona?

EXERCISE 2 Complete each sentence with *who* or *whom*.

1. _____ is the first settler to explore Arizona?

2. By _____ were you told?

3. _____ do you think built ruins?

4. With _____ did you come to the presentation?

5. _____ brought the tortillas?

6. For _____are these remarks intended?

7. _____ should we invite on our canyon hike?

8. _____ can it be?

EXERCISE 3 Complete each sentence by adding the correct demonstrative pronoun. Use the directions in parentheses. Be sure to use the correct number.

1. _____ (near) are some examples of Native American art from Arizona.

2. What kind of doll is _____ (far)?

3. _____ (near) is a kachina doll. And so is _____ (far).

4. Are _____ (far) special kinds of dolls?

5. Yes, in Hopi culture, _____ (near) represent spirits that visit a village to help people live in harmony with nature.

6. What are _____ (far)—the round objects with feathers?

7. _____ (near) are dream catchers. According to Navajo legend, they capture bad dreams and let good dreams pass.

8. What is _____ (far) on the silver bracelet?

9. _____ (far) is a piece of turquoise. It's a traditional gemstone in jewelry of the Southwest.

10. _____ (near) are all fascinating objects with interesting stories.

APPLY IT NOW

Write seven questions about a state that interests you, using at least three different interrogative pronouns. Then find the answers to your own questions.

Tech Tip With an adult, research your state online.

3.9 Relative Pronouns

A **relative pronoun** is used to join a dependent clause to its antecedent in the independent clause. The relative pronouns are *who, whom, that, whose,* and *which.*

> **The Chinese use certain medical treatments *that* are not common practices in the West.**

The relative pronoun *that* joins the dependent clause—*that are not common practices in the West*—to the independent clause—*The Chinese use certain medical treatments.* The antecedent of *that* is *treatments.*

The relative pronouns *who* and *whom* refer to persons.

> **The Chinese, *who* have one of the world's oldest civilizations, have a written history going back more than 3,500 years.**

The relative pronoun *that* refers to people, animals, places, or things. The relative pronoun *whose* often refers to people but also can refer to animals, places, or things. The relative pronoun *which* refers to animals, places, or things.

> **People *that* the Chinese influenced included the Koreans.**
> **The Chinese, *whose* civilization is ancient, developed paper first.**
> **Chinese culture, *which* was respected, influenced many other cultures throughout Asia.**

Which of the following is correct?

> **People who the Chinese influenced included the Japanese.**
> **People whom the Chinese influenced included the Japanese.**

The second sentence is correct. The relative pronoun is the direct object in the dependent clause, so the object form *whom* is correct. Use *who* when the relative pronoun is the subject in a dependent clause. Use *whom* when the relative pronoun is an object in a dependent clause—a direct object, an indirect object, or an object of a preposition.

> **Other Asians, *who* admired the Chinese, adopted aspects of Chinese language and culture.** (subject)
> **The Chinese, for *whom* acupuncture is a common practice, use medical treatments different from those in the West.** (object of a preposition)

EXERCISE 1 Identify each relative pronoun. Then find its antecedent.

1. The Chinese use medical procedures that rely on the body's natural ability to heal itself.

2. Many Westerners also believe in this approach, which is thousands of years old.

3. In the 12th century, Chinese medical information was written down in a huge volume that Chinese practitioners still use today.

4. Anyone who is treated by a Chinese practitioner has probably received acupuncture.

5. The patient is treated with fine needles that are used for pain relief and other therapeutic purposes.

6. They are inserted in areas of the body called meridians, which are considered channels of energy in the body.

EXERCISE 2 Complete each sentence with *who* or *whom*. Then tell how that pronoun functions in the dependent clause.

1. Herbal medicine is popular with people _____ live in the West.

2. Usually, herbal treatments are specially selected for the patient to _____ they are prescribed.

3. Patients typically give detailed case histories to practitioners _____ specialize in herbal medicine.

4. Many of the people _____ practice herbal medicine follow ancient Chinese traditions.

5. A naturopathic doctor is someone _____ you might consult about herbal remedies.

EXERCISE 3 Add dependent clauses that begin with relative pronouns where indicated in the following sentences.

1. Mr. Li, (dependent clause), studies the art of combining medicinal herbs.

2. Special herbs, (dependent clause), help ease his patients of their pain.

3. The Chinese, (dependent clause), commonly use herbs such as ginseng and licorice.

APPLY IT NOW

Look in magazines and newspapers for five sentences containing relative pronouns. For each, underline the dependent clause, circle the relative pronoun, and draw an arrow from that pronoun to its antecedent.

Grammar in Action. Identify the relative pronoun in the p. 260 excerpt.

3.10 Indefinite Pronouns

An **indefinite pronoun** refers to any or all of a group of people, places, or things.

SINGULAR		PLURAL	SINGULAR AND PLURAL
another	neither	both	all
anybody	nobody	few	any
anyone	no one	many	more
anything	nothing	others	most
each	one	several	none
either	other		some
everybody	somebody		
everyone	someone		
everything	something		
much			

Like nouns, indefinite pronouns act as subjects and objects.

> *Many* **have visited the Rock and Roll Hall of Fame and Museum.** (subject)
>
> **I read** *something* **about the museum online.** (direct object)
>
> **I hadn't heard of** *either* **of those musicians.** (object of a preposition)
>
> **She was the** *one* **who sang the anthem.** (subject complement)

Some of these words can also be used as adjectives.

> *Many* **musicians are in the Rock and Roll Hall of Fame.**

Many is an adjective that modifies the noun *musicians.*

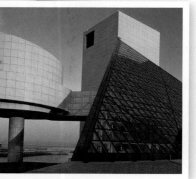

Rock and Roll Hall of Fame and Museum

EXERCISE 1 Identify the indefinite pronouns in these sentences. Not every sentence contains an indefinite pronoun.

1. Few may know that the Rock and Roll Hall of Fame and Museum is fairly new; it was opened in Cleveland in 1995.

2. Someone had the idea for a Rock and Roll Hall of Fame in the 1980s.

3. Its purpose was to honor musicians and others who had contributed to rock-and-roll history.

4. All of those in the hall are acknowledged "greats."

5. Several are elected to the Rock Hall annually as new members.

6. A panel of 1,000 rock-and-roll experts choose them.

7. A big contribution to rock and roll was made by each.

8. The Hall of Fame building impresses everyone.

9. It features bold geometric shapes and a 162-foot tower.

10. Many have performed at the Rock Hall.

11. Each have found the experience to be thrilling.

12. Someday I plan to visit it too.

13. I don't know the names of every rock star elected to the Rock Hall, but I know quite a few.

14. Maybe I will be someone elected to the Hall of Fame.

Chuck Berry

EXERCISE 2 Identify the indefinite pronoun or pronouns in each sentence. Then tell what its function is in the sentence.

1. It should surprise nobody that Elvis Presley was among the original inductees to the Rock and Roll Hall of Fame and Museum.

2. Everybody called him the King for his role in popularizing rock and roll.

3. Actually, some credit Chuck Berry, also an original inductee, with inventing the new musical style.

4. He did something that no one had done before—combine country and western with rhythm and blues.

5. Both of these styles merged to develop into rock and roll in the 1950s.

6. Aretha Franklin was one of the first women members.

7. Most know her as the Queen of Soul.

8. Several of her songs sold more than a million copies.

9. Not all the inductees are actually rock-and-roll musicians; some are placed in a special category.

10. Bessie Smith, a blues singer of the early 1900s, for example, is one of several in the category "Early Influences."

EXERCISE 3 Write sentences using the following indefinite pronouns.

1. everybody
2. somebody
3. all
4. some
5. much
6. each
7. several
8. either

APPLY IT NOW

Talk to seven people about what they know about rock and roll and its musicians and what they think of this type of music. Write a paragraph with your results. Include at least four indefinite pronouns.

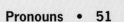 Chart your results on a graph using PowerPoint.

3.11 Agreement with Indefinite Pronouns

Most indefinite pronouns are singular, but some are plural. When an indefinite pronoun acts as the subject of a sentence, the verb needs to agree with it in number.

Singular indefinite pronouns include *another, anybody, anyone, anything, each, either, everybody, everyone, everything, much, neither, nobody, no one, nothing, one, other, somebody, someone,* and *something.* They take singular verbs.

> **No one is able to predict earthquakes.**

In the above sentence, *no one* is followed by *is,* the third person singular form of the verb *be.*

Which verb correctly completes the following sentence?

> **Everyone (want wants) us to be able to predict them.**

The correct answer is *wants.* It is a third person singular verb, to agree with the singular indefinite pronoun. Remember that third person singular verbs end in *s.*

Plural indefinite pronouns include *both, few, many, others,* and *several.* They take plural verbs.

> **Many are working to try to predict earthquakes.**

Some indefinite pronouns can be either singular or plural, depending on how they are used in a sentence. These include *all, any, more, most, none,* and *some.* These pronouns are singular and take a singular verb when they are followed by a phrase with a singular noun or an abstract noun. They are plural and take a plural verb when they are followed by a phrase with a plural noun.

SINGULAR	PLURAL
All of the building was destroyed.	**All of the buildings were destroyed.**

EXERCISE 1 Choose the correct verb to complete each sentence. Make sure the verb agrees with its subject.

1. (Has Have) anybody been able to predict earthquakes?
2. Some (says say) that we don't know much in this area of science.
3. Scientists can tell us where quakes might occur in the future, but no one (is are) really more definite than that.
4. All of the efforts so far (has have) not created anything to predict a quake reliably.
5. Among cultures in earthquake regions, several (has have) tried for centuries to predict quakes.
6. One of those attempts (was were) an ancient Chinese device that actually picked up the earth's vibrations and pointed out the direction of the quake.
7. None of the proposed methods for predicting earthquakes, however, (has have) proved successful.

EXERCISE 2 Identify the indefinite pronoun in each sentence. Then choose the verb that agrees with it.

1. Several of the students (wear wears) parkas in the winter.
2. Neither of the girls (play plays) in the band.
3. Both of the boys usually (forget forgets) their homework.
4. One of the answers (is are) wrong.
5. Many of the employees (eat eats) their lunches in the diner.

EXERCISE 3 Rewrite the sentences to correct errors in agreement between subject and verb. Not all sentences have errors.

1. Nobody is likely to forget being in an earthquake.
2. Nothing feels scarier than having the whole world shaking around you.
3. Many says that the air smells different after an earthquake.
4. Everyone agree that the experience is indescribable.
5. Some experience several quakes in a lifetime.
6. Of my two friends in California, both has firsthand knowledge of this phenomenon.
7. Neither, however, have been hurt by the earthquakes.
8. Everybody in earthquake zones need to learn about emergency procedures.

APPLY IT NOW

Write eight sentences describing a collection of things, such as the contents of your backpack. Use four indefinite pronouns in your paragraph. Underline the verbs with which the indefinite pronouns agree.

Pronoun Review

3.1 Identify each pronoun, and tell its person, number, and gender.

1. I am trying to decide whether to take French or Spanish as an elective.

2. Julia decided to take German because she is going to visit a friend in Hamburg next summer.

3. You should take a foreign-language course.

4. Jack and Ryan think they might take Japanese.

3.2 Choose the correct subject pronoun to complete each sentence.

5. (I Me) am reading *The Hobbit* for my book club.

6. My friends really liked the *Lord of the Rings* movies, and it was (they them) who picked the book.

7. (They Them) will make the discussion exciting.

8. My brother and (I me) really like the book, especially the part about the dragon.

3.3 Identify the underlined pronoun in each sentence as a direct object, an indirect object, or an object of a preposition.

9. Lewis and Clark took a dog with <u>them</u> out West.

10. The Native Americans wanted to trade skins for <u>it</u>.

11. Lewis was the first to observe coyotes, which always saluted <u>him</u> by barking.

12. The grizzly bears gave <u>them</u> a real fright.

13. Once, when a bear came close to camp, Lewis and Clark and several men with rifles killed <u>it</u>.

3.4 Choose the correct pronoun to complete each sentence. Then identify the word to which the pronoun is compared.

14. Jim and Sarah are learning sign language, but Jim is becoming a better signer than (her she).

15. Sarah also takes a Spanish class but thinks the signing class is more exciting than (them it).

16. Ms. Ramos is an excellent teacher, and Sarah wants to be as good as (she her).

3.5 Rewrite the sentences and replace each possessive adjective and noun with the correct possessive pronoun.

17. My Chumbawumba CD is in the car.

18. We switched, and he gave me his Joni Mitchell CD.

19. Our CD collection has more than a thousand titles.

20. We went to our friends' house to see their collections.

3.6 Identify the underlined pronouns as intensive or reflexive. Then tell their antecedents.

21. We prepared ourselves for writing a research paper on American history.

22. My mother herself was amazed that we had to write 10 pages each.

23. I amazed myself when I thought of a good topic and started the paper early.

24. You yourself should start any project at least a month before it is due.

3.7 Complete each sentence with the pronoun that agrees with the antecedent.

25. Josh and Cara wanted a new pet, so _____ went to the animal shelter.

26. _____ wanted a kitten, but he wanted a dog.

27. Josh couldn't decide until a gray cat jumped onto _____.

28. Josh loved the cat, and _____ named it Cannonball.

3.8 Complete each sentence with an appropriate interrogative or demonstrative pronoun.

29. _____ is the book on astronomy?

30. Do you know _____ of the planets are visible tonight?

31. From _____ did you get the book?

32. _____ is a fascinating book.

3.9 Identify the relative pronoun and its antecedent in each sentence.

33. The Chunnel is a train tunnel that connects France and England.

34. People who travel by Chunnel can make the journey in about one hour.

35. Commuters, for whom crossing quickly is important, use this option.

3.10 Identify the indefinite pronoun or pronouns in each sentence.

36. The speaker told the eighth graders that each person should visit a farm at least once.

37. A farm has something to offer everybody.

38. Not just anybody can learn to work on a farm; several skills require a lot of practice.

39. Even among farmers, some say that they have never mastered farming.

3.11 Rewrite the sentences to correct errors between subject and verb.

40. Have anybody ever walked the 3,750 miles atop the Great Wall of China?

41. Nobody know how many people were needed to complete the wall.

42. Some thinks the wall stand as a reminder of the strength of the Chinese people.

 Tech Tip Go to www.voyagesinenglish.com for more activities.

Pronoun Challenge

EXERCISE 1 Read the selection and then answer the questions.

1. Each of you, boys and girls, belongs to two important societies: the family and the state. 2. "What," you may ask, "is the obligation that is imposed by membership in these societies?" 3. The answer is this. 4. You must give a respectful obedience to those in authority, perform your duties conscientiously, and strive to live in harmony with other members. 5. In other words, you must develop in yourself whatever will make you a valued member of each group. 6. Such is the attitude of every worthwhile person. 7. It should also be yours.

1. What kind of pronoun is the first word in the selection?
2. Name the personal pronoun in sentence 1. Is it singular or plural?
3. What is the person and number of the pronoun *you* in sentence 2? How is it used in the sentence?
4. What is the interrogative pronoun in sentence 2? How is it used?
5. What is the relative pronoun in sentence 2? What is its antecedent?
6. What is the demonstrative pronoun in sentence 3?
7. In sentence 4, what personal pronoun is used as a subject?
8. What is the pronoun in sentence 6? What kind of pronoun is it?
9. What is the gender of the pronoun *it* in sentence 7?
10. Find the reflexive pronoun in the selection. What sentence is it in? How is it used in the sentence?
11. Find the possessive pronoun in the paragraph. What sentence is it in?

EXERCISE 2 Do you agree with the paragraph above? Would you add anything else? Follow the instructions below.

Write a short response to this paragraph explaining how you would change it, what you might add or remove, and why. You can also give examples from your own experience. Be sure to include an interrogative pronoun, a subject pronoun, and an object pronoun. Then identify the subject pronoun as either a subject or a subject complement. Identify the object pronoun as a direct object, an indirect object, or an object of a preposition. Finally, correctly use either *who* or *whom* at least once in your response.

Verbs

4.1 Principal Parts of Verbs

Verbs show action or state of being.

> We *read* several Mexican folktales. (action)
> Folktales *are* traditional stories of a people. (state of being)

The principal parts of a verb are the **base form,** the **past,** and the **past participle.** A fourth part, the **present participle,** is formed by adding *-ing* to the base form of the verb. Participles have three functions in sentences. They can be part of a verb phrase, or they can function as an adjective or a noun.

Aztec calendar

BASE	PAST	PAST PARTICIPLE	PRESENT PARTICIPLE
talk	talked	talked	talking

Regular verbs, such as *talk,* form the past and past participle by adding *-d* or *-ed* to the base form. Irregular verbs, such as the ones below, do not form the past and past participle in this way. If you are unsure of the principal parts of a verb, check a dictionary.

BASE	PAST	PAST PARTICIPLE	PRESENT PARTICIPLE
hide	hid	hid	hiding
freeze	froze	frozen	freezing

A **verb phrase** is two or more verbs that work together as a unit. A verb phrase may have one or more **auxiliary verbs** and a **main verb.**

> One folktale *is called* "The Legend of the Volcanoes."

In the sentence above, the main verb is the past participle *called*, and the auxiliary verb *is* is a form of the verb *be*. Note that the past participle is often used with auxiliary verbs, but the past stands alone.

Can you find the main verb and the auxiliary verb in this sentence?

> The volcano has emitted smoke for years.

You are correct if you said that *has* is the auxiliary verb and that *emitted,* a past participle, is the main verb.

Common auxiliary verbs are *be* and *have* and their various forms, as well as *do* and *did.* Other auxiliary verbs include *can, may, might, should, could,* and *will.*

EXERCISE 1 Underline the verbs and verb phrases in the sentences. Then identify the auxiliary verb and the main verb in each verb phrase.

1. The most famous volcano in Mexico is called Popocatépetl.
2. Its name means "smoking mountain."
3. The volcano has been an active one for hundreds of years.
4. It lies close to Mexico City.
5. According to Aztec legends, this volcano was once a warrior that had been transformed into a volcano.
6. Kilauea, the earth's most active volcano, is located in Hawaii.
7. It is the youngest volcano on the big island of Hawaii.
8. This volcano has erupted continuously since 1983!
9. It was believed to be the home of Pele, the Hawaiian volcano goddess, by ancient Hawaiians.

EXERCISE 2 Identify each verb or verb phrase. Tell whether each main verb is the past form or the past participle form.

1. An ancient ruler and his wife had a beautiful baby.
2. The daughter was named Iztaccíhuatl.
3. When she grew up, she fell in love with a warrior, Popoca.
4. Popoca was called to battle.
5. The king had promised Popoca his daughter's hand for a victory.
6. A false message came to the king that Popoca had won but that he had been killed in battle.
7. When Iztaccíhuatl heard the news, she died of sadness.
8. When Popoca arrived back home, he learned of Iztaccíhuatl's death.
9. He died of grief.
10. According to myth, the lovers were transformed into volcanos.
11. Have you noticed his name within the name of the volcano Popocatépetl?

Popocatépetl volcano

APPLY IT NOW

Write a brief summary of a folktale or a legend you know. Use each of the four verb forms at least once, and label them accordingly.

Grammar in Action. Identify three past principal parts in the p. 298 letter.

4.2 Transitive and Intransitive Verbs

A **transitive verb** expresses an action that passes from a doer to a receiver. The receiver of the action is the direct object. To determine whether there is a direct object, ask *whom* or *what* after the verb.

> **The ancient Greeks *created* myths.**

The verb *created* is transitive. Its direct object is *myths*.

Some transitive verbs are phrasal verbs. A **phrasal verb** is a combination of a main verb and a preposition or an adverb, such as *clear out, nail down, nose out, root out, saddle up,* and *win over.* Although it may appear to be the object in a prepositional phrase, the noun or pronoun that follows a phrasal verb is a direct object. In the following sentence, *up this horse* is not a prepositional phrase.

> **Saddle up this horse.** (*Saddle up* is the phrasal verb; *horse* is the direct object.)

An **intransitive verb** does not have a receiver for its action. It does not have a direct object.

> **A family of gods *sat* on Mount Olympus.**

Can you tell whether the verb in this sentence is transitive or intransitive? How can you tell?

> **The myths *provided* explanations of things in the world.**

The verb *provided* is transitive. Its direct object is *explanations*. Some verbs may be transitive or intransitive, depending on their use in the sentence.

> **Hercules *fought* a huge lion.** (transitive)
> **The gods *fought* among themselves.** (intransitive)

EXERCISE 1 Identify the verb, verb phrase, or phrasal verb in each sentence. Then tell whether the verb is transitive or intransitive.

1. The Greek gods watched over human affairs.
2. From high on Mount Olympus, they watched.
3. People still tell the Greek myths.

4. Some of the myths describe such heroes as Hercules and Perseus.
5. People sometimes prayed to the gods for help.
6. The Greeks called the messenger of the gods Hermes.
7. I have read about Greek heroes in class.
8. The lives of Greek gods and heroes make fascinating stories.

EXERCISE 2 Identify the verb, verb phrase, or phrasal verb in each sentence. Tell whether it is transitive or intransitive. For each transitive verb, identify the direct object.

1. The young hero Perseus lived with his mother, Danae.
2. A king wanted Perseus's mother for his wife.
3. The king did not get along with Perseus.
4. He challenged Perseus to an impossible feat.
5. The king was wishing for Perseus's death.
6. The brave Perseus accepted the challenge.
7. The king requested the head of a monster.
8. Medusa, the monster, had snakes for hair.
9. One sight of the monster turned people into stone.
10. Medusa once had boasted of her beauty.
11. The gods had punished her for that boast.
12. The gods now were looking after Perseus.
13. One goddess lent Perseus a bright shield.
14. Perseus was walking along in search of Medusa.
15. Eventually, he came to Medusa's island home.
16. How could he bring about the monster's death?

EXERCISE 3 Identify the verbs. Tell whether they are transitive or intransitive. For each transitive verb, identify the direct object. Identify any transitive verbs that are phrasal verbs.

1. What movies are shown at that theater?
2. Brad Pitt played the Greek hero Achilles in one movie.
3. Achilles and Hector fought against each other in one battle scene.
4. We all cleared out of the theater afterward.

APPLY IT NOW

Write two sentences for each of the verbs *read*, *fight*, and *practice*. In one sentence use the verb as a transitive verb and in the other as an intransitive verb.

4.3 Troublesome Verbs

The following pairs of verbs often cause usage problems. Study the differences to avoid mistakes.

Teach (taught, taught) means "to give knowledge."
Learn (learned, learned) means "to receive knowledge."

> He *taught* history.
> I *learned* a lot in his class.

Take (took, taken) means "to carry from a near place to a more distant place."
Bring (brought, brought) means "to carry from a distant place to a near place."

> Don't *take* that book to Jim's house.
> Please *bring* several sharp pencils for the test.

Lend (lent, lent) means "to let someone use something of yours."
Borrow (borrowed, borrowed) means "to take something and use it as one's own with the idea of returning it."

> Please *lend* me your coat.
> He *borrowed* a warm coat.

Lie (lay, lain, lying) means "to recline." It does not take a direct object.
Lay (laid, laid, laying) means "to place." It takes a direct object. Notice the differences in the principal parts of *lie* and *lay*.

> *Lie* down here.
> *Lay* the blanket on the bed.

Rise (rose, risen) means "to get up." It does not take a direct object.
Raise (raised, raised) means "to lift up" or "to bring to maturity." It takes a direct object.

> Please *rise* now.
> They *raise* the flag each morning.

Sit (sat, sat) means "to take a seat." It does not take a direct object.
Set (set, set) means "to put down." It takes a direct object.

> *Sit* down in the kitchen.
> *Set* the groceries on the table.

EXERCISE 1 Choose the correct verb to complete each sentence.

1. He (learned taught) us how to project our voices onstage and gave lots of other tips about acting.
2. Don't (set sit) the paint can there while you're working.
3. Don't (take bring) that brush; I still need it.
4. Come and (set sit) down; you look exhausted.
5. After painting all afternoon, I had to (lie lay) down and rest.
6. Whose job is it to (rise raise) the curtain?
7. Do you know where I've (lain laid) my script?
8. My sister (borrowed lent) me her silk blouse for the performance.
9. I even (lent borrowed) her best scarf.
10. At the last minute, my mother didn't remember where she (lay laid) the tickets.
11. She had (set sit) them on the hall table.
12. They were (lying laying) there when we looked for them.

EXERCISE 2 Rewrite any incorrect sentence to correct the use of a troublesome verb. Not all the sentences have errors.

1. We're selling T-shirts for the play at the door; we hope to raise money for next term's play.
2. The community center borrowed us extra chairs for the performance.
3. All the members of the audience raised to their feet and applauded.
4. The entire experience learned us a lot about the theater and acting.
5. The experience was so exhausting that I laid in bed resting until 10 o'clock the next morning.
6. The babysitter laid the sleeping infant in the crib.

EXERCISE 3 Choose the correct verb to complete each sentence.

1. Don't forget to _____ your fishing rod with you on your camping trip. (take bring)
2. The audience _____ from their seats and applauded the musician. (raise rose)
3. _____ your boots and socks by the woodstove so they will dry out by morning. (Lie Lay)

APPLY IT NOW

Use each troublesome verb on the preceding page in a sentence to illustrate its correct use.

4.4 Linking Verbs

Not all verbs express action. **A linking verb** joins the subject with a **subject complement.** The subject complement is a noun or pronoun that renames the subject, or an adjective that describes the subject.

SUBJECT	LINKING VERB	SUBJECT COMPLEMENT
Woody Guthrie	**was**	**a folk singer.** (noun)
It	**was**	**he who popularized folk music.** (pronoun)
His songs	**remain**	**popular.** (adjective)

The verb *be* in its various forms (*am, is, are, was, were, will be, has been, had been,* and so on) is the most common linking verb. Other common linking verbs are *appear, become, feel, grow, look, remain, seem, smell, sound, stay, taste,* and *turn.*

Some of these verbs can function as either action verbs or linking verbs.

> **Miriam Makeba's name** *remains* **famous in the music world.** (linking verb)
> **She** *remained* **in the United States for many years.** (action verb—an intransitive verb)
> **Makeba's voice** *sounded* **powerful.** (linking verb)
> **Makeba courageously** *sounded* **her protest against apartheid to the world.** (action verb—a transitive verb with the direct object *protest*)

When words such as *remain* and *sound* are used as linking verbs, a form of the verb *be* can be substituted for the original verb.

> **Miriam Makeba's name** *is* **famous in the music world.**
> **Makeba's voice** *is* **powerful.**

EXERCISE 1 Identify the linking verbs and the subject complements in these sentences. Not every sentence has a linking verb.

1. Woody Guthrie was a songwriter.
2. He became famous for his songs about the United States and its people.
3. Many of his songs are accounts of working people during the Great Depression of the 1930s.
4. His was a voice of protest against injustice.

Woody Guthrie

5. "This Land Is Your Land" remains his most famous song.

6. It is a celebration of the country from one coast to the other.

7. In certain verses the song becomes bitter, lamenting the gap between rich and poor.

8. The song ends on a hopeful note, however.

9. Many people feel proud of their heritage because of the song.

10. To some, the song is our informal national anthem.

EXERCISE 2 Identify the verb or verb phrase in each sentence. Then tell whether that verb is transitive, intransitive, or linking.

1. Miriam Makeba was a famous singer with an incredible voice.

2. She had lived in Johannesburg, South Africa.

3. At that time in South Africa, the system of apartheid separated black people from white people.

4. Makeba voiced her opposition to apartheid.

5. Because of this, she gained enemies.

6. She began a musical career in the United States in the 1950s.

7. She introduced African music to the West.

8. She became popular around the world for her music.

9. Her music blended different styles, including jazz and African strains.

10. Miriam Makeba returned to South Africa after the fall of apartheid.

Miriam Makeba

EXERCISE 3 Identify the linking verb in each sentence. Identify the word to which the verb is linked. Tell whether the verb links the subject with a noun, a pronoun, or an adjective.

1. Noah's guitar is beautiful.

2. We are a popular band.

3. The audience's mood grew enthusiastic during our first set.

4. It was she who chose the songs.

5. A banjo is a string instrument that Noah also plays.

6. Samantha always remains calm onstage.

APPLY IT NOW

Use the linking verbs *was, appear, become, feel, look, seem, sound, smell,* and *taste* in nine sentences. Label each subject complement as a noun, a pronoun, or an adjective.

Tech Tip Post sentences on your class blog for peer review.

4.5 Active and Passive Voices

A transitive verb has voice. When a transitive verb is in the **active voice,** the subject is the doer of the action.

Congress *passed* **the bill.**

In the **passive voice,** the subject is the receiver of the action.

The bill *was passed* **by Congress.**
The bill *was being studied* **in committee.**

In the first sentence, *Congress,* the subject, is the doer of the action *passed.* The verb, therefore, is in the active voice. In the second sentence, the subject *bill* is the receiver of the action *was passed.* The verb, therefore, is in the passive voice.

A verb in the passive voice is formed by combining some form of *be* with the past participle of the main verb. Only transitive verbs can be used in the passive voice. Which of the following sentences is in the passive voice?

Nicole writes articles for the magazine.
The articles for the magazine are written by Nicole.

You are correct if you said the second sentence is in the passive voice. The subject *articles* is the receiver of the action, and the verb consists of a form of *be (are)* plus the past participle of the verb *write (written).*

Sentences in the active voice are generally more alive and direct.

I gave the speech. (active voice)
The speech was given by me. (passive voice)

Sometimes, though, passive voice can be the better choice; for example, when the doer of the action is unknown or unimportant.

Every house on the street was painted a different color.

EXERCISE 1 Identify the verb or verb phrase in each sentence and tell whether it is in the active voice or the passive voice.

1. The Constitution of the United States was ratified in 1788.
2. The original Constitution did not include a bill of rights.
3. Many people wanted a statement of the limitation of the government's power over individuals.

4. For them the American Revolution was fought precisely for these rights.

5. Leaders in favor of ratification promised a bill of rights.

6. Personal rights were outlined in the proposed bill.

7. These rights were incorporated into amendments to the Constitution.

8. The first 10 amendments to the Constitution form the Bill of Rights.

9. Basic freedoms, such as freedom of speech, freedom of religion, freedom of the press, and a right to trial by jury are guaranteed by the Bill of Rights.

10. The rights are recognized as essential to the foundations of American democracy.

EXERCISE 2 **Rewrite each sentence in the voice indicated.**

1. The Constitution established a strong central government. (passive)

2. The Constitution was opposed by revolutionary leaders Patrick Henry and Samuel Adams. (active)

3. The states approved the Constitution only after a long debate. (passive)

4. The small states feared the power of the larger states. (passive)

5. Two houses of the legislature were proposed by the writers of the Constitution. (active)

6. The upper house—the Senate with two senators from each state—ensured strong representation for small states. (passive)

EXERCISE 3 **Rewrite the following sentences. Change the verbs in the active voice to the passive voice or the verbs in the passive voice to the active voice.**

1. The Iroquois nation wrote a constitution that inspired our own.

2. Other ideals were imported from Europe.

3. The two houses of the legislature are similar to England's government.

4. Healthy debate strengthens our civilization.

5. Our respect for one another must not be lost despite our differences.

6. The Constitution protects minorities from the tyranny of the majority.

APPLY IT NOW

Find a science article in a magazine or newspaper and identify four transitive verbs—two active and two passive. Label each one accordingly.

With an adult, find a science article online.

4.6 Simple, Progressive, and Perfect Tenses

Verb forms indicate **tense,** or the time of the action. **Simple tenses** are the **present tense,** the **past tense,** and the **future tense.**

Progressive tenses consist of a form of the auxiliary verb *be* and the present participle of the main verb. Verbs in the progressive tense indicate continuing, or ongoing, action.

Present progressive:	**Alyssa** *is studying* **Italian.**
Past progressive:	**Alyssa** *was studying* **Italian last term.**
Future progressive:	**Alyssa** *will be studying* **Italian for many years.**

Perfect tenses consist of a form of the auxiliary verb *have* and the past participle of the main verb. The **present perfect** tells about an action that took place at an indefinite time in the past or that started in the past and continues into the present. The **past perfect** tells about an action that was completed before another past action. The **future perfect** tells about an action that will be completed before a specific time in the future.

Present perfect active:	**I** *have read* **the book on Venice.**
Past perfect active:	**I** *had read* **the book before my trip.**
Future perfect active:	**I** *will have read* **the book by the time I leave.**

In the perfect tenses, the passive voice is formed by inserting *been* between the auxiliary verb *have* and the main verb.

Present perfect passive:	**A plan to save Venice** *has been undertaken* **recently.**
Past perfect passive:	**The solution** *had been proposed* **a while ago.**
Future perfect passive:	**Perhaps the plan** *will have been implemented* **by the time I visit.**

Progressive forms of the perfect tenses indicate ongoing actions.

Present perfect progressive:	**I** *have been planning* **for months.**
Past perfect progressive:	**I** *had been studying* **Italian for a while before I understood it.**
Future perfect progressive:	**I** *will have been studying* **Italian for a long time before I am fluent.**

EXERCISE 1 Identify the verbs in these sentences. Tell the tense and voice of each verb.

1. Carlos has purchased a new digital camera.
2. The check will have been mailed before the payment is due.
3. Louise had trained hard before the race.
4. The act will have been performed by the time you get there.

EXERCISE 2 Complete the sentences with the verbs in parentheses. Use the tense and voice indicated.

1. Venice _____ (*build*—simple past, passive) on pilings in the marshy ground.
2. The weight of the city buildings _____ (*drive*—present perfect, active) the pilings down into the muddy land.
3. The city's residents and visitors _____ (*use*—present perfect, active) well water from beneath the city.
4. This also _____ (*contribute*—present perfect, active) to the gradual sinking of the city.
5. Global warming now _____ (*cause*—present progressive, active) a rise in the water level in the sea and the lagoon.
6. A plan finally _____ (*decide*—simple past, passive) on in 2001 after many plans _____ (*propose*—past perfect, passive).
7. Workers _____ (*construct*—present progressive, active) gates at entrances to the lagoon.
8. These _____ (*block*—simple future, active) high waters.
9. Some _____ (*oppose*—simple present, active) this plan for environmental reasons.

10. The city _____ (*work*—future progressive, active) on the gates for many years.
11. I _____ (*hope*—simple present, active) the city _____ (*solve*—future perfect, active) the flooding problem with this plan.
12. The beauty of Venice's waterways _____ (*add*—present perfect progressive) romance to this city for centuries.

APPLY IT NOW

Write a paragraph about a place that you plan to visit, using at least six verbs and three different tenses. Include information about the place's history, why you want to visit it, what you plan to do there, and how you are preparing for the trip. Circle the verbs you use and label their tenses.

4.7 Indicative, Imperative, and Emphatic Moods

Verb forms also indicate mood. There are four **moods** in English: indicative, imperative, emphatic, and subjunctive. You will examine the first three in this section and the fourth in the next section.

The **indicative mood** is the form of a verb that is used to state a fact or ask a question.

> **We** *are working* **on the project together.**
> *Have* **you ever** *painted* **a T-shirt?**

Note that all the tenses studied in Section 4.6—simple, progressive, and perfect—are forms of the indicative mood.

The **imperative mood** is the form of a verb that is used to give commands. The subject of a verb in the imperative mood is almost always in the second person, either singular or plural. The subject *you* usually is not expressed. To form the imperative mood, use the base form of the verb. For negative sentences, use *do not* or *don't*.

> *Plan* **your design carefully.**
> *Do not start* **without a definite design.**

In both the above sentences, the subject *you* is understood.

To form a command using the first person, use *let's (let us)* before the base form of the verb.

> *Let's get* **the materials for our project.**

The **emphatic mood** is the form of a verb that gives special force to a simple present or past tense verb. For the present tense, use *do* or *does* before the base form of the verb. For the past tense, use *did* before the base form of the word. Do not confuse this with *do*, *does*, and *did* used as auxiliary verbs in questions or negative sentences.

> **I** *do like* **your idea.**

EXERCISE 1 Identify the verb or verb phrase in each sentence. Then tell whether the sentence is in the indicative, imperative, or emphatic mood.

1. I do hope to paint a T-shirt for the school logo contest.
2. We can work together.
3. What do we need for the project?

4. Get a couple of T-shirts, some fabric paints, and a piece of cardboard.
5. Why do we need the cardboard?
6. Put the cardboard inside the T-shirt.
7. The cardboard stops paint from soaking onto the back of the T-shirt.
8. Do not paint the shirt without the cardboard inside!
9. Please choose a design.
10. I am thinking of a slogan about learning and cooperation.

EXERCISE 2 **Rewrite the following sentences in the imperative mood.**

1. You can apply the fabric paint with a brush or a sponge.
2. It is a good idea to squeeze paint from the tube right onto the shirt to draw lines.
3. You should not put the painted shirt on immediately.
4. It is necessary to let the paint dry first.
5. You can use different colored T-shirts to get different background effects.
6. Would you hand me the fabric paint?
7. Can you tell me which colors you like?
8. You can pick from the rack of paints on the wall.

EXERCISE 3 **Identify the verb or verb phrase in each sentence. Then tell whether the verb is in the indicative or the imperative mood. If the verb is in the emphatic mood, tell its tense.**

1. The soccer team's annual car wash is this afternoon.
2. We need money for new uniforms.
3. The Art Club made signs for us.
4. Hang one sign at each end of the block.
5. Good advertising really does work!
6. Do we have enough buckets and sponges?
7. Put soapy water in the buckets.
8. Rinse the soap off the cars with the hoses.
9. Use these rags to dry the cars.
10. Drivers will be happy about their clean cars!
11. We did have fun last year too.

APPLY IT NOW

Write your school's fire drill instructions, using two of each type of verb: imperative, indicative, and emphatic.

4.8 Subjunctive Mood

The **subjunctive mood** of a verb can express a wish or desire or a condition that is contrary to fact. The past tense is used to state present wishes or desires or contrary-to-fact conditions. The past perfect tense is used to state past wishes, desires, or contrary-to-fact conditions. Note the use of *could* and *would have* in the contrary-to-fact sentences.

Wish or desire:	I wish my new bike *were* here already.
	I wished I *had bought* a computer.
Contrary-to-fact condition:	If I *were* in the market for a bike, I *could research* prices on the Internet.
	If you *had worked* more hours, you *would have earned* enough to buy a computer.

The subjunctive mood is also used to express a demand or recommendation after *that* or to express an uncertainty after *if* or *whether*. The base form of the verb is used in the clause after *that, if,* or *whether*.

Demand after *that:*	I must insist that your mother *be* with you when you buy it.
Recommendation after *that:*	I recommended that James *compare* prices before buying a new bike.
Uncertainty:	Whether Joe's suggestion *be* good or bad, I'm sticking with my decision.
	Whether he *buy* a bike or a computer, James will be happy.

EXERCISE 1 Tell whether each of the following sentences is in the subjunctive, indicative, emphatic, or imperative mood.

1. You could choose from games, clothing, and lots of other things if you were to shop online.
2. I do believe you could order everything you need online.
3. I recommend that he follow simple tips for shopping online.
4. Consumer experts urge that every buyer check out the reliability of online merchants.
5. Experts also suggest that every consumer keep copies of online transactions and purchases.
6. Buy only from well-known companies.
7. Check out the special sales.
8. If he were buying a computer, he says that he would shop online.

9. Many of my friends do shop online.

10. Some things you buy don't fit or are not what you expected.

EXERCISE 2 Identify each verb in the subjunctive mood. Tell what each verb expresses: a wish or desire, a contrary-to-fact condition, a demand, recommendation after *that*, or an uncertainty.

1. Long live the King!

2. My sister would play the piano if she were here.

3. The store clerk recommended that you wash the new jeans before wearing them.

4. May she be happy in her new job!

5. Whether he be honest or not, we have to trust him.

6. Akira insisted that her little sister go to bed after the movie.

7. He looks as if he just swallowed a lemon.

8. If I were you, I would read the assignment.

9. May all your dreams come true.

10. I suggest that she report her missing wallet to the police immediately.

EXERCISE 3 Choose the correct forms to complete the sentences. Tell what each verb expresses.

1. If I (was were) you, I would send those boots back.

2. You wouldn't have to ship them if you (live lived) in the city.

3. You must insist that the company (takes take) them back.

4. You must demand that the company (gives give) you your money back or (sends send) you a pair in a bigger size.

5. I recommend that you (be are) firm with them.

6. Whether the pair of boots (be are) sturdy enough is another question.

7. If the company (was were) in town, I'd talk to the president.

8. I wish that I (own owned) boots like that—but in the right size.

APPLY IT NOW

Write three sentences using the following phrases about consumer issues, such as online shopping. When you have finished, circle all the verbs in the subjunctive mood.
Experts suggest that . . .
If I were . . .
I recommend that . . .

Grammar in Action.  Identify the subjunctive mood in the letter on p. 299.

4.9 Modal Auxiliaries

Modal auxiliaries are used to express permission, possibility, ability, necessity, obligation, and intention. They are used with main verbs that are in the base form.

The common modal auxiliaries are *may, might, can, could, must, should, will,* and *would.* Study the verb phrases in each of these sentences.

Permission:	**Anyone who needs help** *may request* **a tutor.**
Possibility:	**I** *might need* **some help with my math.**
Ability:	**Laurel** *can solve* **equations easily.**
Necessity:	**You** *must complete* **your homework on time.**
Obligation:	**I** *should study* **more.**
Intention:	**Andy** *will help* **you with that paper.**

For verb phrases with auxiliaries, the passive voice is formed by inserting *be, have been,* or *had been* between the modal auxiliary and the past participle.

The homework *could be done* **in an hour.**

The project *must have been completed* **yesterday.**

Some auxiliaries that include forms of *have* indicate contrary-to-fact conditions.

I *could have completed* **my homework on Friday [but I didn't].**

I *should have started* **my homework earlier [but I didn't].**

EXERCISE 1 Identify the verb phrase with a modal auxiliary in each sentence. Tell whether the verb phrase expresses permission, possibility, ability, necessity, obligation, or intention.

1. My parents say that I should get better grades.
2. In fact, they say that I must get better grades.
3. I agree that I could have studied more last term.
4. I should have started on my projects before the deadlines.
5. I will also try to get help if I need it.
6. My teacher said I may ask for help if I need it.
7. Helpful tips like these can be used by any student.
8. Especially for students who may have lost their discipline.
9. My sister can study for hours on end.
10. My grades must be raised by the end of this semester.

EXERCISE 2 Complete each sentence with a verb phrase containing a modal auxiliary. Use the verb in parentheses with the meaning indicated. More than one modal auxiliary may be correct for some sentences.

1. Every student _____ (*have*—obligation) an assignment book.

2. You _____ (*write*—obligation) your assignments down.

3. You even _____ (*write*—possibility) a schedule for completing long-term assignments.

4. That way you know at a glance what you _____ (*do*—necessity) every day to complete projects.

5. You _____ (*have*—obligation) a regular time to do homework.

6. For example, you _____ (*start*—possibility) your assignments right after school.

7. Then you _____ (*have*—ability) the evenings free.

8. My teachers said that I _____ (*sit*—permission) nearer the front in class.

9. This way I _____ (*hear*—ability) them better.

10. You _____ (*ask*—obligation) questions about what you don't understand.

11. You _____ (*make*—possibility) a list of questions as you do your homework.

12. You _____ (*study*—possibility) with someone else.

13. You _____ (*do*—necessity) your tasks; otherwise, you are letting someone else down.

14. I _____ (*do*—ability) math better than my brother, so I help him with math and he helps me with English.

15. Here's another tip that _____ (*help*—possibility) you.

16. You _____ (*review*—possibility) material regularly—not just before tests.

APPLY IT NOW

Write six study tips for a younger student. Use at least four modal auxiliaries in your writing.

4.10 Agreement of Subject and Verb—Part I

A **verb** agrees with its subject in person and number. Remember that a third person singular subject requires the verb form ending -s or -es for a present tense verb.

> Several <u>towns</u> *re-create* **life at different times in the past.** (base form of the verb with a plural subject)
>
> <u>Williamsburg</u> *re-creates* **colonial life.** (base form plus -s with a singular subject)

Doesn't and *Don't*

Use *doesn't* when the subject is third person singular.

> <u>Williamsburg</u> *doesn't* **have automobiles.**

Use *don't* in other cases.

> **I** *don't* **know where Williamsburg is located.**

You as the Subject

Use *are* and *were* with *you* whether the subject is singular or plural. Do not use *is* or *was* with the subject *you*.

> **Were** *you* **at the historic reenactment of our town's founding?**

There Is and *There Are*

When *there is* or *there are* introduces a sentence, the subject follows the verb. Use *there is (was, has been)* with singular subjects. Use *there are (were, have been)* with plural subjects.

> *There is* **a historic** <u>village</u> **in Massachusetts.** (singular subject)
>
> *There are* **several reconstructed colonial** <u>towns</u> **on the East Coast.** (plural subject)

Be careful when using the contraction *there's;* it must be followed by a singular subject.

Phrases Between the Subject and the Verb

When there is an intervening phrase between the subject and the verb, the verb must agree with the subject, not with the noun or pronoun in the intervening phrase.

> **A** <u>place</u> **with historic sites** *is* **Williamsburg, Virginia.**
>
> **Several other towns, including Old Sturbridge Village,** *are* **historic sites.**

EXERCISE 1 Choose the correct form of the verb in each sentence.

1. One of the most famous tourist attractions in the United States (is are) Williamsburg, Virginia.

2. You (was were) at Williamsburg once, (wasn't weren't) you?

3. Williamsburg (takes take) visitors back to life in the 1700s.

4. There (is are) houses there built in the 1700s.

5. The town (doesn't don't) have all original houses; there (is are) also buildings reconstructed in the colonial style.

6. Some interesting sites in the town (includes include) shops of a wig maker, a saddle maker, and a silversmith.

EXERCISE 2 Complete each sentence with *doesn't* or *don't.*

1. _____ you want to visit a historic town?

2. _____ Sturbridge Village have a covered bridge?

3. The village _____ re-create life in the 1700s, but the 1800s.

4. Nat _____ know what a blacksmith does.

5. _____ the town have a Web site?

6. We _____ have to pay to get in because we are students.

EXERCISE 3 Name the subject of each sentence. Then choose the correct form of the verb to complete each sentence.

1. Several members of the staff (practice practices) here on Saturday mornings.

2. The delightful re-creation of the village (account accounts) for the extensive tourist trade.

3. A stack of hot pancakes (was were) placed on the table.

4. Jacqueline's tales of her trip (was were) great.

EXERCISE 4 Rewrite the sentences to achieve correct subject-verb agreement. Not every sentence requires rewriting.

1. Are you interested in visiting Sturbridge Village?

2. Activities includes a horse-and-buggy ride.

3. Was you ever on a horse and buggy?

4. There is places for visitors to see traditional crafts.

5. A task of blacksmiths were to make wheels for buggies.

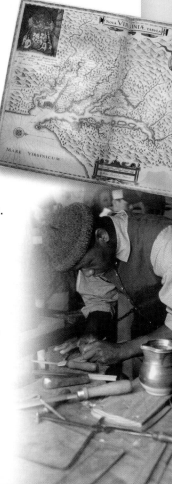

Antique map of Virginia

APPLY IT NOW

Write ten sentences about an interesting place you have visited. Incorporate the phrase below. Make sure that the subjects and verbs agree.
One of the most interesting places . . .

4.11 Agreement of Subject and Verb—Part II

Compound subjects with *and* usually take a plural verb. If the subjects connected by *and* refer to the same person or thing or express a single idea, the verb is singular.

> **Lumber and medicine** *are* just two products of forests.
> **Fire safety and prevention** *is* the subject of the talk.

When *each, every, many a,* or *no* precedes a compound subject connected by *and* or *or,* use a singular verb.

> **Every adult and child** *is* contributing to the cleanup.

When a compound subject is connected by *or* or *nor,* the verb agrees with the subject closer to it.

> **Neither the exhausting work nor the harsh living conditions** *deter* **wildland firefighters from their job.**
> **Neither the harsh living conditions nor the exhausting work** *deters* **wildland firefighters from their job.**

A **collective noun** names a group of people or things considered as a unit. Examples include *audience, band, herd,* and *public.* A collective noun usually requires a singular verb. However, when the meaning suggests that the members are being considered as separate individuals, use a plural verb.

> **The firefighting team** *uses* **tools such as helicopters.**
> **The team** *don't take* **any vacations during fire season.**

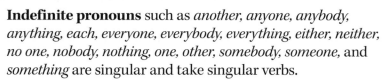

Indefinite pronouns such as *another, anyone, anybody, anything, each, everyone, everybody, everything, either, neither, no one, nobody, nothing, one, other, somebody, someone,* and *something* are singular and take singular verbs.

> **Everyone** *is* **responsible for forest fire prevention.**

Some nouns that are **plural in form are singular in meaning** and require singular verbs. These include *aeronautics, civics, economics, mathematics, measles, news,* and *physics.*

Other nouns that are **plural in form refer to one thing** and require plural verbs. These nouns include *ashes, clothes, goods, pliers, pants, proceeds, thanks, trousers,* and *scissors.*

EXERCISE 1 Choose the correct form of the verb to complete each sentence.

1. The news of a large nearby forest fire (was were) on the radio.
2. My family and I (was were) among those who evacuated the area.
3. When we left, ashes (was were) floating around us.
4. Everyone (was were) worried about what we would find.
5. Neither my brother nor I (was were) really prepared for the devastation we saw as we drove through the forest.
6. After a big fire, nothing in the forest (seems seem) to be alive.
7. Fortunately, everything at our house (was were) OK—just the outside was dirty from smoke.

EXERCISE 2 Identify the subject of each sentence. Then choose the correct form of the verb to complete the sentence.

1. Somebody always (call) when I am asleep.
2. Nobody (want) to drive anywhere in this snowstorm.
3. (Have) anyone taken my ticket?
4. One of her favorite beverages (come) from Brazil.
5. Neither of the children (want) to leave the beach.
6. Each of the clowns (ride) a unicycle.
7. (Be) either of your brothers going on the hike?
8. Someone (keep) asking me your name.

EXERCISE 3 Rewrite the following sentences to correct errors in subject-verb agreement. Not every sentence requires rewriting.

1. Damage from the fire was in the millions, but mathematics alone do not tell the human story.
2. No one living along that road still have a house.
3. From all over the country, goods are arriving to help those who have been left homeless.
4. Thanks is due to all who helped.
5. Every firefighter and police officer have put in heroic and tireless work in protecting the community.

APPLY IT NOW

Write five sentences using one of the following subjects: *each neither, either, somebody, everyone.* Make sure the subjects and verbs agree.

Verb Review

4.1 Identify the principal part of each main verb and the auxiliary verb.

1. I am learning about volcanoes around the world.
2. More volcanoes are located under the sea than on land.
3. Most undersea volcanoes are naturally hidden from view.
4. Undersea volcanoes eventually may grow high enough to break the ocean surface.
5. The Hawaiian Islands formed from volcanic mountains.

4.2 Identify the verbs or verb phrases in each sentence. Then tell whether the verb is transitive or intransitive.

6. In the Middle Ages, nobles controlled vast areas of land.
7. The nobles lived in castles, some of which are still standing today.
8. I have read many stories about knights in the Middle Ages.
9. We read about King Arthur last year in literature class.

4.3 Replace the troublesome verbs in each sentence.

10. My mom borrowed me her Bob Dylan CDs.
11. I set down in the living room and listened to one of his first recordings.
12. My eighth-grade music teacher learned us "Blowin' in the Wind."
13. Just lie that sheet music over on the table.

4.4 Identify the linking verbs and the subject complements. Tell whether the subject complement is an adjective, a noun, or a pronoun.

14. Maria Tallchief was America's first great prima ballerina.
15. It was she who popularized many of the characters in the world's most famous ballets.
16. Her performances remain memorable.
17. Tallchief became enthusiastic about dance after attending a pow-wow of the Osage people.

4.5 Identify each verb or verb phrase, and tell whether it is in the active voice or the passive voice.

18. Last spring a primary election was held to select nominees for the U.S. Senate.
19. Several candidates were slated from each party.
20. My candidate had legislative experience in the state senate.
21. His speeches were delivered to groups all over the state.
22. He won the primary election by a wide margin.

4.6 Complete each sentence with the verb indicated in parentheses. Use the tense and voice indicated.

23. My brother Frank _____ (travel—simple present, active) frequently for business.
24. Over the last 10 years, he _____ (accumulate—present perfect, active) millions of frequent-flier miles.

25. Frank and his fiancée _____ (redeem—future progressive, active) those miles for their upcoming honeymoon trip.

4.7 Identify each verb or verb phrase, and tell whether the sentence is in the indicative or imperative mood.

26. When have you last paddled and portaged in the Boundary Waters Canoe Area Wilderness?

27. Get fit for this kind of trip.

28. Carrying unnecessary items can be maddening.

4.8 Identify the correct form of the verb to complete each sentence. Identify which sentences are not in the subjunctive mood.

29. The counselor recommends that Eric (receive receives) training as a chef.

30. He wishes the institute (was were) closer to home.

31. I insist that someone (be is) with you when you walk home tonight.

32. That kind of training (helps help) a person get a job.

4.9 Complete each sentence with a verb phrase containing a modal auxiliary verb. Use the meaning indicated in parentheses after the sentence.

33. Our class _____ (visit) Washington, D.C. (possibility)

34. We _____ (raise) enough money to finance half of the cost. (necessity)

35. The eighth graders I know _____ (accomplish) this goal easily. (ability)

4.10 Correct the following sentences for subject-verb agreement. Not all the sentences have errors.

36. Was you the one who asked about Mackinac Island?

37. Activities on the island includes biking and sailing.

38. A popular stop for tourists are the Grand Hotel.

39. A race with hundreds of sailboats are held every year.

40. The race across Lake Michigan begins in Chicago.

4.11 Correct the following sentences for subject-verb agreement. Not all the sentences have errors.

41. The sandhill crane and the arctic tern is just two kinds of birds that migrate.

42. Neither the cold nor the wet conditions deters avid birdwatchers.

43. A flock of migrating swans were sighted last week.

44. Everyone here is excited when the birds start arriving.

Tech Tip   Go to www.voyagesinenglish.com for more activities.

Verb Challenge

Read the selection and then answer the questions.

1. You probably have heard the name UNESCO. 2. Do you know the meaning of its letters? 3. They stand for United Nations Educational, Scientific, and Cultural Organization. 4. This organization was founded in 1945, after World War II, at the same time as the United Nations itself. 5. As the many letters in UNESCO's name suggest, the organization's mission is broad. 6. It builds schools in countries devastated by war or poverty. 7. It has helped in the preservation of historic places through the World Heritage program. 8. By 2003 there were more than 700 such sites around the world, including the Grand Canyon and the historic pueblos of the United States. 9. Currently, UNESCO is actively working toward a number of concrete goals. 10. One goal is that by 2015 everyone will have access to free public education. 11. By 2015 UNESCO also hopes that it will have cut in half the number of people in extreme poverty. 12. Its overall goal is even loftier—to help build peace. 13. Let's all work to help it succeed. 14. You can learn more about UNESCO at its Internet site, www.unesco.org. 15. I recommend that everyone read the information at that site.

1. Which principal part of the verb *hear* is used in sentence 1?
2. What is the verb phrase in sentence 2?
3. What is the verb phrase in sentence 4? What are its tense and voice?
4. What is the linking verb in sentence 5? What part of speech is its subject complement?
5. What is the verb in sentence 6? Is it transitive or intransitive?
6. What is the verb phrase in sentence 7? What are its tense and voice?
7. What is the verb phrase in sentence 9? What are its tense and voice?
8. What is the verb phrase in sentence 11? What are its tense and voice?
9. Find the verb in the imperative mood in the selection. What sentence is it in?
10. Find the verb phrase with a modal auxiliary in the selection. What sentence is it in?
11. Find the verb in the subjunctive mood in the selection. What sentence is it in?

Verbals

5.1 Participles

Verbals are words made from verbs to function as another part of speech. There are three kinds of verbals: participles, gerunds, and infinitives.

A **participle** is a verb form that is used as an adjective; it describes a noun or pronoun. Participles often end in *-ing* or *-ed*.

> After graduation from high school, Jason spent some time *assisting* his mother in her classroom.

In this sentence *assisting* is a participle. It resembles an adjective because it modifies the noun *time.*

Just like other verb forms, participles show time through tense. Present participles end in *-ing*, and past participles often end in *-ed*. Participles can also be active or passive.

Present Participle:	*Reading Marjorie Kinnan Rawlings's novels and stories*, **I learned about life in rural Florida.** (active)
	Being treated as an outsider, **Rawlings did not gain her new neighbors' acceptance at first.** (passive)
Past Participle:	*Worried by their views*, **she tried to make friends.** (active)
	Accepted by her new neighbors, **Rawlings started to learn more about their lives.** (passive)
Perfect Participle:	*Having won a Pulitzer Prize*, **Rawlings started to earn a living from her writing.** (active)
	Having been awarded a Pulitzer Prize, **Rawlings gained prestige as a writer.** (passive)

Like appositives, a participle that is **nonrestrictive**—not essential to a sentence—is set off by commas. A participle that is **restrictive**—essential to the meaning of a sentence—is not set off by commas.

A **participial phrase** is made up of the participle, its object or complement, and any modifiers.

> *Left out in the rain*, **the library book is now ruined.**

In this sentence the participial phrase *Left out in the rain* describes the noun *book* and includes the prepositional phrase *in the rain,* which acts as an adverb telling where. A participial phrase can come before or after the word it describes.

EXERCISE 1 Identify the participle in each sentence.

1. Raised around Washington, D.C., Rawlings loved to write stories and submit them to local newspapers.

2. Beginning her career as a journalist, she wrote for newspapers and created a syndicated column.

3. Devoting herself to fiction, Rawlings wrote many notes about her new life in Florida.

EXERCISE 2 Identify the participial phrase in each sentence. Name each participle and tell the noun or pronoun it describes.

1. Writer Marjorie Kinnan Rawlings, becoming tired of city life, went to live in Florida in 1928.

2. Fascinated by the simple way of life on a visit to Florida, Rawlings decided to move there.

3. Having bought an orange grove, she planned to farm.

4. Already inhabited by a couple of cows and some chickens, the orange grove became her home.

5. Having hoped for a quiet life, she soon realized the difficulties.

6. Rawlings, having sold everything for the grove, could only stay and try to solve her problems.

7. Pursuing her ambition as a writer, Rawlings continued to work.

8. The subjects found in her own life and surroundings became the topics in her book *Cross Creek*.

9. A movie based on the book was made in 1983.

EXERCISE 3 Identify the participial phrase in each sentence and tell the noun it describes. Then identify the participle and tell whether it is present, past, or perfect.

1. Rawlings's novel *The Yearling,* set in rural Florida in the 1800s, is perhaps her most famous book.

2. Having lost its mother, a fawn is adopted by a boy.

3. For the boy, living on an isolated farm with his parents, the fawn becomes the center of his life.

4. Facing problems with the deer, the boy has to make a decision.

5. Having been recommended by a librarian, *The Yearling* became the first book I read this year.

APPLY IT NOW

Write six sentences, each using one of the following participles in a participial phrase: *arriving, crying, having lost, written, having finished, starring.*

5.2 Placement of Participles

If a participle is used alone as an adjective before or after the word it modifies, or after a linking verb, the participle is a **participial adjective.**

> I made my ceramic pot on a *spinning* wheel.
> My ceramic project did not produce the results *desired.*
> Miriam, on the other hand, is *delighted* with her pot.

A participial adjective after a linking verb should not be confused with a participle that is part of a verb phrase.

> This exercise is *relaxing* to me. (participial adjective modifying *exercise*)
> This exercise is *relaxing* my tense muscles. (part of the verb phrase *is relaxing*)

Asking these questions can help determine whether a participle is a participial adjective or as part of a verb phrase:

- Can the participle be used in front of the noun *(relaxing exercise)?*
- Does it makes sense when used after *seems (seems relaxing)?*
- Can it be compared *(most relaxing)* or modified *(very relaxing)?*

If the answer to these questions is yes, the participle is a participial adjective.

A participial phrase acts as an adjective and therefore must describe a noun or pronoun. A participial phrase that does not appear to modify any word in the sentence is called a **dangling participle**—something to avoid in your writing.

> Dangling participle: *Having worked hard on the ceramic project,* **the finished pot was disappointing.**
>
> Correction: *Having worked hard on the ceramic project,* **I was disappointed in the finished pot.** (The participial phrase modifies *I.*)

A **misplaced participle** is a participial phrase that seems to modify the wrong word or more than one word in a sentence.

> Misplaced participle: *Covered with a glaze,* **the instructor put the pot into the kiln.**
>
> Correction: *Covered with a glaze,* **the pot was placed into the kiln. OR**
> **The instructor put the pot,** *covered with a glaze,* **into the kiln.**

Notice that in both sentences, some words had to be added or changed.

EXERCISE 1 Identify the participial adjective in each sentence.

1. Vincent van Gogh was not a known painter during his lifetime.
2. Today he is an admired artist.
3. The striking colors of his paintings draw many to them.
4. Their vibrating surfaces, often with thick brush strokes visible, seem to have a life of their own.
5. The tortured artist of these works had a difficult life.
6. A caring brother helped support him.
7. Van Gogh felt increasingly isolated.
8. The rejected artist experienced a mental breakdown.
9. One of his famous paintings is the moving *Starry Night*.
10. It is full of life with its swirling forms.

Vincent van Gogh, a self-portrait

EXERCISE 2 Rewrite the sentences to correct dangling participles. Not all the sentences need correcting.

1. Having seen van Gogh's painting *Sunflowers*, a copy is now hanging in my room.
2. Being a lover of art, museum visits aren't boring to me.
3. I know many techniques, having taken art classes at the museum.
4. Inspired by the works in the museum, I began one myself.
5. Desiring vivid colors, acrylic paints were chosen for the work.
6. Having been assigned an art project at school, a collage seemed a good idea to me.
7. Making my collage, lots of colorful magazines were needed.
8. I spent hours deciding on the right subjects looking at magazines.

EXERCISE 3 Rewrite the following paragraph. Revise any sentences that contain a misplaced participle.

Hanging on the walls, the students studied the works of art. Then a judge looked at my collage carrying his clipboard. Smiling, he looked at it for a long time. He pointed to my collage waving a blue ribbon. I shook the judge's hand wearing a big grin.

APPLY IT NOW

Write a short review of a movie, a book, or a TV program. Use at least two of the following words as participial adjectives: *bored*, *surprising*, *exhilarating*, *confused*, and *breathtaking*.

Grammar in Action. Find two participial adjectives in the p. 337 model.

Verbals • 87

5.3 Gerunds as Subjects and Subject Complements

A **gerund** is a verb form ending in *-ing* that is used as a noun. Because it acts as a noun, a gerund can be used in a sentence as a subject, a subject complement, a direct object, an object of a preposition, or an appositive. You will study the first two functions in this section and the remaining three in the next section.

> *Running* **is his main form of exercise.** (subject)
> **Currently my favorite exercise is** *swimming*. (subject complement)

A **gerund phrase** may have objects and complements, and it may contain modifiers. The entire gerund phrase acts as a noun. In the first sentence below, *Reading books* is the gerund phrase; *Reading* is the gerund and *books* is its direct object. In the second sentence below, *skateboarding in the park* is the gerund phrase, and *skateboarding* is the gerund.

> *Reading books* **is Mom's favorite form of recreation.**
> **Lynne's favorite activity is** *skateboarding in the park*.

How do the gerunds function in the above sentences? You are right if you said the gerund acts as the subject of the first sentence and as the subject complement in the second.

Gerunds can be active or passive.

> *Making the team* **is Kevin's goal.** (active)
> *Being chosen for the team* **is Kevin's goal.** (passive)

EXERCISE 1 Identify the gerund or gerund phrase in each sentence. Tell whether each is a subject or subject complement.

1. Getting some exercise every day is important.
2. Exercising every day will keep the heart healthy.
3. A common exercise for people of all ages is biking.
4. Participating in a sport is a good exercise also.
5. Being inactive much of the time can make you feel tired.
6. Remaining active can restore energy.
7. A good way to exercise may be walking to school.
8. According to Mom, the best exercise for me is cleaning my room.

EXERCISE 2 Identify the gerund phrase in each sentence.
Rewrite the sentence by substituting the gerund phrase for
the subject.

EXAMPLE **My favorite activity is running long distances.**
Running long distances is my favorite activity.

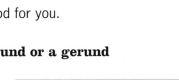

1. An important warm-up routine is stretching all the muscles.
2. The best part of the workout was finishing the course.
3. My evening routine has been jogging quickly around the block.
4. A characteristic of good runners is refusing to quit.

EXERCISE 3 Identify the gerund or gerund phrase in
each sentence. Tell whether each is a subject or a subject complement.
Identify any direct objects in the gerund phrase.

1. Eating properly is essential to good health.
2. Staying away from fats and sweets is a good idea.
3. Choosing fruits and vegetables for snacks can be a
   healthful alternative to junk food.
4. Another good idea is snacking on low-fat popcorn.
5. Eating a good breakfast gives you energy in
   the morning.
6. A basic health habit is brushing your teeth after
   every meal.
7. Another good health habit is getting enough sleep.
8. One function of sleep is restoring energy to your body.
9. Relaxing is important too.
10. Taking time for some favorite activity every day is good for you.

EXERCISE 4 Complete each sentence with a gerund or a gerund
phrase. Tell how it functions in the sentence.

1. My favorite free-time activity is _____.
2. _____ is my least favorite activity.
3. The best way to spend an afternoon is _____.
4. _____ is a boring way to exercise.
5. _____ is my favorite way to exercise.
6. _____ is one food habit I should change.
7. One health habit I need to change is _____.
8. _____ is a good way to stay active.

APPLY IT NOW

What do you think are
important health tips for
students your age to follow?
Make a list of five tips.
Use gerunds in your tips.
Compare your tips with those
of your classmates.

 Post your tips on the class blog for comparison.

5.4 Gerunds as Objects and Appositives

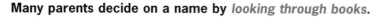

A gerund can be used as a direct object.

> **Many parents consider** *naming their children after family members*.

The gerund phrase *naming their children after family members* is the object of the verb *consider*.

A gerund can be used as the object of a preposition.

> **Many parents decide on a name by** *looking through books*.

The gerund phrase *looking through books* is the object of the preposition *by*.

A gerund can be used as an appositive, a word or group of words that renames a noun and gives more information about it.

> **Genealogy,** *exploring one's family roots*, **often involves research into last names.**

The gerund phrase *exploring one's family roots* explains the noun *genealogy*.

What are the gerund phrases in these sentences? Can you identify their functions in the sentences?

> **Abernathy's wish, being called Abe, seems understandable.**
> **He prefers being called by his nickname rather than by his given name.**

You are correct if you said that in the first sentence, the gerund phrase *being called Abe* is used as an appositive. It explains the noun *wish*. You are also correct if you said that in the second sentence, the gerund phrase *being called by his nickname* is the direct object of the verb *prefers*.

EXERCISE 1 Identify the gerund phrase in each sentence. Tell whether the gerund phrase is used as a direct object, an object of a preposition, or an appositive.

1. People began using nicknames a long time ago.
2. The idea behind a nickname, using a name other than a person's given one, suggests a desire for informality.
3. Some parents like naming their children after relatives and friends.
4. Parents, however, may get tired of repeating a child's given name.

5. They may consider finding a short, informal name, or one may present itself as a term of endearment.

6. The practice of shortening a name is common; for example, Samantha to Sam.

7. One common practice, calling people by a physical trait, produces names such as Red (a person with red hair).

8. With the use of irony, Shorty may become the way of designating an extremely tall person.

9. Sometimes a particular action leads to obtaining a specific nickname.

10. For winning a battle at a place named Tippecanoe, President William Henry Harrison was given that as a nickname.

11. The famous Beatle Ringo Starr loved wearing lots of rings—and so came his nickname.

12. Usually one person starts calling a person by a nickname, which is then picked up by others.

EXERCISE 2 **Complete each sentence with an appropriate gerund phrase used as a direct object.**

1. Do you enjoy _____?

2. We should avoid _____.

3. Have they begun _____?

EXERCISE 3 **Complete each sentence with a gerund. Then tell whether it is used as a direct object, an object of a preposition, or an appositive.**

1. I am really good at _____.

2. I really dislike _____.

3. My favorite pastimes include _____.

4. The latest style, _____, is something I might try.

5. I am thinking of _____ next year.

6. I spent my entire day _____.

Ringo Starr

APPLY IT NOW

Write five sentences about your morning routine. Use four gerunds and identify how they are used.

5.5 Possessives with Gerunds, Using *-ing* Verb Forms

Gerunds may be preceded by a possessive form—either a possessive noun or a possessive adjective. These possessives describe the doer of the action of the gerund.

> *Our choosing Florida as a vacation spot* **was a good idea.** (not *Us choosing Florida*)
>
> **The worst moment was** *Kendra's getting lost at the park.* (not *Kendra getting lost*)

What is the correct choice of word in these sentences?

> **(You Your) offering to feed the cat is much appreciated.**
>
> **I was surprised by (Ian Ian's) calling to wish me a good trip.**

If you chose *Your* and *Ian's,* you are correct. These are the possessive forms, the form to use before a gerund.

Whether an *-ing* form of a verb is a participle or a gerund depends upon the emphasis in the sentence. When the emphasis is on the doer, the word is a participle; when it is on the action, the word is a gerund.

> **The coach watched the girls** *swimming.* (The girls—the doers—are the center of the coach's attention; therefore, *swimming* is a participle modifying *girls.*)
>
> **The coach watched the girls'** *swimming.* (The swimming of the girls—the action and not the girls themselves—is what the coach is watching; therefore, *swimming* is a gerund and *girls'* must be possessive.)

EXERCISE 1 Choose the correct word to complete each sentence.

1. My (family family's) getting ready to go on a trip was a huge task.

2. First, (us our) deciding on Florida as a destination required a lot of negotiation.

3. My (brother brother's) finally agreeing to a Florida vacation which made it possible for us to start making plans.

4. (Dad Dad's) making reservations at a beach resort sounded great to me.

5. (Us Our) packing for the trip also was a major task.

6. (Gina Gina's) taking so many clothes is silly, and it just means more stuff to carry.

7. I said, "(You Your) worrying so much about clothes is not necessary, Gina."

8. (Me My) calling the hotel to ask what one wears in Florida in April is probably not the best plan.

9. I think that (Mom Mom's) suggesting that we watch the weather forecast is a good one.

10. (Milly Milly's) offering to check the newspaper is another helpful idea.

EXERCISE 2 Tell whether the italicized word in each sentence is a gerund, a participial adjective, or part of a verb phrase.

1. *Running* around all day has left me exhausted.

2. Thoughts about Florida's beaches have been *running* through my head.

3. I would prefer to be relaxing near the *running* water of a river.

4. Many flights are now *running* between Chicago and Miami.

5. *Sitting* in the plane was not an exciting experience for me.

6. Then *sitting* on the beach, I realized how tranquil the sun, sand, and water felt.

7. After my family had been *sitting* for dinner, we all took a walk on the beach path.

EXERCISE 3 Read the directions after each sentence. Then tell which word correctly completes each sentence.

1. On the plane we listened to the (babies babies') crying. (Emphasis is on the doer.)

2. We also listened intently to the (pilots pilot's) speaking. (Emphasis is on the action.)

3. At the beach my family enjoyed watching the (teens teens') surfing. (Emphasis is on the doer.)

4. Above us we could hear the (birds birds') calling. (Emphasis is on the action.)

5. I could hear my (siblings siblings') laughing as they splashed in the surf. (Emphasis is on the doer.)

APPLY IT NOW

Use the word *driving* in three sentences—as a gerund, a participial adjective, and part of a verb phrase. Have a partner identify how the word is used in each sentence.

5.6 Infinitives as Subjects and Subject Complements

An **infinitive** is a verb form, usually preceded by *to,* that is used as a noun, an adjective, or an adverb.

> *To cook* **is a necessary skill.** (infinitive used as noun)
> **I have a meal** *to prepare.* (infinitive used as adjective)
> **I went** *to get a cookbook from the library.* (infinitive used as adverb)

Like participles and gerunds, infinitives can appear alone or in phrases. An **infinitive phrase** consists of the infinitive, its object, and any modifiers. In the examples above, *to cook* and *to prepare* are examples of infinitives used alone. *To get a cookbook from the library* is an infinitive phrase.

When infinitives are used as nouns, they function as subjects, complements, objects, or appositives.

> *To make an appetizing meal* **was my goal.** (subject)
> **My task was** *to learn a few recipes.* (subject complement)
> **I want** *to surprise my family.* (direct object)
> **My goal,** *to prepare a whole meal,* **was ambitious.** (appositive)

Are the infinitives in the following sentences subjects or subject complements?

> **My hope is to learn some easy recipes.**
> **To make a pie seems too difficult right now.**

You are right if you said that the infinitive in the first sentence, *to learn some easy recipes,* is a subject complement and that the one in the second sentence, *to make a pie,* is a subject.

Infinitives can be active or passive, and they can also have perfect forms.

Simple active:	**My job is** *to peel* **the potatoes.**
Simple passive:	**These potatoes are** *to be peeled* **for the stew.**
Perfect active:	**My goal is** *to have peeled* **the potatoes by six o'clock.**
Perfect passive:	**Those potatoes were** *to have been peeled* **by my sister.**

EXERCISE 1 Identify the infinitive phrase in each sentence. Tell whether it is used as a subject or a subject complement.

1. To read about the history of spices can be fascinating.
2. One basic use of spices such as cinnamon, ginger, cloves, and pepper has been, of course, to flavor food.
3. Another use was to be put into medicines.
4. For centuries, to own spices was like owning gold.
5. To possess a few peppercorns gave one significant wealth.
6. During the Middle Ages, to control the spice trade to the West was the prerogative of the Arabs.
7. To find a sea route to the riches—and spices—of the East was a race.
8. The Portuguese plan was to travel east around Africa.
9. To find a shorter route west was Columbus's goal.
10. Queen Isabella was displeased with Columbus's attempt to enslave the natives of the New World, however.
11. She ordered officers to arrest him and to bring him back to Europe.

Christopher Columbus

EXERCISE 2 Complete each sentence with an appropriate infinitive or infinitive phrase.

1. _____ is an accomplishment.
2. _____ is a good feeling.
3. _____ can be dangerous.
4. _____ requires a lot of studying.
5. _____ makes me happy.

EXERCISE 3 Complete the sentences with infinitives. Tell if they are used as subjects or subject complements.

1. Something I would like to learn is _____.
2. _____ is a dream of mine.
3. _____ would be very fascinating.
4. _____ is an important skill.
5. One way to study for a test is _____.

APPLY IT NOW

Imagine describing emotions to a robot that does not understand them. Write a poem to the robot that explains an emotion. Follow this model, using three infinitives in the description.
Sadness is
    to lose a friend,
    to see the dying leaves in fall,
    to feel alone.

5.7 Infinitives as Objects

When an infinitive functions as a noun, it can be used as a direct object.

> In the 1900s Mahatma Gandhi **tried** *to obtain freedom for India.*
> He also **hoped** *to gain rights for all Indians.*
> He **wanted** *to make the world aware of the issues.*

An infinitive used as a direct object may be preceded by a noun or a pronoun. This noun or pronoun, the subject of the infinitive, tells the doer of the action of the infinitive. The infinitive and its subject form an **infinitive clause**. This construction always follows the main verb of the sentence, and a pronoun used as its subject is always in the object form.

> Gandhi **encouraged** <u>people</u> *to engage in protest.*
> He **urged** <u>them</u> *to act in nonviolent protest of unjust laws.*

In the second sentence, *them to act in nonviolent protest of unjust laws* is an infinitive clause, and *them,* the object form of *they,* is the subject.

Mahatma Gandhi

EXERCISE 1 Identify the infinitive phrase and the main verb in each sentence.

1. Mahatma Gandhi hoped to secure India's independence from British rule.
2. The British had begun to rule in India in the 1700s.
3. As a young man, Gandhi failed to do well in college.
4. Gandhi eventually managed to get a law degree in England.
5. Back in India, he failed to become a successful lawyer because of his shyness.
6. Taking a job in South Africa, he learned to talk effectively in public.
7. He wanted to gain rights for Indians in South Africa.
8. He tried to make service to others his primary goal.
9. In 1914 Gandhi decided to give up his now successful law practice in South Africa.
10. He wanted to go back to his homeland, India.
11. He was determined to bring freedom to his country.

EXERCISE 2 Identify the infinitive phrase or clause used as a noun in each sentence. Note whether it is a subject, a subject complement, or a direct object.

1. To end the inequities of the Indian caste system became one of Gandhi's goals, along with independence.
2. Gandhi started to study famous religious works.
3. He refused to accept material items as essential.
4. To reject violence was a goal that Gandhi adopted after an incident in South Africa.
5. He had refused to move from a first-class car to a third-class car on a train.
6. Officials had forced him to leave the train.
7. As a result of that incident, Gandhi had resolved never to use violence as a way of action.
8. His plan was to change society without violence.
9. Gandhi convinced others to join his struggle for rights.
10. He urged Indians to participate in a program of civil disobedience.
11. The British leaders' response was to put him into prison because of his acts of civil disobedience.
12. Gandhi managed to gain world attention for his cause.
13. He decided to lead a 24-day march to the sea against the British monopoly on salt.
14. To pick up some salt from the shore was a symbol of protest.
15. People began to ignore the law against homemade salt.
16. Eventually the British invited Gandhi to participate in a conference on India's fate.
17. After World War II, the British promised to grant independence to India.

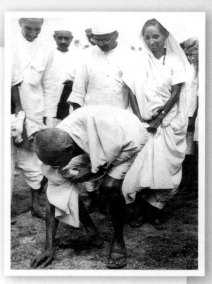

Mahatma Gandhi breaking the salt law by picking up a lump of natural salt at Dandi, Gujarat

EXERCISE 3 Complete each sentence with an appropriate infinitive or infinitive phrase used as a direct object.

1. Gandhi intended _____.
2. Officials vowed _____.
3. The British managed _____.
4. The Indians continued _____.
5. From Gandhi, people should try _____.

APPLY IT NOW

Write six sentences about a person you admire for helping others. Include three infinitives as direct objects in your writing.

5.8 Infinitives as Appositives

Washington, D.C., as originally laid out, from a 1793 engraving

An infinitive that functions as a noun can be used as an **appositive.** An appositive is a word or group of words put after a noun or pronoun to rename it or to give more information about it.

> **My suggestion,** *to do a project on Washington, D.C.,* **was accepted by the group.**

The infinitive phrase in red acts as an appositive, renaming and telling something about the noun *suggestion*.

Infinitive appositives appear in various positions.

> **Subject: The team's goal,** *to win first place in the conference,* **meant practicing every day.**
>
> **Subject complement: Improvement was our aim,** *to do better at each meet.*
>
> **Direct object: The team set its own rules,** *to practice daily and to work hard.*
>
> **Indirect object: We gave the objective,** *to bring home a trophy,* **our best efforts.**

EXERCISE 1 Identify the infinitive phrase used as an appositive in each sentence. Tell what word the appositive renames.

1. The government leaders expressed their desire, to build a magnificent capital for the new country.

2. The final choice, to build a city between Virginia and Maryland, was made in the 1790s.

3. Pierre L'Enfant's task, to design the capital of the United States, was given to him by George Washington.

4. L'Enfant had a vision, to create a city of wide avenues and vistas.

5. His original plan, to have three separate areas for the three branches of government, was not implemented.

6. Pennsylvania Avenue, a wide boulevard connecting the Capitol Building to the White House, had a special purpose, to serve as a place for ceremonial processions.

The Capitol when first occupied by Congress in 1800

EXERCISE 2 Identify the infinitive phrase or clause used as a noun in each sentence. Tell whether it is used as a subject, a subject complement, a direct object, or an appositive.

1. The purpose of the Liberty Bell, to mark the 50th anniversary of Pennsylvania's charter, showed the importance of the charter's freedoms to the colony.

2. In 1751 the colony's assembly ordered the bell to be made.

3. The assembly planned to place the bell in the State House, now Independence Hall, in Philadelphia.

4. Their decision was to order the bell from England.

5. A flaw in the bell caused it to crack during its hanging.

6. To recast the bell was the task given to two Philadelphia foundry workers.

7. The tone of the recast bell failed to please people.

8. Despite the arrival of a new bell from England, the final decision was to keep the recast bell in place.

9. To ring for these major events became the fabled task of the bell: the Battles of Lexington and Concord and the Declaration of Independence on July 8, 1776.

10. The fate of the bell, to ring for all important occasions, made it a national relic.

11. People began to call it the Liberty Bell in the 1830s.

12. No one knows for sure when the bell began to crack.

13. People continued to use it until 1846.

14. To give the bell a symbolic tap is a tradition on July 4.

15. Now visitors from all over the country want to view it on visits to Philadelphia.

EXERCISE 3 Identify the infinitive used as a noun in each sentence and tell its function.

1. To reach the finish line of the Philadelphia marathon was reward enough for Ty.

2. He tried to run at an even pace.

3. He seemed to collapse at the halfway point.

4. Yao's job was to pace him though the last two miles.

5. Karl's task, to bring water along, was crucial.

APPLY IT NOW

Write five sentences about a specific historical topic. Use four infinitives as nouns in your writing.

Tech Tip With an adult, research your historical topic online.

5.9 Infinitives as Adjectives

Infinitives can be used as adjectives to describe nouns and pronouns. These infinitives follow the words they describe.

> I got a **chance** *to read* a book by Dorothy M. Johnson.
> The book was a great **way** *to learn* about the West.
> The book, *Buffalo Woman*, was definitely **one** *to recommend* to others.

Native American buffalo skin tepees on the Great Plains in the 1800s

In the first two sentences, the infinitives modify the nouns *chance* and *way.* In the third sentence, the infinitive modifies the indefinite pronoun *one.*

Can you find the infinitives or infinitive phrases used as adjectives and the nouns they describe in the sentences below?

> **Johnson had the ability to take readers into the past.**
> **Lists of Western novels to read always include her books.**

The infinitive phrase *to take readers into the past* acts as an adjective describing *ability* in the first sentence. *To read* acts as an adjective describing the noun *novels* in the second sentence.

A pronoun used as the subject, subject complement, or direct object of an infinitive is always in the object form.

> **Juanita's parents expected the winner to be** *her.*
> **Our team cheered for the winner to be** *her* **or** *me.*

EXERCISE 1 Identify the infinitive phrase used as an adjective in each sentence. Then tell the noun it describes.

1. A decision to go to Montana influenced Dorothy M. Johnson's life.

2. Her family's move led to her desire to study the West.

3. Writing gave her a way to share her fascination with the American West.

4. Johnson wrote stories to entertain both lovers of Western novels and general readers alike.

5. One of her books to be made into a film was *The Man Who Shot Liberty Valance.*

6. She was praised for her efforts to portray Native Americans correctly.

EXERCISE 2 Identify the infinitive phrase or clause in each sentence. Tell whether each is used as an adjective or a noun. For those used as adjectives, tell the word that the infinitive phrase describes.

1. A huge monument to honor Native Americans is being built in South Dakota.

2. The project to build the memorial began in 1948.

3. Sioux chief Henry Standing Bear asked a sculptor to make it.

4. Korczak Ziolkowski accepted the invitation to carve the sculpture.

5. The chief wanted to portray Crazy Horse.

6. The Sioux consider him to be a great leader.

7. Crazy Horse's efforts to serve his people and protect their culture earned him the honor.

8. The final design was to show the chief on horseback.

9. Korczak Ziolkowski's task, to carve a gigantic statue out of a mountain, was an immense one.

10. Work to make the face of the chief began in 1988.

11. To carve out just the face took 10 years.

12. The ceremony to dedicate the face took place in 1998.

13. Ziolkowski, having died in 1982, failed to see this stage of work.

14. Work to carve the sculpture continues.

15. The money to build the statue comes from private contributions.

16. Blasts to remove stone take place several times a week.

17. The date to see the finished statue is still far in the future.

EXERCISE 3 Identify the infinitive phrase in each sentence.

1. The Crazy Horse sculpture is a great monument to visit in South Dakota.

2. The Sioux want to share his history with the public.

3. Preserving his culture is an important issue to the Sioux.

Crazy Horse Memorial in Black Hills, South Dakota

Korczak Ziolkowski

APPLY IT NOW

In a paragraph describe a community service project in which you would like to participate. Pick three of the sentence starters below to explain why, using infinitive phrases.

With this project, I want . . .
This is a chance . . .
It is important . . .
Our community deserves . . .
My idea is . . .
I volunteer . . .

Tech Tip Post your paragraph on the class blog.

5.10 Infinitives as Adverbs

An infinitive can be used as an adverb to describe a verb, an adjective, or another adverb. These infinitives follow the words they modify.

> **Butch went to Montana** *to take a special vacation on a dude ranch*. (describing the verb *went*)
>
> **He was excited** *to ride a horse for the first time*. (describing the adjective *excited*)
>
> **He wasn't experienced enough** *to stay on the horse at first*. (describing the adverb *enough*)

Identify the infinitives used as adverbs in these sentences. What does each infinitive phrase describe?

> **I didn't know enough to write about the Oregon Trail.**
>
> **I was determined to learn more about it.**
>
> **I visited the library to get a book on traveling west.**

In the first sentence, the infinitive phrase *to write about the Oregon Trail* describes the adverb *enough*. In the second sentence, the infinitive phrase *to learn more about it* describes the adjective *determined*. In the third sentence, *to get a book on traveling west* explains the verb *visited*. An infinitive that describes a verb often answers the questions *why* or *how* about the verb.

EXERCISE 1 Identify the infinitive phrase used as an adverb in each sentence. The word it describes is italicized. Give its part of speech: adjective, adverb, or verb.

1. Susan *traveled* to the West last summer to participate in a historic adventure tour.

2. She *went* to take a trip in a covered wagon.

3. Susan was *eager* to try the pioneer experience.

4. She was *happy*, however, to learn about the wagons.

5. Rubber wheels *were used* to make the ride less bumpy.

6. A farmhand *was provided* to drive each wagon.

7. Each participant *could sit* in the front to drive the horses.

8. On her turn Susan was strong *enough* to control the horses on her own.

EXERCISE 2 Identify the infinitive phrase used as an adverb in each sentence. Then tell the word the infinitive phrase describes and the word's part of speech.

1. At night everyone sat around the campfire to tell stories.
2. Mattresses were provided to sleep on in the wagons.
3. The wagon train stopped regularly to give participants chances for hiking and exploring.
4. The pace of the wagon train was easy to manage.
5. It traveled slowly to allow time for enjoying nature—10 miles a day instead of the 15 miles a day of the pioneers.

EXERCISE 3 Identify the infinitive phrase in each sentence. Tell whether each is used as a noun, an adjective, or an adverb.

1. The original pioneers faced hardships to get to the West.
2. People hoped to have a better life in the West.
3. The dangers to be faced on the trip included harsh weather, accidents, disease, and sometimes starvation.
4. The wagons, with springs only under the driver's seat, were bumpy to ride in.
5. Usually people chose to walk alongside the wagons with their cattle and sheep.
6. The pace was sometimes difficult to maintain.
7. A train usually began to move at seven in the morning.
8. At five the train stopped to rest for the night.
9. At longer stopovers women had the chance to do chores.
10. To arrive at a watering hole was excuse enough to stop.

EXERCISE 4 Identify the infinitive phrase used as an adverb in each sentence. Then tell the word the infinitive phrase describes and the word's part of speech.

1. Some pioneers struggled to establish new lives.
2. Grass was needed to feed the horses and cattle.
3. Some areas were too difficult to pass through.
4. Travelers shared goods to lighten their loads.
5. Many pioneers were anxious to return to the East.

APPLY IT NOW

Choose two of the following infinitive phrases. Write three sentences for each, using it as a noun, an adjective, and an adverb.

to study a foreign language
to see the new museum
to play the guitar
to go to a rock concert

Grammar in Action. Find an infinitive phrase functioning as an adverb in the p. 337 excerpt.

5.11 Hidden and Split Infinitives

The word *to* is called the sign of the infinitive, but sometimes infinitives appear in sentences without the *to*. Such infinitives are called **hidden infinitives.**

After verbs of perception such as *hear, see,* and *feel,* the infinitive is used without a *to*. This is also the case for the verbs *let, make, dare, need,* and *help.*

> We **heard** the astronomer *talk* about the comet.
> We would not **dare** *use* Marshall's telescope without his permission.

The *to* is also omitted after the prepositions *but* and *except* and the conjunction *than.*

> Marshall does little but *talk* about the comet these days.
> I'd rather do an experiment than *read* about science.

An adverb placed between to and the verb results in a **split infinitive**. Good writers try to avoid split infinitives. To avoid a split infinitive, put the adverb where it sounds best.

> Split infinitive: We were told to carefully view each star.
> Improved: We were told to view each star carefully.
>
> Split infinitive: Marshall told us to not damage his telescope.
> Improved: Marshall told us not to damage his telescope.

Where to place the adverb you remove from the middle of the infinitive depends on the meaning of the sentence.

> Split infinitive: We started to optimistically watch the sky for the comet.
> Improved: Optimistically we started to watch the sky for the comet. OR
>   We started to watch the sky for the comet optimistically.

EXERCISE 1 Identify the hidden infinitive in each sentence.

1. Many people saw the comet appear in the sky.
2. Watching the comet streak across the sky made us feel small.
3. Marshall let us borrow his telescope for one night to see Halley's comet.

4. I prefer to see the comet in the sky firsthand rather than view a video of it.

5. We knew that we would see the comet shine more clearly with a telescope.

6. We dared not damage it.

7. He need not worry about us—we are always careful with things we borrow.

8. My father helped us place the telescope in our window.

9. I did nothing all day but think about viewing the comet.

10. When will people watch the comet blaze across the sky again?

EXERCISE 2 Rewrite the sentences so that they do not contain split infinitives.

1. I was determined to safely view the next solar eclipse.

2. I knew enough to not look directly at the sun.

3. I went to the library to thoroughly research the topic so that I could do so safely.

4. I was warned to constantly keep my back to the sun throughout the eclipse.

5. I managed to easily make a pinhole projector.

6. I was able to readily obtain the two necessary pieces of cardboard needed to make it.

7. I needed to simply cut a small hole in one piece.

8. I needed to properly place the two pieces in alignment during the eclipse.

9. I would look through the hole to clearly see the sun's reflection on the other piece of cardboard.

10. I wanted to immediately test out the device—but I had to wait for the eclipse, of course.

EXERCISE 3 Rewrite each sentence to include the adverb in parentheses. Avoid creating a split infinitive.

1. Gail hopes to become a professional astronomer. (eventually)

2. She plans to identify all the constellations. (correctly)

3. She appears to have most of them identified. (already)

4. Her uncle, Captain Matthews, learned how to land planes. (skillfully)

5. He has landed planes in bad weather. (carefully)

APPLY IT NOW

Write a short description of what you see, hear, and feel while outside at night. Use two hidden infinitives in your writing and identify them.

Verbal Review

5.1 Identify each participial phrase, each participle, and the noun or pronoun each participle describes. Then identify the participle as present, past, or perfect.

1. Walking through the open-air market, Jin stopped at each stall.
2. Having decided to make empanadas, she needed fresh ingredients.
3. Filled with meat, cheese, or fruit, empanadas are popular Latin American pastries.
4. Having purchased the ingredients, Jin went home.

5.2 Identify the participial adjective or participial phrase in each sentence. Correct any sentences that have a dangling participle.

5. The conductor quieted the waiting audience.
6. Tapping his baton, the orchestra began to play.
7. Being a fan of classical music, the concert was enjoyable.

5.3 Identify each gerund phrase. Tell whether each gerund is a subject or a subject complement.

8. Training for a 26.2-mile race is a serious commitment.
9. Stretching before a race can help prevent injuries.
10. A recommendation is drinking enough water to stay hydrated.

5.4 Identify the gerund phrase in each sentence and tell whether it is used as a direct object, an object of a preposition, or an appositive.

11. In many countries people enjoy drinking tea.
12. According to folklore, the Chinese accidentally discovered the drink by dropping some leaves of the plant into hot water.
13. The practice, drinking tea, was at first only for the wealthy.
14. Some Americans began serving tea over ice cubes.

5.5 Choose the correct word to complete each sentence.

15. (Me My) writing the winning story would be great.
16. I was happy with (Carl's Carl) editing of my story.
17. (Her She) entering the contest took courage.
18. We applauded (his him) winning the award.

5.6 Identify each infinitive phrase and tell whether it is used as a subject or a subject complement.

19. To explore west of the Mississippi was one of President Thomas Jefferson's goals.
20. As Jefferson's personal secretary, Meriwether Lewis's main duty was to help plan for westward expansion.

21. To serve as a commander for the expedition was an honor for Lewis.

22. The purpose of the expedition was to gather information about the West.

23. William Clark's responsibility as chief cartographer was to map the expedition.

5.7 Identify each infinitive phrase and the verb of which it is a direct object.

24. Henry Ford first attempted to establish an auto manufacturing company in 1899.

25. He hoped to revolutionize the manufacturing industry.

26. He wanted to use standardized parts and division of labor.

27. In 1903 he founded Ford and managed to start the world's first moving assembly line.

5.8 Identify each infinitive phrase and tell the word each appositive explains.

28. My idea, to write a report on the Normandy Invasion, required a great deal of research.

29. The plan, to turn the tide in favor of the Allies, succeeded.

30. The decision to postpone the invasion because of the weather was a good one.

31. The purpose of Memorial Day, to honor soldiers killed in battle, seemed especially important on the 60th anniversary of D-Day.

5.9 Identify the infinitive phrases used as adjectives. Tell the noun each infinitive phrase describes.

32. Felicity got the chance to browse London's famous flea markets.

33. Rummaging through the stalls is a great way to find hidden treasures.

34. She bought items to fix and resell at her store.

35. Bargaining is one technique to get a good deal.

5.10 Identify the infinitive phrases used as adverbs. Tell whether the phrase modifies a verb, an adjective, or an adverb.

36. Pedro was anxious to work toward his goal.

37. He practiced enough to become proficient.

38. The surfers thought some waves were too big to ride.

39. The surfers met on the shore to pack up their gear.

5.11 Identify any hidden infinitives. Rewrite any sentence to correct a split infinitive.

40. Magdalena helped the club organize a fund-raiser for charity.

41. The volunteers were told to seriously consider their duties.

42. Do you think they'll let me sell tickets?

43. I decided to definitely donate an item.

Tech Tip · Go to www.voyagesinenglish.com for more activities.

Verbal Challenge

Read the selection and then answer the questions.

1. Ever since fourth grade, I have been wanting to visit the battle monument in Concord, Massachusetts. 2. We were expected to memorize the "Concord Hymn" by Ralph Waldo Emerson. 3. I enjoyed reciting it, and I still know it by heart. 4. Emerson wrote the poem in 1837 for the dedication to be put on the battle monument. 5. The monument was raised to honor the Minutemen, soldiers who fought for America's independence from England, at the battles of Lexington and Concord in 1775.

6. Traveling through New England last year, my family was passing near Concord. 7. This made it possible for me to realize my dream to see the monument. 8. It was the dead of winter, and the setting sun cast a reddish-orange glow over everything. 9. Wearing only our thin jackets, Dad, my little sister, and I were freezing, but nobody complained. 10. I cannot think of a better way to see this historic site. 11. I recited a verse of the poem in honor of visiting this piece of American history.

1. In sentence 1, what is the infinitive phrase? How is it used in the sentence?

2. In sentence 3, what is the gerund phrase? How is it used in the sentence?

3. In sentence 4, what is the infinitive phrase? How is it used in the sentence?

4. In sentence 5, what is the infinitive phrase? How is it used in the sentence?

5. How does the phrase *Traveling through New England last year* function in sentence 6?

6. How is the word *passing* used in sentence 6?

7. How is the word *setting* used in sentence 8?

8. What is the participial phrase in sentence 9? What words does it describe?

9. In sentence 10, what is the infinitive phrase? How is it used in the sentence?

10. How is the phrase *visiting this piece of American history* used in sentence 11?

Minute Man National Historical Park in Concord, Massachusetts

Adverbs

6.1 Types of Adverbs

An **adverb** is a word used to describe a verb, an adjective, or another adverb. It is also called a simple adverb. There are several types of adverbs.

> **Many stories are told** *orally*. (The adverb *orally* describes the verb phrase *are told*.)
>
> **Oral storytelling has an** *extremely* **long history.** (The adverb *extremely* describes the adjective *long*.)
>
> **Jackson tells stories** *very* **dramatically.** (The adverb *very* describes the adverb *dramatically*.)

An **adverb of time** tells when or how often. Some adverbs of time are *again, early, frequently, now, then,* and *weekly.*

> **I** *recently* **heard a strange story.**

An **adverb of place** tells where. Some adverbs of place are *above, away, up, forward, here, nearby,* and *there.*

> **Sit** *down*, **and listen to the story.**

An **adverb of manner** tells how or in what manner. These adverbs include *carefully, slowly,* and *enthusiastically.*

> **Everyone listens** *attentively* **to Jackson's stories.**

An **adverb of degree** tells how much or how little. Some adverbs of degree are *almost, hardly, many, quite, seldom,* and *very.*

> **Some of his stories are** *quite* **scary.**

An **adverb of affirmation** tells whether a statement is positive or expresses consent or approval. The adverbs of affirmation include *allegedly, indeed, positively, undoubtedly,* and *yes.*

> **This author** *undoubtedly* **has traveled widely.**
>
> *Indeed*, **his biography refers to him as a world traveler.**

An **adverb of negation** expresses a negative condition or refusal. Among the adverbs of negation are *no, not,* and *never.*

> **I** *never* **expect to see any science fiction books by him.**
>
> **That is** *not* **where his interests lie.**

EXERCISE 1 Identify the italicized words in each sentence as adverbs of time, place, degree, manner, affirmation, or negation.

1. Bill was *not* able to recall the story *recently*.
2. He started *quite calmly*.
3. *Allegedly*, the lion had *never* been seen running *away*.
4. Walking *confidently* toward the lion, she talked *steadily* to it.
5. The lion *undoubtedly* was curious and *slowly* stood *up*.

EXERCISE 2 Identify the adverb in each sentence and tell whether it is an adverb of time, place, manner, degree, affirmation, or negation.

1. The highly unusual stories that make the rounds throughout the country are called urban legends.
2. You certainly have heard some of these.
3. People sometimes hear stories about alligators living in sewers.
4. According to legend, baby alligators once were given as pets.
5. When families got tired of tending to the alligators, they irresponsibly abandoned them.
6. The alligators eventually got into the sewer system.
7. Alligators quickly multiplied.
8. They grew terribly large.
9. Rumors spread of the extremely dangerous threat.
10. Some people claimed that the alligators occasionally entered houses through the plumbing system.

EXERCISE 3 Identify the adverb or adverbs in each sentence. Tell the word that each adverb describes and give the word's part of speech.

1. People frighten one another with totally untrue stories.
2. The legends still persist despite emphatically strong denials by police.
3. Such tales are told confidently by the storytellers.
4. Tellers usually have heard them from a "friend of a friend."
5. The accounts simply may appeal because they are scary.

APPLY IT NOW

Write a brief paragraph about a story you like to tell. Use adverbs of manner such as *calmly, happily, hesitantly, determinedly,* and *rapidly* to add detail to your writing.

 Tech Tip Post your story on the class Web site.

6.2 Interrogative Adverbs and Adverbial Nouns

An **interrogative adverb** is used to ask a question. The interrogative adverbs are *how, when, where,* and *why.* Interrogative adverbs are used to express or to query reason, place, time, or method.

Reason: *Why* did the railroads lose some of their importance?
Place: *Where* did first public railroads run?
Time: *When* did your train arrive?
Method: *How* do you usually travel long distances?

An **adverbial noun** is a noun that acts as an adverb by describing a verb. Adverbial nouns are used to express time, distance, measure, value, or direction.

Time: I spent 21 *hours* on the train.
Distance: We traveled nearly 1,000 *miles* on the trip.
Measure: The container held two *quarts* of water.
Value: The meal cost several *dollars* more than we expected.
Direction: The train traveled *west* throughout the night.

An adverbial noun should not be mistaken for a direct object. A direct object follows a transitive verb and answers the question *what.*

Her cold lasted three *weeks*.
He crossed out three *weeks* on the calendar.

In the first sentence, *three weeks* is an adverb telling how long the cold lasted. In the second sentence, *three weeks* is a direct object telling what was crossed out.

EXERCISE 1 Identify the adverb or adverbs in each sentence. Point out which ones are interrogative adverbs.

1. The rusty car rolled forward slowly.
2. When did the car start to approach the corner?
3. It barely scraped Tom's car.
4. Tom quickly jumped out and started sadly, shaking his head.
5. How long did he chase the empty car?
6. The car just kept rolling away from him.

EXERCISE 2 Identify the interrogative adverbs and adverbial nouns in these sentences. Tell what each interrogative adverb expresses—reason, place, time, or method. Tell what each adverbial noun expresses—time, distance, measure, value, or direction.

1. When was the great era of railroads?

2. It started approximately 200 years ago.

3. Where did the first successful railroad trip by steam engine take place?

4. A load might weigh thousands of pounds—including ten tons of iron and five wagons—and be pulled by a single engine.

5. The first trip covered nearly 10 miles of track.

6. The tracks went many miles across the United States.

7. Where did the two ends of the transcontinental railroad finally meet?

8. The railroads took settlers west across the United States.

9. In the United States today the largest number of train passengers moves north and south along the East Coast.

10. Some passenger trains travel 267 miles an hour; however, airplanes are often more convenient for long distances.

11. Why are railroads still important?

12. Although they cost millions of dollars to maintain, trains still carry many tons of freight from place to place.

EXERCISE 3 Complete the sentences with interrogative adverbs or adverbial nouns. Use the clues in parentheses.

1. _____ did you travel on your last vacation? (method)

2. _____ did you go? (place)

3. We traveled approximately _____. (distance)

4. The trip took _____. (time)

5. _____ did you choose to visit a theme park? (reason)

6. We paid _____ to rent a campsite. (value)

7. I researched the location for _____. (time)

8. _____ did you finally decide? (time)

9. _____ did you make your decision? (method)

APPLY IT NOW

With a partner, interview each other about trips you have taken. Write five interview questions using interrogative adverbs. Use at least one adverbial noun in each of your answers.

 Post your interview on the class blog or wiki.

6.3 Comparative and Superlative Adverbs

Some adverbs can be compared. Like adjectives, they have **comparative** and **superlative** forms.

Positive:	My sister packs *quickly*.
Comparative:	My mom packs *more quickly* **than my sister.**
Superlative:	I pack *most quickly* **of all in the family.**

The comparative and superlative forms of most adverbs that end in *ly* are formed by adding *more* or *most* (or *less* or *least*) before the positive form of the adverb. The comparative and superlative forms of many adverbs that do not end in *ly* are formed by adding *-er* or *-est*. Using *more* or *most* (or *less* or *least*) with adverbs that end in *er* or *est* is incorrect. Avoid constructions such as *more faster* and *more better*.

POSITIVE	COMPARATIVE	SUPERLATIVE
carefully	more (or less) carefully	most (or least) carefully
hastily	more (or less) hastily	most (or least) hastily
fast	faster	fastest
late	later	latest

Some adverbs have irregular comparisons.

ADVERB	COMPARATIVE	SUPERLATIVE
well	better	best
badly	worse	worst
far	farther	farthest
little	less	least
much	more	most

EXERCISE 1 Write the comparative and superlative forms of the following adverbs.

1. easily
2. noisily
3. hurriedly
4. early
5. beautifully
6. soon
7. cautiously
8. well
9. effectively
10. desperately
11. simply
12. nervously
13. high
14. powerfully
15. sloppily

EXERCISE 2 Identify the adverb in each sentence. Tell whether the adverb is positive, comparative, or superlative.

1. The editor examined the manuscript closely.
2. The wind blew more strongly as we reached the open water.
3. Are you adequately prepared for this test?
4. The judge listened most attentively.

EXERCISE 3 Complete each sentence with the correct comparative or superlative form of the adverb in parentheses.

1. With Mom in the Army, we move much _____ (frequently) than most other families.
2. My mom always works _____ (hard) of all of us.
3. No one plans a move _____ (carefully) than she does.
4. She is the _____ (highly) organized person I know.
5. She works _____ (good) than any moving company.
6. Of cleaning, doing laundry, and packing, I don't know which is my _____ (little) favorite task.
7. What I find _____ (much) distressful is saying good-bye.
8. I can make friends _____ (readily) now that I'm getting older.

EXERCISE 4 Rewrite the sentences to correct the use of adverbs in comparisons. Not all the sentences have errors.

1. Of all publications *The Guinness Book of World Records* probably covers world records most comprehensive.
2. For example, it tells about people who have traveled most farthest.
3. Arthur Blessitt has walked farther than anyone else—about 37,502 miles in 310 countries.
4. In addition to traveling most farthest, he probably also has traveled the longest time—about 30 years.
5. Of all the books I own, I read the record books more eagerly.

APPLY IT NOW

Write six sentences using the following adverbs. Use the degree of comparison indicated in parentheses.

carefully (comparative)
well (superlative)
little (superlative)
sloppily (superlative)
confidently (comparative)
effectively (superlative)

6.4 *As . . . As, So . . . As, and Equally*

The Nile River in Egypt

Both adjectives and adverbs can be used in comparisons.

A particular usage problem may come up in comparisons with *as . . . as* or *so . . . as.* Study the following examples of adverb comparisons.

> **The Yukon River flows** *as far in North America as* **the Orinoco River does in South America.**
> **The Nile River doesn't flow quite** *so forcefully as* **the Amazon River does.**
> **The Nile River doesn't flow quite** *as forcefully as* **the Amazon River.**

In the first sentence, the comparison is positive. In that sentence only *as . . . as* may be used. In the second and third sentences, the comparison is negative; the sentences contain *not.* In a sentence with a negative comparison, either *as . . . as* or *so . . . as* may be used.

The same rules for using *as . . . as* and *so . . . as* apply to adjectives used in comparisons. A positive comparison may use only *as . . . as.* A negative comparison may use *as . . . as* or *so . . . as.*

> **The Chang Jiang River is nearly** *as long as* **the Amazon.**
> **The Mississippi River isn't** *so long as* **the Amazon.**

Equally is also used in comparisons. Never use *as* between *equally* and the adverb or adjective.

> **The two rivers are** *equally* **impressive.**
> **Both rivers are** *equally* **dangerous.**

EXERCISE 1 Complete each sentence with *so* or *as.*

1. The Monongahela River is not _____ long as the Allegheny River.

2. The Allegheny River, however, doesn't flow _____ powerfully as the Monongahela River.

3. The use of the rivers for transportation is _____ old as the history of the country.

4. Pittsburgh, where the Monongahela and the Allegheny meet, is _____ historic as any city west of the Appalachians.

5. The ocean is not _____ accessible as a river.

EXERCISE 2 Choose the word or words that correctly complete each sentence.

1. The two rivers that meet at Pittsburgh, the Allegheny and the Monongahela, are (equally impressive equally as impressive).

2. In the 1700s the area where the two rivers meet to form the Ohio River was (as so) strategic as any in the West.

3. During the French and Indian War, the French and the British were (equally desirous equally as desirous) to control it.

4. In fact, there wasn't any outpost (as so) important to the French as it was, because it allowed passage from their northern to their southern colonies.

5. Few attacks ended (as so) disastrously as that of British General Edward Braddock on French-held Fort Duquesne in 1754.

6. His army, however, was not (as so) large as the British army that successfully captured the fort in 1758.

7. Pittsburgh did not figure (so as) importantly as did cities farther east during the Revolutionary War.

8. More recent periods in history are not (as so) fascinating to me as the colonial period.

9. I say that is because I'm (as so) much of a history buff as my father.

10. My father and mother tell me that the 1700s suit me (as so) well as my own time.

11. People today do not work (as so) rigorously to survive as they did in the 1700s, so I'm not sure I agree.

The Allegheny River in Pittsburgh, Pennsylvania

EXERCISE 3 Choose the word or words that correctly complete each sentence.

1. Cedric's bicycle is (as equally as) good as mine.

2. That end of the pool is not (equally so) deep as this end.

3. Tia and Max play the drums (equally equally as) well.

4. San Francisco has (as so) much fog as London.

APPLY IT NOW

Use *as . . . as* or *so . . . as* in sentences to compare one of the following sets of items. Choose items that you have opinions about.

two songs   two sports
two books   two school subjects
two movies   two music groups

Grammar in Action. Find the adverb comparison in the p. 374 excerpt.

6.5 Adverb Phrases and Clauses

Prepositional phrases can be used as adverbs to describe verbs, adjectives, or other adverbs. Prepositional phrases used in this way are called **adverb phrases**. They tell *when, where, why,* and *how.*

> **Monarch butterflies return north** *in the spring.* (describes the verb *return*— tells *when*)
>
> **Some monarch butterflies migrate** *from Canada.* (describes the verb *migrate*—tells *where*)

What are the adverb phrases in these sentences? What does each describe?

> **Many butterflies travel to Mexico.**
>
> **They are vulnerable to habitat loss.**
>
> **They begin their migration early in the autumn.**

You are correct if you answered as follows: In the first sentence, the adverb phrase *to Mexico* describes the verb *travel.* In the second sentence, the adverb phrase *to habitat loss* describes the adjective *vulnerable.* In the third sentence, the adverb phrase *in the autumn* describes the adverb *early.*

A **clause** is a group of words containing a subject and a predicate. A **dependent clause** is one that does not express a complete thought and that cannot stand alone. A dependent clause that acts as an adverb is called an **adverb clause**. Like adverbs and adverb phrases, adverb clauses tell *how, when, where, why, to what extent,* or *under what condition.*

> **Unlike most other insects, monarch butterflies migrate** *because they cannot survive the cold.* (The adverb clause tells *why* and describes the verb *migrate* in the main clause.)
>
> *When it gets cold,* **the butterflies begin migration.** (The adverb clause tells *when* and describes the verb *begin.*)

Some common conjunctions used to introduce adverb clauses are *after, although, as, because, before, if, in order that, provided that, since, so that, unless, until, when, whenever, where, wherever, whether,* and *while.*

EXERCISE 1 Identify the adverb phrase in each sentence. Name the word the adverb phrase describes.

1. Monarch butterflies spend summer in North America.
2. During the summer they are spread over a wide area.
3. In the fall they migrate to their winter homes.
4. Some monarch butterflies fly to the same winter homes used by the previous generation of butterflies.
5. During the flight they are, of course, vulnerable to predators.
6. Many monarch butterflies fly to Mexico in large groups.
7. Most monarch butterflies winter in a Mexican forest.
8. Millions congregate in the same place.

Monarch butterflies in the Sierra Chincua Butterfly Sanctuary in Angangueo, Michoacan, Mexico

EXERCISE 2 Identify the adverb clause in each sentence. Name the word or words the adverb clause describes.

1. Because they make a long migratory flight rather quickly, monarch butterflies born at the end of summer have special features.
2. Although they look like their parents, they differ in some ways.
3. Because their bodies store a lot of fat in the abdomen, they have enough fuel for their long flight.
4. They leave for the south before the weather gets cold.
5. If they stay too long, they cannot make the trip.
6. Butterflies cannot fly in cold weather because they are cold-blooded animals.
7. As they migrate southward, they stop to get nectar and actually gain weight on the trip.

EXERCISE 3 Identify the underlined words in each sentence as an adverb phrase or adverb clause. Name the word it describes.

1. Strike while the iron is hot.
2. The greyhound ran faster than the rabbit could.
3. The ants climbed over my sandwich.
4. An honest woman speaks as she thinks.
5. Raphael acted with courage.

APPLY IT NOW

Find an article about an animal that interests you. Try to identify all the adverb phrases and clauses in it. Write a five-sentence summary of the article without looking back at it. Use at least one adverb phrase and one adverb clause in your summary.

Adverb Review

6.1 Identify the simple adverb in each sentence. Tell its type and the word the adverb describes.

1. Erin frequently walks her dog on the trail.
2. Her dog, Rufus, waits enthusiastically at the door in the morning.
3. The sun is hardly up when they begin their walk.
4. Rufus scampered away from Erin.
5. Rufus is certainly happy on those morning walks.
6. Their morning walks are never short.
7. They walk far from home.
8. Rufus tugs playfully on his leash.
9. They are quite tired at the end of their walk.
10. Erin and Rufus travel everywhere together.
11. They usually run around the park.

6.2 Identify the underlined word in each sentence as an interrogative adverb or an adverbial noun.

12. <u>When</u> will Donna arrive home from school?
13. <u>Why</u> was her bus so late?
14. It had to stop many <u>times</u>.
15. <u>Why</u> did the traffic jam occur?
16. Donna spent two <u>hours</u> on the bus.
17. In that time the bus traveled three <u>miles</u>.
18. <u>Where</u> was the bus stuck?
19. The bus moved only <u>inches</u> at a time.
20. Donna's trip usually takes 30 <u>minutes</u>.
21. <u>How</u> did Donna feel when she <u>finally</u> arrived home?
22. It seemed like she was riding the bus all <u>night</u>.
23. Donna only lives 12 <u>blocks</u> from school.

6.3 Write the comparative and superlative forms of the following adverbs. If the comparative form is given, write the superlative form.

24. skillfully
25. less carefully
26. fast
27. far
28. well
29. much
30. little
31. badly
32. simply
33. less readily
34. soon
35. actively
36. less effectively
37. early
38. slow

6.4 Complete each sentence with *so, as,* or *equally.*

39. This year's art fair wasn't _____ crowded as last year's.

40. The painting was _____ realistic as a photograph.

41. The artists are _____ talented, judging from the exhibits.

42. This mosaic isn't _____ colorful as the other one.

43. She sculpts _____ well as she paints.

44. Larry doesn't like art _____ much as he likes music.

45. Pottery and quilts are _____ remarkable.

46. This painting is _____ striking as that one.

47. The judges thought the two paintings were _____ impressive.

48. Sarah's paintings aren't _____ interesting as her sculptures.

49. Sarah doesn't work on her paintings _____ often as she works on her sculpture.

50. Kim's collage was _____ colorful as her photograph.

51. The crowd believed her two pieces were _____ striking.

6.5 Identify the adverb phrase or adverb clause in each sentence. Tell whether each is a phrase or a clause, and identify the word it describes.

52. Julia spent her vacation at her grandparents' house.

53. When Julia arrived, her grandparents hugged her.

54. Her grandparents live in San Francisco.

55. Their house looks over the bay.

56. Although Julia enjoys the hot weather of southern California, she appreciates San Francisco's cooler air temperature even more.

57. Julia goes sightseeing whenever she visits San Francisco.

58. She usually goes to Chinatown with her grandparents.

59. They also take a ferry to Angel Island Park.

60. Angel Island Park is where her grandparents first arrived when they immigrated to America.

61. After they go to Chinatown, they often walk along the wharf.

62. That is where they catch the ferry to Angel Island State Park.

63. Because Julia likes animals, they also go to the San Francisco Zoo.

64. Before Julia goes home, they all go shopping.

65. In the shopping bags are many souvenirs.

Go to www.voyagesinenglish.com for more activities.

Adverb Challenge

American astronaut Edwin "Buzz" Aldrin walking near the lunar module on the moon

EXERCISE 1 Read the selection and answer the questions.

1. The first astronauts had to be very brave. 2. They ventured to places where no one had ever been. 3. Carefully trained physically and scientifically, they began to explore parts of the universe that previously were seen only from a distance. 4. They were indeed modern pioneers. 5. They were probably more thoroughly trained than the recent astronauts who have left Earth's atmosphere on space shuttles.

6. As space exploration has advanced, inhabited Earth-orbiting stations that were once idly dreamed about have become a reality. 7. The possibility of space travel is not so much a question anymore as that of how long human bodies can stay in space without damage.

1. What is the adverb in the first sentence? What part of speech is the word it describes?

2. In sentence 2 is *where* an interrogative adverb, a conjunction, or an adverbial noun? What word does it describe?

3. In sentence 2 which adverb shows time? What does it describe?

4. In sentence 4 find an adverb. What type of adverb is it?

5. In sentence 5 find the adverb in the comparative form. Give its positive and superlative forms.

6. In sentence 5 find the adverb phrase. What does it describe?

7. In sentence 6 find the adverb clause.

8. In sentence 6 find the adverb of manner.

9. In sentence 7 is *without damage* an adverb phrase or adjective phrase? What does it describe?

EXERCISE 2 Write a paragraph, following these instructions.

Describe an extracurricular activity you enjoy. In your description, use at least two simple adverbs, a comparative adverb, a superlative adverb, an adverb phrase, and an adverb clause. Explain how, when, and where you participate in the activity, as well as why you participate.

7.1 Single and Multiword Prepositions

A **preposition** shows the relationship between a noun or pronoun and some other word in the sentence. In this sentence the preposition *of* shows the relationship between *goddess* and *Greeks*.

Gaia was the earth goddess *of* the ancient Greeks.

A **prepositional phrase** is composed of the preposition, the object of the preposition, and words that describe the object. In the example the phrase consists of the preposition *of*; its object, *Greeks*; and *the* and *ancient*, which describe *Greeks*. The entire phrase acts as an adjective describing the noun *goddess*.

Here are some common prepositions.

about	behind	from	since
above	beside	in	through
across	between	into	throughout
after	beyond	near	to
against	by	of	toward
among	down	off	under
around	during	on	up
at	except	over	with
before	for	past	without

Multiword prepositions are made up of more than one word but are treated as single words. In each of the following sentences, the prepositional phrase is in red italics and the preposition is underlined.

In addition to Gaia, another early deity was her consort, Uranus.
According to Greek mythology, the Titans were their children.

Here are some common multiword prepositions.

according to	in addition to	in spite of	out of
because of	in front of	instead of	outside of
by means of	in regard to	on account of	prior to

EXERCISE 1 Identify the preposition or prepositions in each sentence. Name the object of each preposition.

1. Because of the princess's beauty, many men fell in love with her at first sight.
2. A shepherd living near the king's palace sang to the princess.

3. The princess responded to his singing with smiles.

4. On account of the princess's need for happiness and because of the shepherd's cleverness, the king allowed the marriage.

EXERCISE 2 Identify the prepositional phrase or phrases in each sentence. Name the preposition.

1. The Titans ruled the universe before the gods of Mount Olympus.

2. Zeus was a son of the Titan Cronos.

3. It was prophesied that Cronos would be overthrown by a son.

4. Because of the warning, Cronos swallowed his children.

5. Zeus escaped this fate through the aid of his mother.

6. Eventually, Zeus did revolt against his father.

7. The three one-eyed Cyclopes and the three hundred-armed Hecatoncheires gave aid to Zeus.

8. The Cyclopes provided Zeus with thunderbolts for weapons.

9. During a battle Hecatoncheires hurled rocks from cliffs onto the Titans.

10. The Titans thought the mountains were falling on them and fled out of fear.

11. By means of this victory, Zeus became ruler.

12. To punish the Titans, he sent them underground, to the lowest level of the universe.

EXERCISE 3 Choose the best preposition to complete each sentence. Use each preposition once.

from	on	throughout
in	up	on account of

1. _____ his part in the revolt, the Titan Atlas was punished.

2. His punishment was different _____ that of the other Titans.

3. He was given the task of holding _____ the sky.

4. The weight of the world is on his shoulders _____ all eternity.

5. Some say that earthquakes and tidal waves are signs of Atlas's faltering _____ his duty.

6. Because Atlas's image was _____ the cover of many medieval collections of maps, such books are now called atlases.

APPLY IT NOW

Brainstorm with a partner at least 10 prepositional phrases. Then write a humorous story, using as many of those phrases as possible.

7.2 Troublesome Prepositions

Beside and **Besides**   *Beside* means "next to." *Besides* means "in addition to."

> Plant the hyacinths *beside* the daffodils.
> *Besides* my mother, my brother likes to garden.

In and **Into**   *In* means "within" or "inside." *Into* means "movement from the outside to the inside."

> The dog was *in* its cage.
> We didn't dare put the puppy *into* the same cage.

Between and **Among**   *Between* is used to speak of two people, places, or things. *Among* is used to speak of more than two.

> What is the difference *between* daffodils and jonquils?
> Choosing *among* the many colors of crocuses was not easy.

Between   *Between* implies a connection between at least two things and should never be used with the singular *each* or *every*.

> Leave a space *between* the boards. (not *between each board*)
> We rested *between* laps. (not *between every lap*)

Differ with, Differ on, and **Differ from**   You *differ with* someone when you disagree. You usually *differ on* things. *Differ from* describes differences between people or things.

> I *differed with* mother over the prettiest tulip.
> We *differ on* the kinds of herbs to plant.
> This lily *differs from* that one in its type of petal.

Like, As if, and **As though**   *Like* is a preposition and is used in phrases. *As if* and *as though* are conjunctions used to introduce clauses.

> Her hat looked *like* a lamp shade.
> She moved *as if* she had all the time in the world.

Angry with and **Angry at**   One is *angry with* a person but *angry at* a thing.

> I was *angry with* my brother over his stubbornness.
> Mother is *angry at* our inability to get along.

EXERCISE 1 Choose the correct preposition to complete each sentence.

1. My mother, brother, and I order bulbs and seeds; (between among) the three of us, we receive many gardening catalogs.

2. We have a large pile of them (beside besides) the phone.

3. We each draw a diagram of our backyard, planning what new plants to grow (beside besides) those that are already there.

4. (Beside Besides) flowers, we also grow herbs and vegetables.

5. Our plans usually differ (on from) one another somewhat.

6. We talked about planting shrubs (between each walkway between walkways).

7. I differed (with from) my brother on what bulbs to plant.

8. A heated argument broke out (among between) us.

9. Mother looked (like as if) she was going to yell at us.

10. Since we differed (on from) the plan, she made the final decision.

11. Mother chided us for getting so easily (angry with angry at) each other.

12. At first I was (angry with angry at) her decision.

13. The garden will look (like as if) a rainbow.

14. Our yard will look (like as though) it was professionally landscaped.

Tulip bulbs

EXERCISE 2 Rewrite the sentences to correct errors in preposition usage. Not all the sentences have errors.

1. I read my mother's book about tulips like it were a novel.

2. I learned about the differences between "broken," "parrot," and "regular" tulips.

3. Beside information on types of tulips, the book explained how in the 1600s in the Netherlands, tulips were more valuable than gold.

4. My mother is now angry at me because I left the book in the garden, and it got damp with dew.

5. I, of course, differ with my mother on whether my admittedly careless action merits punishment.

APPLY IT NOW

Choose four sets of troublesome prepositions. Write eight sentences showing the correct use of the prepositions in each set.

Grammar in Action. Identify the prepositions in the last sentence of the excerpt on p. 374.

7.3 Words Used as Adverbs and Prepositions

Some words can be either adverbs or prepositions.

> **As we sat on the mountaintop, an eagle flew** *below* **us.**
> **As we sat on the mountaintop, an eagle flew** *below*.

In the first sentence, the adverb phrase *below us* contains the preposition *before* and the object *us*. The phrase describes the verb *flew*. In the second sentence, the word *below* functions as an adverb describing *flew*.

What part of speech is the word *beneath* in each of these sentences?

> **We dug** *beneath* **the porch in search of treasure.**
> **We really had no idea what lay** *beneath*.

You are correct if you said that in the first sentence, the word *beneath* is a preposition, part of the phrase *beneath the porch*. In the second sentence, *beneath* is not part of a phrase. You are correct if you said that it is an adverb describing the verb *lay*.

To distinguish between a preposition and an adverb, remember that a preposition is always part of a phrase that ends with a noun or pronoun as its object.

EXERCISE 1 In the following sets of sentences, the word italicized in the first sentence is used as an adverb. Use the word as a preposition in the second sentence by adding an object.

1. Let's climb *up*.
   Let's climb up _____.

2. Let's rest *after*.
   Let's rest after _____.

3. We can look *around*.
   We can look around _____.

4. The cabin is *near*.
   The cabin is near _____.

5. I would rather stay *inside*.
   I would rather stay inside _____.

EXERCISE 2 Tell whether each italicized word is an adverb or a preposition.

1. Have you ever wanted to climb *up* a mountain?
2. You get to the top, look *down,* and feel that you have achieved something special.
3. Some beginners start climbing *indoors.*
4. There are special places for climbing *in* some gyms.
5. Perhaps there is such a gym *near* your home.
6. Many kids start climbing *with* special harnesses.
7. It can be a bit scary at first when you look *below.*
8. Many gyms have lower walls *with* bigger grips for kids.

EXERCISE 3 Identify the adverb or preposition in each sentence.

1. The rain splashed down while we were running toward shelter.
2. Inez piled the reports on my desk.
3. Sheila left the note outside your door.
4. Suddenly, the door opened, and in rushed Michelle.
5. The gorilla and his band stood outside.
6. Is that your snake slithering in the sand under the porch?
7. Her father got a new job so Jane is moving away.

EXERCISE 4 Choose the best word to complete each sentence. Use each word once. Tell whether each word is used as an adverb or a preposition.

before   down   from   toward   within

1. Have you ever sat _____ at a local beach or park and unexpectedly heard the sound of music?
2. It might be coming _____ a bandstand, a café, or a street corner.
3. The sound may be carried _____ you on a breeze.
4. As the sound continues, it may appeal to something _____ you.
5. It may remind you of something that happened _____.

APPLY IT NOW

Imagine that you are a world-class mountain climber. Write 10 sentences about your adventures and accomplishments. Use some of the following words as prepositions or adverbs in your description: *above, after, before, below, down, in, off, through, under, up.* Identify the use of each of these words.

7.4 Prepositional Phrases as Adjectives

A prepositional phrase that describes a noun or pronoun is an **adjective phrase**.

> Flowers are the large, showy blossoms *on a plant*.
> The function *of the flowers* is to produce seeds.

Both of the italicized prepositional phrases are adjective phrases. In the first sentence, the prepositional phrase *on a plant* tells something about *blossoms,* a noun. In the second sentence, the prepositional phrase *of the flowers* describes the noun *function*.

In the following sentences, what are the adjective phrases, and what do they describe?

> The meaning of flowers can vary.
> The lotus, a water lily, is the national flower of India.

You are correct if you said that *of flowers* describes the noun *meaning*. In the next sentence, *of India* describes *flower*.

EXERCISE 1 Identify the adjective phrase or phrases in each sentence.

1. The international customs for flowers vary.
2. Suppose friends in Japan invite you home.
3. A small gift from the guest is expected.
4. It is best not to take a gift of cut flowers, however.
5. Cut flowers are usually considered gifts for sick people or for courting couples.
6. A popular custom in France takes place on May 1.
7. People exchange bunches of lilies of the valley.
8. The flowers are a sign of friendship.
9. Carnations are not a good gift for Europeans because many think the flowers are a sign of bad luck.
10. Purple has associations with mourning, so don't give flowers of that color unless it is appropriate.
11. People in the United States often give gifts of flowers or candy on special occasions.

EXERCISE 2 Identify the adjective phrase or phrases in each sentence. Name the noun or pronoun the adjective phrase describes.

1. The appearance of some flowers is truly weird.
2. Yet some gardeners have a taste for the exotic.
3. The plants in their gardens might include unusual flowers.
4. One from Borneo is called *Rafflesia arnoldii.*
5. The blossom on this Malaysian parasitic plant can be three feet across.
6. A cavity at its center holds several quarts of water.
7. That's not the most unusual feature of the flower, however.
8. The flower's foul odor resembles that of rotting flesh.
9. Why would a flower give off a scent like that?
10. The repugnant smell is actually an attraction for flies.
11. The plant requires pollination by flies.

Rafflesia arnoldii

EXERCISE 3 Rewrite each group of words as an adjective phrase.

1. garden gate
2. rose garden
3. tree bark
4. plant food
5. flower bed
6. flower box
7. water bottle
8. gardening catalog

Write an adjective phrase to describe each noun.

9. tree
10. flower
11. house
12. garden
13. path
14. row
15. bed
16. bag

EXERCISE 4 Write an adjective phrase using each preposition. Use the adjective phrase in a sentence.

1. beside
2. between
3. among
4. into

APPLY IT NOW

Write a brief paragraph about a custom related to flowers for holidays or gift giving. Use at least five adjective phrases in your writing.

With an adult, research customs online.

7.5 Prepositional Phrases as Adverbs

Adverb phrases are prepositional phrases that are also used as adverbs—to describe verbs, adjectives, or other adverbs.

Like single-word adverbs, adverb phrases answer the questions *how, when, where, why, to what extent,* and *under what condition.*

> **Adverb: The abolitionists worked** *dedicatedly* **to free slaves.**
>
> **Adverb phrase: The abolitionists worked** *with dedication* **to free slaves.**

What are the adverb phrases in the sentences below? What does each describe?

> **Antislavery action began in colonial times.**
>
> **Many people were angry at slavery's existence.**
>
> **The movement gained momentum early in the 19th century.**

In the first sentence, the adverb phrase *in colonial times* describes the verb *began.* In the second sentence, the adverb phrase *at slavery's existence* describes the adjective *angry.* In the third sentence, the phrase *in the 19th century* modifies the adverb *early.*

EXERCISE 1 Tell what each italicized adverb phrase describes.

1. Charlotte Forten went *to the South* during the Civil War.
2. As an African American, she was committed *to the abolitionist cause.*
3. She was very sensitive *to the needs* of others.
4. She brought her ideals *to her work.*
5. Forten came *from an influential and affluent family.*
6. Early *in her life* she lived in Philadelphia.
7. She went *to Massachusetts* and attended a school for teachers.
8. She began her teaching career *in the Salem schools.*
9. There she taught grammar school until the onset of tuberculosis forced her to return *to Philadelphia.*
10. Forten taught successfully *during many phases* of her life.

A U.S. Army officer explains the duties of freedom to former slaves after the Emancipation Proclamation in 1863.

EXERCISE 2 Identify the adverb phrase or phrases in each sentence. Name the word or words the adjective phrase describes.

1. In 1862 Charlotte Forten went to South Carolina.

2. She was acting on her deepest beliefs.

3. She helped other African Americans by means of her teaching skills.

4. In spite of her commitment, she faced many difficulties.

5. Her pupils spoke in a special local dialect.

6. Forten was unfamiliar with the language.

7. Normal school routines were strange to her students.

8. Forten did not bond closely with the islanders.

9. Under physical and emotional stress, she grew ill.

10. She left the island of Saint Helena after two years.

11. She departed in disappointment.

12. Forten spoke for equality in many forums for many years.

13. Forten is now famous for her diaries.

14. Later in her life she married Presbyterian minister Francis J. Grimké.

Charlotte Forten Grimké

EXERCISE 3 Rewrite each italicized adverb as an adverb phrase. Use the phrase in a sentence.

1. acted *courageously*
2. studied *diligently*
3. worked *determinedly*
4. wrote *clearly*
5. wrote *honestly*
6. wrote *regularly*

EXERCISE 4 Identify the prepositional phrase or phrases in each sentence. Tell whether the prepositional phrase is being used as an adjective or an adverb.

1. Thor Heyerdahl led the *Kon-Tiki* expedition from Peru to Polynesia on a raft made of balsa logs.

2. The purpose of the expedition was to prove that the Inca Peruvians were the settlers of Polynesia.

3. Worshipping the Sun god Kon was a practice of the early South American Indians, according to legend.

4. The *Kon-Tiki* was damaged on a reef, but the men survived and completed their voyage.

APPLY IT NOW

Use an encyclopedia, a textbook, or the Internet to get more information on the abolitionists or on Charlotte Forten. Write seven sentences about what interests you. Use at least five adverb phrases and underline them.

7.6 Prepositional Phrases as Nouns

A prepositional phrase can be used as a noun.

> **Before dinner is my usual time to do homework.**

Before dinner is a prepositional phrase used as the subject of the verb *is*.

A prepositional phrase may appear in any position where a noun can be used in a sentence.

> **My time for playing the guitar is *after dinner*.**

In the above sentence, the prepositional phrase acts as a subject complement.

Which of these sentences uses a prepositional phrase as a noun?

> **Inside the display case lay a beautiful antique quilt.**
> **On the lawn was the best place to take the class photos.**

You are correct if you chose the second sentence. The prepositional phrase *on the lawn* is the subject of the verb *was*.

EXERCISE 1 Identify the prepositional phrase used as a noun in each sentence. Tell how the prepositional phrase functions in the sentence.

1. In front of the camera sometimes seems an uncomfortable place.
2. Behind the camera can also be a difficult place to be.
3. During bad weather is usually not a good time to take pictures.
4. Because of the light, a good time to take landscapes is in the early morning or the early evening.
5. A bad place to pose a subject is in front of a cluttered background.
6. In front of a strong sun is usually a bad place to take a picture.

EXERCISE 2 Identify the prepositional phrases in these sentences. Then tell whether each prepositional phrase is an adjective phrase, an adverb phrase, or a noun phrase.

1. A surprising time to receive a gift that changes one's life is at age 48.
2. However, that is exactly what happened to Julia Cameron.
3. Cameron's life changed with the gift of a camera.
4. Cameras of the 1860s were quite different from those of today.

5. Cameron gained mastery of their use, however, and became fascinated with photography.

6. On Cameron's estate's lawn was a wonderful place to take photos.

7. She took pictures of her family and friends.

8. Often her friends and relatives dressed up for these photographs.

9. Sometimes they would choose a work of literature and dress as the characters in it.

10. The results of her efforts are dreamy and romantic photographs that spark the imagination.

11. She also began to take photographs of famous people.

12. There are photos by her of the naturalist Charles Darwin and the philosopher Thomas Carlyle.

13. Her portrait of the poet Alfred, Lord Tennyson is her most famous and is counted among her greatest work.

14. She received praise and awards for her work.

15. Some people have remarked that Cameron's portraits capture the vitality of the sitter.

16. Some people, however, criticize her work for the out-of-focus technique of certain pictures.

17. She used long exposures, and because of this, her sitters had to remain still for long periods of time.

18. According to her, however, behind the camera was the most difficult place to be.

Alfred, Lord
Tennyson portrait
by Julia Cameron

EXERCISE 3 Write sentences using the following prepositional phrases as indicated in parentheses.

1. in the box (adjective phrase)
2. over the hill (adverb phrase)
3. inside the house (noun phrase)
4. after school (adverb phrase)
5. next to the fire (adjective phrase)
6. on the road (noun phrase)

APPLY IT NOW

Write seven sentences about a photo that is important to you. It may be one you took, one given to you, one with you in it, or one of an important event. Identify the prepositional phrases in your writing and tell how they function in the sentence.

Tech Tip   Post your writing and photo on the class blog.

Preposition Review

7.1 Identify the prepositional phrase or phrases in each sentence. Name the preposition.

1. According to experts, the giant squid is the largest invertebrate on earth.

2. From end to end, the giant squid can measure 75 feet long.

3. Through research, scientists have tried to learn more about the mysterious creature.

4. In spite of scientists' efforts, no one has seen a giant squid alive in its natural habitat.

5. It is believed that giant squid live in much deeper waters.

6. On account of its unusual appearance, humans have long been fascinated by the creature.

7. Recently, scientists have filmed a giant squid alive in its habitat for the first time.

8. They were rarely seen but had been occasionally caught by fishers.

9. Giant squid are found throughout the world but are rare in polar and tropical regions.

7.2 Choose the correct preposition to complete each sentence.

10. How does crocheting differ (with from) knitting?

11. (Beside Besides) a different number of needles, the two crafts require different skills.

12. Take the ball of yarn (from off) the pile and bring it to your grandmother.

13. I was angry (with at) my mother for making me wear the ugly, handmade sweater.

14. While learning how to knit, I sat (beside besides) my grandmother.

15. (Between Among) the three of us, there was enough knitting skill to produce one scarf.

16. My mother and grandmother differ (with on) which craft they like better.

17. (Between Among) you and me, I am a better knitter than my mother.

18. (Besides Beside) scarves, it is better to buy professionally made knit items.

19. Put the leftover yarn (in into) the sewing box.

20. I differ (on with) my mother about the best kinds of items to knit.

7.3 Tell whether each underlined word is an adverb or a preposition.

21. The horses galloped <u>around</u> the pasture.

22. Excited about riding the horses, we saddled <u>up</u>.

23. Because it was our first time horseback riding, we stayed <u>near</u> the barn.

24. We rode <u>along</u> a path.

25. We rode <u>around</u> for a half hour or so.

26. Let's brush <u>down</u> the horses.

27. They rode <u>beneath</u> the hot sun.

28. After the long ride, the horses rested <u>inside</u>.

29. We went <u>in</u> and had a cool drink.

7.4 **Identify the adjective phrase in each sentence. Name the noun the adjective phrase describes.**

30. People from the United States often visit European countries.

31. France is a country in Europe.

32. Paris has many museums for art lovers.

33. Chocolate from Belgium is delicious.

34. Rome is an ideal spot for a vacation.

35. The beaches along the Mediterranean Sea attract many tourists.

36. Hikers enjoy the mountains of Switzerland.

37. Travel on European trains is inexpensive and convenient.

7.5 **Identify the adverb phrase in each sentence. Name the word or words each phrase describes.**

38. Marcy is known for her cooking.

39. She went to the grocery store.

40. She shopped with attention to freshness and quality.

41. Marcy went to the produce section.

42. She cooked with confidence.

43. The meal was served with fanfare.

44. The guests ate the food with gusto.

45. The food was praised by all the guests.

46. Marcy was happy at the outcome.

47. Marcy invited us to her next party.

7.6 **Identify the prepositional phrase in each sentence. Tell whether each phrase is an adjective phrase, an adverb phrase, or a noun phrase.**

48. After school is the best time to do homework.

49. Kara wrote the answers in her notebook.

50. She always reads with a dictionary nearby.

51. The students studied for two hours.

52. To stay organized, Louis puts his books and pencils in his backpack.

53. The assignment for English homework is page 230.

54. Do you know the answer to the last question?

55. Put your homework on the teacher's desk.

Go to www.voyagesinenglish.com for more activities.

Preposition Challenge

EXERCISE 1 Read the selection and then answer the questions.

1. Less than a minute remained in the final Northern League basketball game of the season. 2. The contest had been an exciting, hard-fought battle between our Mayfair team and the Lincoln players. 3. At that game was definitely the place to be that January night. 4. Everything depended on what we did in the next few seconds, because Lincoln held a one-point lead. 5. In spite of close guarding, one of our players made a deft hook shot into the basket. 6. Spectators stood up and cheered loudly as those two precious points put us in the lead by one point. 7. Lincoln, now in possession of the ball, certainly was desperate to score. 8. The ball sailed harmlessly through the air and over the basket, however. 9. It fell into eager hands from our team as a loud blast from a horn announced not only the end of the game but also a victory for Mayfair. 10. Our team had come through.

1. Name the prepositions in sentence 1.
2. What is the prepositional phrase in sentence 2? Is it used as an adverb, an adjective, or a noun?
3. How is the prepositional phrase *at that game* used in sentence 3?
4. How is the prepositional phrase *into the basket* used in sentence 5?
5. Name the multiword preposition in sentence 5.
6. In sentence 6 is the word *up* used as an adverb or a preposition? How do you know?
7. Find two adverb phrases in sentence 8. What does each describe?
8. How many adjective phrases can you find in sentence 9? Name them and the words they describe.

EXERCISE 2 Prepositional phrases add important details to sentences in a narrative or an expository essay. Follow these instructions.

Think of an important or eventful story about your family that was told to you by a relative. In one to three paragraphs, record the story and its importance to you and your family. Use prepositional phrases as nouns, adjectives, and adverbs. Label each.

Sentences

8.1 Kinds of Sentences

A sentence is a group of words that expresses a complete thought. The essential parts of a sentence are the subject and the predicate. The **subject** tells who or what the sentence is about. The **predicate** names an action or a state of being. In this sentence the simple subject is the noun *Web site*. The simple predicate is the verb *lists*.

A special *Web site* | *lists* the times in major world cities.

The **complete subject** is the simple subject plus all the words and phrases that go with it. The **complete predicate** is the verb and all the words and phrases that go with it. In the sentence above, a vertical line separates the complete subject and complete predicate.

A **declarative sentence** makes a statement. It ends with a period.

I have a new watch.

An **interrogative sentence** asks a question. It ends with a question mark.

Are you late for school?

An **imperative sentence** gives a command. It usually ends with a period but may end with an exclamation point. In imperative sentences the subject *you* is understood.

(You) Tell me the time of the game.

An **exclamatory sentence** expresses a strong emotion. It ends with an exclamation point.

We are so late!

EXERCISE 1 Tell whether each sentence is declarative, interrogative, imperative, or exclamatory.

1. For most of the 19th century, each community in the country determined its own time.
2. What unbelievable confusion there was!
3. Two neighboring towns might have different times.
4. Why did the situation change?
5. Guess the answer.

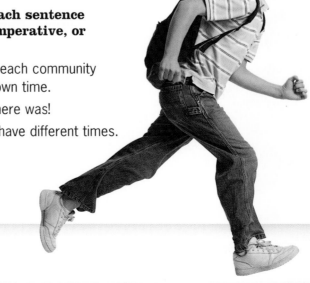

6. In the 1880s, the railroads demanded standardized time.

7. How were the changes decided?

8. In 1884, delegates from more than 27 countries met in Washington, D.C.

9. They divided the earth into 24 time zones.

10. What a historical event it was!

EXERCISE 2 **Identify the complete subject and the complete predicate in each sentence. Then name the simple subject and the simple predicate.**

1. Imaginary lines on the globe separate the 24 time zones.

2. The prime meridian runs through Greenwich, England.

3. Zero degree longitude marks the start of time zones.

4. The continental United States has four time zones: eastern, central, mountain, and Pacific.

5. One hour is lost for every time zone to the west.

6. You can determine the different times fairly easily.

7. New York City is three hours later than Los Angeles.

8. At the same moment, Denver is one hour earlier than Chicago.

9. Variations still exist in the United States, however.

10. Some places don't change to daylight saving time in the spring.

EXERCISE 3 **Identify the complete subject and complete predicate in each sentence. Then tell whether each sentence is declarative, interrogative, imperative, or exclamatory.**

1. My family and I drove from Florida to New Mexico.

2. The scenery was amazing!

3. My father asked us a hard question.

4. Who knows how many time zones we will cross?

5. Look at a map and guess again.

6. The correct answer was two time zones.

APPLY IT NOW

Write six sentences about a time when you were either too late or too early. Use at least one of each of the four sentence types: declarative, interrogative, imperative, and exclamatory. Identify the simple subjects and the simple predicates in your writing.

Tech Tip Post your paragraph on the class blog for peer review.

Sentences • **141**

8.2 Adjective and Adverb Phrases

A **phrase** is a group of words that is used as a single part of speech. Unlike a sentence or a clause, a phrase does not contain a subject or a predicate. Several types of phrases function as adjectives and as adverbs.

A **prepositional phrase** is made up of a preposition, the object of the preposition, and modifiers of the object.

> **The Marine Corps was established** *in 1798*.
> (adverb phrase describing the verb *was established*)
>
> **The initial corps was a group** *within the United States Navy*. (adjective phrase describing the noun *group*)

A **participial phrase** is made up of a present or past participle and any words that go with it. Participial phrases always act as adjectives.

> *Participating in every major war*, **the Marine Corps has a long history.**
> (participial phrase describing the proper noun *Marine Corps*)

An **infinitive phrase** is made up of an infinitive—*to* and the base form of a verb—and any words that go with it. An infinitive phrase acts as an adjective, an adverb, or a noun.

> **A good place** *to find information about songs* **is the Internet.**
> (infinitive phrase acting as an adjective describing the noun *place*)
>
> **There wasn't time enough** *to find all the information this afternoon*.
> (infinitive phrase acting as an adverb describing the adjective *enough*)
>
> *To earn a dog biscuit* **is the reason my dog performs tricks for me.**
> (infinitive phrase acting as a noun)

EXERCISE 1 Tell whether each italicized phrase is prepositional, participial, or infinitive. Then tell whether the phrase is used as an adjective or an adverb.

1. The Barbary Coast is part *of North Africa*.
2. Tripoli, Morocco, Algiers, and Tunis, *bordering the Mediterranean Sea*, made up the Barbary States.
3. *In the 1700s and early 1800s*, pirates from the Barbary States robbed and terrorized the ships of other countries.
4. Countless efforts *to stop these raids* failed.
5. The North Africans, *dubbed "the Barbary pirates,"* ruled the sea.
6. The pirates' offers *to spare U.S. ships* were rejected.

7. *To let the ships pass,* the pirates demanded payment.

8. The offers were greeted *with the slogan* "Millions for defense but not a cent for tribute."

9. Several countries finally banded together *to stop the pirates.*

10. A fleet of U.S. warships commanded *by Stephen Decatur* set out for the Barbary Coast.

11. *Joining European warships,* the U.S. fleet helped drive the pirates from the sea.

12. When you hear the words *to the "Marine Hymn,"* you will now understand "to the shores of Tripoli."

Burning of the American ship *Philadelphia* held by Barbary pirates in Tripoli Harbor in 1804

Stephen Decatur

EXERCISE 2 Identify the phrases in these sentences. Tell whether each is prepositional, participial, or infinitive and whether it acts as an adjective or as an adverb.

1. I am studying the songs of the military services.

2. I searched the Internet to find the lyrics.

3. Reading the lyrics, I had some questions about their meaning.

4. My desire to understand the lyrics sparked new research.

5. I even studied about the Barbary pirates for hours.

EXERCISE 3 Use these phrases in sentences of your own. Tell whether each phrase is prepositional, participial, or infinitive. Then tell whether the phrase is used as an adjective or an adverb.

1. to rescue captives

2. guarding our shores

3. at sea

4. with secret maps

5. to find buried treasure

6. sailing the seas

7. to explore new lands

8. throughout the world

9. in a day

10. changing the course of history

APPLY IT NOW

Write six sentences explaining your after-school routine. Use at least one prepositional phrase, one participial phrase, and one infinitive phrase. Identify each phrase and tell whether it acts as an adjective or as an adverb.

8.3 Adjective Clauses

A **clause** is a group of words that contains a subject and a predicate. An **independent clause** is one that expresses a complete thought and so can stand on its own.

Boston has many historic sites.

A **dependent clause** cannot stand alone.

One site *that tourists visit* **is south of town.**
Some events *about which I studied* **occurred in Boston.**

Notice that neither of the groups of words in red expresses a complete thought, even though each has a subject and a verb.

An **adjective clause,** one type of dependent clause, describes a noun or a pronoun. Most adjective clauses begin with one of the **relative pronouns** *who, whom, whose, which,* or *that.* The word in the independent clause to which the relative pronoun relates is its **antecedent**. In this sentence the adjective clause modifies *Madison.* *Madison* is the antecedent of the relative pronoun *which.*

Madison, *which is in Wisconsin,* **has several lakes.**

Can you identify the adjective clause, the relative pronoun, and the antecedent of the pronoun in this sentence?

I visited the school that my mother attended.

The adjective clause is *that my mother attended.* The relative pronoun is *that,* and *school* is its antecedent.

Some adjective clauses begin with a subordinate conjunction such as *when, where,* or *why.*

Madison is the place *where my mother went to school.*

EXERCISE 1 Identify the adjective clause in each sentence. Name the noun or pronoun that the adjective clause describes.

1. I traveled to Newfoundland with my uncle Joel, who had invited me on the trip.

2. Joel is a person whose ideas for adventures always turn out well.

3. His plan, which he presented as a trip to Newfoundland during the winter, was unusual.

4. It seemed suited to people who love cold weather.
5. I, however, am not a person who likes cold weather.
6. We headed to New England, which was blanketed in snow.
7. A blizzard, which hadn't been forecast, forced us to stop.
8. So New Brunswick was the place where we stayed for several days—indoors.
9. We eventually made it to the ferry that would take us across the Gulf of St. Lawrence to Newfoundland.
10. The ferry, which had an icebreaker on its bow, chopped through the ice floes.
11. Our plan, which was to see the winter landscape, was hindered by another few days of bad weather.
12. This was the one adventure of Uncle Joel's that didn't please me.

EXERCISE 2 Identify the adjective clause in each sentence. Tell whether it begins with a relative pronoun or a subordinate conjunction.

1. Quebec, which is located in Canada, sits on the banks of the St. Lawrence River.
2. It is a city where people enjoy dogsled races and other winter activities.
3. It is in a region that is very cold.
4. Quebec is the Canadian city where many Americans travel for Winter Carnival.

EXERCISE 3 Rewrite the following sentences, inserting an adjective clause after the italicized words.

1. The *trip* was my favorite one.
2. I remember the *day*.
3. I'll never forget the *place*.
4. The *hotel* was a lovely one.
5. Every day we went to the *park*.
6. The *pool* was a welcome sight.
7. I watched the *game* in the lobby.
8. She wrote the *guidebook*.

APPLY IT NOW

Choose one of the following sightseeing attractions.
Write five sentences about it, each containing an adjective clause.
Mount Rushmore
Golden Gate Bridge
Niagara Falls
Lake Placid
Gateway Arch
Mississippi River
Manhattan
Great Plains

Tech Tip With an adult, research one of the places online.

8.4 Restrictive and Nonrestrictive Clauses

Some adjective clauses, called **restrictive clauses,** are essential to the meaning of the sentences in which they appear. Without them, the sentences no longer make sense. An adjective clause that is not essential to the meaning of the independent clause and that can be removed without affecting the sense of the sentence is a **nonrestrictive clause.**

> **A large arena** *that stands in modern Rome* **has survived through centuries.** (restrictive clause)
>
> **The Coliseum,** *which is a major tourist attraction,* **was built by the ancient Romans.** (nonrestrictive clause)

Can you tell which clauses are restrictive and which are nonrestrictive in the following sentences?

> **The ancient Romans,** *who created a large empire,* **left buildings throughout much of the Mediterranean.**
>
> **The empire** *that they created* **lasted for centuries.**
>
> **The structures** *that the Romans built* **included aqueducts and arenas.**

The adjective clause in the first sentence is nonrestrictive, and those in the second and third sentences are restrictive. In the first sentence, the adjective clause can be removed without changing the basic meaning of the sentence. Removing the adjective clauses from the other sentences would make the sentences unclear.

Note the following characteristics of adjective clauses:

- A nonrestrictive clause is set off by commas.
- A restrictive clause does not have commas.
- A proper noun is usually followed by a nonrestrictive clause.
- The relative pronoun *that* is generally used for restrictive clauses, and *which* is used for nonrestrictive clauses.

EXERCISE 1 Identify the adjective clause in each sentence. Tell whether the adjective clause is restrictive or nonrestrictive.

1. The Coliseum, which is one of the most famous buildings in the world, stands in central Rome.

2. It is a magnificent monument that was left by the ancient Romans.

3. The Romans, whose skill at building was famous, created a great empire.

The Coliseum

4. Roman structures that are still standing include amphitheaters, aqueducts, arches, and roadways.

5. The Coliseum, which was built in only 10 years, has been standing since the first century AD.

6. The emperor who started the building was Vespasian.

7. The huge structure, which rises more than 187 feet in the air, is about 600 feet long and about 500 feet wide.

8. It had more than 80 entrances, which were numbered for easy access.

9. The structure could hold more than 45,000 people, who came for public entertainments provided by the emperor.

10. The entertainment that it provided for audiences included combats between gladiators and frequently with wild animals.

EXERCISE 2 Identify the adjective clause in each sentence and tell whether the clause is restrictive or nonrestrictive. Rewrite the sentences with nonrestrictive clauses, adding commas where necessary.

1. Gladiators whose name comes from the Latin word for *sword* were a class of professional fighters.

2. Pairs of gladiators would fight each other in games that were part of the public entertainment of Rome.

3. The pairs which could sometimes number up to 5,000 couples in one amphitheater were trained in fighting.

4. A gladiator who was defeated was killed by the victor.

5. Some gladiators were slaves that had been sold to gladiator schools.

6. Spartacus who was forced to fight as a gladiator escaped with 70 other gladiators.

7. It was Spartacus and his followers who eventually freed 100,000 slaves before being captured by the Roman army.

8. The bloody gladiator games which continued until 404 AD were finally banned by the emperor Honorius.

APPLY IT NOW

Copy five sentences with adjective clauses that you locate in books. Underline the adjective clauses and indicate whether each is restrictive or nonrestrictive.

8.5 Adverb Clauses

Dependent clauses may act as adverbs, describing or giving information about verbs, adjectives, or other adverbs. These clauses, called **adverb clauses,** tell *where, when, why, in what way, to what extent (degree),* or *under what condition.*

> *Wherever they went,* **King Arthur's knights helped the weak and the poor.**

The adverb clause tells *where* and describes the verb *helped* in the independent clause.

Adverb clauses are introduced by subordinate conjunctions, some of which are listed below.

after	because	since	until
although	before	so long as	when
as if	even though	so that	whenever
as long as	if	than	where
as soon as	inasmuch as	though	wherever
as though	in order that	unless	while

A **subordinate conjunction** joins an adverb clause to an independent clause. Find the subordinate conjunctions in these sentences. What does each adverb clause tell about?

> **Even though there may have been a real King Arthur, the stories we read about him are legends.**
> **People have loved the tales of King Arthur since they were written down during the Middle Ages.**

In the first sentence, the subordinate conjunction *even though* introduces an adverb clause that tells a condition—*even though there may have been a real King Arthur.* In the second sentence, the subordinate conjunction *since* introduces an adverb clause that shows time—*since they were written down during the Middle Ages.*

An adverb clause can come before or after the independent clause. When an adverb clause begins a sentence, it is usually followed by a comma.

> *Since they were written down during the Middle Ages,* **the tales of King Arthur have been popular.**

EXERCISE 1 Identify the adverb clause in each sentence. Name the subordinate conjunction.

1. If you want to read some good stories, read the tales about King Arthur and the Knights of the Round Table.

2. Here is one version of the ending, although there are other versions.

3. As the years passed, Arthur's knights died or went away.

4. An evil knight, Mordred, plotted so that he could have power.

5. Because Mordred wanted to take the throne from Arthur, a great battle occurred.

6. After the day-long battle ended, only Arthur, two of his knights, and Mordred were left standing.

7. When Arthur saw Mordred on the battlefield, he was able to strike a fatal blow to the evil knight's heart.

8. As Mordred was falling, however, he swung one last blow with his sword and wounded Arthur.

9. While he lay wounded, Arthur told his loyal knight Sir Bedivere to throw Excalibur, Arthur's magic sword, into the nearby lake.

10. After Bedivere dragged Arthur to the shore, a boat appeared with three women who carried Arthur away.

Tintagel Castle in Cornwall, England, which is associated with the legend of King Arthur

EXERCISE 2 Identify the dependent clause in each sentence. Tell whether it is an adjective clause or an adverb clause.

1. No one knows Arthur's fate after he disappeared into the mists.

2. Perhaps the women healed his wounds unless it was too late.

3. In some versions Arthur lives on Avalon, which is an island of mists and mystery.

4. The version of the legend that I read ends with no clear answer.

5. Even though the ending is unclear, Arthur's values of honor, fairness, and bravery live on.

6. Another version of the King Arthur myth, from the viewpoint of his sister, was written in 1982.

7. The book, which is called *The Mists of Avalon*, was a best seller.

APPLY IT NOW

Choose a passage from another textbook and list the adjective and adverb clauses in it.

8.6 Noun Clauses as Subjects

Dependent clauses can be used as nouns. These clauses, called **noun clauses,** function as subjects, complements, appositives, direct objects, indirect objects, and objects of prepositions. Although a noun clause is a basic part of the independent clause and cannot be eliminated, it is still a dependent clause. A noun clause used as a subject generally takes the singular form of the verb.

Compare these sentences.

> My *worry* **must have been evident from my facial expression.**
>
> *That I was worried* **must have been evident from my facial expression.**

In the first sentence, the noun *worry* is the subject. In the second sentence, the clause *that I was worried* is the subject. The clause does the work of a noun, and so it is a noun clause.

Most noun clauses begin with one of the following introductory words: *that, who, whom, whoever, whomever, how, why, when, whether, what, where,* and *whatever.*

Compare the noun clauses in these sentences. How do the noun clauses, which are in red, function?

> <u>That</u> *we needed entertainment for my little brother's birthday party* **was never in doubt.**
>
> <u>Whoever</u> *suggested a clown* **had a good idea.**

Both noun clauses are subjects: in the first sentence, the subject of the verb *was,* and in the second sentence, the subject of *had.*

In the first sentence, *That* introduces the clause but serves no specific function within the dependent clause. In the second sentence, however, *Whoever* acts as the subject of the dependent clause. What is the verb? You are right if you said *suggested.*

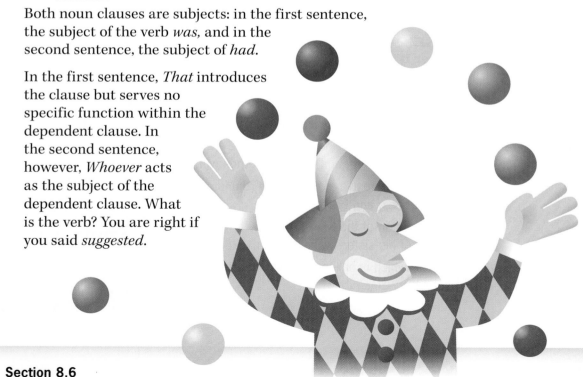

EXERCISE 1 Identify the noun clause used as the subject in each sentence.

1. That the magician was late for Angelica's party surprised us all.
2. What we should do next was the question.
3. How we could keep the children quiet was our greatest concern.
4. That they were happy playing games soon became clear.
5. Whether they would pay attention to the magician was uncertain.
6. Why he did not call to explain his lateness disturbed me, especially since we had talked the day before.
7. That he had lost the address and phone number did not occur to us.
8. How he finally found the house was in itself a mystery.
9. That the children enjoyed the performance was obvious in their laughter.
10. That our food arrived cold was disappointing.
11. Whoever chose the movie deserves the credit too.
12. Whether I'll ever help out at another birthday party is a big question.

EXERCISE 2 Complete each sentence with an appropriate noun clause used as the subject.

1. _____ was my favorite slogan.
2. _____ continues to be important to me.
3. _____ has always interested me.
4. _____ disturbs me.
5. _____ is puzzling.
6. _____ seems to be what I enjoy about school.
7. _____ is what I am most proud of.
8. _____ was thinking ahead.
9. _____ is what I was trying to achieve.
10. _____ will involve everybody.

APPLY IT NOW

Use each noun clause as the subject of a sentence.

- that we would win the game
- how I mastered that skill
- whether I'll ever learn French
- what pleases me the most
- why I like my best friend

8.7 Noun Clauses as Subject Complements

Noun clauses can be used as subject complements.

> **The issue in the balance was** *the control of the Roman world*.
> **The issue in the balance was** *who would control the Roman world*.

In the first sentence, the subject is *issue*. The verb *was* links the subject to the subject complement, the noun *control*. In the second sentence, *issue* is again the subject. The linking verb *was* joins the subject to the subject complement, the entire noun clause *who would control the Roman world*.

What are the subject complements in the following sentences? Which one is a noun clause?

> **The ruler would be the winner of the battle of Actium.**
> **The ruler would be whoever won the battle of Actium.**

In the first sentence, the noun *winner* is the subject complement. In the second sentence, the noun clause *whoever won the battle of Actium* is the subject complement. Its subject is *whoever,* and its verb is *won.*

EXERCISE 1 Identify the noun clause in each sentence. Tell if it is a subject or a subject complement.

1. My teacher's belief is that American history is the most exciting subject to share with students.
2. Why the study of ancient civilization is more interesting to me is a puzzle.
3. My suspicion is that where an American grows up makes a real difference.
4. That they are somehow participants in Revolutionary history might be the feeling of people from Boston.
5. My guess is that my interest in science fiction has something to do with my interest in ancient civilizations.
6. How such things influence each other is something to explore.
7. The fact is, I suppose, that you can't really account for taste.
8. The lucky thing is that my preferences enable me to learn about both topics.

Boston antique engraving, 1854

EXERCISE 2 Identify the noun clause used as the complement in each sentence. Name the subject about which the noun clause gives information.

1. The fact is that the battle of Actium changed the world.
2. The question was who would rule Rome.
3. Mark Antony's hope was that he would defeat Octavius.
4. The situation was that he had been living in Egypt with Cleopatra.
5. Cleopatra's advice was that they fight a battle at sea.
6. Her belief was that Antony's forces would win.
7. Cleopatra's hope was that she would be queen of Rome.
8. The generals' concern was that Cleopatra couldn't be trusted.
9. The truth is that Antony might have won.
10. The surprising event was that Cleopatra sailed away.
11. The big question was why Antony and his ships followed her.
12. The outcome was that Octavius and his navy won the battle.

EXERCISE 3 Complete each sentence with an appropriate noun clause used as the subject complement.

1. My teacher's greatest characteristic is _____.
2. The best attribute of our school is _____.
3. My favorite saying used to be _____.
4. What I've always wondered is _____.
5. The best lesson I've learned is _____.
6. The fact remains _____.
7. Still, it seems _____.
8. My hope is _____.
9. The question remains _____.
10. An answer might be _____.
11. The outcome might be _____.
12. My biggest wish is _____.

Sea battle of Actium in 31 BC, in which Octavius defeated Antony and Cleopatra

APPLY IT NOW

Write five sentences using noun clauses as complements to describe a friend, a teacher, or a family member.

8.8 Noun Clauses as Appositives

Noun clauses can be used as appositives. An **appositive** is a word or group of words that follows a noun and renames it, or gives more information about it.

> **The theme of many folktales is** *that people have moral and social responsibilities*. (subject complement)
>
> **The theme** *that people have moral and social responsibilities* **is important in folktales.** (appositive)

In the first sentence, the italicized noun clause is a subject complement. It describes the subject *theme* and follows the linking verb *is*. In the second sentence, the italicized noun clause is an appositive. It explains the noun that precedes it, *theme*.

Can you identify the noun clause used as an appositive in the following sentence and what it explains?

> **The principle that friendship is essential is in many folktales.**

You are correct if you said the noun clause is *that friendship is essential* and that it follows and renames the noun *principle*.

Adjective clauses are sometimes confused with noun clauses used as appositives. An appositive renames the noun or pronoun it follows. An adjective clause describes a noun or pronoun.

> **The folktale** *that I read* **was about the trickster Spider Ananse.** (adjective clause)
>
> **The theme** *that weakness can overcome strength* **is developed in some of the Ananse tales.** (noun clause)

In the first sentence, *that* acts as a relative pronoun. Its antecedent is *folktale,* and it is the object of the verb *read* in the adjective clause. In the second sentence, *that* introduces the noun clause but has no other function in the clause; it is strictly an introductory word.

EXERCISE 1 Identify the noun clauses used as appositives in these sentences. Not all sentences have noun clauses.

1. It is a fact that folktales are popular.
2. Many folktales from around the world have themes and plots that are similar to one another.
3. It is a fact that African folktales have universal themes.
4. The people's hope that they could communicate with the sky god led them to build a high tower in an old Nigerian tale called "Why the Sky Is Far Away."

5. The punishment that people have to plow fields and that the sky is far away was the result of their action.

6. The tale's theme that people will be punished for wasting resources has a lesson for all of us today.

7. The message that people accepting society's values are rewarded is another common theme in African folktales.

8. Qualities that are valued in African tales include wisdom, friendship, love, and heroism.

9. Qualities that are not valued include foolishness and disloyalty.

10. It is a fact that wit and trickery are sometimes rewarded in African tales.

11. Characters that try to trick others are also sometimes fooled or punished, however, as in the Ananse tales.

12. The moral that caution is needed along with good sense is found in West African tales of Zomo the Rabbit trickster.

EXERCISE 2 Complete each sentence with a noun clause used as an appositive.

1. The theme _____ is important in folktales.

2. The saying _____ is important to me.

3. I read a folktale, and I appreciated its message _____.

4. The fact _____ is surprising to me.

5. Did you hear the legend _____?

6. Claudia's story _____ was a big hit around the campfire.

7. Do you believe the story _____.

8. The moral _____ is sometimes forgotten among friends.

9. It was my grandfather's hope _____.

10. The rumor was _____.

APPLY IT NOW

Choose a folktale that you have enjoyed. Write an e-mail recommending the story to a friend. Use at least two noun clauses as appositives.

Sentences • 155

8.9 Noun Clauses as Direct Objects

A noun clause can act as a direct object. Recall that a direct object receives the action of the verb and answers the question *who* or *what* after a verb.

> **We wondered** *how we would raise money for new computers.*
> **We decided** *that we would hold a car wash.*

The introductory word *that* is frequently dropped from a noun clause used as a direct object.

> **I think** *our fund-raising activity was a success.*

When verbs such as *feel, learn, say, see,* and *think* are followed by a noun clause, be careful to retain *that* if omitting it changes the meaning.

> **I see** *you study in the library.*
> **I see** *that you study in the library.*

The words in red in each sentence are noun clauses that serve as the direct object of the verb. How do the meanings of the sentences differ?

Which of these sentences contains a noun clause used as a direct object?

> **Each student will do whatever he or she has the time or talent for.**
> **Each student will do the task that he or she has the time or talent for.**

In the first sentence, the action of the verb is received by the noun clause *whatever he or she has the time or talent for.* In the second sentence, the noun *task* is the object, and it is followed by the adjective clause *that he or she has the time or talent for.*

EXERCISE 1 Identify the noun clause used as a direct object in each sentence.

1. Our class decided that it wanted to organize a fund-raising project for new computers for classrooms.

2. The class decided whether it would hold a car wash or do some other fund-raising activity.

3. Jo suggested that we make and sell a cookbook.

4. Although the idea wasn't popular at first, the class eventually decided that it was a good idea.

5. Then we discussed how we would make and sell the book.

EXERCISE 2 Identify the direct object in each sentence. Tell whether the direct object is a noun or a noun clause.

1. We knew that we wanted to collect favorite recipes from as many people as possible.
2. We asked whoever was involved with the school for recipes—parents, teachers, and others in the community.
3. We of course asked that the cafeteria workers submit recipes.
4. We requested whatever were people's very best recipes.
5. We wondered how we should organize the recipes.
6. We received multiple recipes from many people.
7. We got many recipes that were repeats, for example, 10 recipes for zucchini bread.
8. One teacher suggested that we divide our cookbook into sections.
9. So we put the recipes into categories that we labeled Appetizers, Soups, Main Courses, and Desserts.
10. Now we hope that people will buy the printed books for themselves and as gifts.
11. We will use all the money that we collect for computers.
12. Our bills include only the cost of printing the book.
13. Everyone agrees that the project was a lot of hard work.
14. My family has tried out several dishes that were in the book.
15. Now someone has proposed that we have a fund-raising dinner with foods from the recipes.

EXERCISE 3 Identify the noun clause in each sentence. Tell whether the noun clause is used as a direct object, a subject, a subject complement, or an appositive.

1. Keisha's fear that the frame would fall off the wall seemed unreasonable.
2. How such a thing might happen was not clear to us.
3. The fact was that the frame was too heavy.
4. That it wobbled and fell to the floor surprised us.
5. Keisha showed us that the frame was heavier than the nails we used to hold it in place.
6. She suggested that we find anchors to hold up the frame.

APPLY IT NOW

Write a paragraph about a class project in which you participated. Include five noun clauses as direct objects in your writing.

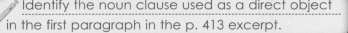
Grammar in Action
Identify the noun clause used as a direct object in the first paragraph in the p. 413 excerpt.

8.10 Noun Clauses as Objects of Prepositions

Noun clauses can function as objects of prepositions.

> **We learned** *about desert biomes*.
> **We learned** *about what the characteristics of desert biomes are*.

What is the noun clause in this sentence? How is it used?

> **I am interested in how animals adapt to dry environments.**

The noun clause is *how animals adapt to dry environments.* The entire noun clause is the object of the preposition *in.*

An adjective clause can be confused with a noun clause used as the object of a preposition. An adjective clause describes a noun or pronoun in the independent clause. The introductory word of the adjective clause, usually a relative pronoun, has an antecedent in the independent clause.

> **A desert** *in which temperatures are low* **is called a cold desert.**
> (adjective clause)
> **We studied about** *which animals can survive in the Red Desert.* (noun clause)

In the first sentence, *which* is a relative pronoun. Its antecedent is *desert,* and it acts as the object of the preposition *in.* In the second sentence, *which* introduces the noun clause but has no antecedent in the independent clause.

What is the correct choice of pronoun in this sentence?

> **The vaccine was taken by (whoever whomever) had a chance of contracting the disease.**

You are correct if you said *whoever.* In the noun clause, *whoever* acts as the subject of the verb *had.* The form of the pronoun is determined by its role in the subordinate clause.

EXERCISE 1 Identify each noun clause used as the object of a preposition. Not all sentences have such a clause.

1. Many species of animals make their homes in what is sometimes referred to as the American Serengeti.
2. Wyoming's Red Desert covers more than five million acres.
3. It is a basin with what are considered bad winters.
4. Surrounding the basin are mountains with rugged gaps where the wind whistles.

5. There are steppes that antelope graze on.

6. Scientists explain about how the antelope migrate hundreds of miles each spring.

7. The animals move to where they can find food.

8. Horned toads and rattlesnakes make their homes in what is an unusual environment for reptiles.

9. Reptiles are usually found where climates are warmer.

10. Nevertheless, the Red Desert is an area that needs protection.

EXERCISE 2 Complete each sentence with an appropriate noun clause used as the object of a preposition.

1. Jesse will give her tickets to _____.

2. We could not see the stage from _____.

3. There was a disagreement about _____.

4. We should make use of _____.

EXERCISE 3 Identify the noun clause in each sentence. Tell if the noun clause is the subject, an appositive, the direct object, or the object of a preposition.

1. Jonas Salk was interested in how polio could be prevented.

2. That the disease had been around since ancient times was well documented.

3. Salk believed that his vaccine could prevent it.

4. Whoever volunteered to do so took part in the tests.

5. That he tried it on his own family early on is remarkable.

6. He found that none of them got sick.

7. That his vaccine was a success became known rather quickly.

8. In 1954 the U.S. government decided that all school children should be inoculated.

9. That the disease is incurable is still true.

10. The fact that polio is now rare is due primarily to Jonas Salk.

Jonas Salk standing in front of the Salk Institute in La Jolla, California

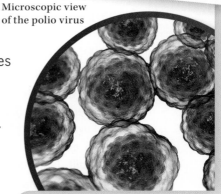

Microscopic view of the polio virus

APPLY IT NOW

Write five sentences about a job that interests you. Use a noun clause as a subject, a direct object, and the object of a preposition at least once each.

8.11 Simple, Compound, and Complex Sentences

Sentences can be classified according to their structure. In the examples below, subjects are in red and verbs are underlined.

A **simple sentence** is a single independent clause. It has a subject and a predicate, either or both of which can be compound.

> *Chicago* <u>borders</u> Lake Michigan.
>
> *Willis Tower* and the *John Hancock Center* <u>are</u> among the city's tall buildings.
>
> Many *Chicagoans* <u>swim</u> and <u>sunbathe</u> along Lake Michigan.

A **compound sentence** contains two or more independent clauses. The independent clauses in compound sentences are commonly connected in one of three ways: (1) by a comma and one of the coordinating conjunctions *and, or, but, nor, so,* or *yet;* (2) by a semicolon; or (3) by a semicolon followed by an adverb such as *therefore, however,* or *nevertheless* and a comma.

> *Chicago* <u>boasts</u> many old skyscrapers, but *it* also <u>has</u> many modern ones.
>
> *Chicago* <u>was</u> on the main railroad lines; consequently, its *industries* <u>grew</u> rapidly in the mid-1800s.

A **complex sentence** has one independent clause and at least one dependent clause, which may function as an adjective, an adverb, or a noun.

> Because *Chicago* <u>welcomes</u> immigrants from all over the world, it boasts many ethnic restaurants. (adverb clause *Because Chicago welcomes immigrants from all over the world*)
>
> The *city, which* <u>burned</u> in a fire in 1871, <u>was</u> quickly <u>rebuilt</u>. (adjective clause *which burned in a fire in 1871*)
>
> Originally, many *people* <u>claimed</u> that the *fire* <u>was caused</u> by a cow. (noun clause *that the fire was caused by a cow*)

The Chicago Water Tower, built in 1869 by architect William W. Boyington

EXERCISE 1 Tell whether each sentence is simple, compound, or complex.

1. The Chicago River system is 156 miles long.

2. The river was originally only 2 feet deep, but now it has been dug to a depth of 26 feet.

3. In the 19th century, the river was a source of disease because it was so polluted.

4. The river flowed into Lake Michigan, and the lake was the source of water for the city of Chicago.

5. In 1900 sanitary engineers reversed the flow of the river; therefore, it now runs backward, out of Lake Michigan.

6. Although cities downriver complained, this feat reduced the number of epidemics in the Chicago metropolitan area.

7. At one time Chicago had 52 movable bridges across the river.

8. There are only 45 of those bridges left, but that is still the highest number of any city in the world.

9. Chicago is like a museum of movable bridges because it has so many different styles, including swing bridges and lift bridges.

10. On St. Patrick's Day the river is dyed green in celebration.

Heron

EXERCISE 2 Combine each pair of simple sentences into one compound sentence.

1. A lake, like Lake Michigan, is a large body of standing water. A pond is a small body of standing water.

2. In Chicago, summer days are warm. Winters are very cold.

3. The Chicago Cubs play baseball in the National League. The Chicago White Sox play in the American League.

4. Chicago has warm, beautiful summers. Chicago has very cold, windy winters.

EXERCISE 3 Identify the clauses in each sentence and tell whether they are dependent or independent.

1. Carp, goldfish, catfish, and sunfish are the main fish species in the Chicago River, although other kinds also live there.

2. Birds that have been seen along the banks include herons, kingfishers, warblers, and ducks.

3. The river had been too polluted for recreational use, but now boaters paddle throughout its length.

4. The city hopes that new walkways and riverside restaurants will attract visitors to the riverbanks.

5. Beaver and muskrat live in the river, and even mink have been seen there.

APPLY IT NOW

Write two examples each of simple, compound, and complex sentences. Identify each type of sentence, circle the subjects, and underline the verbs, including those within dependent clauses.

Sentence Review

8.1 Add the correct end punctuation to each sentence. Then identify the complete subject and complete predicate.

1. Do you know what to do in case of severe weather

2. Go to the basement, please

3. What are the warning signs of severe weather

4. Funnel clouds develop from the colliding of hot and cold air

5. Destructive tornados occur frequently in spring

8.2 Identify the adjective phrase or adverb phrases in these sentences. Tell whether each is prepositional, participial, or infinitive.

6. They sailed before daybreak.

7. Watching through binoculars, the Coast Guard captain spotted a boat.

8. The captain's efforts to call for assistance were successful.

9. The crew lowered lifeboats into the water.

10. Reaching safety, the crew was relieved.

8.3 Identify the adjective clause in each sentence and the noun or pronoun that the adjective clause describes.

11. Willis Tower, which is in Chicago, is a world-famous skyscraper.

12. Wacker Drive is the street where it is located.

13. The views from the buildings that overlook Lake Michigan are spectacular.

14. A tourist, who was from China, viewed the distant skyline through a high-powered telescope.

15. The floor where visitors can see the entire city is called the Skydeck.

8.4 Identify the adjective clause in each sentence. Tell whether the adjective clause is restrictive or nonrestrictive. Add commas where necessary.

16. His garden which was at the back of the lot contained a wide variety of vegetables.

17. The beans that did so well last year are not available.

18. Tomatoes, strawberries, and rhubarb are plants that grow hardily.

19. Mulch is organic material that has decomposed.

20. Weeding which is my least favorite gardening task must be done frequently.

8.5 Identify the adverb clause in each sentence and each subordinate conjunction.

21. Whenever you want to leave, I will be ready.

22. As soon as she puts on her coat, we can leave.

23. Make certain that you have your keys before we lock the door.

24. Dad did the grocery shopping while Mom ran errands.

25. We'll buy peaches if they look ripe.

8.6 Identify the noun clause used as the subject in each sentence.

26. Whoever alerted the fire-fighters will receive a commendation.

27. That they were able to extinguish the fire relieved us.

28. That residents were still inside the building was our worry.

29. How everyone escaped was a miracle.

30. Whether they will be able to go back inside is yet to be decided.

8.7 Identify the noun clause used as a complement in each sentence. Name the subject it describes.

31. The doctor's advice was that he exercise and watch his diet.

32. The doctor's belief is that walking is the best exercise.

33. The thought is that walking at least 10,000 steps a day is beneficial.

34. What I wonder is how people count their steps.

35. The fact is that a pedometer makes it easy to count them.

8.8 Identify the noun clause used as an appositive in each sentence.

36. It is a fact that kindness is contagious.

37. The theme that good defeats evil is common in literature and movies.

38. The advice, how to avoid insect bites, was quite timely.

39. The saying that old friends and new friends are special in different ways is probably true.

8.9 Identify the direct object in each sentence. Tell whether it is a noun or a noun clause.

40. Jasmine wondered how she would get to school on time.

41. She knew that she was late.

42. She gave excuses to explain her lateness.

43. Jasmine promised that she would not dawdle anymore.

8.10 Identify the noun clause used as the object of a preposition in each sentence.

44. We learned about how long the life of a fruit fly is.

45. There are stages through which a fruit fly must go.

46. Our group reported on how the various changes take place.

47. I am interested in what are the possible benefits from fruit flies.

8.11 Tell whether each sentence is simple, compound, or complex.

48. Most tulips bloom in the spring.

49. The flower originated in Holland, but it is extremely popular in the United States.

50. Because tulips must be exposed to cold in order to blossom, gardeners plant their bulbs in the fall.

51. Tulips, which are available in many colors, make wonderful flower arrangements.

Tech Tip · Go to www.voyagesinenglish.com for more activities.

Sentence Challenge

Read the selection and then answer the questions.

1. New Year's celebrations vary around the world, and they even occur at different times. 2. Still, there are some similarities among the many customs.

3. One way to celebrate the new year is with fireworks. 4. In the past the belief that the noise of fireworks scared off evil spirits was a reason for their use. 5. Now although the fireworks are still part of the celebrations, people seem to use them more for their visual entertainment aspects.

6. What people eat on New Year's is also important. 7. In many places people eat foods that are sweet. 8. Why do they do this? 9. The reason is that they want a "sweet," or good, new year. 10. People in Israel, for example, dip apples into honey. 11. Sometimes foods that are eaten symbolize hoped-for wealth. 12. People in many places eat lentils, which look like tiny coins. 13. In other places people eat cabbage because it looks like paper money. 14. Others eat round foods, such as doughnuts, that symbolize the cycle of life.

15. Think about how and when your family and culture celebrate the new year. 16. Whatever you do, have a happy new year!

1. Is sentence 1 a simple, compound, or complex sentence?
2. Identify the infinitive phrase in sentence 3. Is it used as an adjective or as an adverb?
3. What is the noun clause in sentence 4? How is it used?
4. Is sentence 5 a simple, compound, or complex sentence?
5. Find the dependent clause in sentence 7. How is it used?
6. What is the noun clause in sentence 9? How is it used?
7. Identify the simple and complete subjects and simple and complete predicates in sentence 10.
8. Is sentence 11 a simple, compound, or complex sentence?
9. Find the adjective clause in sentence 12. Is it restrictive or nonrestrictive?
10. What is the dependent clause in sentence 13? How is it used?
11. Is sentence 15 a simple, compound, or complex sentence?
12. Find any sentences that are interrogative, imperative, or exclamatory in the selection.

Conjunctions and Interjections

9.1 Coordinating Conjunctions

A **conjunction** is a word used to connect words or groups of words. The four types of connectors are coordinating conjunctions, correlative conjunctions, conjunctive adverbs, and subordinate conjunctions.

A **coordinating conjunction** joins words or groups of words that are similar. The coordinating conjunctions are *and, but, or, nor, so,* and *yet.* Coordinating conjunctions connect words and phrases.

> **Adventurers sought gold *or* glory.** (words)
> **They searched in northern South America *and* along the Amazon River for the legendary city of El Dorado.** (prepositional phrases)
> **They wanted to find the city *and* to gain its wealth.** (infinitive phrases)

Coordinating conjunctions can also connect independent clauses to form compound sentences.

> **No one found that city, *yet* the search continued.**
> **Francisco Coronado searched for the fabled Seven Cities, *and* Ponce de Leon searched for the Fountain of Youth.**

Can you identify what is connected in these examples?

> **The Seven Cities were supposedly rich in gold and in jewels.**
> **Coronado searched for the cities in what is present-day New Mexico, but he never found great riches.**

In the first example, the conjunction connects prepositional phrases. In the second example, the conjunction connects clauses.

EXERCISE 1 Identify the coordinating conjunction in each sentence. Tell the words, phrases, or clauses that the conjunction connects.

1. Explorers and adventurers searched for the golden city of El Dorado.

2. People of many nations heard and believed tales of this rich city.

3. The dream of a city of gold was intriguing, and the search for it was undertaken by many.

4. Explorers searched long but fruitlessly for El Dorado.

5. *El Dorado* means "the gilded one," and it supposedly referred to the king of this gold-rich city.

6. Every year in a special ceremony, the king supposedly appeared, covered with ointments and sprinkled with gold dust.

7. He then bathed and washed off the gold in a lake.

8. From a boat he threw gold and jade objects into the lake as offerings to the gods.

9. El Dorado now refers to a place of fabulous wealth or to the land of one's dreams.

10. This fabulous quest for El Dorado went on primarily during the 16th and 17th centuries.

11. Some scholars believe a city like El Dorado probably existed but it didn't have the great wealth of the legends.

12. Great works of literature like *Paradise Lost* by John Milton and *Candide* by Voltaire reference El Dorado.

13. The name of El Dorado has been given to many cities in Latin America and to one county in the state of California.

14. One explorer who tried to search for the great city was Sir Walter Raleigh, yet he was unsuccessful in his task.

15. Other great mythical cities besides El Dorado were said to have existed, but they were never found by the explorers who looked for them.

16. Many explorers were unsuccessful in their quest to find El Dorado, but they helped discover many parts of the Americas we now know today.

Sir Walter Raleigh
(1552–1618)

EXERCISE 2 Complete each sentence with a coordinating conjunction and an appropriate word, phrase, or clause as indicated.

1. The curtain rose, _____. (clause)

2. Will you meet me in the park _____? (phrase)

3. Learning the new game was slow _____. (word)

4. Should I sit near the window _____? (phrase)

5. I tossed the stone into the water, _____. (clause)

6. We looked for the missing contact lens slowly _____. (word)

7. We searched meticulously, _____. (clause)

8. I walked into the bookstore, _____. (clause)

9. Would you rather eat Chinese food for dinner, _____? (phrase)

10. Mother stirred the beef stew on the stove carefully _____. (word)

APPLY IT NOW

Choose a topic you enjoy, such as sports, movies, or TV. Write a sentence using each coordinating conjunction. Include examples of words, phrases, and clauses connected by the conjunctions.

9.2 Correlative Conjunctions

Correlative conjunctions are conjunctions that are used in pairs to connect words or groups of words that have equal importance in a sentence. The parts of the sentence that are connected should have parallel structure. Correlative conjunctions emphasize the relationship between the connected words.

> Lemonade *or* juice is a good drink for a picnic.
> *Either* lemonade *or* juice is a good drink for a picnic.

In the first sentence, the coordinating conjunction *or* joins two nouns, *lemonade* and *juice*. In the second sentence, the pair of conjunctions *either* and *or* also connects *lemonade* and *juice* but gives greater emphasis to the relationship.

These are the most commonly used correlative conjunctions:

both . . . and	**not only . . . but also**
either . . . or	**whether . . . or**
neither . . . nor	

Correlative conjunctions generally appear immediately in front of the words or phrases that are connected.

> *Neither* Sue *nor* Linda is on the picnic committee.
> *Whether* young *or* old, all students are welcome.
> Alexa is bringing *not only* fruit *but also* veggies.
> You can leave the food *either* on the table *or* in the refrigerator.

EXERCISE 1 Identify the correlative conjunctions in each sentence.

1. Both Lisa and I are on the class picnic committee.
2. We are planning not only the food but also the games.
3. Both my father and my mother have volunteered to help us.
4. Whether rain or shine, the picnic will be held.
5. In case of rain, we can use either the school basement or the gym.
6. Neither the principal nor the assistant principal can attend.
7. Both Mr. Alvarez and Mrs. Marini are helping the committee.
8. The picnic will be held on a school day— either on a Thursday or on a Friday.
9. Whether we play dodgeball or have relay races, we will have a good time.

EXERCISE 2 Identify the correlative conjunctions in these sentences. Not every sentence contains correlative conjunctions.

1. We asked for volunteers to bring either ice or charcoal.
2. Jason has signed up to bring both hot dogs and hamburgers.
3. Several parents and teachers will bring grills from home.
4. We will grill beef burgers, turkey burgers, and veggie burgers.
5. Most students are preparing either salads or desserts.
6. Neither ice cream nor milk is on the menu this year because many of our classmates are allergic to dairy products.
7. There will be both rides and races for fun.
8. We will have not only a trampoline but also a slide.
9. Either Jane's dad or my dad will be supervising the games.
10. Jessica or Luis will be in charge of obtaining prizes.
11. We are collecting money to pay for both the prizes and the drinks.

EXERCISE 3 Add correlative or coordinating conjunctions to complete these sentences.

1. _____ food and drink will be available at our picnic.
2. Most of the food will be donated by volunteers, _____ some of the food will be purchased.
3. _____ will we have a lot of food at the picnic _____ beverages.
4. We need separate committees for _____ collecting money and cleaning up.
5. I will be in charge of _____ the money-collection committee or the cleanup committee.
6. Jane asked Mr. Alvarez if _____ kickball _____ potato sack races could be played at the picnic.
7. We are all looking forward to _____ the games and races.
8. _____ Jessica _____ Lisa can guess who will win.
9. _____ outside _____ indoors, we will have a great time.

APPLY IT NOW

Plan an activity such as a party, a meal, or a field trip. Write five sentences using both correlative conjunctions and coordinating conjunctions in your writing.

Tech Tip Plan and organize your activity on a spreadsheet.

Conjunctions • 169

9.3 Conjunctive Adverbs

A **conjunctive adverb** connects independent clauses. It helps make clear the relationship between the clauses. When a conjunctive adverb connects clauses, a semicolon is used before it and a comma after it.

> **Cities offer many attractions;** *nevertheless*, **some people prefer to live in the country.**

Common conjunctive adverbs include the following:

also	hence	later	otherwise
besides	however	likewise	still
consequently	in fact	moreover	subsequently
finally	indeed	nevertheless	therefore
furthermore	instead	nonetheless	thus

Parenthetical expressions, also called explanatory expressions, are used in the same way as conjunctive adverbs. Among these are *for example, namely, on the contrary, in fact, that is,* and *on the other hand.* When a parenthetical expression joins independent clauses, it must be preceded by a semicolon and followed by a comma.

> **Missy often illustrates her compositions;** *in fact*, **she would rather draw than write.**

EXERCISE 1 Identify the conjunctive adverb in each sentence.

1. Rome was founded in 753 BC; thus, it is one of Europe's oldest cities.
2. The city has many old buildings; however, it has many modern ones.
3. In the past, residents used stones from old buildings to build new ones; nevertheless, many old buildings still stand.
4. The Circus Maximus, a huge oval area for races, no longer stands; indeed, its site is now preserved only as an open space.
5. Cars buzz around the city at all hours; also, riders on small motorcycles add to the congestion and noise level.
6. Rome is one of the world's richest cities in art and history; therefore, it is a magnet for tourists.
7. The Colosseum, a freestanding amphitheater, was begun between AD 70 and AD 80; moreover, it could seat 50,000 spectators.
8. The Trevi Fountain is one of the most beautiful fountains in Rome; consequently, many tourists come to see it and marvel at its many statues.

Trevi Fountain in Rome, Italy

EXERCISE 2 **Rewrite these sentences, choosing the correct conjunctive adverb or parenthetical expression. Add semicolons and commas where needed.**

1. Manhattan is only 13 miles long and 2 miles wide (consequently otherwise) land space is scarce.

2. One solution to the lack of space is to construct buildings high into the air (therefore nevertheless) land is still scarce.

3. Tall buildings were originally places to work (still later) they became places to live.

4. The Chrysler Building is no longer the tallest building in Manhattan (however moreover) it is still one of the most beautiful.

5. Some space was left for green areas (in fact nevertheless) there are more than a hundred parks in New York City.

6. Central Park is right in the middle of busy Manhattan (however moreover) it has many quiet and peaceful areas.

7. The human traffic in Central Park includes a never-ending flow of panting joggers (moreover however) there are many inline skaters on the park's roads and paths.

8. Many other cities in the United States have gained recognition; (namely instead) Los Angeles, Chicago, and Houston.

9. Because of its warm climate, Los Angeles attracts many residents (otherwise also) the work opportunities in many industries bring new residents.

10. Bright outdoor light was needed to film early motion pictures (therefore however) Los Angeles's sunny climate was perfect for the movie industry.

11. At one time land near Los Angeles was almost desert (in fact nevertheless) only snakes, lizards, and a few rabbits lived there.

12. Now irrigation pipes divert water to support the large city population (furthermore however) reservoirs save rainwater for use by residents.

APPLY IT NOW

Write six sentences about your town, city, or state. Use conjunctive adverbs in your sentences.

Grammar in Action. Identify the conjunctive adverb in the script on p. 451.

9.4 Subordinate Conjunctions

A **subordinate conjunction** is used to join an independent clause and a dependent clause and to indicate their relationship. Subordinate conjunctions typically introduce adverb clauses. These clauses describe verbs, adjectives, or adverbs in the independent clause. They tell *how, why, to what extent,* and *under what condition.* The subordinate conjunctions *where* and *when* may introduce adjective clauses, and noun clauses may be introduced by subordinate conjunctions such as *how, when,* and *whether.*

<u>When</u> we studied about prehistoric humans, **we learned about their cave paintings.**
I am fascinated by this time period <u>when</u> *written language was in its earliest form.*

In the first sentence, the subordinate conjunction *When* introduces the dependent clause *When we studied about prehistoric humans.* The dependent clause is an adverb clause, and it modifies *learned.* In the second sentence, *when* introduces an adjective clause that modifies *period* in the independent clause.

Cave painting in Lascaux, France

Common subordinate conjunctions include the following:

after	in order that	till
although, as though	once	unless
as, as long as	provided (that)	until
as if, as far as	since	when, whenever
as soon as	so long as	where, wherever
because	so (that)	whether
before	than	while
how	that	why
if, even if	though, even though	

EXERCISE 1 Identify the subordinate conjunction in each sentence. Then identify the dependent clause and the independent clause.

1. Experts studied the paintings in the caves at Lascaux, France, so that they could determine the early painters' techniques.

2. After those first artists had ground up charcoal and colored rocks, they mixed the resulting powders with saliva.

3. Once they had made the colors they wanted, they blew the colored liquid onto the cave walls and ceilings.

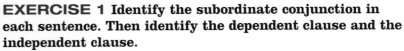

4. Bumps in the limestone walls were utilized by the artists so that some of the creatures seem almost three-dimensional.

5. Though most of the figures in the caves represent animals, there are some stylized human figures.

6. While most creatures are painted in lifelike detail, one figure has the head of a buffalo and the legs of a human.

7. As soon as the caves' discovery became widely known, many visitors arrived.

8. Because the carbon dioxide in human breath caused the walls of the caves to deteriorate, there was a need for action.

9. If immediate action had not been taken, the artwork might have disappeared completely.

10. The public has not been able to view the paintings firsthand since the caves were closed to visitors in 1963.

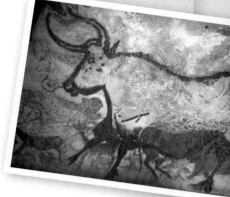
Cave painting in Lascaux, France

EXERCISE 2 Identify the connectors in these sentences and tell whether each is a coordinating conjunction, a correlative conjunction, a conjunctive adverb, or a subordinate conjunction.

1. Although the paintings are the first thing to attract attention, Lascaux also contains an altarlike stone.

2. There were no signs that people had actually lived in the caves; still, fires had been built in them.

3. Either worship or some other form of ritual took place there.

4. All these things are interesting, yet the major source of wonder remains the paintings.

5. The colors are still brilliant; moreover, the lifelike creatures have been captured in motion.

6. While the cave paintings are mostly positioned on walls and ceilings, experts think that scaffoldings were used to reach the higher portions of the cave.

7. Not only are there close to 600 painted animals and symbols but also nearly 1,500 engravings.

8. Because the caves were closed to the public, there was a partial replica that opened in 1983 called Lascaux II.

APPLY IT NOW

Write a brief paragraph about an amazing or a surprising experience. Use and identify subordinate conjunctions.

Post your paragraph on the class blog.

9.5 Troublesome Conjunctions

Some conjunctions are frequently misused or confused.

Unless* and *Without The word *without* is a preposition and introduces a prepositional phrase.

> **No family should be *without* an emergency kit.**

Without introduces the prepositional phrase *without an emergency kit.*

The word *unless* is a subordinate conjunction, and it introduces a dependent adverb clause.

> **No family is prepared for a disaster *unless* it has an emergency kit.**

Which word correctly completes the following?

> **Don't leave (without unless) I accompany you.**

The correct answer is the subordinate conjunction *unless,* used to introduce an adverb clause.

Like, As If,* and *As The word *like* is a preposition, and it introduces a prepositional phrase.

> **Julio looks *like* his brother.**

As if is a subordinate conjunction, and it introduces a clause.

> **Sam looks *as if* he is worried.**

As can function as a conjunction or as a preposition.

> **I crawled under a table *as* the earth shook.** (conjunction introducing a clause)
> **We studied emergency procedures *as* part of our health class.**
> (preposition in a phrase)

EXERCISE 1 Choose the correct item to complete each sentence.

1. (Without Unless) you have felt the ground under you heave and roll, it is hard to imagine an earthquake.

2. You feel (as if like) the ground under you is not solid.

3. In fact, the ground moves (as if like) a carpet of wavelike jelly.

4. You may not realize how scary earthquakes can be (unless without) you have lived through one.

5. It may seem to be the end of the world (as like) whole buildings wobble wildly or collapse entirely.

6. Objects fall (as if like) they are being thrown down.

7. Scientists (as if like) Charles F. Richter have devised various scales for measuring the size of earthquakes.

8. (Without Unless) you understand the scale, you may not realize that an earthquake measuring 7 is 10 times greater than one measuring 6.

9. (Without Unless) such measures, there would be no way to compare the magnitude of earthquakes.

10. The destructive force of earthquakes is clear (as like) you look at photos of their aftermath.

EXERCISE 2 Use one of the following terms to complete each sentence: *as, as if, like, unless, without*.

1. In the aftermath of an earthquake, people find themselves _____ services such as power, gas, water, and cable.

2. People debate how much preparation for disasters _____ earthquakes is useful or even possible.

3. _____ older buildings are retrofitted, they remain dangerous.

4. We must always behave _____ the next earthquake is near.

5. _____ a supply of drinking water, nonperishable food, and warm clothing is kept on hand, people are not ready for an earthquake.

6. It is important we keep the hallway of homes clear _____ this is one of the safest places to be during an earthquake.

7. One of the worst earthquakes in California took place in 1906, leaving many people _____ homes, food, or jobs.

8. The earthquake reduced San Francisco to rubble and made it appear _____ the city was crushed.

9. The earthquake occurred at 5:13 in the morning _____ many people were just starting their day or were still sleeping.

10. Buildings began to sway _____ they were dancing.

11. Other towns did not go _____ damage; San Jose, Salinas, and Santa Rosa all felt the earthquake's impact.

APPLY IT NOW

Complete these sentences to show you can use the troublesome conjunctions and prepositions correctly.

I won't go unless _____.
I won't go without _____.
You look like _____.
You look as if _____.

9.6 Interjections

An **interjection** is a word or phrase that expresses a strong or sudden emotion. Interjections can be used to convey happiness, delight, anger, disgust, surprise (of a good or an unpleasant sort), impatience, pain, wonder, and so on. They can also be used to get or hold attention.

> *Hey!* **You dropped your ticket.**

What do you think is expressed by the above interjection? It might be used to get attention.

Interjections may be set off from the rest of a sentence by an exclamation point.

> *No!* **I can't find my ticket.**
> *Ouch!* **I just stubbed my toe.**

An interjection may also be part of an exclamatory sentence. If the sentence is exclamatory, the interjection is followed by a comma, and the exclamation point is put at the end of the sentence.

> *Oh,* **how exciting the game is***!*
> *Yes,* **I will marry you***!*

These are some common interjections:

Ah!	Hey!	Oh!	Yes!
Alas!	Hooray!	Oh, dear!	Yikes!
Beware!	Hush!	Oops!	Yippie!
Bravo!	Indeed!	Ouch!	Yum!
Dear me!	Never!	Rats!	Well!
Enough!	No!	Sh!	What!
Good grief!	No way!	Stop!	Whew!
Hello!	Nonsense!	Ugh!	Wow!

EXERCISE 1 Identify the interjection in each sentence. Indicate the emotion that you think is expressed in each.

1. Great! We have really good seats for the game.
2. Oh, dear! Someone tall is sitting in front of us.
3. Oh, well! I can still see well enough.
4. Wow! That was a great shot.
5. Hooray! We are leading the game.
6. No! I can't believe the referee's call.

7. Bravo! Joan just made a great shot for our team.

8. Ah, that's another foul on our team!

9. Goodness! It's a close game.

10. Great! Edwards is coming into the game.

11. No! Our best player looks as if she might be injured.

12. Wonderful! She's back in the game.

13. Hey! Sit down in front.

14. Oh, there are only two seconds left!

15. Yes, we've won the game!

16. Yippee! We have such a good team.

17. Indeed, the coach is the best we've ever had!

18. No way! Joan received the Most Valuable Player Award.

19. Fantastic! She deserves the award for her hard work today.

20. Ah, I hope we win the game next week!

EXERCISE 2 Write an interjection to go with each sentence. Use an exclamation point at the end of each interjection.

1. _____ We got places in the front row.

2. _____ We can really hear the band.

3. _____ The parade is starting.

4. _____ I took a picture of the cheerleaders.

5. _____ I don't have the right film in my camera.

6. _____ I would like to take a picture of that float.

7. _____ Those people riding on it are waving.

8. _____ It's getting hot.

9. _____ I drank all the water.

10. _____ It's the end already.

APPLY IT NOW

Imagine that you have just won a great prize. Draft an e-mail telling your friends the good news. Use interjections and exclamatory and interrogative sentences to show the different emotions associated with each.

Grammar in Action. Identify one interjection in the p. 451 script.

Conjunction and Interjection Review

9.1 Identify the coordinating conjunction in each sentence. Tell whether it connects words, phrases, or clauses.

1. The sun was shining, yet the forecast called for rain.

2. Tanya wanted to dig beds and to plant flowers.

3. She planted petunias in the beds and in containers.

4. She knew purple or white petunias would look best.

5. Tanya tried to finish and to clean up before the storm.

6. The clouds rolled in, and the wind picked up.

7. It rained heavily, so the flowers didn't need to be watered.

8. Tanya stored her gardening tools and gloves in the shed.

9. It rained all afternoon and into the next day.

10. Tanya was tired from her hard work, yet she looked forward to watching her garden grow.

9.2 Identify the correlative conjunctions in each sentence.

11. Either math or science is Pablo's favorite subject.

12. Neither the beaker nor the slide was cleaned after the experiment.

13. Whether you finish or not, please leave your worksheets on the desk.

14. Tom was not only studying for the exam but also practicing for the big race.

15. Both his mom and his dad help him with homework.

16. Tom wants to ace both the exam and the race.

17. Whether Pablo is my study partner or not, I will make flash cards.

18. Not only did Tom review his science homework, but also he reread the chapter.

9.3 Rewrite these sentences, choosing the correct conjunctive adverb. Add commas and semicolons where needed.

19. Stonehenge was built thousands of years ago (also nevertheless) it still stands.

20. Stonehenge may mark solar and lunar alignments (otherwise consequently) it may have been used as a calendar.

21. Stonehenge was carefully constructed (therefore still) it must have been important.

22. No one knows for sure what purpose it served (later still) many people visit Stonehenge.

23. The stones used to build the structure were large (moreover however) they were heavy.

24. Stonehenge is close to London (therefore besides) many tourists come for a day trip.

25. It is important to experience ancient history up close (thus indeed) a trip to Stonehenge would be ideal.

26. Stonehenge is an ancient relic (however finally) London is also filled with historic landmarks.

9.4 Identify the subordinate conjunction and the dependent clause in each sentence.

27. As if one cat weren't enough, now there are three more on the deck.

28. As long as we feed the stray cats, they will continue to come to the back door.

29. Because it was so skinny, Jeff fed the kitten.

30. Although stray cats are usually afraid of people, the kitten walked right up to Jeff.

31. Jeff took the kitten to the veterinarian before he adopted it.

32. If we can catch the adult cats, we will take them to the veterinarian as well.

33. There will be more kittens soon, unless the cats are spayed.

34. Jeff has always loved cats, while his sister prefers dogs.

35. Provided that you can care for a pet, local shelters are a good place to look for a cat to adopt.

36. A shelter will help find a new home for a stray cat, once it receives proper vaccinations.

9.5 Choose the correct item to complete each sentence.

37. No one should be caught (unless without) an umbrella on a rainy day.

38. Jane's feet will become wet (unless without) she wears boots.

39. Don't leave (unless without) checking the forecast.

40. Meteorologists (as like) John's dad are busy when it storms.

41. The sky looks (as if like) it might open at any minute.

42. Juan waited under an awning (as if as) the raindrops fell.

43. Molly says it looks (as if like) our game will be canceled.

44. Coach won't allow us to play the game (without unless) we get an all-clear from the referee.

45. The sky looks (as if like) it will stop soon.

9.6 Identify the two ways to correctly punctuate each sentence.

46. Hey we can't find our tickets

47. Oh dear we will miss the start of the play

48. Hooray the tickets were in my coat pocket

49. Hush I can't hear the actors

50. Bravo you were very good as the lead

51. Hush talking is not permitted in the theater

52. Rats I forgot my ticket at home

53. Indeed the director is very talented

54. Wow what a great finale

 Go to www.voyagesinenglish.com for more activities.

Conjunction and Interjection Challenge

Read the selection and then answer the questions.

1. What could be more typically ethnic than Italian tomato sauce or Swiss chocolate? 2. When we think of tomatoes and chocolate, we think of Italy and Switzerland. 3. These ideas seem natural; however, both tomatoes and chocolate originated in the Americas.

4. Yes! Tomatoes are, in fact, native to Mexico and Central America, and the Aztecs grew them by AD 700. 5. Chocolate was made into a sacred drink by the Aztecs; moreover, the emperor Montezuma is said to have drunk some 50 cups of it a day. 6. Because chocolate was so precious, the cocoa bean was used even as currency. 7. The Spaniards found these products in the Americas, and they introduced them to Europeans in the 1500s. 8. Although chocolate become popular as a drink in Europe, it was only made into solid-bar form in the 1800s in the Netherlands. 9. Shortly thereafter the Swiss entered the picture. 10. It was a Swiss confectioner who made the first milk chocolate. 11. By that time the Italians had long discovered the tomato and were using it both as a fruit and as the main ingredient in savory sauces.

1. Identify the coordinating conjunction in sentence 1. Does it connect words, phrases, or clauses?

2. What is the subordinate conjunction in sentence 2? Identify the clause it introduces. What kind of clause is it?

3. What is the conjunctive adverb in sentence 3?

4. Identify the correlative conjunctions in sentence 3.

5. Identify the two coordinating conjunctions in sentence 4. What does each connect—words, phrases, or clauses?

6. Identify the connector in sentence 5. What type is it?

7. Identify the conjunction in sentence 6. What type is it?

8. Identify the conjunction in sentence 7. What type is it?

9. Identify the subordinate conjunction in the last paragraph. What sentence is it in?

10. Identify the correlative conjunctions in the last paragraph. What sentence is it in?

11. Find the interjection in the selection. What sentence is it in?

Punctuation and Capitalization

10.1 Periods and Commas

A **period** is used at the end of a declarative or an imperative sentence, after an abbreviation, and after the initials in a name.

> The poem is about a shipwreck. Recite the poem.
> Mrs. Eleanor Roosevelt
> R. A. Anaya

Commas are used for the following:

- to separate words in a series of three or more and to separate adjectives of equal importance

> Inez, Patricia, and Roberto wrote about sea disasters.
> My favorite trees are tall, leafy, green elms.

- to set off the parts of addresses, place names, and dates

> The big flood in Johnstown, Pennsylvania, occurred on May 31, 1889, and lasted no more than 10 minutes.

The *Titanic* striking an iceberg in thick fog off Newfoundland

- to set off words of direct address and parenthetical expressions

> Lizzie, the *Titanic* disaster took place in 1912.
> The *Titanic* was called unsinkable; on the contrary, it struck an iceberg and sank in 2 hours.

- to set off nonrestrictive phrases and clauses

> Johnstown, a town in southwestern Pennsylvania, was the site of a major flood. (nonrestrictive appositive)
> The flood, which occurred because of a burst dam, left many people dead and homeless. (nonrestrictive clause)

- to set off a direct quotation or parts of a divided quotation

> "I remember a big flood," my grandmother said.
> "We evacuated our home," she continued, "in a boat!"

- before coordinating conjunctions when they are used to connect clauses in a sentence and after conjunctive adverbs in compound sentences

> The South Fork dam broke, and the city of Johnstown was flooded.
> People living below the dam felt secure; consequently, they ignored the alarm.

- after the salutation in a friendly letter and after the closing in all letters

> Dear Miriam,   Yours truly,

EXERCISE 1 Rewrite these sentences. Add periods and commas where needed.

1. "Our history contains songs poems and stories about ships and tragedy" said Mrs Nelson our history teacher

2. "Some of these" she continued "we'll examine class"

3. Henry W Longfellow a famous American poet of the 1800s wrote a poem about a ship that sank during a storm

4. Name some other works by Longfellow

5. The poem which was based on an actual event is called "The Wreck of the *Hesperus*" and it is one of Longfellow's best-known poems

6. The characters are a ship captain his daughter and an old sailor

7. "The Sinking of the *Reuben James*" a song by Woody Guthrie tells of another tragedy at sea

8. The song tells of a US ship torpedoed by a German submarine on October 31 1941 near Iceland

9. The song focuses on individuals involved in the tragedy and originally its verses named the crew members

10. The *Reuben James* was the first US Navy ship lost during World War II and only 44 members of the crew survived

Out of the 2,228 people onboard the *Titanic*, only 705 survived. The ship sank on April 14, 1912.

EXERCISE 2 Rewrite the following sentences to correct any errors in punctuation.

1. On November 10 1975 the *Edmund Fitzgerald* a large freighter sank in a sudden powerful storm on Lake Superior

2. The storm damaged the ship's communication system and no one knows how the ship sank

3. Yes the ship's sinking remains a mystery.

4. The *Arthur Anderson* the *William Clay Ford* and the *Hilda Marjanne* all helped search for the missing boat and its crew

5. Great Lakes Engineering Works the company commissioned to build the great ship had over 1,000 men working on the job

6. Gordon Lightfoot a Canadian folksinger did not personally know any of the 29 dead but he wrote a tribute to them nonetheless.

7. Lightfoot's song which was written not long after the tragedy is still one of his most-requested works

APPLY IT NOW

Write a letter to a friend. Include lists and information about your favorite musical performers. Punctuate your letter correctly.

10.2 Exclamation Points, Question Marks, Semicolons, and Colons

Exclamation points are used after most interjections and to end exclamatory sentences.

> **Hooray! We are going to visit California.**
> **No, I can't find my suitcase!**

Question marks are used to end interrogative sentences.

> **Who put my suitcase in the basement?**

A **semicolon** is used for the following:

- to separate clauses in a compound sentence when they are not joined by a conjunction

  > **We left early in the morning; the roads were empty.**

- to separate clauses in a compound sentence that are connected by conjunctive adverbs

  > **Truckers carried freight along Route 66; furthermore, families used the highway for vacation trips.**

- to separate phrases or clauses of the same type that include internal punctuation

  > **Several significant dates in World War II are December 7, 1941; May 5, 1945; and August 14, 1945.**

- before parenthetical expressions such as *for example* and *namely* when they are used to introduce examples

  > **We traveled through several states; namely, Texas, New Mexico, Arizona, and Nevada.**

A **colon** is used for the following:

- before a list when terms such as *the following* or *as follows* are used

  > **The following are places I'd like to visit: Grand Canyon, Yellowstone National Park, and Hawaii.**

- after the salutation of a business letter

  > **Dear Professor Rosenfeld:**

EXERCISE 1 **Rewrite the following sentences. Add exclamation points, question marks, semicolons, and colons where needed.**

1. Route 66 was a highway however, it was far more than that.
2. It represented many things namely, the romance of the open road, a chance for adventure, and a new life in the West.
3. It was one of the first highways across the United States it was commissioned in 1926.
4. Where did the highway start and end
5. It started near Lake Michigan in Chicago, Illinois it ended near the Pacific Ocean in Santa Monica, California.
6. The cities that Route 66 went through included the following Tulsa, Amarillo, Albuquerque, and Flagstaff.
7. What a great road it was

EXERCISE 2 **Rewrite these sentences, using the correct punctuation.**

1. Other names for Route 66 are these the Main Street of America the Mother Road and the Will Rogers Highway
2. There have been songs written such as "Will Rogers Highway" by Woody Guthrie and "Route 66" by Bobby Troup which helped immortalize this historic highway
3. Hotels restaurants and gas stations opened along the highway which catered to truck drivers and travelers alike
4. John Steinbeck wrote *The Grapes of Wrath* the characters in this book travel along Route 66
5. A writer has said the following about Route 66: "It's a station wagon filled with kids wanting to know how far it is to Disneyland a wailing ambulance fleeing a wreck on some lonely curve It's yesterday today and tomorrow Truly a road of phantoms and dreams, 66 is the romance of traveling the open highway"
6. Route 66 was officially ended in 1985 new interstate highways replaced it
7. The old highway exists in many places however various sections have been renumbered

APPLY IT NOW

Choose a well-known or scenic street in your community. Write five sentences using each of these punctuation marks: exclamation point, question mark, semicolon, and colon.

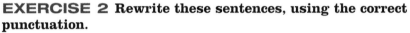

Tech Tip With an adult, find a map of the original Route 66 online.

10.3 Quotation Marks and Italics

Quotation marks are used for the following:

- before and after direct quotations and around the parts of divided quotations

  "This," Mr. Small cried, "is just the sweater I've been looking for."

- to set off the titles of stories, poems, songs, magazine and newspaper articles, episodes of TV series, and radio programs

  We learned the spiritual "Deep River."
  They read Edgar Allan Poe's poem "The Bells."
  "Thanksgiving Disaster" would be a good title for my story.

Single quotation marks are used to set off quoted material within a quotation.

"Have you read the story 'To Build a Fire'?" Mary Margaret asked.
Mick said, "Explain the proverb 'A penny saved is a penny earned.'"

Indirect quotations do not use quotation marks.

Mark said that his favorite literature was science fiction.

Edgar Allan Poe

Italics are used for the titles of books, magazines, newspapers, movies, TV series, ships, and works of art.

We prayed for those aboard the aircraft carrier *Hornet*.
Today's *Washington Post* has a photograph of Michelangelo's *Pietà*.

If you are handwriting, use underlining for italics.

You should read the article "Sitting Pretty" in Hearth and Home.

EXERCISE 1 Rewrite these sentences. Add punctuation marks where needed.

1. Bottlenose dolphins the scientist explained are fascinating.
2. She continued They are known for their intelligence.
3. Do they live in families? asked a student.
4. Not exactly, but they travel in groups ranging from a dozen to several hundred individuals explained the scientist.
5. You may see these dolphins playing at the oceanarium said the scientist because they are very social creatures.

EXERCISE 2 Rewrite these sentences. Add quotation marks and italics where needed. You can use underlining to indicate italics.

1. In the book Tales and Stories for Black Folks I especially enjoyed the story Raymond's Run by Toni Cade Bambara.
2. George's favorite poem is The Willow and the Gingko.
3. Nat Hentoff's novel The Day They Came to Arrest the Book is about the book The Adventures of Huckleberry Finn and a group of censors.
4. Several films tell the story of the sinking of the Titanic.
5. The Walt Disney movie Sleeping Beauty featured music by Tchaikovsky.
6. The movie Minority Report was based on the short story The Minority Report, which appeared in The Variation Man.
7. No one knows who is portrayed in Leonardo da Vinci's famous painting Mona Lisa.
8. When U.S. and Canadian teams play each other, fans sing both The Star-Spangled Banner and O Canada.

EXERCISE 3 Rewrite each sentence, using correct punctuation.

1. The author of Harry Potter and the Order of the Phoenix was on the Today Show yesterday
2. The article The Magic of Potter appeared in Time magazine
3. Do you know asked Carol how Harry got to Hogwarts School
4. Brendan remarked My cousin said that Harry Potter and the Goblet of Fire is his favorite Harry Potter novel
5. Carla said We wrote a song called Help Me, Hedwig
6. My favorite book is James and the Giant Peach said Theresa
7. The book by Roald Dahl explained Mike was written for his children in 1961
8. The main character and hero of this book said the teacher is named James Henry Trotter
9. There are many other characters in the book for example some talking bugs Aunt Sponge and Aunt Spiker.

APPLY IT NOW

Make a list of all your favorite books, songs, movies, plays, works of art, and magazines. Check the punctuation of all the titles.

Grammar
in Action. Rewrite two lines from the play on p. 451, using quotation marks correctly.

10.4 Apostrophes, Hyphens, and Dashes

An **apostrophe** is used for the following:

- to show possession

    Grady's toy soldiers   my cousins' cat

- to show the omission of letters or numbers

    can't   I'll   class of '08

- to show the plural of lowercase letters but not of capital letters unless the plural could be mistaken for a word

    a's   u's   Ps   Ns   (Exceptions: *U's* and *I's*)

A **hyphen** is used for the following:

- to divide a word between syllables at the end of a line

    My grandfather, who lives in California, will be visit-
    ing in July.

- in compound numbers from twenty-one to ninety-nine and to separate parts of some compound words

    sixty-three   mother-in-law

- to form some temporary adjectives

    The project will take *four years*.
    A *four-year* project is a big undertaking. (adjective)

A **dash** is used for the following:

- to indicate a change in thought or an interruption

    I turned suddenly—I'm still surprised I did—and left the room.

- to surround a series of words, phrases, or clauses in apposition

    Children's pets—cats, dogs, birds, and fish—are first in popularity.

EXERCISE 1 Rewrite these sentences. Add apostrophes, hyphens, and dashes where needed.

1. My father in law gave a terrific party.
2. There was a merry go round in the yard, and each child got a five minute ride.

3. My mother in law hung a star shaped piñata from a tree.

4. At first the children couldnt break it a surprise to us all.

5. Finally it broke, and different colored candies fell out.

6. I counted eighty nine candy wrappers on the ground under the piñata after the children left the party.

7. My brother in laws band played songs a real treat for all.

8. Well remember the peppermint flavored ice cream.

9. The children went home at six oclock.

10. Theyll never forget this great birthday party.

EXERCISE 2 Rewrite the following sentences, adding the correct punctuation.

1. Members of Mrs. Carters eighth grade class chose their favorite works of art.

2. Carlas favorite movie is The Wizard of Oz.

3. Several nominated the book A Wrinkle in Time.

4. Ana has seen Rodins famous statue The Thinker a wonderful experience.

5. Keshawn remarked My dads favorite piece of music is the Beatles Good Day Sunshine.

6. Carol and Christine both selected Robert Frosts poem Stopping by Woods on a Snowy Evening.

7. Mrs. Carter reported My brother in law loves Jack Londons short story To Light a Fire.

8. The novel Great Expectations by Charles Dickens received a number of votes a surprise to Mrs. Carter.

9. The song America the Beautiful was more popular than The Star Spangled Banner.

10. The Newtown Gazette reported the results of the poll.

EXERCISE 3 Write sentences using the following prompts.

1. A sentence that uses a temporary adjective

2. A sentence that uses a dash

3. A sentence to show possession

4. A sentence that uses a hyphen

APPLY IT NOW

Rewrite the following sentence using correct hyphens and dashes: My seventy two year old grand-father if you can believe it walks northbound on Main Street for two miles every day.

Grammar in Action. Identify how the dash is used in the script on p. 460.

10.5 Capitalization

A **capital letter** is used for the following:

- the first word in a sentence, the first word in a direct quotation, and the first word of most lines of poetry and songs

  My favorite sport is baseball. The coach yelled, "*Slide*!"

  And somewhere men are laughing and somewhere children shout;
  But there is no joy in Mudville—mighty Casey has struck out.
  —Ernest Lawrence Thayer

- proper nouns and proper adjectives, including names of people, groups, specific buildings, particular places, months, and holidays

  Mary's **bat**   *American* **sports**
  Seattle, *Washington*   *Flatbush Avenue*
  the *Baseball Hall* **of** *Fame*   *Japanese* **food**

- a title when it precedes a person's name

  Senator **Hamilton** (*but* The senator said . . .)

- the directions north, south, east, and west, when they refer to sections of the country

  My sister went to the college in the *South*. (*but* Go east on Oak Street.)

- the names of deities and sacred books

  Holy Spirit   *Bible*   *Koran*   *Old Testament*

  - the principal words in titles of works (but not the articles *a, and,* and *the;* coordinating conjunctions; or prepositions unless they are the first or last word)

    To Kill a Mockingbird   *Lord of the Flies*

  - abbreviations of words that are capitalized

    U.S.A.   *Dr.*   *Ave.*   *Jan.*

Do not capitalize the names of subjects unless they come from proper names.

  science   **math**   *Spanish*

EXERCISE 1 Rewrite the following sentences, adding capital letters where needed.

1. watching baseball ranks high among leisure-time activities in the united states.

2. when we are not watching baseball, we may be reading stories about it, such as gary soto's "baseball in april" or judith viorst's "the southpaw."

3. songs like "take me out to the ball game" are classics.

4. take me out to the ball game.
   take me out with the crowd.
   buy me some peanuts and cracker jack.
   i don't care if I never get back.

5. sadly, many historic ballparks such as ebbets field in brooklyn, forbes field in pittsburgh, and crosby field in cincinnati no longer exist.

6. in some cases the original teams moved to the west, and their old parks in the east fell to the wrecking ball.

7. it is a tradition to go to ballparks on such holidays as memorial day, the fourth of july, and labor day.

8. baseball is played in many places, including japan, puerto rico, and mexico.

9. some people say that baseball evolved from an english sport called rounders, but others say that abner doubleday invented it in cooperstown, new york, in the 1800s.

10. roberto clemente, a famous hispanic baseball player, died in a plane crash while carrying supplies to earthquake victims in nicaragua in central america.

11. the national baseball hall of fame and museum, located in cooperstown, new york, displays old bats, balls, and baseball jerseys of famous players like greg maddux.

12. joe dimaggio was a famous player and was part of the new york yankees, but he is also known for marrying film starlet marylin monroe.

13. many famous movies like *field of dreams* and *a league of their own* celebrate baseball and are popular with fans of the game.

14. *a league of their own* is about women who played in the all-american girls professional baseball league.

APPLY IT NOW

Copy a passage from a book, magazine, or newspaper, without the capital letters. Trade papers with a partner. See whether your classmate can correct your passage while you correct your classmate's passage.

Use a camera to photograph capital letters in street signs.

Punctuation and Capitalization Review

10.1 **Rewrite each sentence. Add periods and commas where needed.**

1. W B Yeats was a famous Irish poet

2. Yeats was born in Dublin Ireland on June 13 1865

3. The poet as you may guess wrote mainly about Irish topics

4. Maxwell please read one of his poems aloud

5. "I would like to read this one" he said

6. Maxwell finished reading "Easter 1916" and the class showered him with applause

7. "Your reading" the teacher commented "was magnificent"

8. My other favorite Irish writers are Oscar Wilde James Joyce and Patrick Kavanagh

9. Dear Mary
Here is a poem I wrote for you and your family

10. "Poetry" explained the teacher "is another way to tell a story"

10.2 **Rewrite each sentence. Add exclamation points, question marks, semicolons, and colons where needed.**

11. What do we need to make pound cake for the bake sale

12. These are the main ingredients butter eggs sugar and flour.

13. Look Half the eggs are broken.

14. The eggs were fine at the store they must have broken on the way home.

15. We don't have enough eggs therefore I must buy more.

16. Please mix all the wet ingredients namely butter and eggs.

17. How did the pound cake turn out

18. Oh my this pound cake is delicious

19. We sold a slice of cake to Steve from Carson City Nevada.

20. Other treats at the bake sale included cookies tarts pies and brownies.

21. The last bake sale was April 14 2009 and the next one is on September 7.

22. Ugh I'm so full from snacking too much

10.3 **Rewrite each sentence. Add quotation marks and underlining to show italics where needed.**

23. How many students read the newspaper every day? asked Mrs. Filippo.

24. Most students read The Daily Herald or the Morning Star each morning.

25. A few students listened to Morning Edition on the radio.

26. Mrs. Filippo brought several issues of Newsweek to the classroom.

27. She asked the class to read the article Ruffled Feathers in Birding for homework.

28. Yesterday's Daily Times featured a photograph of Michelangelo's sculpture David.

29. Tommy and Hunter write for the school paper, The Janesville High Gazette.

30. May I interview you, Principal Markham? asked Keisha.

31. I like to read the comics and the column Money Sense.

32. There was a large photograph of Rodin's The Thinker to accompany the article.

33. I read the Los Angeles Times and Time magazine whenever I can says Mrs. Filippo.

10.4 **Rewrite each sentence. Add apostrophes, hyphens, and dashes where needed.**

34. My sister in law went to Charlie's school.

35. She graduated in 99.

36. It was the fifty fifth class to graduate from the school.

37. There were ninety seven students in her class.

38. Several students graduated with straight As.

39. Many students my brother is one went to the same high school.

40. They have known each other since they were in a high level math class together.

41. They had their 10 year reunion last week can you believe it?

42. My friends sisters were both star athletes in high school.

43. His sisters who are twins played basketball and soccer.

44. "I graduated college in 09," she said, "with a major in prelaw"

10.5 **Rewrite each sentence. Add capital letters where needed.**

45. the u.s. team trained for the summer olympics that were held in athens, greece, in 2004.

46. several training facilities are located in the west.

47. i think some swimmers train in boulder, colorado.

48. is it near the university of colorado?

49. athletes received a good-luck message from senator glenn thompson.

50. coach philips wants us to train at the mountain view aquatic center in loveland, colorado.

51. andre and wendy swim on a team called the boulder poseidons.

52. If you take pearl street south, you can reach the base of the flatirons foothills.

Tech Tip

Go to www.voyagesinenglish.com for more activities.

Punctuation and Capitalization Challenge

Copy these paragraphs, adding whatever punctuation and capital letters are needed for clarity and correctness.

weak and thin and pallid, he awoke at last from what seemed to have been a long and troubled dream feebly raising himself in the bed with his head resting on his trembling arm he looked anxiously around

what room is this where have I been brought to said Oliver this is not the place I went to sleep in

he uttered these words in a feeble voice being very faint and weak but they were overheard at once the curtain at the bed's head was hastily drawn back and a motherly old lady, very neatly and precisely dressed, rose as she undrew it, from an arm-chair close by in which she had been sitting at needlework

—oliver twist by charles dickens

Oliver Twist asks for a second helping of porridge in this illustration by J. Mahoney.

11.1 Simple Sentences

A **diagram** is a visual outline of a sentence. It shows in a graphic manner the relationships among the various words or groups of words in a sentence. Diagramming serves two purposes. First, it helps you understand how a sentence is put together. Second, it identifies errors in a sentence and makes clear why they are errors.

In a diagram the subject, the verb, the direct object, and the subject or the object complement go on the main horizontal line. The subject is separated from the verb by a vertical line that cuts through the horizontal line. The line to separate a verb from a direct object is also vertical but does not cut through the line.

SENTENCE **Galaxies contain stars.**

The line to separate a subject complement from a verb slants left.

SENTENCE **The Milky Way is a galaxy.**

An object complement is placed on the horizontal line after a line slanting right.

SENTENCE **The astronomy club elected Jaime president.**

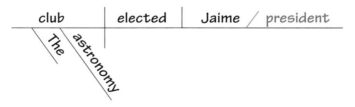

An indirect object is placed on a horizontal line under the verb.

SENTENCE **The astronomer gave the class a talk.**

Adjectives, adverbs, and articles are placed under the words that they describe. In this sentence the adjective *large* describes *radish*. The adverb *slowly* describes the phrasal verb *pulled up*. The adverb *very* describes *large*.

SENTENCE **He slowly pulled up a very large radish.**

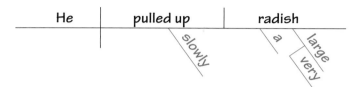

Prepositional phrases can act as adjectives or adverbs. In this sentence *in San Francisco* is an adjective phrase describing *commuters*. *On cable cars* is an adverb phrase describing *ride*.

SENTENCE **Commuters in San Francisco ride on cable cars.**

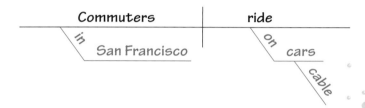

EXERCISE 1 Diagram the sentences.

1. An important crop of France is the grape.
2. My friend in Australia sent me a birthday card by e-mail.
3. My aunt named the baby Ava.
4. Colorful pennants decorated the walls of the gym.
5. My brother composes songs for the guitar.
6. Okefenokee Swamp in Florida is an animal sanctuary.
7. The soda pop from the pop machine was warm.
8. The octopus squirts an inklike substance for its defense.
9. Mars is the fourth planet in the solar system.
10. The Empire State Building in New York is my favorite place.
11. My sister baked cookies for the school fund-raiser.
12. Tourists in St. Louis visit the very impressive Gateway Arch.

APPLY IT NOW

Write and diagram five simple sentences. Include at least one object complement, one prepositional phrase used as an adjective, and one prepositional phrase used as an adverb.

11.2 Appositives

An **appositive** is a word or a group of words that follows a noun or a pronoun and further identifies it or adds information. An appositive names the same person, place, thing, or idea as the word it explains.

In a diagram an appositive is placed in parentheses to the right of the word it identifies. Words that describe the appositive go under it. In this sentence the appositive renames the proper noun *Shel Silverstein,* which is the subject.

SENTENCE **Shel Silverstein, a humorous poet, wrote *A Light in the Attic*.**

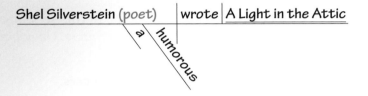

An appositive can appear in all the places in a sentence where nouns occur. In this sentence the appositive, the proper noun *Walk Two Moons,* explains the word *novel,* which is a direct object.

SENTENCE **We read the novel *Walk Two Moons* for class.**

What word does the appositive in this sentence rename? How does that word function?

SENTENCE **We read poems by Maya Angelou, an American poet.**

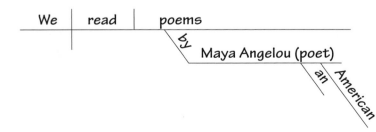

The appositive, *poet,* explains the proper noun, *Maya Angelou,* which is the object of a preposition.

EXERCISE 1 Diagram the sentences.

1. Eudora Welty, a Southern writer, lived in rural Mississippi.
2. Our senator is proposing an amendment, a change to the Constitution.
3. Bernini, an Italian artist, created sculptures based on stories from Roman mythology.
4. Monkeys live in the canopy, the uppermost layer of a rain forest.
5. Robinson Crusoe, a shipwrecked sailor, was a character in an early novel by Daniel Defoe.
6. In our studies of World War II, we learned about D-Day, the day of a major Allied invasion.
7. Monks copied books onto parchment, a paperlike material.
8. My cousin now lives in Berlin, the capital of Germany.
9. Cerberus, a dog with three heads, guarded the entrance to the underworld of Greek mythology.
10. Capillaries, the smallest blood vessels, carry nutrients to cells.
11. Jane Eyre, a governess, is the main character in that novel.
12. Frodo Baggins, a hobbit, carried the ring to Mount Doom.
13. We planned a trip to Key West, the southernmost point in Florida.
14. Liberty Island, a national park, is open to the public.
15. We'll meet at our usual place, the clock tower on State Street.
16. Aspen, a ski resort, is a great place for a winter vacation.
17. Santorini, a Greek island, may be the site of Plato's Atlantis.
18. A labrys, a double-headed ax, is exhibited in the archaeological museum.
19. Claude Monet, a famous painter, was a leader of the Impressionist movement.
20. Rome, a historic city, has many tourists during the year.

Robinson Crusoe

Santorini, Greece

APPLY IT NOW

Write and diagram four sentences with appositives: one describing a subject, one describing a direct object, one describing a subject complement, and one describing an object of a preposition.

Grammar in Action. Identify the appositives in the excerpt on p. 489.

11.3 Compound Sentences

A **compound sentence** contains two or more independent clauses.
An independent clause has a subject and a predicate and can stand
on its own as a sentence. Clauses in a compound sentence are usually
connected by a coordinating conjunction.

In a diagram each independent clause has its own horizontal line with
its subject and verb as well as any objects and complements.

- The coordinating conjunction is placed on a vertical dashed line
  at the left edge of the diagram.
- The line connects the main horizontal lines of the two clauses.

In the first clause of this sentence, *tourists* is the subject, *visited* is the
verb, and *Philadelphia* is the direct object. In the second clause, *they* is
the subject, *saw* is the verb, and *Liberty Bell* is the direct object.

SENTENCE **The tourists visited Philadelphia, and they
saw the Liberty Bell.**

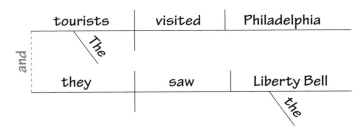

Independent clauses connected by a conjunctive adverb and a semicolon
are also compound sentences. A conjunctive adverb is diagrammed in
the same way as a coordinating conjunction.

SENTENCE **Our team was winning; however, it lost in the ninth inning.**

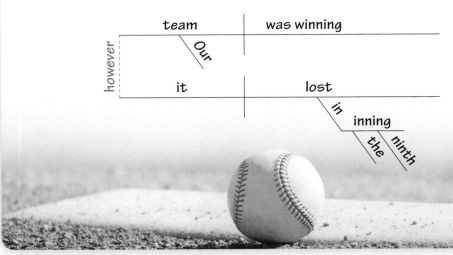

SENTENCE **I recited a poem, "The Highwayman"; in addition, other performers presented musical numbers.**

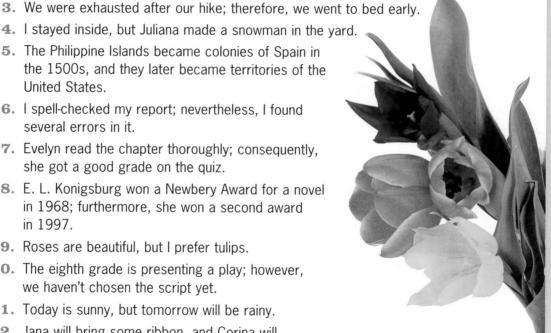

EXERCISE 1 Diagram the sentences.

1. I have read the Harry Potter books, but I haven't seen the movies.
2. Summer days are warm in the mountains, but the nights are cool.
3. We were exhausted after our hike; therefore, we went to bed early.
4. I stayed inside, but Juliana made a snowman in the yard.
5. The Philippine Islands became colonies of Spain in the 1500s, and they later became territories of the United States.
6. I spell-checked my report; nevertheless, I found several errors in it.
7. Evelyn read the chapter thoroughly; consequently, she got a good grade on the quiz.
8. E. L. Konigsburg won a Newbery Award for a novel in 1968; furthermore, she won a second award in 1997.
9. Roses are beautiful, but I prefer tulips.
10. The eighth grade is presenting a play; however, we haven't chosen the script yet.
11. Today is sunny, but tomorrow will be rainy.
12. Jana will bring some ribbon, and Corina will buy the glitter.
13. I slept after the game, but José started his homework.
14. They sky looks cloudy; however, it will not rain.
15. The spaghetti tastes delicious; nevertheless, I wanted vegetable stir-fry.

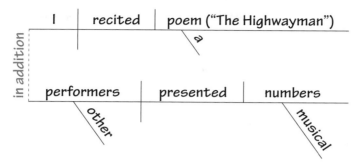

APPLY IT NOW

Write and diagram six compound sentences. Use coordinating conjunctions in three sentences and conjunctive adverbs in the other three.

11.4 Compound Sentence Elements

The subject and the predicate in a sentence may be compound. They may consist of two or more words connected by a coordinating conjunction. Remember that a sentence with a compound subject or a compound predicate is still a simple sentence.

In a diagram the compound parts are placed on two separate lines joined to the main line. The conjunction is placed on a vertical dashed line between them. In the first sentence, the subject is compound. In the second sentence, the verb is compound.

SENTENCE **Phil and Paul are forwards on the soccer team.**

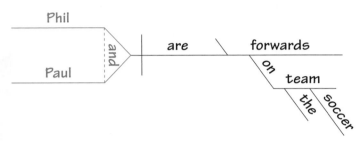

SENTENCE **The chef washed and cut vegetables for the stew.**

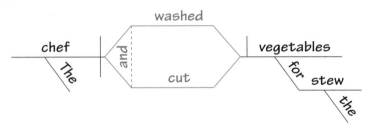

Both the subject and the verb may be compound, and each verb may have its own object.

SENTENCE **My sister and I bought groceries and prepared supper.**

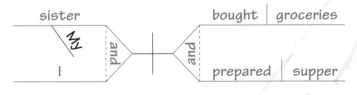

Words other than subjects and verbs may also be compound, and they are diagrammed in a similar way. In this sentence compound adjectives function as subject complements.

SENTENCE **The day was warm and sunny.**

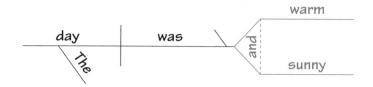

EXERCISE 1 Diagram the sentences.

1. King Richard and King John were brothers.
2. Belize and Guatemala are located in Central America.
3. Nick sat down and read.
4. Is Sacramento or Los Angeles the capital of California?
5. Copper and zinc together form brass.
6. A telescope gathers and focuses light into a tiny point.
7. I can play the violin and the trumpet.
8. Norita ate slowly but finished the plate of linguine.
9. Kevin and Elaine are good dart players.
10. The butler cleaned and polished the silver.
11. Maria and Rosa are entering the competition.
12. Tony and Andy deliver newspapers before school.
13. I will find more silverware and set the table.
14. Mr. Kenney advises the drama club and the debate team.
15. We can read the Sunday comics or watch cartoons.
16. Stanley Stevens was the class president but is now the treasurer.
17. Our class went to the Miller Aquarium and went to the dolphin show.
18. Sarah scored many goals and celebrated with her team.
19. John and Katie studied for the test and then played outside.
20. Uncle Bill should mow the lawn or clean the garage.

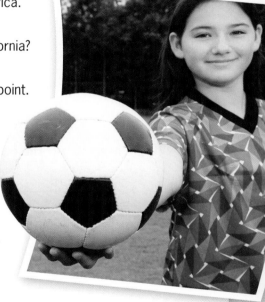

APPLY IT NOW

Write and diagram four sentences: two with compound subjects and two with compound predicates.

11.5 Participles

A **participle** is a verbal that is used as an **adjective**. A participial phrase is made up of the participle and its objects, complements, and any modifiers. The entire phrase acts as an adjective.

In a diagram a participial phrase goes under the noun or pronoun it describes on a slanted line connecting to a horizontal line.

- The participle starts on the slanted line and extends onto the horizontal line.
- A direct object or a complement is placed after the participle.
- Any word that describes the participle or its object or complement goes on a slanted line under the correct word.

SENTENCE **Lying in the hammock, I watched the clouds in the sky.**

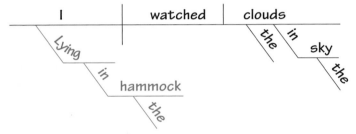

SENTENCE **The cat, stretched across the cushion, was sleeping.**

SENTENCE **The students, having removed litter from the grounds, next cleaned litter from the park.**

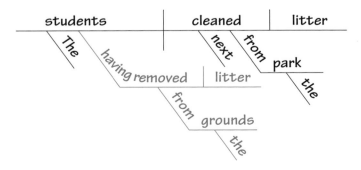

Participial adjectives, which often precede the nouns they describe, are placed just as other adjectives are.

SENTENCE **The firefighters ran into the burning building.**

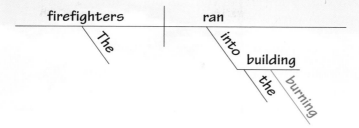

EXERCISE 1 Diagram the sentences.

1. Toby, having explained the problem, was questioned by the student council.
2. Sitting in the sun for several hours, I got a bad sunburn.
3. Driving rain is in the forecast announced on the radio.
4. Congress cannot make laws prohibiting freedom of speech.
5. Afflicted with allergies, Luis sneezed and sneezed.
6. Having eaten breakfast, Melinda packed herself a lunch.
7. New Orleans, located near the mouth of the Mississippi, controls much river trade.
8. *Common Sense* is a pamphlet written by Thomas Paine during the American Revolution.
9. Urging separation from England, Paine captured the imagination of the colonists.
10. Studying for the test, I stayed up quite late.
11. Having overslept, I missed the school bus.
12. Erasing the board, Ms. Catania scolded the class.
13. Having ridden along the bike path, Matt arrived at the picnic area.
14. Saugatuck, located on the Kalamazoo River, is a resort town.
15. Walking through the art museum, we saw paintings and sculpture.
16. Playing baseball, Keith hurt his ankle.

APPLY IT NOW

Write and diagram four sentences with participial phrases.

11.6 Gerunds

A **gerund** is a verb form ending in *ing* that is used as a noun. A gerund can be used in a sentence as a subject, a subject complement, an object of a verb, an object of a preposition, or an appositive.

In a diagram a gerund is placed according to its function.

- The gerund is placed on a stepped line that extends onto a horizontal line.
- A direct object or a complement is placed after the gerund.
- Words that describe the gerund or its object or complement go on slanted lines.

A gerund that functions as a subject, a direct object, or a subject complement is placed on a stepped line above the main horizontal line in the appropriate position. The gerund in this sentence is used as the subject.

SENTENCE **Playing the trumpet is my favorite hobby.**

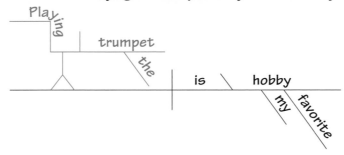

The gerund in this sentence is used as the direct object. A gerund used as a subject complement would go in a similar position, but the line before it would be slanted left. A gerund used as an appositive goes next to the word it describes in parentheses, as other appositives do.

SENTENCE **I remember writing the e-mail.**

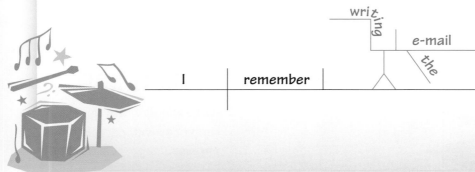

A gerund used as the object of a preposition is part of the prepositional phrase, which goes under the word it describes. A stepped line is still used, but it is not raised.

SENTENCE **Windmills are used for pumping water.**

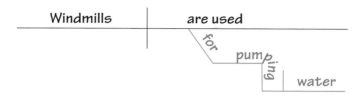

EXERCISE 1 Diagram the sentences.

1. I had a scary dream about riding on a roller coaster.
2. Traveling to new places is exciting.
3. The city forbids swimming in the lagoon.
4. Do you prefer taking the bus?
5. An important industry in Australia is raising sheep.
6. Organizing ideas, an early step in the writing process, is essential.
7. Walking to school provides me with good exercise.
8. She followed the directions for assembling the bike.
9. My job at the animal shelter, answering the phones, is a hectic one.
10. My favorite kind of vacation is camping in the mountains.
11. Sonja's next task is baking a birthday cake for Garret.
12. My extra chore is walking the dog.
13. A popular activity at picnics is playing volleyball.
14. Glazing the pot is the trickiest part of the job.
15. Clara enjoys knitting scarves as a hobby.
16. My science teacher wrote a book about building telescopes.
17. Joseph likes building model airplanes.
18. Jenna enjoys sewing cotton shirts for Girl Scouts.
19. Sarina was excited at finding her lost car keys.
20. An interesting pastime is collecting stamps.

APPLY IT NOW

Write and diagram eight sentences with gerunds. Have at least one gerund for each of these functions: subject, direct object, object of a preposition, and appositive.

Identify three gerunds in an online newspaper article.

11.7 Infinitives

An **infinitive** is a verb form, usually preceded by *to*, that is used as a noun, an adjective, or an adverb.

In a diagram an infinitive is placed according to its function in the sentence.

- An infinitive itself is diagrammed like a prepositional phrase. The *to* goes on a slanted line, and the verb goes on a horizontal line.
- A direct object or a complement is placed after the verb on the horizontal line.
- A word that describes the infinitive or part of the infinitive phrase goes under the horizontal line.

An infinitive used as a subject, a direct object, a subject complement, or an appositive is placed on a stepped line above the main horizontal line in the appropriate position. In the first sentence, the infinitive is a direct object, and in the second sentence, the infinitive is an appositive.

SENTENCE **I planned to leave early.**

SENTENCE **My plan, to start a babysitting service, requires organization.**

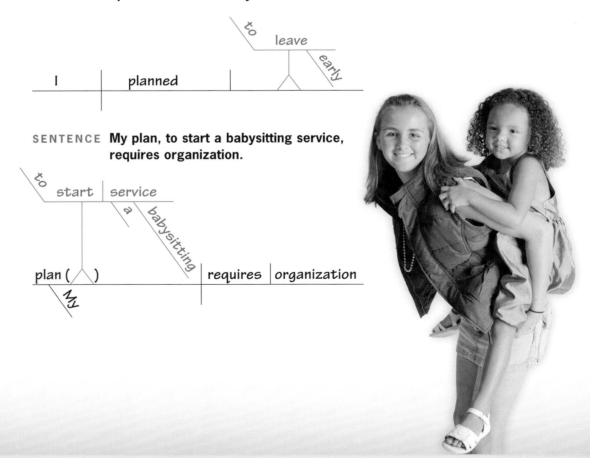

Infinitives used as adjectives or adverbs are placed under the words they modify.

SENTENCE **I was pleased to receive the invitation.**

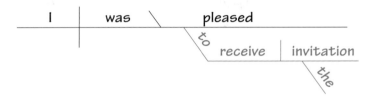

EXERCISE 1 Diagram the sentences.

1. Many people in the stands rose to applaud the team.
2. The boy's aim was to rescue the dog.
3. To practice anything daily requires discipline.
4. I want to read the new mystery.
5. Leo's task, to paint scenery for the play, is an important one.
6. The runners are ready to start.
7. Color blindness is the inability to distinguish certain colors.
8. Athletes need skill and a will to succeed.
9. My family went to the museum to see an exhibit on filmmaking.
10. To be chosen for the student council is a real honor.
11. Troy wants to finish his math homework before dinner.
12. The bookstore will open at midnight; however, we do not plan to go until tomorrow.
13. You forgot to put that banana in my lunch box.
14. Sandy wants to swim, but the waves are too high.
15. My little sister was happy to see *Snow White* at the movie theater.
16. David's idea, to begin an opera club, requires a teacher sponsor.
17. Our family wanted to vacation in Sweden.
18. Carla decided to try out for the basketball team.
19. To go to the Super Bowl was Rodney's dream.
20. John needed to ride the bus, but he lost his money.

APPLY IT NOW

Write and diagram 10 sentences with infinitives. Use at least one infinitive for each of these noun functions: subject, direct object, object of a preposition, and appositive. Use at least one infinitive as an adjective and one as an adverb.

11.8 Adjective Clauses

An **adjective clause** is a dependent clause that describes or limits a noun or a pronoun. An adjective clause usually begins with one of the relative pronouns *(who, whom, whose, which,* or *that)* or with a subordinate conjunction *(when, where,* or *why).*

In a diagram the adjective clause and the independent clause are on separate lines, with the dependent clause beneath the independent clause.

- A dashed line connects the relative pronoun or the subordinate conjunction in the dependent clause to the word in the independent clause that is modified by the adjective clause.
- A relative pronoun is placed in the diagram according to its function in the adjective clause.

In the first sentence, *Lake Erie* is the antecedent of *which. Which* acts as the subject in the adjective clause. In the second sentence, *pictures* is the antecedent of *that. That* acts as the direct object of the verb *took* in the adjective clause.

SENTENCE **Lake Erie, which was once fairly polluted, is now much cleaner.**

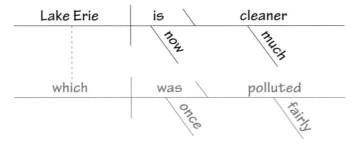

SENTENCE **Molly showed me the pictures that she took in Italy.**

The relative pronoun *whose*, like other possessives, goes under the noun it is associated with.

SENTENCE **This is the boy whose pumpkin won the top prize.**

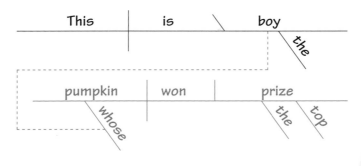

EXERCISE 1 Diagram the sentences.

1. Norway is a country that has many fjords.
2. The train, which leaves for Toronto in five minutes, is already full.
3. The person who wrote the letter to the editor remained anonymous.
4. The directions that the passerby gave me were incorrect.
5. Pablo Picasso, who was a very famous artist of the 20th century, worked in many styles.
6. Matt read the poem that he had written.
7. Willis Tower, which is the tallest building in the United States, is in Chicago.
8. The original White House, which the British burned in 1814, was first used by John Adams and his wife, Abigail.
9. Animals that live in polar regions are usually extremely hairy and have thick hides.
10. The artist whose painting won first prize in the local fair is my cousin.
11. The house, which has been abandoned, is rumored to be haunted.
12. Grandmother Harris enjoyed the postcards that Uncle Mike bought in Greece.
13. Aunt Susan gave me the canvas that she had painted.
14. The sweater that Lillian wore was prettier than mine.
15. We quickly entered the concert hall where the band had played.

APPLY IT NOW

Write and diagram eight sentences with adjective clauses. Use *whose* in at least one of them.

11.9 Adverb Clauses

An **adverb clause** is a dependent clause that acts as an adverb; it describes a verb, an adjective, or another adverb. Adverb clauses begin with subordinate conjunctions, such as *after, although, as, because, before, if, since, so that, unless, until, when, whenever, wherever,* and *while.*

In a diagram an adverb clause goes on its own horizontal line under the independent clause.

- The subordinate conjunction is placed on a slanted dashed line that connects the two clauses.
- The line goes from the verb in the adverb clause to the word in the independent clause that the adverb clause describes, which is usually the verb.

In the first sentence, the subordinate conjunction is *Although.* The dependent clause modifies *was.* In the second sentence, the subordinate conjunction is *after.* The independent clause modifies *should hammer.*

SENTENCE **Although I got up early, I was too late to see the sunrise.**

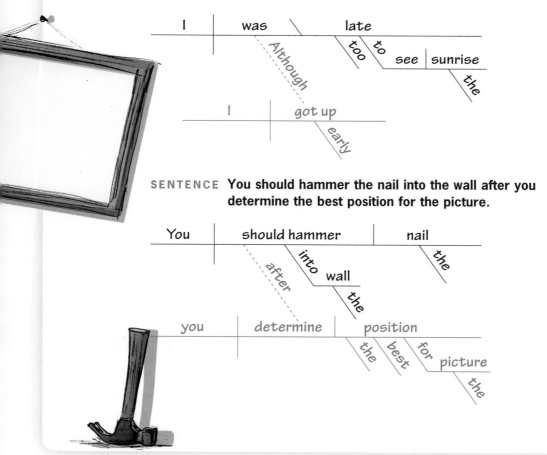

SENTENCE **You should hammer the nail into the wall after you determine the best position for the picture.**

I want to see the movie because *The Hobbit* is my favorite book.

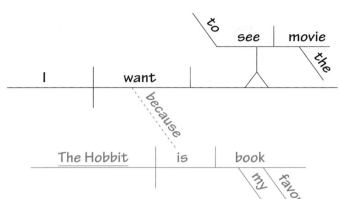

EXERCISE 1 Diagram the sentences.

1. Dylan bent the frame of his bike when he crashed into the fire hydrant.

2. Before individual cakes of soap were manufactured, grocers would cut pieces of soap from a huge block.

3. Margie played the same polka on her accordion until she memorized it.

4. When ancient Egyptian kings died, their bodies were mummified.

5. The Great Wall was built so that China would have protection from invaders.

6. The graduates tossed their caps into the air after they had received their diplomas.

7. If you need help with math, you can get a tutor.

8. The moon is visible because it reflects sunlight.

9. Will you lend me your red marker since mine is out of ink?

10. When I watch ice-skaters, I want to learn to skate.

11. Corinne became a skier when she lived in Canada.

12. I will enter the photo contest although I have little hope of winning.

13. Larry will feed Amy's cat, Snoopy, while she visits Aunt Ruth.

14. Although the dog was friendly, I was too scared to pet it.

15. We will go to the movies when school is finished.

APPLY IT NOW

Write five sentences with adverb clauses and diagram the sentences.

Grammar in Action. Identify the adverb clause in the last sentence in the fourth paragraph of the model on p. 489.

11.10 Noun Clauses

Dependent clauses can be used as nouns. **Noun clauses** work in sentences in the same way that nouns do. Among the words that commonly introduce noun clauses are *that, whoever, whomever, how, whether, what, whatever, when, where, which, who, whom, whose,* and *why.*

In a diagram the noun clause is placed according to its function in the sentence.

- The clause has its own horizontal line that rests on a stem connecting it to the independent clause. Except for clauses used as objects of prepositions, noun clauses are placed above the independent clause.
- If the word that introduces a noun clause has no function in the clause, it is placed on the vertical line connecting the noun clause to the independent clause. If the word that introduces the noun clause has a specific function, it is placed in the diagram according to that function.

In this sentence the noun clause is the subject. Noun clauses used as complements or direct objects are diagrammed in a similar way. Noun clauses used as appositives go in parentheses next to the nouns they describe.

SENTENCE **That the school needs a new computer lab is evident from the crowding in the old lab.**

In this sentence the noun clause is the object of the preposition *to*. The word *whoever,* which introduces the noun clause, acts as its subject.

SENTENCE **The principal gave a special certificate to whoever had perfect attendance.**

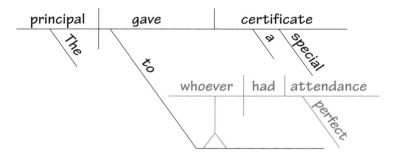

EXERCISE 1 Diagram the sentences.

1. I decided that I wanted a large yogurt smoothie.
2. That Martha is a good singer is obvious.
3. Did you hear about what Tiffany did on her vacation?
4. You should give a reward to whoever returned your wallet.
5. My hope is that we finish this work soon.
6. The textbook explains how the kidneys function.
7. Lance cannot buy a bicycle with what he has saved.
8. The fact that George Washington was honest is clear.
9. I didn't hear the announcement that the bus was leaving.
10. After I had written my haiku, I noticed that the second line had an extra syllable.
11. I hope that our class presentation will be successful.
12. Seth wondered what iguanas eat.

Iguanas eat mainly fruits and leaves, and enjoy an occasional treat such as the hibiscus.

APPLY IT NOW

Write six sentences with noun clauses and diagram the sentences. Use at least three different words to introduce the clauses.

Tech Tip Diagram a noun clause, using a PowerPoint presentation.

11.11 Diagramming Practice

Let's review some of the basics of diagramming. Subjects, verbs, direct objects, subject complements, and object complements go on the main horizontal line. Adjectives, adverbs, prepositional phrases, participles, and some infinitives go under the words or phrases they modify.

Gerunds and infinitives used as subjects, objects, or complements go above the main horizontal line of a diagram. Gerunds used as objects of prepositions and infinitives used as adverbs and adjectives go on lines below the horizontal main line. Can you identify a gerund and an infinitive in this sentence? How are they used?

SENTENCE **To study for the test is our reason for meeting at noon.**

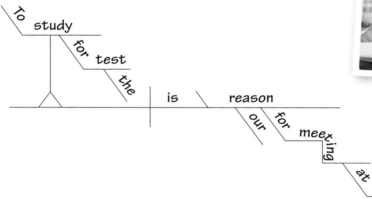

Diagrams of compound sentences and of sentences with adjective clauses, adverb clauses, and noun clauses have two horizontal lines. Review the various ways the two lines are connected. What kinds of clauses are in this sentence?

SENTENCE **Students can take lessons in French or Spanish before regular classes begin.**

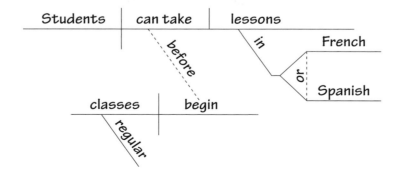

EXERCISE 1 Write out the sentences.

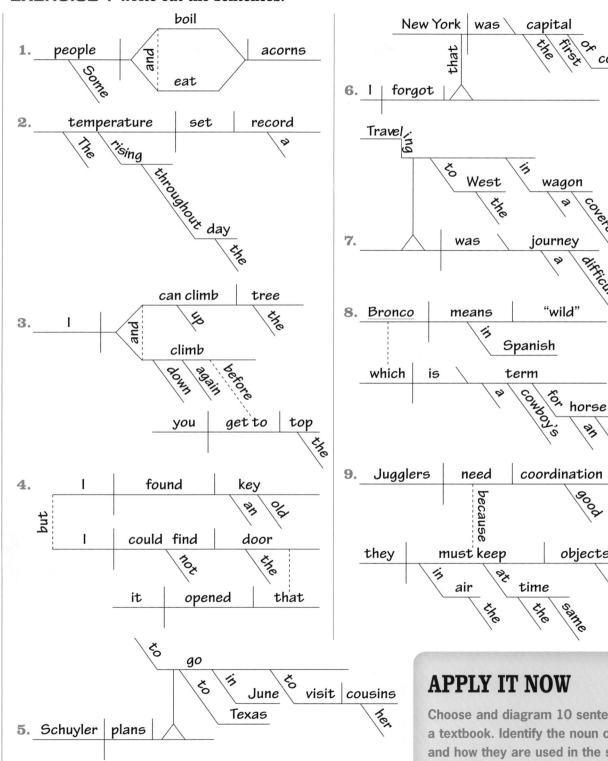

APPLY IT NOW

Choose and diagram 10 sentences from a textbook. Identify the noun clauses and how they are used in the sentences.

Diagramming Review

Diagram the sentences.

11.1
1. Horses run fast.
2. Smarty Jones is a horse.
3. Smarty Jones won many races.

11.2
4. Amelia Earhart, a famous pilot, disappeared with her plane.
5. We read the book *Amelia Earhart: A Biography* at school.

11.3
6. Javier planted a garden, and he grew vegetables.
7. The beans grew; however, rabbits ate them.

11.4
8. Pete washed and waxed the car.
9. Jenny and I cleaned the garage.

11.5
10. Sitting on the dock, we watched boats on the lake.
11. Tony, showing his skill, steered the boat with ease.
12. Enjoying the sand, Samantha stayed on the shore.

11.6
13. Tapping my foot is an easy dance move.
14. Lessons are useful for teaching dances.

11.7
15. Shauna wanted to make some bread.
16. The next step, to knead the dough, seemed difficult.

17. England, which was once separated from France, is now connected by a tunnel.

18. The explanation that Mr. Johnson gave was fascinating.

19. Since Tate was staying overnight, she packed a toothbrush.

20. She arrived for the slumber party after the family had eaten dinner.

21. Although the girls wanted to watch the late show, they fell asleep early.

22. That Tom was a good artist was obvious.

23. The resident artist gave guidance to whoever asked for help.

11.11 **Write out the sentences.**

24.

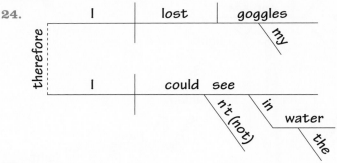

25.

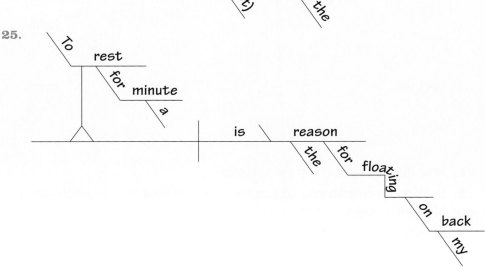

Go to www.voyagesinenglish.com for more activities.

Tech Tip

Diagramming • 219

Diagramming Challenge

Study the diagram and then answer the questions.

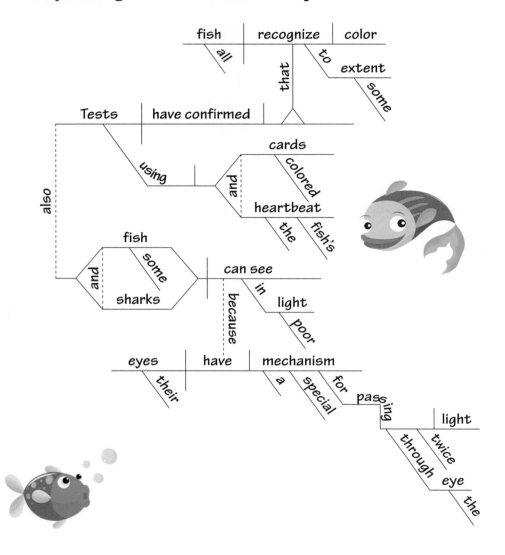

1. How many clauses are in the sentence?
2. Look at the coordinating conjunctions. Identify what they connect—words, phrases, clauses, or sentences.
3. Identify the adverb clause.
4. Identify the noun clause.
5. How is *using* used in the sentence?
6. Name the gerund phrase in the sentence. How is it used?
7. Write out the sentence.

WRITTEN AND ORAL COMMUNICATION

Chapters

Personal Narratives

LiNK **The Story of My Life**
by Helen Keller

I had now the key to all language, and I was eager to learn to use it. Children who hear acquire language without any particular effort; the words that fall from others' lips they catch on the wing, as it were, delightedly, while the little deaf child must trap them by a slow and often painful process. . . .

At first, when my teacher told me about a new thing I asked very few questions. My ideas were vague, and my vocabulary was inadequate; but as my knowledge of things grew, and I learned more and more words, my field of inquiry broadened, and I would return again and again to the same subject, eager for further information. Sometimes a new word revived an image that some earlier experience had engraved on my brain.

I remember the morning that I first asked the meaning of the word, "love." This was before I knew many words. I had found a few early violets in the garden and brought them to my teacher . . . Miss Sullivan put her arm gently around me and spelled in my hand, "I love Helen."

> This excerpt by Helen Keller, who lost her sight and hearing as a young child, is a good example of a personal narrative.

THE STORY OF MY LIFE

HELEN KELLER

ENRICHED CLASSIC

CHAPTER 1

Room: 123

Name: Kerrie Knight

Tossed by a Twister

A certain pressure or scent in the air will remind me instantly of the afternoon of April 3, 1974. My Weimaraner, Tucker, and I had been strolling in the fields near our house in Elmira, Oklahoma, when the air became strangely still. It smelled peculiar, like it was heavy with gases, and breathing was difficult. Then bam! A sudden thunderstorm drenched us. As I was charging back to the house, soaked and shivering, an alarming sound told me that nature wasn't through with us yet. The sound was like a million bees streaming from a giant hive. Living as I do in a tornado alley, I knew what was happening. A mean tornado was approaching, and it was coming fast.

I was petrified and a little awestruck as I looked up at the sky. I saw a vast dark reddish-gray funnel cloud, perhaps a quarter mile high, coming towards me. The deafening sounds seemed to originate from its tail, which had a circular opening at least 50 feet wide. I threw myself down to the ground on top of Tucker to protect him. The wind was so strong that Tucker was pulled from under me. There was nothing I could do to get him back.

As quickly as it had hit, the twister passed over us. I stood up carefully, brushed off my arms and legs, and took a cautious look around. A narrow path of trees was down, but everything else seemed untouched. My first thoughts were of Tucker. What had the tornado done to my dog? I finally heard a muffled bark. There was Tucker, hiding in a hole just his size, under the limb of a fallen oak tree. He was trapped by branches but uninjured. Had he dug the hole for protection, or had the twister done it for him? I never found out. Whatever the case, I was relieved to find that Tucker and I had survived the most frightening experience of our lives.

What Makes a Good Personal Narrative?

LiNK

The Story of My Life

"What is love?" I asked. She drew me closer to her and said, "It is here," pointing to my heart, whose beats I was conscious of for the first time. Her words puzzled me very much because I did not then understand anything unless I touched it.

I smelt the violets in her hand and asked . . .

"Is love the sweetness of flowers?"

Helen Keller

A personal narrative is a first-person account of an event in a writer's life. It invites readers to share the writer's experiences and his or her reactions to them.

Following are some points to keep in mind when you write a personal narrative. How closely did the writer of the personal narrative on page 223 follow these suggestions?

Topic

A good personal narrative relates an event that was unusual, memorable, or significant to the author's life. The best narratives use the incident to illustrate an idea, or theme, that many people could relate to.

Audience

Know the audience of your narrative. Is it your teacher and classmates, a close friend, or the readers of a favorite magazine? How do you want your audience to react: with smiles, tears, nods of recognition, or all three? How will you relate the events that occurred? The tone, or overall feeling, of your personal narrative depends on your answers to these questions.

Structure

A good personal narrative has a definite structure. It begins with an introduction that lures the reader in and hints at the story to come. The body, or main section, of the narrative tells what happened step-by-step. The conclusion tells the outcome of the incident and may show why the incident was significant.

Coherence

A personal narrative should maintain coherence, which means that each part of the narrative builds on what came before it. The story should be told in a logical way, usually in chronological order. Any details that aren't important to the story being told should be left out.

Title

Don't underestimate the power of a title. A title is like a snapshot of your personal narrative—it creates a first impression. If the title is short, creative, and focused on the subject or theme, the first impression will be positive.

ACTIVITY A Explain why each topic below could or could not be used for a personal narrative.

1. my favorite year in school
2. the pets I've had growing up
3. my worst basketball practice
4. the family vacation that wasn't
5. five reasons to study American history
6. the day I met my best friend
7. how my parents met
8. surviving my aunt's visit
9. all the times my mom supported me
10. my first piano lesson
11. the difference between alligators and crocodiles

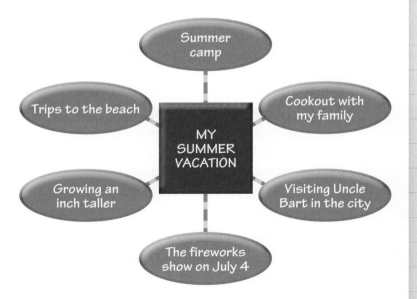

Tech Tip Use a computer program to map out your ideas.

ACTIVITY B Read this personal narrative. Then answer the questions that follow.

My Favorite Disaster

It took a force of nature to bring your grandpa and me together. Ray had been delivering groceries to my house for months, and I'm certain he noticed me. I surely noticed him, with his turquoise eyes and curly blond hair. But we two pitifully shy people had never muttered more than a few words to each other.

One stormy autumn evening, more than 40 years ago now, Ray delivered the groceries as usual. The wind was howling like a lonely wolf. As he put the last cardboard box of groceries on the kitchen table, we heard a sharp crack. The lights went out, and the room went dark. As I looked up, heavy drops of rain fell onto my face.

An oak had gouged a huge hole in the roof. During the time it took to find and light candles, assess the damage, and figure out what to do, Ray and I overcame our shyness. That was the beginning of our romance—a day, I sometimes say, when an ill wind brought some good.

1. What does the title tell you about this narrative?
2. Who is the intended audience?
3. How would you describe the tone?
4. Does the first sentence entice readers to continue reading? Why or why not?
5. In what way does the first sentence hint at what's to come?
6. What sensory details does the writer include?
7. Does the narrative maintain coherence? Explain how.
8. Which sentence gives the theme?
9. Identify two chronological steps that the narrator describes in the main body.
10. How is the personal narrative concluded?

ACTIVITY C Read each title for a personal narrative. Tell why you think it is or isn't effective.

1. My First and Only Scuba Dive
2. June 3, 1954
3. Why I Ran Away
4. A Rather Dull Afternoon
5. The Day My Dream Became a Nightmare
6. My Brother Is Born!
7. What Happened to Me One Day

ACTIVITY D Read the following paragraphs for coherence. Do the events flow logically? Are only relevant details included? Edit each paragraph to make it more coherent.

1. Because I live in Hawaii, I'd seen snow in movies and on TV, but I'd never seen it firsthand. I live right near the beach, which is wonderful. Nevertheless, two months ago, armed with parka and boots, I flew from Waikiki to Minneapolis. We had to switch planes in Chicago. Three feet of snow was on the ground in Minneapolis, and more was on the way. My heart was racing. I didn't know how snow felt, tasted, or even smelled. But I was going to find out.

2. My three-year-old son Danny was screaming. People in the crowd were looking either sympathetic, annoyed, or amused—and I was sweating. How was I going to get Danny's blankie back from that innocent-looking but criminal baby elephant? Eventually, we did get it back. Dangling a bag of peanuts over the fence at the animal had accomplished nothing. So I dug our lunch out of my backpack, unwrapped a sandwich of corned beef on rye, and waved it back and forth. I still had a piece of fruit and a drink saved for later. The elephant exchanged the blanket for the sandwich, and my friend May pulled the blanket through the fence with a stick. Teamwork and ingenuity saved the day.

LiNK

The Story of My Life

Again I thought. The warm sun was shining on us. "Is this not love?" I asked, pointing in the direction from which the heat came. "Is this not love?" It seemed to me there could be nothing more beautiful than the sun, whose warmth makes all things grow. But Miss Sullivan shook her head . . .

Helen Keller

WRITER'S CORNER

Choose at least three favorite topics from the web of subjects you brainstormed on page 225. Think of some catchy titles for each possible topic.

Introduction, Body, and Conclusion

Introduction

The introduction of a personal narrative sets the reader's expectations. If the introduction is bland or tedious, readers have no incentive to continue reading. The introduction may include just one sentence, or it may consist of several sentences or even paragraphs. The introduction should help the reader understand the topic of the narrative and lead the reader into the body of the narrative.

Body

The body is the core of a personal narrative, and it is generally the longest part. It uses sensory details that let the reader see, smell, hear, feel, and taste what the writer experienced. Depending on the topic and tone, the body may include dialogue, flashbacks, and other literary devices as ways to tell an effective story. Though in many ways it is similar to a fictional story, a personal narrative describes something that actually happened to the writer. Every sentence in the body should advance the narrative. Irrelevant details are like dead weight on a sinking ship. Good writers throw them overboard!

Conclusion

The conclusion of a personal narrative is the writer's last chance to leave an impression. The conclusion can summarize the event, or it can tie the narrative together. The writer can also use the conclusion to comment or reflect upon the event, and share what he or she may have learned.

ACTIVITY A Imagine that you are writing a personal narrative. Choose two of the following incidents and write a short introduction in paragraph form for each.

1. helping to cook a meal for your family
2. overhearing a classmate saying something mean and untrue about you
3. going on a long road trip
4. playing in a championship game
5. moving because your mother got a new job
6. finding or losing something
7. meeting someone new

ACTIVITY B Below are two introductions for personal narratives. Choose the less effective paragraph and rewrite it to make it stronger.

1. I woke up to the sounds of a scratchy weather report on the radio and my mom insisting I get up and get dressed. The winds outside were slapping gusts of rain against our house, and my dad was packing the car with food and blankets. You'd think I'd be used to participating in an abrupt exodus alongside my fellow Dade County residents during a hurricane. But the last serious one that hit our section of Florida happened when I was too young to remember. Even with all of my family's preparations for this one, I was still in for quite a ride.

2. Ever since I learned to read, I've studied snakes, especially my favorite, the king cobra. When I was given the opportunity last year to go to India with a group from school, I hoped finally to see one up close. It was a long, tiring trip. The airplane food was bad, and I sat next to someone who talked during the whole flight. I never want to take such a long flight again.

WRITER'S CORNER

Choose a topic and title from the list of possibilities you created on page 227. Write two introductions to begin your personal narrative. Be sure the first sentence of each entices your audience to continue reading. Later you can select your favorite introduction and revise it to make it even more effective.

Tech Tip Post your introductions on the class blog for peer review.

ACTIVITY C These are paragraphs from personal narratives. Identify the topic of each, as well as the sensory details (words or phrases) used to enliven the descriptions of events.

1. Lisa and I had spoken in our made-up language many times but never in a crowd. So at the homecoming football game last week (where the most fascinating dialogue we heard was "Woo, go team!"), we decided to try some made-up French. We walked to the opposing team's side and tried hard not to crack up as we spouted vaguely French-sounding gibberish. Besides attracting a bit of attention, our goal was to converse in our invented language so convincingly that people who heard our slurred speech thought we were foreign exchange students. Lisa and I turned up our noses and pretended to insult the other team, all while masking our giggles. Then suddenly we felt a tap on our shoulders. It was a real Frenchman, with the biggest smirk on his face I had ever seen.

2. After the department store disaster, Mom, Javi, and I raced breathlessly back to the car. Actually, we raced back to the space where the car had been. Mom checked the parking receipt on which she had jotted C-7. Yes, we were standing (bug-eyed) in front of parking space C-7, but it was empty. The car was missing. Mom's forehead wrinkled like she was ready for steam to start pouring out of her ears. We huddled together miserably and discussed what to do next.

ACTIVITY D These are conclusions to personal narratives. Write a satisfying ending to complete each conclusion.

1. We'd hiked to the summit and eaten our picnic, and now we were taking a well-deserved nap in the sun before thinking about our descent. Have you ever felt as though someone was watching you when you were sleeping? That feeling was making the hairs on the back of my neck stand up. I opened my eyes cautiously and looked straight into the golden eyes of a bobcat, which was standing no more than 15 feet away from me. We looked at each other for what felt like an eternity but surely was less than a minute. I whispered, "What do you want?" Then the big cat turned and ambled off, looking over its shoulder once before disappearing into the underbrush.

2. When we finally filed onstage, heads up and smiling, I completely forgot the months of practice, the fund-raising, and the social life I'd given up. Our small chorus from a small town in a small state was at Carnegie Hall, and we were about to perform for a sold-out crowd. I felt both ecstatic and a bit melancholy as I wondered whether life would ever again present me with an occasion as great as this.

3. I still have no idea what made me suspicious of the paper bag that sailed out the window of the pickup truck or why I pulled over to find out what it was. The greater mystery is how the tiny black puppy inside the bag survived the fall. He had only minor injuries and trusted me enough to lie quietly in my lap as we sped to the animal hospital. If I hadn't been busy going to school and working part-time, I would have put myself first on the list to adopt Chance (so named because my lucky discovery gave him a second chance at life).

4. After months of mowing lawns, weeding flower beds, and cleaning out old toolsheds, my day finally came. I went around to each of the houses that I had done work for and collected my wages. Mrs. Lewis offered me a "Congratulations" as she handed me an envelope. Mr. Ediza looked surly as usual, but he handed me the money without complaint. As my bag grew heavier, a feeling of pride swept over me, knowing that I had reached my goal.

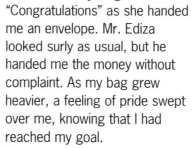

5. When I got home, I slumped on the couch and told Mom that all the barbershops were closed on Monday. My hair was going to look awful for family photos that night. My mother smiled. She told me my grandmother had cut hair when she was younger. I was nervous when Grandma grabbed the scissors, but I sure looked great that night.

Grammar in Action. Identify the objects of prepositions in the excerpt on p. 224.

WRITER'S CORNER

Pick your or your classmates' favorite introduction from the ones you wrote for the previous Writer's Corner. Think of the directions your narrative might take and the themes you might want to express. Add sensory details to enhance it. Reread "Tossed by a Twister" on page 223 as a model for ideas.

Time Lines

For almost any project you set out to do, the right tools can help you. Just as maps and compasses help hikers chart their course, time lines help writers chart their narrative course by arranging events. Time lines are constructed by numbering events in chronological order on a vertical, a horizontal, or a diagonal line. In the example below, Keisha has created a time line to organize her personal narrative into a coherent structure. In this time line, she has recorded her memories of a scary experience she had while sailing on Lake Michigan.

Reviewing Your Time Line

When Keisha reviewed her original time line, she found some details missing. She added steps to show how the storm got worse.

When you create a time line, go over it again to jog your memory. Are any steps or details missing? Don't be afraid to add more details.

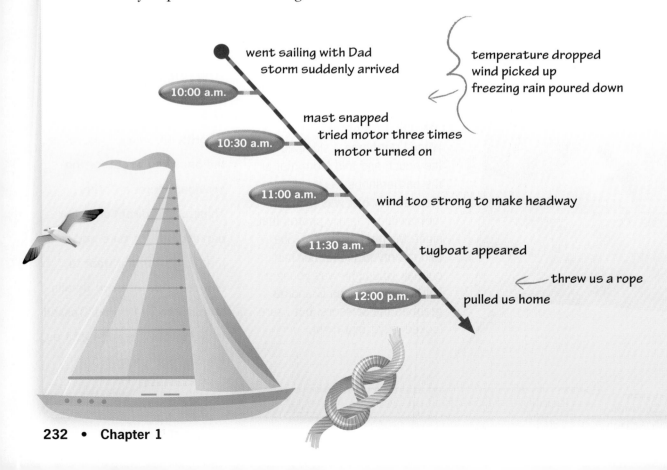

went sailing with Dad
storm suddenly arrived

temperature dropped
wind picked up
freezing rain poured down

10:00 a.m.

mast snapped
tried motor three times
motor turned on

10:30 a.m.

11:00 a.m. wind too strong to make headway

11:30 a.m. tugboat appeared

threw us a rope

12:00 p.m. pulled us home

ACTIVITY A The events from the personal narratives below were listed out of order. Rearrange each set of events in the order in which they would have occurred. Construct a time line for each set.

The Big Game

1. I slid safely into second base just as the winning run was scored.
2. I stepped to the plate and took a deep breath.
3. Cheering wildly, my teammates rushed onto the field.
4. The opposing pitcher stared at me menacingly.
5. He blew the first two pitches right by me, and the other team cheered.
6. When the coach called my name with the game tied, I knew this could be my chance.
7. I popped the ball up behind third base and started to run.
8. The third baseman tripped, and the ball dropped to the ground.

A Very Bad Day

1. By the end of the day, I was thinking I should have just stayed in bed.
2. My mother shook me awake long after I should have woken up.
3. I had to run to catch the bus.
4. We were out of my favorite cereal, so I had to eat oatmeal instead.
5. When I got to class, I realized I had forgotten my homework.
6. At lunch I found I had forgotten my lunch money too.
7. I raced to get dressed so quickly that I slammed the closet door on my finger.

WRITER'S CORNER

Create a time line listing the events for the personal narrative you picked in the previous Writer's Corner.

Transition Words

When a writer turns a series of events into a narrative, transition words help each event flow into the next. Some of these words are *first, then, later, before, during, while, next, finally, suddenly, after,* and *when*. You can also use phrases such as *at once, at last,* or *in the end* to create transitions.

Keisha used transition words to turn her time line into a narrative paragraph. Notice that she sometimes combined several events into the same sentences and added a few details.

Caught in the Storm

I was out sailing with my Dad when a storm suddenly arrived. The temperature dropped, the wind started howling, and a freezing rain pelted against our little sailboat. Suddenly, we heard a sharp crack. The mast had snapped! We knew we had to get out of there. First, we tried the motor. After three attempts, it finally caught, but we couldn't make any headway. Then out of nowhere a tugboat miraculously appeared. The captain threw us a rope, and I hitched it to our boat. Finally, we were headed home, trailing along behind the tugboat that had saved the day.

ACTIVITY B Answer the following questions about the personal narrative "Caught in the Storm."

1. What transition words were used in the paragraph?
2. What details were added that were not in the time line?
3. Which events from the time line were combined into the same sentence?

ACTIVITY C Rewrite the following paragraphs, using transition words and combining sentences so that they flow logically.

1. I had never been to a haunted house before. I told my friends that I wouldn't be scared. We waited in line. Spooky music played. I started to feel nervous. We went into the haunted house. A giant spider fell from the ceiling. I screamed. A scary clown reached out from behind a metal bar. My heart pounded. I raced through the rest of the house as fast as I could. I decided that was enough haunted houses for one year.

2. I was talking to my friend Marcy on the playground. The wind picked up. My fancy new hat blew off. I went running after it. It skipped across the playground. It rolled across the street. It landed in a puddle. I caught up to it and shook off the water. I decided not to wear it for the rest of the day.

3. The Saint Patrick's Day parade was downtown. We got there early. We set up our lawn chairs in front of a bank. The high school band marched past playing the school fight song. A pickup truck with hay and cowboys in back rumbled by. My little brother said he wanted to see the leprechauns. A clown passed us selling balloons. A man dressed like a fish came by selling bottled water. Several men rode by on mopeds, waving to the crowd. I spotted several men dressed as leprechauns near the end of the line. I held my little brother up over my head so he could see.

ACTIVITY D Choose one of the time lines from Activity A and turn it into a narrative paragraph. Use transition words and phrases to make the events flow together logically.

WRITER'S CORNER

Write two or three paragraphs of your narrative, using the time line you created in the previous Writer's Corner. Use transition words to make your paragraph flow logically. Reread the narratives at the beginning of this chapter for ideas.

Varied Sentences

Most readers prefer variety in their sentences. Too many simple sentences in a row can be boring to read, but so can too many compound sentences. Too many short sentences can be choppy. Turn them all into longer sentences, however, and you may find your reader drifting to sleep. The key is to punctuate long, compound and complex sentences with shorter, simpler ones. The reader will appreciate the break.

A simple sentence has one subject and one predicate.

> **Students at the private school wear uniforms.**

A compound sentence has two or more independent clauses joined together with a coordinating conjunction (*and, but, or, nor,* and *yet*).

> **Paul loves snowstorms, but Keegan detests them.**

Complex sentences are formed by joining dependent and independent clauses (groups of words with subjects and predicates). They are joined with a subordinate conjunction (*after, although, as, because, for, if, so, than, which, while, unless,* and *until*) that can appear at the beginning or middle of the sentence. When the conjunction comes at the beginning of the complex sentence, a comma is usually added between the two phrases.

> **Though they are too young for licenses, many kids who live on ranches and farms drive.**

In the sentence, *Though they are too young for licenses* is the dependent clause. It does not make sense on its own. *Many kids who live on ranches and farms drive* is the independent clause. It makes sense by itself.

See if you can identify the structure of each sentence below. Identify conjunctions and changes in punctuation.

A **I could paint the living room, or I could use wallpaper.**

B **Since we can't see every snowflake, how do scientists know that no two are alike?**

C **Thomas and Juwan, who look like twins, aren't.**

D **Hurricanes, tornadoes, and earthquakes cause billions of dollars in damages every year.**

ACTIVITY A Rewrite each pair of sentences as a compound sentence. Delete and add words as needed.

1. What are earthquakes? What causes earthquakes?

2. One type of earthquake is tectonic. Another type is volcanic.

3. I think intensity is the most significant measure of an earthquake. Magnitude is also important.

4. Seismographs record the waves from earthquakes. They help people determine how powerful an earthquake is.

5. The focus of an earthquake is the place where the first movement happens. The epicenter is the point on the surface above the focus.

6. The type of earthquake depends on where it happens. It depends on the geology of that place as well.

7. Earthquakes that occur beneath the sea are often harmless. Some cause giant destructive waves called tsunamis.

ACTIVITY B Rewrite each pair of sentences as a complex sentence. Delete and add words as needed.

1. My distant relative Ferdinand Foch was a famous WWI general. Foch was a French military leader.

2. I couldn't see the flounder's flat body. Its body blended with its surroundings.

3. We saw the Parthenon while on vacation. The Parthenon overlooks Athens.

4. My family visited the Sears Tower. The Sears Tower is located in Chicago, Illinois.

5. I learned that Ponce de León gave Florida its name. *Florida* means "full of flowers" in Spanish.

6. Our West Highland terrier is very energetic when she plays. She is also very gentle.

7. I rejoined the drama club. I had taken a year off to play basketball.

WRITER'S CORNER

Review the narrative paragraphs you wrote for the Writer's Corner on page 235. Revise them to include compound and complex sentences. Reread the personal narratives at the beginning of this chapter for ideas.

ACTIVITY C Rewrite the paragraphs to make them more interesting by varying the structure and length of the sentences. Add or delete words, and combine or rearrange sentences as necessary.

1. We went hiking through the woods in the state park. We went hiking this weekend. The sun was shining. The air was cool. It felt good. The leaves were already changing. Green was changing to red. Green was changing to yellow and brown too. Many leaves had fallen. They smelled wonderful. We tramped through them. We saw squirrels foraging for nuts. We also saw chipmunks foraging for nuts. A flock of geese flew over. The geese were headed south. Fall was here. The signs were everywhere. Winter was approaching fast.

2. A storm was heading our way. I could see lightning in the distance. The wind was howling. The waves were choppy. Dad and I decided to stay a while longer. Dad got a bite at last. He tugged furiously. The boat rocked. Dad almost fell overboard. I held the net. My brother stood by. My uncle stood by. They waited to see if they should bring in the fish. Or should they cut the line? I looked over the side of the boat. I began to laugh. Dad pulled in the line. He had hooked the boat's anchor.

ACTIVITY D The sentences below begin personal narratives. Write two sentences of varying lengths to follow each first sentence. Your sentence types should include simple, compound, and complex sentences.

1. Who would have suspected that a family reunion could turn into such a disaster?

2. Getting a part-time job was the best and worst decision I made last year.

3. I remember the day I learned the difference between teasing and tormenting.

4. We had traveled hundreds of miles to ski, and now we were stuck.

5. Here's how an uninvited guest ruined my birthday party and my whole year.

6. An evening scuba dive seemed exciting, but also a bit scary.

7. How hard can babysitting one small boy be?

8. I arrived at the party, but I never imagined that I'd see him there dressed like a scuba diver.

ACTIVITY E Write a body paragraph based on each time line below. Use a variety of long and short sentences.

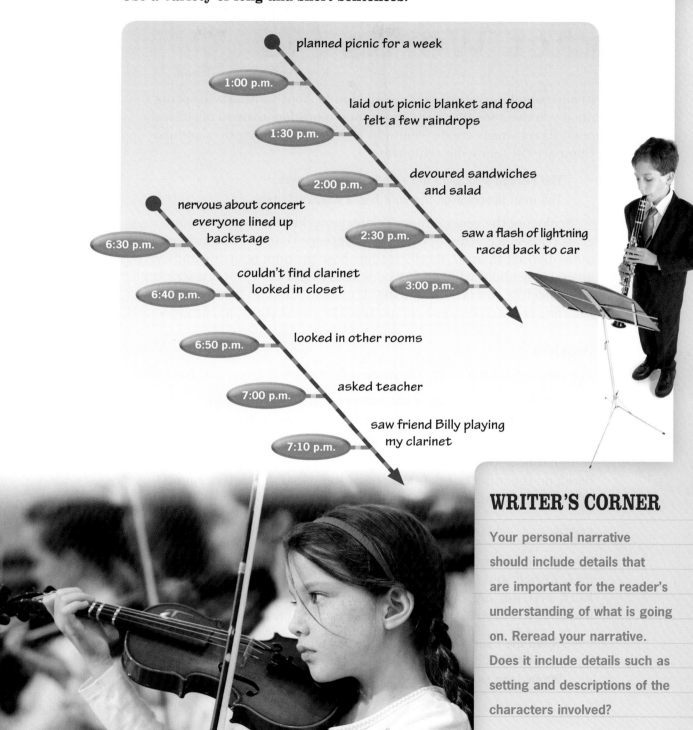

planned picnic for a week

1:00 p.m.

laid out picnic blanket and food
felt a few raindrops

1:30 p.m.

devoured sandwiches
and salad

2:00 p.m.

nervous about concert
everyone lined up
backstage

6:30 p.m.

2:30 p.m.

saw a flash of lightning
raced back to car

couldn't find clarinet
looked in closet

6:40 p.m.

3:00 p.m.

looked in other rooms

6:50 p.m.

asked teacher

7:00 p.m.

saw friend Billy playing
my clarinet

7:10 p.m.

WRITER'S CORNER

Your personal narrative should include details that are important for the reader's understanding of what is going on. Reread your narrative. Does it include details such as setting and descriptions of the characters involved?

Exact Words

In a personal narrative, every word counts. Your writing will spring to life if you use specific nouns, verbs, and modifiers instead of general ones. Exact words create clear and vivid pictures in readers' minds. Compare the following sentences:

The person sitting on the sofa has a nice smile.

The man perched on the sofa has a dazzling smile.

Replacing the general noun *person* with the more specific noun *man* gives readers a picture of whom the sentence is about. The verb *perch* is more distinct than *sit*. It tells readers how the man is sitting and even gives a clue about what sort of person he might be. What is a *nice* smile? The adjective *nice* is so vague that it calls to mind no particular image. *Dazzling* is exact. Readers can picture the man's stunning, bright smile.

Nouns

The more exact the noun, the more information it gives. For example:

Kendra thinks wearing a hat makes her look sophisticated.

Kendra thinks wearing a beret makes her look sophisticated.

What sort of picture does the noun *hat* call to mind? None. Unless you picture a specific kind of hat, you can't create a picture at all. A beret, on the other hand, is a certain kind of hat. It is a flat, round hat often worn to one side.

Verbs

Specific verbs tend to be action-packed and colorful. The verbs *raced, fled, dashed,* and *jogged* are livelier than *ran*. Using forms of the verb *be* (such as *is, am, are,* or *were*) will make a sentence passive and dull. Try to use an active verb instead. Which sentence below is livelier?

When the cookie was snatched by John, he was scolded by his mother.

When John snatched the cookie, his mother scolded him.

ACTIVITY A Replace each general noun below with a more specific one. Think creatively. Use a thesaurus if you need ideas.

1. sport
2. animal
3. shoe
4. food
5. color
6. vehicle
7. relative
8. furniture

ACTIVITY B The following paragraph, which is the body of a personal narrative, lacks specific sensory details. Change and add sentences to insert livelier verbs.

I was very nervous at lunch last Tuesday. I knew I needed to build some energy for the debate coming up. What could I have been thinking when I ordered beef stew? I know cafeteria stew is bad. Just looking at it made me feel sick, but I was so hungry that I ate it anyway.

ACTIVITY C Replace the italicized verb in each sentence below with a more exact verb.

1. When we noticed the sky, we *came* inside instantly.
2. "Watch out for the undertow!" I *said.*
3. Andi *looked* at the presents hidden in the closet.
4. The rock climber *went* up a formidable cliff.
5. For nearly a week, rain *came* down without stopping.
6. The toddler was so shy he *talked* into his mother's ear.
7. The baby goats *ran* in the field for hours.
8. Lightning *hit* the old barn last week.
9. Lila *worked* for a month on her science fair project.
10. The goldfish *came* to the top of the bowl as I approached.

WRITER'S CORNER

Go over your narrative and circle words you feel are weak or inexact. Use a thesaurus or synonym finder to replace them. Then have a partner read your narrative and circle any words he or she feels could be replaced with more vivid or exact words. Use a thesaurus or other reference book to replace any of these as well.

Grammar in Action. Identify the comparative adjective in the excerpt on p. 237.

Adjectives

Specific adjectives strengthen descriptions of the nouns they precede. Describing your brother as your *little* brother gives readers important information, but describing him as your *sniveling little* brother really sharpens the image. Some adjectives are so commonplace that writers should avoid them. Adjectives such as *pretty, good, cute, great,* and *bad* are often overused. They do not really contribute to a reader's "mental picture" of the noun either. What are some other weak or overused adjectives?

Adverbs

Adverbs also help to enliven a piece of descriptive narrative, but like all modifiers, they should be used in moderation. Remember that one well-chosen, particular verb can usually accomplish more in a sentence than one or more adverbs modifying a commonplace verb.

Use adverbs sparingly to strengthen the verbs they follow.

Dana laughed at my joke.
Dana laughed *uproariously* at my joke.

Avoid using an adverb when a more exact verb would accomplish the job.

Koi smiled slightly at my joke.
Koi *grinned* at my joke.

ACTIVITY D Write an adjective that adds a specific detail to the italicized noun in each sentence.

1. A *cloud* hovered over our heads.
2. Justin is practicing jumps on his *skateboard*.
3. My *puppy* loves to doze in front of the fire on cold winter nights.
4. Have you seen the *film* about Mars exploration?
5. I got a *wet suit* and flippers for my birthday.
6. Do you think this *sweater* and shirt match?
7. We vacationed at a *ranch* in Montana.
8. One of the *fish* in the class aquarium ate another fish.
9. It's amazing that *butterflies* migrate from Canada to Mexico.
10. I hope it rains today so I can wear my *slicker*.
11. My new laptop has a *screen saver* from our climb up Mount Everest.

ACTIVITY E Add an adverb that strengthens the italicized verb in each sentence.

1. My two-year-old sister *talks*, but she's not easy to understand.
2. Our dog *runs* to the door when the doorbell rings.
3. "Buy me some ice cream," Gabriel's sister *said*.
4. Marta *sang*, and she didn't need a microphone.
5. Dwayne *followed* behind me on the narrow trail.
6. The audience *clapped* after Marcus finished his speech.
7. Emotional people *cry* at sad movies.
8. The cat jumped from the bookcase just as it *fell* to the ground.
9. Justin *threw* his broken MP3 player onto the ground.
10. The pollution pouring out of the old factory *smelled*.

ACTIVITY F Select five sentences you revised in Activity E. Replace the verb and adverb with a single specific verb. Make sure the new word does not contradict or lose the meaning of the original sentence.

ACTIVITY G Below is a paragraph from a personal narrative. Rewrite it, replacing vague and overused words with specific and more interesting choices. Add detail by using adjectives and adverbs.

I was just starting to eat lunch when the Daly City earthquake happened. I heard a noise that got louder and louder. Then the shaking began. Mom got me and we went to the doorway. We lay down on the floor, and she put her body over mine. I heard lots of noises. I looked under Mom's arm. Kitchen supplies were moving, and the kitchen windows were opening and shutting. Then there was silence. The earthquake was over. When Mom opened the kitchen cabinets, broken glass and china came out. We laughed, happy to be safe.

WRITER'S CORNER

Choose three sentences from Activity D. Rewrite them, using different adjectives that change the meaning of the sentences. Then review your personal narrative. Add detail with adjectives and adverbs.

Grammar in Action. Identify the abstract nouns in the excerpt on p. 237.

Oral Personal Narratives

You tell stories from your life, or personal narratives, every day. When you describe to your friend what happened at a party, when you tell your parents about your day at school, when you explain to your teacher why you were late for school, you are delivering a personal narrative. To tell your story well, you must remember what happened, describe it to your audience in an understandable way, and answer their questions. It takes planning and practice to guarantee success.

Purpose

Having a clear purpose will help you deliver a focused and an effective personal narrative. The purpose of your narrative can guide your word choices, imagery, and organization. The purpose of your narrative may be to relate a story about an event. It may be to share with your audience what an event has taught you. Try to have a clear purpose in mind as you begin your narrative.

Structure

An oral personal narrative is structurally organized like a written one, though the language may differ slightly. Lure your listeners with an engaging introduction. Introduce your topic and tell the story logically, using interesting details. Conclude by describing what you learned or by offering an overall message.

Audience

Who is your audience? How will your words affect them? Sometimes speaking requires a more careful choice of words than does writing. Identify your audience so that your tone and word choice will be appropriate. Some of your favorite words on paper may sound stiff or awkward when you read them aloud. Make changes to your narrative so that sentences flow and words do not sound awkward.

ACTIVITY A Below are titles of personal narratives to be presented to a large audience. Write a short introduction for each title. Have each introduction appeal to one of the following audiences: classmates, judges at a storytelling contest, or a community group.

1. I Was an Archaeologist for a Day
2. How I Learned to Live with My Little Brother
3. That Snap Was My Leg!
4. Two Long Weeks as a Camp Counselor
5. My Garden and How It Grew
6. A Day When Everything Went Wrong

ACTIVITY B Read aloud these sentences from personal narratives. Rewrite them so that they sound smoother and more natural when read aloud.

1. As I climbed hand over hand up the side of the cliff wall, my hand came in contact with something bumpy and warm, which turned out to be an iguana.

2. Folding laundry in my family is a complicated process and one that should not be engaged in without training because every single family member likes his or her clothes folded in a different way.

3. I was too frightened to take notice of the beauty of the spectacular branch of lightning that illuminated the sky.

4. That's the manner in which I learned that the first and most important rule to follow when cooking from a recipe is to read through all the steps slowly and with deliberation.

5. "Write the way you speak" is a phrase I have heard on many occasions from my teacher Mr. Whittaker, but he fails to understand that the advice does not always work due to the fact that my jumbled speech never sounds good when written down.

Tech Tip With an adult, go online for synonyms of boring words.

SPEAKER'S CORNER

Read your introductory paragraphs aloud several times to a partner. Ask your partner what kind of tone he or she identifies from the introduction, and what words or sentences help capture his or her interest. Replace words or sentences your partner finds boring or awkward. Reread the narratives at the beginning of this chapter for further practice.

Prepare

Don't read your narrative directly from your paper. It will sound monotonous and dull. Instead, write key phrases for each idea on a sheet of paper or on note cards. You may wish to bring a visual, such as a photograph or a small object related to your story. Plan how you will use your visual beforehand.

Present

Present your personal narrative to a partner or small group. Ask your audience to critique both the content of your story and your presentation. Keep these speaking tips in mind:

- Establish eye contact with your audience. Scan across everyone in the group instead of locking eyes with one person.
- Speak clearly and slowly so that everyone can follow your narrative. Avoid saying *um, ah, well,* or *you know.*
- Vary your pitch and pace for emphasis. For example, you might slow down at a quiet moment in your story or speak with more urgency during a climactic part. Use facial expressions, gestures, and movements to reinforce your intended meaning.

Listening Tips

Just as you can become a better speaker, with practice you can become a better listener. Here are some suggestions for improving your listening skills.

- Look at the speaker. Give him or her the same attention you would want if you were speaking. Show that you are listening by smiling, nodding, or responding in some other nonverbal way at appropriate times.
- Pay close attention. Try to picture what the speaker is describing and listen for key words that signal important ideas. Figure out where the story is heading and identify the main ideas or theme of the speech.
- Don't interrupt the speaker. If you have a question or want to critique a point, write a quick note to yourself.
- At the end of the talk, ask questions or give feedback if you are invited to do so. Mention a few things you liked about the presentation and include suggestions for improvement.

ACTIVITY C Read aloud each of the following sentences twice, expressing a different emotion each time you read. Vary the pacing, volume, and emphasis, as well as expressions, gestures, and movements. Ask a classmate to identify the emotions you are expressing.

1. Will a puppy that tiny survive?
2. I can see the finish line and the cheering crowd up ahead.
3. Is that really a cheesecake?
4. My eyes widened as I saw all the fish around me.
5. The grapes those people are stamping with their bare feet will become wine.

ACTIVITY D Present an extemporaneous, or unplanned, talk (about one minute long) to a partner. Keep in mind what you have learned about being a good listener when your partner is speaking. Choose from the following topics for your talk:

1. why I was late for school
2. an adventure I'll never forget
3. my first day at a new school
4. the funniest person I've ever met
5. clothes shopping with a parent
6. a great triumph playing a sport
7. something about me that people would never guess
8. the weirdest food I ever ate
9. a time when my best friend and I had a fight
10. the strangest day of my life

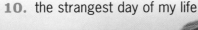
Record a podcast of your personal narrative.

SPEAKER'S CORNER

Present the personal narrative idea you completed and revised in the Writer's Corner on page 237. Write your introductory sentence and some key phrases on a sheet of paper or note cards. Then present your personal narrative aloud to a small group. Reread the narratives at the beginning of this chapter for extra practice.

Prewriting and Drafting

In this chapter you have considered the characteristics of personal narratives, ways to organize your thoughts, and writing skills that will help you make your writing colorful and concise. Now you will use everything that you have learned so far to draft, revise, and publish a personal narrative.

Prewriting

Prewriting is a time to brainstorm, choose a writing topic, and freewrite to explore ideas. It is also a time to develop a plan for how you will organize

Ideas and structure your writing. There are several prewriting techniques that you can use: lists or charts, doodles or drawings, graphic organizers, or simply jotting down ideas on paper.

Writer's Tip Brainstorming is quickly generating many ideas, recording anything that comes to mind.

Freewriting is generating more information about your brainstormed ideas.

Brainstorming

Brainstorming can assist you in choosing a topic. When you brainstorm, quickly jot all possible ideas for your topic. The following steps can assist you in brainstorming:

- Start writing ideas. Write anything that comes to mind. Use a graphic organizer such as a clustering web to help you pursue ideas and develop themes.
- When you have run out of ideas, carefully read what you have written. Do you notice any themes or incidents that keep cropping up?

Jacob, an eighth grader, needs to think of a topic for a personal narrative. His brainstorming web is shown here. What topics for a personal narrative do they suggest to you?

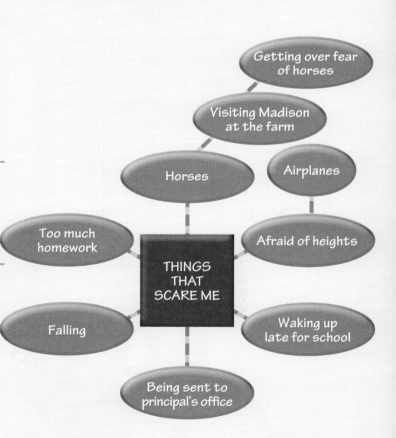

Things that scare me:
- Getting over fear of horses
- Visiting Madison at the farm
- Horses
- Airplanes
- Too much homework
- Afraid of heights
- Falling
- THINGS THAT SCARE ME
- Waking up late for school
- Being sent to principal's office

Freewriting

After choosing a topic, begin freewriting. When you freewrite, you explore and expand on ideas about the topic that you chose. Record whatever comes to mind about the topic. The more ideas you have, the more material you have to work with when you begin to write your narrative. Use graphic organizers as freewriting tools to record events, details, and other ideas.

 **Organization** After a productive freewriting session, you can begin arranging your ideas into a narrative structure. One way to do this is to create a time line for your narrative. Your time line will help you put your story in chronological order.

Jacob created the time line below for his narrative.

Your Turn

Brainstorm some topics for a personal narrative. Then use freewriting to flesh out your ideas. Organize your ideas, using a time line. Use the following suggestions:

- Use one of these prompts as you brainstorm topics:
  The first, last, only time I . . .
  My worst, best, most surprising day
  A person, place, experience I'll never forget
  My greatest accomplishment or biggest mistake
- After choosing your topic, spend three minutes freewriting. Write whatever comes into your head. You can use different graphic organizers to help you.
- Organize your thoughts in chronological order by creating a time line.

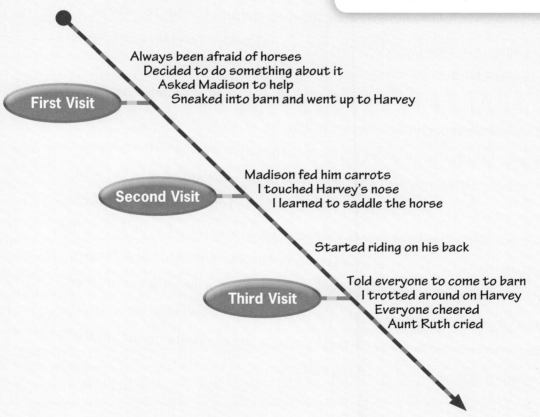

First Visit
Always been afraid of horses
Decided to do something about it
Asked Madison to help
Sneaked into barn and went up to Harvey

Second Visit
Madison fed him carrots
I touched Harvey's nose
I learned to saddle the horse

Started riding on his back

Third Visit
Told everyone to come to barn
I trotted around on Harvey
Everyone cheered
Aunt Ruth cried

Prewriting
Drafting
Content Editing
Revising
Copyediting
Proofreading
Publishing

Drafting

A draft is your first chance to develop and organize your prewriting notes into a coherent narrative. Jacob had brainstormed a topic, used freewriting to think of details, and created a time line to organize his narrative. How did these steps help Jacob write his first draft below? When do you think he decided on his title? Read Jacob's draft and reflect on these questions.

Not Too Scary

I have no idea where my fear of horses came from. Fear of horses is called equinophobia. Maybe a horse thought I was a bucket of oats when I was a baby! Just kidding. Since I live in the suburbs of Philadelphia, this fear wasn't really a big problem, at least not during the school year, but in the summer I usually visit Aunt Ruth and Uncle Henry's farm, and that's when my equinophobia became a problem. Last summer I decided to do something about my problem. I couldn't go on trail rides with my cousins. Heck, I couldn't even go on hayrides. I couldn't go anywhere on or near a horse.

I asked for the aid of my cousin Madison. Madison is 16. She promised not to tell anyone about our project. For over two weeks, we got up before anyone else. We went off to the barn together. On the first day, we just went near Harvey's stall. We thought a 15-year-old shetland pony would be the easiest to get used to. I went as close to him as I could before my mouth got dry and my heart started beating overtime. Madison fed him carrots. I watched. Then we went back to the house. The next day Harvey nickered when we approached his stall. I touched Harvey's nose, which was nice, while Madison fed him carrots. The rest of the week went that way. I got a bit more comfortable with Harvey. Harvey really is a sweet and nice pony. The next week I learned to saddle the horse and walk him around the paddok. By the beginning of week three I was riding the horse.

At the end of that week, Madison and me called everyone down to the barn. They couldn't believe it when I put the saddle and bridle on Harvey, led him into the paddok, and got on. We trotted! I know we'll be cantering soon. My cousins were surprised. They jumped up and down. They cheered. Aunt Ruth even teared up a little, just because she was so proud of me, she said. I was proud of me! And if you break down something you're afraid of into tiny steps and do it little by little, you'll soon be proud of yourself too.

Everyone has a distinctive way of speaking that is unique. Similarly, every writer uses a distinctive voice. This voice is based on word choice, descriptions, tone, pace, punctuation, and other stylistic devices. It is the "personality" of the narrator. If your writing sounds flat or unnatural, it does not reflect voice.

Voice

Writer's Tip Many writers find writing introductions and conclusions difficult. If that's true of you, write the body first and tackle the other parts later.

Your Turn

Look back at your freewriting and your time line as you plan to write a draft of your personal narrative. Before you begin writing your draft, recall the following characteristics of effective personal narratives:

- first-person point of view
- tone appropriate for audience
- apparent theme or purpose
- sensory details
- specific word choices

Now begin to write. If you are using a pen and paper, leave extra space between lines so you have room to edit later. If you are typing, use double-spacing. Write quickly and clearly to get all your good ideas recorded.

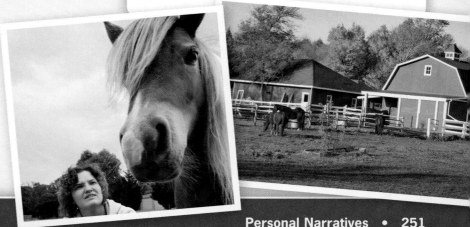

Prewriting

Drafting

Content Editing

Revising

Copyediting

Proofreading

Publishing

Editor's Workshop

Content Editing

When you content edit, you edit ideas for logic, order, and clarity. A content editor notices how well the ideas of a piece are expressed and checks to make certain that all of the necessary information is included. To help you make corrections and improvements to a personal narrative, use the checklist below as you revise your draft.

Jacob was pleased with the draft of his personal narrative. However he knew he could improve it. Armed with a red pen, the draft, and the Content Editor's Checklist, Jacob began content editing. First, he read his draft aloud and made marks beside parts of the draft that he felt needed to be deleted, replaced, or rearranged. Then he reread his draft and fine-tuned it some more. Based on the Content Editor's Checklist and your reading of his draft, what changes do you feel he needed to make?

Next, Jacob traded drafts with his classmate Cody. He knew Cody could help him by pointing out the confusing, repetitive, and awkward parts in the draft.

Writer's Tip Exact, descriptive words will make your ideas more clear and complete.

Content Editor's Checklist

☐ Does the introduction make the reader want to read more?

☐ Does the body of the narrative tell the events clearly?

☐ Is the order of events logical?

☐ Are additional details needed for clarity?

☐ Are there unnecessary details that keep the narrative from flowing?

☐ Are the ideas clearly conveyed through the choice of words?

☐ Are transition words used to help the reader follow the events?

☐ Is there a coherent balance of simple, compound, and complex sentences?

☐ Does the conclusion leave the audience with something to remember?

Cody read a copy of Jacob's draft silently as well as aloud. Next, Cody used the Content Editor's Checklist to help him edit the draft. He made some notes on the copy and some on a separate sheet of paper.

After Cody had finished editing, he and Jacob conferred. Cody offered positive feedback first. He told Jacob that he chose a great incident to write about, one that was important to Jacob and interesting to readers. Then Cody offered the following suggestions for improving Jacob's draft:

- I like the sentence *Maybe a horse thought I was a bucket of oats as a baby!* It is funny, and it made me want to keep reading.

- Think about moving the sentence *Last summer I decided to do something about my problem.* It doesn't seem to fit. Otherwise, the way you have organized your narrative makes it easy to read.

- Can you include more description about Harvey? Some sensory words might help a reader picture what you are describing.

- Replace words like *went* and *nice* with more exact words that explain your ideas more clearly.

- I thought that your conclusion was effective. You gave some really good advice about how to do something that you were afraid to do.

Your Turn

Use the Content Editor's Checklist to guide the editing of your own draft as you follow these steps:

- Read your draft silently and aloud several times as you edit. Each time you read, you will notice something new.
- Trade drafts with a classmate. If possible, have your partner write corrections on a copy of your draft and do the same for him or her.
- Meet with your partner to discuss the drafts and make suggestions for improving them.

When you content edit your partner's draft, begin by pointing out a few things that you liked. Be honest and courteous in your comments.

Prewriting

Drafting

Content Editing

Revising

Copyediting

Proofreading

Publishing

Revising

This is Jacob's edited draft, which he revised based on his own and Cody's suggestions.

Not Too Scary

I have no idea where my fear of horses came from *, or equinaphobia*. ~~Fear of horses is called equinophobia.~~ Maybe a horse thought I was a bucket of oats when I was a baby! ~~Just kidding.~~ Since I live in the suburbs of Philadelphia, this fear wasn't ~~really~~ a big problem, ~~at least not~~ during the school year, but in the summer I usually visit Aunt Ruth and Uncle Henry's farm, and that's when my equinophobia ~~became a problem~~ *really bothered me*. ~~Last summer I decided to do something about my problem.~~ I couldn't go on trail rides with my cousins *, and* ~~Heck,~~ I couldn't ~~even~~ go on hayrides. *In fact,* I couldn't go anywhere on or near a horse. *Last summer I decided to do something about it.*

I asked for the aid of my *16-year-old* cousin Madison. ~~Madison is 16.~~ She promised not to tell anyone about our project. For over two weeks, we got up before anyone else. ~~We went~~ *and sneaked* off to the barn together. On the first day, we just ~~went near~~ *stood at* Harvey's stall. (We thought a 15-year-old shetland pony would be the easiest to get used to.) I went as close to him as I could before my mouth got dry and my heart started beating overtime. Madison fed him *crunchy* carrots, *as* I watched *his huge teeth grind them up.* Then we ~~went~~ *crept* back to the house, *before anyone woke up.* The next day Harvey nickered when we approached his stall. I touched Harvey's nose, which was ~~nice~~ *soft and velvety*, while Madison fed him carrots. The rest of the week ~~went that~~ *proceeded the same* way. I ~~got~~ *became* a bit more comfortable with *the gentle* Harvey. ~~Harvey really is a sweet and nice pony.~~ The next week I learned to saddle the horse and walk him around the paddok. By the beginning of week three I was riding the horse.

At the end of that week, Madison and me called everyone ~~down~~ to the barn.

They couldn't believe it when I put the saddle and bridle on Harvey, led him into the paddock, and ~~got on. We trotted! I know we'll be cantering soon. My cousins were~~ *climbed aboard. We trotted briskly around the field. My Cousins were so* ~~surprised. They jumped up and down. They cheered.~~ Aunt Ruth even teared up a *astonished they stood dumbfounded for a moment. Then they jumped up and down and cheered* *noisily.* little, ~~just because she was so proud of me, she said.~~ *"I'm just so proud of you" she sniffed.* I was proud of me! ~~And if you~~ ~~break down something you're afraid of into tiny steps and do it little by little,~~ *If you conquer something you're afraid of,* you'll ~~soon~~ be proud of yourself too.

Here are some ways that Jacob improved his draft:

- Jacob appreciated Cody's compliment, but as he reread his draft, he noticed that he could make his introduction stronger. How did he accomplish this?
- He agreed with Cody about the sentence *Last summer I decided to do something about my problem.* How did he revise this sentence?
- What descriptive words did he add about Harvey?
- Jacob had already found more descriptive

   Word Choice

  words for *nice*, but he agreed that he used the word *went* too often. How did he address this problem?

As Jacob revised his draft, he noticed that Cody had missed the checkpoint about unnecessary details on the Content Editor's Checklist. What unnecessary information or details did Jacob delete? What are some other changes Jacob made to his draft? What other changes might you suggest?

Grammar in Action

Jacob's use of appositives adds clarity to his narrative. Identify one example of an appositive from Jacob's narrative. Can you find a second?

Your Turn

Read your own and your partner's edits.

- Decide which edits to include in your revision.
- Ask yourself the questions on the Content Editor's Checklist once again to decide whether additional changes would improve your narrative.
- Write or type a revised draft of your narrative.

Prewriting

Drafting

Content Editing

Revising

Copyediting

Proofreading

Publishing

Copyediting and Proofreading

Copyediting

When you copyedit, you should look for accuracy in word meaning, word choice, and sentence structure, and review the overall logic of the piece. After making extensive changes to his draft, Jacob wanted to make sure that his work was logical and coherent. He used the following checklist to copyedit his draft.

Conventions

Writer's Tip Unique words that suggest a feeling or tone can enhance the narrator's voice.

Copyeditor's Checklist

- ☐ Are transition words used correctly?
- ☐ Do any words seem out of place or awkward?
- ☐ Do the chosen words or phrases convey their intended meaning?
- ☐ Are there any run-on or rambling sentences?
- ☐ Do the verb tenses agree?
- ☐ Are the structures of sentences logical and grammatically correct?

What verbs did he change to more accurately convey his intended meaning?

Your Turn

Use the Copyeditor's Checklist to copyedit your draft. If possible, read the draft aloud to an editing partner. What words do you want to change? Are the sentences coherent? What does your editing partner notice?

Proofreading

Writers proofread to find mistakes in spelling, grammar, punctuation, and capitalization. They also check to make certain that no new errors have been introduced during revising. Jacob used the Proofreader's Checklist to catch mistakes in the revised draft.

A proofreader can offer a new set of eyes when editing a piece of writing. Jacob asked his friend Miles to proofread his draft. Jacob knew that because Miles had a fresh perspective, he might spot errors that Jacob and Cody had missed. After Miles had proofread Jacob's draft, Jacob used a dictionary, a thesaurus, and a language arts textbook to check the things that Miles had marked.

Proofreader's Checklist

- ☐ Are the paragraphs indented?
- ☐ Have any words been misspelled?
- ☐ Are the beginnings of sentences and proper nouns capitalized?
- ☐ Is the grammar accurate?
- ☐ Is punctuation correct?
- ☐ Were new errors introduced during editing?

Your Turn

Proofread your revised draft.

- Use the Proofreader's Checklist to help you or make one of your own that includes the kinds of errors that you make most frequently.
- If you can, proofread with a partner as Jacob and Miles did.
- Use a note card or sheet of paper so that you scan the draft one line at a time. Reading line by line will keep you from reading too quickly and missing mistakes.

Prewriting
Drafting
Content Editing
Revising
Copyediting
Proofreading
Publishing

Common Proofreading Marks

Symbol	Meaning	Example
¶	begin new paragraph	over. Begin a new
◡	close up space	close u p space
∧	insert	students think (should)
℘	delete, omit	that the the book
/	lowercase letter	Mathematics
∼	letters are reversed	letters are reversed
≡	capitalize	washington
⌄⌄	quotation	I am, I said.
⊙	period	Marta drank tea

Writer's Workshop

Publishing

Publishing is the moment when you decide to share your final work. You know it is your best work and you are ready to show it to your audience. After several editing sessions, Jacob felt he had done his best. See if you can find the spelling and punctuation errors he corrected while proofreading. It was now time for the finished version. Jacob typed it on a computer and printed it out. Then he proofread it one more time to make sure there were no errors. Finally, he was ready to publish his work.

Not Too Scary

I have no idea where my fear of horses, or equinophobia, came from. Maybe a horse mistook me for a bucket of oats when I was a baby! Since I live in the suburbs of Philadelphia, this fear wasn't a big problem during the school year. But in the summer I usually visit Aunt Ruth and Uncle Henry's farm, and that's when my equinophobia really bothered me. I couldn't go on trail rides with my cousins, and I couldn't enjoy hayrides. In fact, I couldn't travel anywhere on a horse or even be anywhere near one. Last summer I decided to do something about my phobia.

I asked my 16-year-old cousin Madison for help and made her promise not to tell anyone. For over two weeks, we got up before anyone else and sneaked off to the barn together. We thought a 15-year-old Shetland pony would be the easiest horse to get used to, so that's why we chose Harvey. On the first day, we just stood at Harvey's stall. I went as close to him as I could before my mouth got dry and my heart started beating overtime. Madison fed him crunchy carrots as I watched his huge yellow teeth grind them up. Then we crept back to the house before anyone woke up.

The next day Harvey nickered when we approached his stall. I touched Harvey's nose, which felt soft and velvety, while Madison fed him. The rest of the week proceeded the same way. Each day I became a bit more comfortable with the gentle Harvey. The next week I learned to saddle the horse and walk him around the paddock. By the beginning of the third week, I was riding.

At the end of that week, Madison and I summoned everyone to the barn. They couldn't believe it when I put the saddle and bridle on Harvey, led him into the paddock, and climbed aboard. We trotted briskly up around the field. My cousins were so astonished they stood dumbfounded for a moment. Then they jumped up and down and cheered noisily. Aunt Ruth became a little teary-eyed. "I'm just so proud of you," she sniffed. I was proud of myself! If you conquer something you're afraid of, you'll be proud of yourself too.

When you have finished, share your personal narrative by publishing it. Choose a publishing option from the list below.

 Create a class magazine with your classmates. Work together to decide on a name for your magazine and to design a cover illustration. Consider distributing copies of your finished magazine to other classes and the school library.

 You can give your narrative as a gift. This is a good idea if you are giving it to a person featured in your narrative. Jacob decided he would give his narrative to his aunt, uncle, and cousin Madison.

 Create a personal portfolio on your class blog and post your narrative in it for classmates to read. You can include pictures and a brief bio of yourself to accompany your narrative.

 Submit your personal narrative to a professional magazine or a Web site that publishes student writing. There are also many student writing competitions in which you can enter your work. Ask your teacher or librarian to help you find a suitable contest for your work.

 Create a class book for a younger grade.

Writer's Tip Before you submit your personal narrative to a professional publisher, read a sample copy online or in a library to see whether the publication is the right one for your work. Then find out what the submission guidelines are and follow them exactly.

Your Turn

Eventually, a professional writer submits his or her work to **Presentation** a magazine, newspaper, or publisher. The final purpose of any writing is presenting it to an audience.

Although the writing you do in school might not be printed in a book or magazine, the moment you share your work with your class or other audience should be an exciting moment. Make sure that your work is in its best form before you present it. To publish your work, follow these steps:

- Use your neatest handwriting or a computer to make a final copy of your work.
- Proofread your copy one more time for correct spelling and punctuation. If you are using a computer, use the spell-checker and grammar-checker. Reread the final hard copy for printing problems such as cut-off margins or sentences.

Prewriting

Drafting

Content Editing

Revising

Copyediting

Proofreading

Publishing

How-to Articles

LiNK Electrical Kite

by Benjamin Franklin
Article from *The Pennsylvania Gazette*
October 19, 1752

Make a small cross of two light strips of cedar, the arms so long as to reach to the four corners of a large thin silk handkerchief when extended; tie the corners of the handkerchief to the extremities of the cross, so you have the body of a kite; which being properly accommodated with a tail, loop, and string, will rise in the air . . . To the top of the upright stick of the cross is to be fixed a sharp pointed wire . . . To the end of the twine, next the key may be fastened. This kite is to be raised when a thunder-gust appears to be coming on, and the person who holds the string must stand within a door or window . . . care must be taken that the twine does not touch the frame of the door. As soon as any of the thunder clouds come over the kite, the pointed wire will draw the electric fire from them, and the kite, with all the twine, will be electrified . . .

Benjamin Franklin

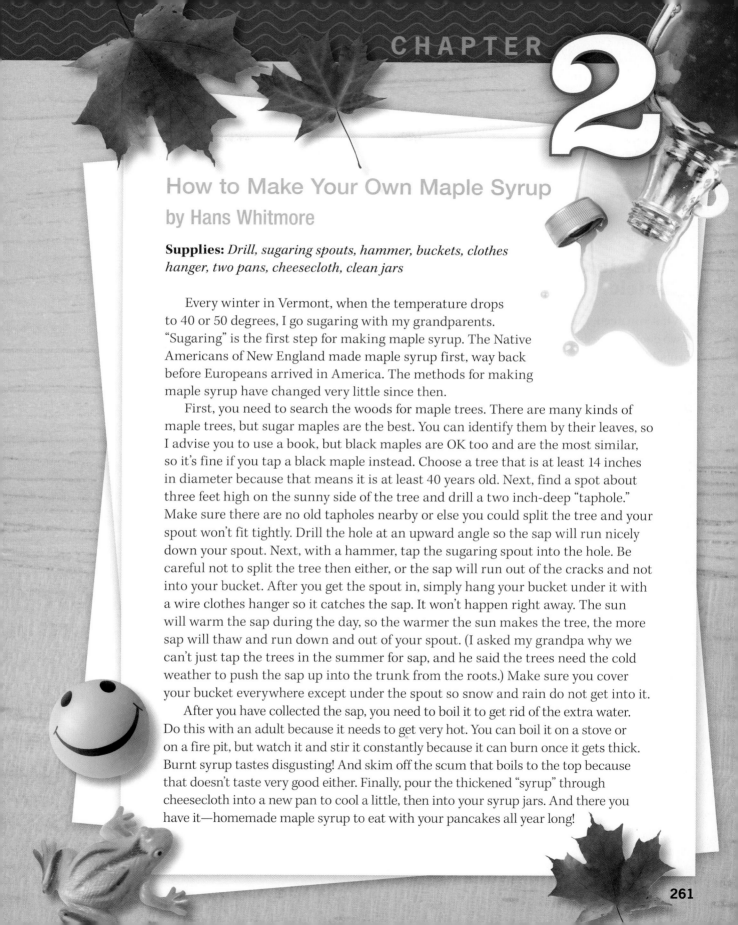

CHAPTER 2

How to Make Your Own Maple Syrup
by Hans Whitmore

Supplies: *Drill, sugaring spouts, hammer, buckets, clothes hanger, two pans, cheesecloth, clean jars*

Every winter in Vermont, when the temperature drops to 40 or 50 degrees, I go sugaring with my grandparents. "Sugaring" is the first step for making maple syrup. The Native Americans of New England made maple syrup first, way back before Europeans arrived in America. The methods for making maple syrup have changed very little since then.

First, you need to search the woods for maple trees. There are many kinds of maple trees, but sugar maples are the best. You can identify them by their leaves, so I advise you to use a book, but black maples are OK too and are the most similar, so it's fine if you tap a black maple instead. Choose a tree that is at least 14 inches in diameter because that means it is at least 40 years old. Next, find a spot about three feet high on the sunny side of the tree and drill a two inch-deep "taphole." Make sure there are no old tapholes nearby or else you could split the tree and your spout won't fit tightly. Drill the hole at an upward angle so the sap will run nicely down your spout. Next, with a hammer, tap the sugaring spout into the hole. Be careful not to split the tree then either, or the sap will run out of the cracks and not into your bucket. After you get the spout in, simply hang your bucket under it with a wire clothes hanger so it catches the sap. It won't happen right away. The sun will warm the sap during the day, so the warmer the sun makes the tree, the more sap will thaw and run down and out of your spout. (I asked my grandpa why we can't just tap the trees in the summer for sap, and he said the trees need the cold weather to push the sap up into the trunk from the roots.) Make sure you cover your bucket everywhere except under the spout so snow and rain do not get into it.

After you have collected the sap, you need to boil it to get rid of the extra water. Do this with an adult because it needs to get very hot. You can boil it on a stove or on a fire pit, but watch it and stir it constantly because it can burn once it gets thick. Burnt syrup tastes disgusting! And skim off the scum that boils to the top because that doesn't taste very good either. Finally, pour the thickened "syrup" through cheesecloth into a new pan to cool a little, then into your syrup jars. And there you have it—homemade maple syrup to eat with your pancakes all year long!

What Makes a Good How-to Article?

LiNK

Magic Card Trick

What you need:
Two decks of cards. It's probably a good idea to make them full decks, too.

To Perform:

1. Give your friend the choice of either pack of cards. It doesn't matter, really. Then, ask him to shuffle his pack; you shuffle yours. Really mix them up, too. . . .

(continued on page 269)

How-to writing is a form of exposition, or informative writing, that gives directions for doing something. How-to writing can offer non-technical guidance, as in "How to Be a Good Leader," or provide step-by-step instructions, as in "How to Make Chocolate Chip Pancakes." It can be as simple as "How to Color Eggs" or as complex as "How to Build a Model of the White House." How-to writing is all around us: in the user's guides that accompany products, in magazine recipes, in craft instructions, in student handbooks. Where do you most often encounter how-to writing?

Here are a few points to keep in mind when you write a how-to article. How closely did the author of "How to Make Your Own Maple Syrup" follow these guidelines?

Audience

Before you begin, consider the audience you are writing for. This will affect both the level of detail and the tone of your writing. An audience that knows how to cook won't need to be told how to turn the oven on. An audience that has never been to your community will need more details when you give directions. If you're writing to a friend, you can use a friendly, informal tone. However, writing an instruction booklet will require a more formal tone.

Introduction

The title and the first paragraph should state clearly the purpose of the how-to article—that is, it should say what is being explained. If necessary, emphasize why the topic is significant. Why would your reader benefit from following the steps you describe? You may want to engage readers with a fascinating first sentence, which should provide background information or stress the significance of your topic.

Body

In the body of a how-to article, describe the steps required to accomplish the goal. Use imperative sentences, which are sentences written in the form of commands. Present the steps in chronological order, providing just enough detail for readers to understand clearly. Organize each step or each group of similar steps into a paragraph.

Conclusion

In the conclusion assure your audience that by following the steps as given, they will be successful, or make a prediction about the impact of their success.

ACTIVITY A Read the list of titles for how-to articles. To what audience would each appeal? Choose five titles and write engaging introductory sentences for each.

1. Recipes for Gourmet Sandwiches
2. You Can Create and Use a Blog
3. Learning to Dress Well
4. How to Run for Political Office
5. Clean the Messiest Bedroom in Less Than 15 Minutes
6. Basic Figure Skating
7. Simple Steps to a Perfect Pie Crust
8. How to Make Friends and How to Keep Them

ACTIVITY B Choose three titles from Activity A. For each title write two questions you would expect to learn the answers to if you read a how-to article on the topic.

WRITER'S CORNER

Brainstorm a list of things you know how to do. Choose a few that would make interesting and unique how-to articles.

 Use an online word web program to brainstorm ideas.

The How-to Article Checklist

When you write a how-to article, there are many questions to keep in mind that will help make your writing clear and engaging. Use the following checklist when you evaluate your writing:

Title and Introduction

☐ Does the title clearly state the topic?

☐ Does the introduction explain the purpose of the how-to article?

☐ Does the introduction engage readers in the topic?

Body

☐ Are the steps in the right order?

☐ Are they clear?

☐ Are all the important steps included?

☐ Is there any unnecessary information?

☐ Does each step give the right level of detail?

☐ Is the tone appropriate?

Conclusion

☐ Is there a conclusion?

☐ Does it sum up the process or invite the readers to make use of or enjoy what they've learned to do?

ACTIVITY C Use the How-to Article Checklist to evaluate the following paragraph. Search for any places where the writer failed to follow the checklist. Then discuss your findings with a small group.

How to Make Hot Chocolate

Here's something you can make. Put some chocolate along with about 1/4 cup of water into a double boiler. A double boiler is two pots that fit together. You heat water in the bottom pot so that whatever you put in the top heats or melts gently. You should probably use semisweet or bittersweet chocolate. My favorite is milk chocolate, but don't use that. Oh, and chop the chocolate. Melt the chocolate. Stir it every so often. Is it smooth yet? Go ahead and stop stirring. Whisk in some hot water into the top of the double-boiler pan, which you have removed from the stove. If you think people will want to add sugar or whipped cream, serve those so people can add their own. Since this recipe makes 4 cups, stir 3/4 cup of milk into each mug. Be sure to use 6 ounces of chocolate. And be sure the milk in the mugs is heated so that the drink will be warm enough.

ACTIVITY D Read these directions and check them over, using the How-to Article Checklist. Then evaluate other aspects of the how-to article by answering the questions that follow.

Getting to the Party

I hope you can come to my birthday party. These are directions to help you get here the quickest and most direct way. If you need help with the directions, just give us a call at (615) 555-0309.

Since most of you will be coming from the city, I'll start from there. Take I-96 north to the Bennett Avenue exit (#87). Then proceed east (right) for about five miles. You will go through three stoplights. After a small strip mall and a gas station on the north (left), you'll see Canfield Road. Turn north (left) onto Canfield. Keep going for two or three miles until you see a sign that reads Forest Park on the east (right). That's the entrance to our subdivision. Turn into the subdivision. You'll be on Parkview Place. Follow Parkview as it curves past Meadowdale and Goldenrod Lane. Just after Goldenrod cuts in, you'll find 1001 Parkview, our big yellow house with green shutters.

Finally, you're here! We'll have a sign out front and plenty of food, music, and fun inside.

1. In which sentence is the purpose stated?
2. What is the tone of the how-to article?
3. How does the writer's audience affect the level of detail she provides?
4. What are some ways the writer clarifies the directions?
5. How well would you be able to follow these directions? Explain.
6. Can you think of ways the directions might be improved?

WRITER'S CORNER

Choose one of the how-to article ideas from the list you wrote in the Writer's Corner on page 263. Write an introduction to your article that clearly states the topic and purpose of the article, and engages the reader.

Grammar in Action. Name the pronouns in the p. 262 excerpt.

Making Instructions Clear and Concise

When writing the steps of a how-to article, the key is to make your instructions clear and concise. As you write, keep in mind the following points to make sure that the steps are logical and easy to follow.

Use Chronological Order

While writing, mentally go through the process step by step, making sure that each step is told in the order in which it should be completed. If you remember something that has been omitted, go back and add it where it belongs.

Divide Steps into Paragraphs

If your how-to article is short, you may be able to fit all the directions into a single paragraph. However, if you have long or complicated directions, put each step or group of steps in a separate paragraph.

Use Transition Words and Phrases

Using transition words such as *first, next,* and *finally,* or phrases such as *when you have finished,* helps clarify the steps in the process.

Provide Enough Detail

Don't assume that somebody will know how much water is "a little" (in a recipe) or where Main Street is (when giving directions). Be specific and use exact words when explaining a step.

Omit Unnecessary Information

Leave out any information that distracts the reader from accomplishing the task you are describing.

ACTIVITY A Arrange the steps of the following recipes in chronological order. Then write the steps in paragraph form, using transition words and phrases to help the steps flow logically. (Hint: The final step in both recipes is in the correct position.)

Hard-boiled Eggs

Turn off stove.

Bring eggs and water to a boil.

Put on lid.

Cover eggs with water.

Place eggs in pot.

Turn on stove.

Remove pot from heat. Let eggs stand for a half hour.

Chewy Nutty Popcorn Balls

Melt caramels over medium heat.

Stir caramel until smooth.

Pour caramel over 10 cups of popcorn.

Wait about 30 seconds for caramel to cool slightly.

Place 1 pound of caramels and 3 cups of water in a double boiler.

Roll popcorn balls in chopped nuts.

Put butter on your hands so the caramel mixture won't stick.

Form popcorn/caramel mixture into balls.

Store at room temperature.

ACTIVITY B Sometimes the activities that we practice daily can be the hardest to explain. Choose one of the suggested activities or come up with your own. Create a list of steps, and then write the steps in paragraph form. Be sure to make them clear and concise. Use transition words and phrases.

Tying your shoes   Making a bed   Folding a T-shirt

Tech Tip Post your article on a class blog or wiki for peer review.

ACTIVITY C Rewrite the following how-to article. First, take the transition words and phrases below and insert them in the spaces where they belong. Then divide the how-to article into three paragraphs, putting each step or set of steps in a separate paragraph.

How to Make Perfect Coffee

Follow these steps for a delectable cup of coffee each time you brew. _____, use clean equipment. Wash your coffeemaker with vinegar and water at least once a week. _____, grind the beans, which should be as fresh as possible. Make sure the grind you are using matches your brewing method: grind for 5 to 10 seconds for percolators, 10 seconds for drip and French press coffeemakers, 15 seconds for vacuum methods, and 25 to 40 seconds for espresso machines. _____, measure the ground coffee. Use 2 level tablespoons for every 6 ounces of coffee. _____, brew the coffee with clear, pure water, following the instructions for the method you are using. _____, warm the cup. Pour the coffee into the cup. _____, enjoy your perfectly brewed cup of coffee. To enjoy the rest of the pot just as much, don't let the coffee sit on a warmer for longer than 15 or 20 minutes, and never reheat it.

Transition words and phrases

Next	Once you have measured the coffee grounds
First	While the coffee is brewing
Finally	Just before you brew the coffee

ACTIVITY D The steps presented here on how to catch a fish are out of order. First, put the steps in their proper order. Then rewrite each step as a complete sentence, using transition words or phrases in each sentence. Add detail when necessary.

1. Reel in fish.
2. Bait hook.
3. Release fish.
4. Land fish and remove hook.
5. Choose a fishing rod and reel.
6. Cast your line into the water.

ACTIVITY E Rewrite the instructions for using electronic voting machines to make the steps easier to understand. Use the Body portion of the How-to Article Checklist to help you.

How to Use Electronic Voting Machines

Welcome to your friendly new electronic voting machine! Follow this procedure for each office you are voting for. You'll see small square touch pads that look like buttons instead of levers as in previous elections. But really, touching a square is easier than pulling a lever. Go into the voting booth. After you touch a square, a pleasant green light will come on. Touch the square at the right of the name of each candidate you want to vote for. If you change your mind, too bad! I'm kidding. Just touch the square again, and the green light will go off. Make another selection and touch the square again.

For write-in votes, go to the Personal Choice column and touch the square marked "write in." If you make a mistake, touch the write-in square again and start over. You can spend all day making changes if you want to. Use the keypad to enter the name.

When you are satisfied with your selections, touch the large red square at the bottom of the screen to cast your vote. You will hear a click that indicates your vote has been counted. Exit the polling booth. Congratulations! You've just cast your vote.

Magic Card Trick

(continued from page 262)

2. Switch packs, but as you do, glimpse the bottom card of your pack. Don't make a "move" out of this. Just casually tilt the deck, glimpse the card and memorize it. (If you forget this card, you're sunk!)

3. Ask your friend to fan the cards towards his face, remove any card and place it at the top of the pack. You do the same. (But don't memorize your card; keep the card in mind from Step 2). . . .

(continued on page 276)

WRITER'S CORNER

Write the steps for the topic you chose in the Writer's Corner on page 267. Use transition words and phrases. Trade your work with a partner for peer review. Save your work and partner's comments to use later.

Revising Sentences

In how-to articles, as in all writing, sentences should be clear and to the point. A sentence should usually focus on one idea or event, instead of going on and on (as this one does), because if the sentence is too long, the reader will not only run out of breath (if he or she is reading aloud), but also may become confused and forget what the sentence was about in the first place.

Run-on Sentences

Run-on sentences connect more than one independent clause without using conjunctions or appropriate punctuation. A run-on sentence is grammatically incorrect.

> **Read the directions carefully before you begin to assemble the model airplane, you should have newspaper laid out on the table.**

Rambling Sentences

A rambling sentence is a sentence with many ideas that, while it may be grammatically correct, should be shortened into several sentences for clarity.

> **Gather your paints and glue on the newspaper, then open the box, take the pieces out, and lay them on the table, and begin painting the body of the airplane whatever color you want.**

Run-on and rambling sentences are undesirable in any type of writing because they confuse the reader. They cause particular problems in how-to writing because the reader needs to understand each step before moving on to the next. How would you rewrite the run-on and rambling sentences on this page?

ACTIVITY A Divide these rambling sentences into several sentences.

1. To learn an acting role, you must first read over the part several times, consider the motivations of the character, then study the lines until you have memorized them and rehearse the role frequently with other actors.

2. Plan out what you will say before you go into the job interview, and bring with you a résumé and some samples of your previous work, and remember to shake the interviewer's hand and maintain frequent eye contact while you are talking.

3. To make an origami dove, take a square sheet of paper, then fold it into a rectangle and unfold it again and fold two corners into the center line.

4. I never told my brother he couldn't ever come into my room, but I asked him to knock first and wait for me to answer instead of just barging in because I need to be able to concentrate on my homework.

ACTIVITY B Correct the following run-on sentences by separating them into more than one sentence.

1. Wait for the paint to dry before you glue the pieces together, be sure you are wearing gloves.

2. A bill is first introduced by a member of Congress and must be passed by both the Senate and the House of Representatives, if different versions of the bill are passed, then members of both chambers will meet in a committee to resolve any differences, it is then sent to the president to sign or veto.

3. Make sure not to park your car on the left side of the street there is a no-parking zone.

WRITER'S CORNER

Rewrite Ben Franklin's "Electrical Kite," on page 260, breaking down his run-on and rambling sentences into shorter sentences. Compare your results with a partner's results.

Grammar in Action, Name the object pronouns in the second paragraph of the p. 261 excerpt.

Making Every Word Count

In describing the steps in a process, every word counts. If important details are left out, readers won't be able to follow the directions. Distracting and unnecessary words can also cause confusion because readers may not be able to wade through them to figure out what to do and how to do it.

Each of the three items below describes the final steps in baking muffins. Which set of directions is the clearest and most useful?

1. Take the muffins out of the oven when they are done, and let them cool for 5 minutes. Then let them cool on a rack for a while.
2. Are your muffins ready yet? If they are, you can think about taking them out and cooling them off. It's probably a good idea to cool them for about 5 minutes in the muffin pan and then move them to a rack (if you don't have a cooling rack, you can improvise) for another 15 minutes.
3. Take the muffins out of the oven when they are golden brown, and let them cool in the muffin pan for 5 minutes. Then move them to a wire cooling rack to continue cooling for 15 minutes longer.

The first set of directions is incomplete. It leaves out critical details, such as when to take the muffins out of the oven. The next set has unnecessary information. Its first sentence is not needed, and the information in parentheses is not helpful. The last set of directions explains exactly what, when, and why. Every word counts.

ACTIVITY C Choose which set of instructions in each group is the clearest and easiest to understand. Discuss reasons for your choices.

1. a. Stir the paint, whatever color it is. Make sure you like the color you picked. Pour the paint into a roller tray, or you can use a bucket or something else. But a roller tray is best. Paint the ceiling before you paint the walls. Use tape to keep paint from getting where you don't want it to be.

    b. Whenever you paint, you should start with the ceiling. Before you begin painting, tape off the wall. Stir the paint. Then pour it into a roller tray. Use a roller as you paint the ceiling.

    c. Start with the ceiling. Use tape. If you're a really good painter, you don't have to use tape. Stir the paint, and then pour it. Paint the ceiling. Don't forget to clean the roller after you have finished using it.

2. a. Combine 4 cups of shredded Monterey jack cheese, 4 beaten eggs, and 4 ounces of canned, chopped green chilies. Spread the ingredients into an 8-inch-square baking pan. Bake at 350°F for 30 minutes.

   b. You need Monterey jack cheese. You also need 4 eggs. You need 4 ounces of green chilies. First, beat the eggs. Make sure the chilies are chopped. Combine everything and spread the mixture into an 8-inch-square baking pan. Turn the oven to 350°F. Then put in the mixture and bake it for 30 minutes.

   c. Stir together some cheese, eggs, and a bunch of chopped green chilies or another kind of chili if you like. Put the ingredients into an 8-inch-square pan. Then bake it for a while in an oven.

ACTIVITY D Identify the unnecessary sentences in the how-to article below.

Setting up an aquarium is easy, but it requires patience. Although large saltwater tanks prove to be the easiest to maintain, they are tougher to set up. You have to add salt and make sure the pH is just right, and there is other stuff to do too. So I will tell you how to set up a freshwater aquarium, which is where a novice should begin. But saltwater aquariums are very cool. First, rinse the aquarium and the gravel thoroughly because the dust will negatively affect the water quality. Never use any kind of soap, not even glass cleaner, on the outside of the aquarium. Always use gravel bought at a store because gravel from your yard can contain chemicals or bacteria that will make your fish sick. There are many medications for curing sick fish. Cover the bottom of the tank with gravel, one inch deep. Next, fill the tank with water, adding a few drops of dechlorinator or simply let the water sit for a day because chlorine evaporates from water fairly quickly. Next, rinse and add decorations. While you are waiting for the chlorine to evaporate, rinse and install the filter and heater. There are many different types of filters and heaters, so follow the directions on the box. Turn them both on, and set the heater to 78 degrees. By the way, you can choose different colors of gravel. I prefer natural colored gravel, but white is also OK. Check the water pH to make sure it is between 6.8 and 7.0. Most tap water is around this pH anyway. If not, there are chemicals you can add. Once the water has reached the proper temperature, you can purchase and add your fish. But be sure to put a hood over the top of the tank to prevent water from evaporating too quickly or fish from jumping out. And float the bags with new fish in the water for a while first so the fish can adjust gradually. I like cichlids the most. Angelfish are pretty too. An octopus is a good choice for saltwater aquariums also.

WRITER'S CORNER

Look back at the steps you wrote in the Writer's Corner on page 267. Look for any unnecessary words or phrases. Add detail for clarity. Revise your steps so that every word counts.

Roots

Knowing the meaning of a word's root and its origin can help you understand the word and use it properly in your writing. For example, knowing that the root *fort* means "strong" can help you figure out that *fortitude* means "strength" or "endurance." The meaning of *somnambulist*, "sleepwalker," is clear if you know that *somnus* means "sleep" and *ambul* means "walk."

Many roots come from Latin and Greek, and some have interesting stories behind them. In the word *companion*, for example, *com* means "with" and *pan* means "bread," so *companion* means "someone you share bread with." Knowing the roots of the word *preposterous* will show you just how preposterous the word is. The roots *pre* and *post* mean "before" and "after." The word itself is a contradiction!

ACTIVITY A Read the list of roots and example words. Write a logical definition for each root, and then check the definition in a dictionary to see how accurate you were.

Root	Examples
1. *migr*	migrate, immigrant
2. *dent*	dentures, dentist
3. *loc*	local, location
4. *fract*	fraction, fracture
5. *cise*	scissors, incision
6. *son*	consonant, resonate
7. *urb*	urban, suburb
8. *mech*	mechanic, mechanism
9. *ject*	inject, reject
10. *leg*	legal, legislate
11. *ambi*	ambivalent, ambidextrous
12. *auto*	automatic, autograph

ACTIVITY B Read the list of roots, their meanings, and example words. Write a second example for each root.

Root	Meaning	Example
1. *therm*	heat	thermometer
2. *sign*	mark	signature
3. *gen*	born	genesis
4. *imag*	likeness	image
5. *fid*	faith	fidelity
6. *terra*	earth	territory
7. *tox*	poison	intoxicate
8. *grat*	pleasing	gratuity
9. *geo*	earth	geometry
10. *civ*	citizen	civilian
11. *bibl*	book	bibliography
12. *fin*	end	final
13. *voc*	call	vocal
14. *tempo*	time	temporary
15. *nov*	new	renovate
16. *dict*	speak	predict
17. *nat*	born	innate
18. *omni*	all	omniscient
19. *man*	hand	manual

ACTIVITY C Choose five words from the Example column of Activity B. Explain what you think each word means and then look it up in a dictionary and compare that definition with yours.

ACTIVITY D Choose five roots from Activity B. Write as many words as you can that contain each root. Check your answers in a dictionary.

WRITER'S CORNER

Examine one of the how-to articles you have written. How many words can you find with the roots from this lesson?

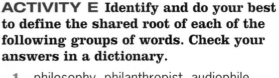

Magic Card Trick

LiNK

(continued from page 269)

4. Tell him to cut his pack; you do the same.
5. Switch decks again.
6. Tell your friend to fan the cards towards himself as before and locate his card. When your friend finds it, he should place it face-down onto the table.
7. You do the same, but you are looking for the card memorized in Step 2. When you locate that card, remove the card directly to the right of it and place it face-down on the table.

(continued on page 285)

ACTIVITY E Identify and do your best to define the shared root of each of the following groups of words. Check your answers in a dictionary.

1. philosophy, philanthropist, audiophile
2. antonym, pseudonym, anonymous
3. exclamation, clamor, proclamation
4. current, concur, incur
5. dermatology, hypodermic, epidermis
6. liberal, liberation, liberty
7. hospital, hospitality, hospice
8. final, define, infinite
9. mental, demented, mentality
10. destruction, construct, structure
11. habit, habitat, inhabit
12. suspend, pendulum, pendant
13. orthodontist, unorthodox, orthopedics
14. autograph, photograph, graphic
15. proceed, exceed, succeed
16. democracy, epidemic, demography
17. carnivore, voracious, herbivore
18. biology, zoology, anthropology

ACTIVITY F Choose four of the word groups from Activity E and use a dictionary to find two additional words with the same root words.

ACTIVITY G Choose two different word groups from Activity E. Write a sentence for each word.

ACTIVITY H Add roots, examples, and meanings to complete the following chart. Use a dictionary if necessary.

	Root	Meaning	Example	Meaning
1.		hear	audible	able to be heard
2.	ven		convene	assemble
3.	port	carry		carry across
4.	rupt	break	erupt	
5.		father	paternity	fatherhood
6.	multi	many		having many colors
7.	lit, liter	letters	literature	
8.	hydr		hydrant	water faucet
9.		year	anniversary	yearly recurring date
10.		sea	marine	of the sea
11.	lat	side		four-sided
12.	cred		credible	believable
13.		life	biography	story of someone's life
14.	cardi	heart	cardiology	
15.	spec		spectator	observer to an event
16.		new	neonate	a newborn baby
17.	mut	change		to undergo change
18.		death	immortal	living forever
19.	mot	move	motivate	
20.	pan		panorama	

ACTIVITY I Use a dictionary to find five roots that did not appear in Activities A–H. Define each root and think of at least two examples of words with the root.

WRITER'S CORNER

Work with a partner to expand the chart above by adding other examples of words with the same roots. Define the words you add. Keep in mind the meaning of the words and use as many as you can in your writing.

Dictionary

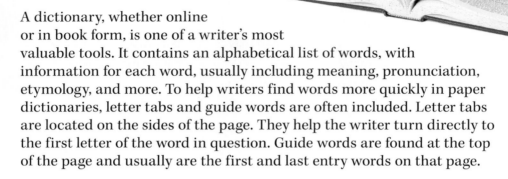

A dictionary, whether online or in book form, is one of a writer's most valuable tools. It contains an alphabetical list of words, with information for each word, usually including meaning, pronunciation, etymology, and more. To help writers find words more quickly in paper dictionaries, letter tabs and guide words are often included. Letter tabs are located on the sides of the page. They help the writer turn directly to the first letter of the word in question. Guide words are found at the top of the page and usually are the first and last entry words on that page.

Examining an Entry

Below is a sample entry of the word *wheeze*. The key on the right identifies each part of the entry. While most dictionaries will have this information, its order sometimes varies. Some dictionaries may have other information such as synonyms or variant spellings. Find each part of the entry listed in the key below. Then look up the word in a classroom dictionary. Does it include all these parts? Can you find any others?

   A   B   C   D
wheeze (hwēz, wēz) *v.* **wheezed, wheez•ing.** To breathe with
difficulty, emitting a whistling sound: *The old man wheezed*   E
when he climbed the stairs. n. **1.** A sound of wheezing.
2. *Informal* An old joke or trite saying. [Middle English,   F
whesen] **wheez´er** *n.* **wheez´i•ly** *adv.* **wheez´i•ness** *n.*
wheez´y *adj.*

A. Syllabication
B. Pronunciation
C. Part of speech
D. Word definition
E. Sample usage
F. Etymology
G. Other forms

Pronunciation

Pronunciations are an important part of a dictionary entry. To read the pronunciation symbols, use the pronunciation key, usually found at the beginning of a dictionary. Short keys are frequently given at the bottom of every other page as well.

a	cat	ō	go	ʉ	fur	ə	a *in* ago
ā	ape	ô	fall, for	ch	chin		*in* agent
ä	cot, car	oo	look	sh	she		*in* pencil
e	ten	ōō	tool	th	thin		*in* atom
ē	me	oi	oil	*th*	then		*in* circus
i	fit	ou	out	zh	measure		
ī	ice	u	up	ŋ	ring		

ACTIVITY A **Look up the following words in a dictionary and answer these questions for each word.**

splendid   cosmetic   forward   occlude   chamois

1. How is this word pronounced?
2. How many parts of speech does the word have? What are they?
3. How many definitions are there for each part of speech?
4. What are the other forms of the word if any?
5. What root does the word contain? What is the meaning of the root?
6. From what language or languages does the root word come?

Tech Tip Post and switch sentences, using a class blog or wiki.

ACTIVITY B Look up the etymologies of the following words. What is the original meaning of the word, and from what language does each word come?

theory   meander   shadow   denouement   occupy

ACTIVITY C Use each word from Activity B in a sentence that accurately illustrates one of its meanings.

Online Dictionaries

Online dictionaries don't need aids such as tabs and guide words because the computer finds the word for you. You only need to have some idea of how the word is spelled when you type it into the search window. If you misspell a word, the online dictionary site will usually provide you with possible alternatives, based on the spelling you provided.

Online dictionaries may have an audio feature that will allow you to listen to a pronunciation of the word in question. Often they provide links to other resources such as a thesaurus, an encyclopedia, or other dictionaries.

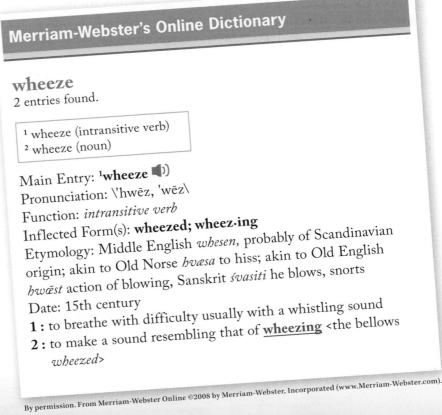

Merriam-Webster's Online Dictionary

wheeze
2 entries found.

> ¹ wheeze (intransitive verb)
> ² wheeze (noun)

Main Entry: ¹**wheeze**
Pronunciation: \\'hwēz, 'wēz\\
Function: *intransitive verb*
Inflected Form(s): **wheezed; wheez·ing**
Etymology: Middle English *whesen*, probably of Scandinavian origin; akin to Old Norse *hvæsa* to hiss; akin to Old English *hwǣst* action of blowing, Sanskrit *śvasiti* he blows, snorts
Date: 15th century
1 : to breathe with difficulty usually with a whistling sound
2 : to make a sound resembling that of **wheezing** <the bellows *wheezed*>

By permission. From Merriam-Webster Online ©2008 by Merriam-Webster, Incorporated (www.Merriam-Webster.com).

ACTIVITY D Answer the questions about the entry for *wheeze* and about the online dictionary page that *wheeze* is on.

1. When *wheeze* functions as a verb in a sentence, what kind of verb is it?
2. Where would you click on the page to find the definition of the noun form of *wheeze*?
3. Where would you click to hear the pronunciation of the word?
4. What is the difference between the two pronunciations of *wheeze*?
5. From what languages does *wheeze* originate? What languages have words that are akin to *wheeze*?

ACTIVITY E Use an online dictionary to answer the following questions about the word *forte*.

1. As what parts of speech can *forte* function?
2. How many pronunciations does *forte* have?
3. What is the origin of the noun form of *forte*?
4. When *forte* means "part of a sword or foil blade," how many syllables does it have?
5. What is the meaning of the adjective form of *forte*?
6. How many different definitions does *forte* have as a noun?
7. As an adjective, on which syllable is *forte* accented?

ACTIVITY F Use an online dictionary to answer the following questions about the word *license*.

1. As what parts of speech can *license* function?
2. How many variant spellings does *license* have?
3. What is the origin of the noun form of *license*?
4. Write two sentences using different forms of the word *license*.

 Use an online dictionary to check unfamiliar words.

How-to Talks

In many ways telling people how to do something is easier than writing instructions, especially if you can demonstrate as you speak. It is much easier, for example, to show someone how to change a bike tire than it is to write instructions for changing a bike tire. Just as in written instructions, you have to be clear, concise, and logical. Here are some guidelines for a successful how-to talk.

Identify Your Audience

Will you have an audience of your peers? Will your audience be expert in the topic or know little about it? You must know the answers to questions like these before you can tailor your talk to your audience.

Introduce Your Topic

Identify the topic of your how-to talk for the audience immediately. Then tell them why the topic is worth their attention. How will the audience benefit?

Explain the Steps

Use visual aids to support your how-to talk. Ideally, you would demonstrate the activity, but this is not always possible. Showing how to fold napkins is easy, but showing how to discourage a bully isn't easy. If you are able to demonstrate the task, make sure everyone can see what you are doing at every step of the way.

If you can't give a demonstration, you could use a diagram, drawing, PowerPoint graphics, poster, or other visual aid. It will help your audience visualize the steps. In a PowerPoint presentation, you can use bulleted lists for any supplies needed, a series of slides to demonstrate different steps, diagrams detailing the order of steps, and clip art or photos as additional visual aids.

Be sure the steps in accomplishing the goal you set out are in chronological order.

Sum Up

Avoid ending your talk with a flat statement such as "It's finished" or "That's all." Instead, remind your audience briefly of what you accomplished ("Look at the lovely basket we just made together") and how you did it ("We used bent willow branches and twine and didn't spend a cent").

ACTIVITY A **Read the topics below and decide who would benefit from the following talks. What type of visual aids would you use?**

1. Build a Picnic Table
2. How to Send a Text Message
3. Become a Hackey Sack Champ in Three Easy Lessons
4. How to Protect Your Computer from Viruses
5. Manage Your Time So You Have More Leisure
6. Give a Party Everyone Will Love
7. Rock Climbing
8. Steps to Keeping Computer Time Under Control
9. Quick and Easy No-Bake Recipes

ACTIVITY B **Choose a title from Activity A. Choose an appropriate audience for a how-to talk on your chosen topic. Then write notes that include the steps for your talk. Present your talk to a partner, describing the visual aids you would use. Take notes on the improvements your partner suggested and save your notes for later.**

SPEAKER'S CORNER

Present a talk on the how-to article you completed in the Writer's Corner on page 273. Even though your demonstration may be as simple as how to tie a shoe, make sure to break down your explanation into understandable, chronological steps. To prepare, write notes to remind yourself of your introduction and the necessary steps.

Tech Tip Make a PowerPoint presentation.

Preparing Your Notes

Creating a set of prepared notes on note cards can help you present your how-to talk smoothly and clearly. When you prepare your notes, you might begin by listing the steps, numbering them in order from start to finish. When you have finished, review your steps, making sure you have them in the correct order.

Preparing Your Visual Aids

Presenting your visual aids clearly is just as important as speaking clearly. If you are presenting a diagram or flowchart, be sure it is large enough and placed in a position where everyone can see it. If you are demonstrating an action, make sure everyone will have a clear view. You don't want to demonstrate how to tie a shoe from the floor. If you're demonstrating how to fold a napkin, you may need to walk around the room to make sure everyone can see the napkin.

Practice

To make sure your talk goes smoothly, it will be helpful to practice it a few times. Practicing will help you be certain that you have all the materials you need and that the steps you describe will produce the goal you intend. As you practice, keep these questions in mind:

- Have I tailored my talk to my audience?
- Do I introduce my topic immediately?
- Am I speaking at a volume and pace so everyone can hear and understand me?
- Are all the steps in the right order?
- Have I eliminated all unnecessary steps?
- Do I present the visual aids clearly?
- Does my conclusion sum up what I explained?

Present

When you present your how-to talk, respond to your audience. If they are straining to hear you, speak more loudly and clearly. If they struggle to see your visual aid, raise it up or pass it around the room. If they seem bored, vary your pitch and pass quickly over steps that may be obvious. If your audience seems confused, repeat difficult steps or explain them in a different way. You can also point out common mistakes made in your activity. Stop occasionally to answer questions. In a how-to talk, understanding is the key.

Listening Tips

In any presentation the listener's role is just as important as the speaker's role. Follow these steps when listening to a how-to talk:

- Closely watch what the speaker is doing and listen carefully. If you miss a step, you may not understand what the speaker is explaining or demonstrating.
- Do not interrupt the speaker. If you are confused by a step, raise your hand or wait for the speaker to ask for questions.
- Give the speaker the same kind of attention and feedback that you would appreciate.

ACTIVITY C **Evaluate the following notes for a how-to talk. Identify any unnecessary, omitted, or out-of-order steps. Then consider a visual aid. What would you use? When would you use it?**

Fried Peanut Butter and Banana Sandwich

1. Assemble ingredients/equipment
   bread, peanut butter, bananas
   frying pan

2. Make sandwich
   Spread peanut butter on two pieces of bread
   Put bananas on one piece
   Slice bananas

3. Cook sandwich
   Put sandwich in pan
   Smell the delicious scent of browning butter
   When golden brown, turn over
   When the second side is cooked, the sandwich is done

4. Eat sandwich
   Great with applesauce
   Great with a big glass of milk
   Some people prefer chocolate milk

LiNK

Magic Card Trick

(continued from page 276)

8. Now, recap—in any "You Do As I Do" trick, it's best to review what has happened: "We both shuffled our cards thoroughly. Then, we both removed a card and placed it on the top of our own deck. We then each cut our pack of cards. All the same steps, right? Next, we switched packs and looked for our chosen card and placed it face-down on the table. Since you did exactly as I did, we should have the same card, right? Let's see . . . !"

9. Ask your friend to turn over both cards and they match.

The Magnificent Montie

SPEAKER'S CORNER

Improve the how-to talk you presented for the Speaker's Corner on page 283. Use the tips you learned in this lesson. Note whether your audience's response improves.

Prewriting and Drafting

Teaching someone how to do something is one of the most basic functions of writing. Often the only way to learn how to do something new is to have someone teach us how. Through writing we can teach others about games and sports, arts and crafts, and all kinds of other activities. You have practiced aspects of how-to writing throughout this chapter. Now you can use what you have learned as you share your skills and knowledge in a how-to article.

Before you prepare your how-to article, choose a topic that's just right for you and plan your article so that readers will understand the steps.

Prewriting

Prewriting is the time to choose your topic, to decide what you want to say about it, and to organize the way that you will present your ideas. For how-to articles, you brainstorm to determine what topic you know enough about to teach to someone else. Then you review the steps in the process, making certain that nothing is left out. Finally, you organize your notes to make sure the steps are in the proper sequence.

Choosing a Topic

Nearly everyone is an expert at something, whether it's constructing a model of the Taj Mahal out of sugar cubes

or training a puppy to roll over. If you select a topic

👀 Ideas

for your how-to article that you know well and genuinely care about, writing it will be fun, not a chore.

Planning the Article

Miguel, an eighth grader, has trained his dog Lobo to perform tricks. He has decided the topic of his how-to article will be how to teach a dog to wave. To help him visualize the steps in order, he used a sequence chart like this one.

Teaching Your Dog to Wave
Need: dog treats

Tell dog to sit, then pick up dog's paw.

⬇

Say "give paw."

⬇

Repeat, and give treats, praise, each time.

⬇

Second Session: Say "give paw" while putting out hand.

⬇

When dog puts paw in hand, give praise and a treat.

⬇

Tell dog "sit" then say "give paw wave."

⬇

Hold out your hand higher so dog must lift his paw up higher too.

⬇

Praise him for trying, but don't grab his paw.

⬇

Repeat, saying just "wave."

Miguel entered his topic and any necessary supplies above the first box. Then he listed

Organization

each step in a separate box of the sequence chart in order. He didn't worry about using full sentences because it was more important that he capture his thoughts on paper first.

Your Turn

Brainstorm a list of possible topics for your article. Think about your interests and the skills that help you pursue those interests. If you get stuck, think about what you did during the week or what you did last summer. Then use a sequence chart to help you visualize the steps in order.

Miguel read over his sequence chart of steps. As he walked through the steps, he noticed that he had mixed up a couple, included a few unnecessary comments, and left out a few important points. From his sequence chart, Miguel created the list on the right, fixing each of these problems. He also made sure to use complete sentences at this point. Look at the list. Which steps did Miguel add? Which ones did he delete?

1. Before you can teach your dog to wave, you have to teach him what "give paw" means.
2. Have the dog sit. Say "give paw." Pick up the dog's paw. Feed your dog a treat and praise him.
3. Repeat this. Praise him and give him a treat each time. That's enough training for one day.
4. Next time say "give paw," put your hand out, and see if the dog remembers to put his paw in it. If he doesn't, take his paw and say, "give paw."
5. Once he gets "give paw," you can go on to "wave."
6. Have your dog sit. Say "give paw wave."
7. Instead of taking his paw, move your hand a little higher so he has to lift his paw up to reach your hand. Don't grab his paw, but praise him for trying to put his paw in your hand. Don't raise your hand too high, or he will stop trying.
8. Repeat. Remember, every time your dog does what he is supposed to, praise him and give him a treat.
9. After a few more repeats, drop the "give paw" part and just say "wave."
10. Practice every day, or nearly every day, for several weeks.

Your Turn

Go over your sequence chart and make notes of steps you left out, unnecessary comments to be removed, and any steps that are out of order.

Make a numbered list of the steps. Use complete sentences for each step.

Prewriting
Drafting
Content Editing
Revising
Copyediting
Proofreading
Publishing

Drafting

Miguel felt confident because he took the time to develop and organize his prewriting notes into a coherent how-to article. He revised the steps involved in teaching a dog to wave, and now he knew they worked. Read the draft of Miguel's article. After writing the body of the article first, what did Miguel add next?

Teaching Your Dog to Wave

It's not hard to teach your dog to wave, and it's a pretty nice trick. As with all dog tricks, praise your dog every time he responds correctly and give him a treat every time, or at least most of the time. Is your dog's attention starting to wander? Stop the training session. Begin again when he is rested.

Before you can teach your dog to wave you have to teach the command "Give paw." Have the dog sit. Say, "Give paw." Pick up the dog's paw. Feed your dog a treat and praise him. Repeat this, praising him and giving him a treat each time. That's enough training for one day.

Next time, say, "Give paw," put your hand out, and see whether the dog remembers to put his paw in it. If he doesnt, take his paw and say "Give paw."

Once he obeys "Give paw," you can go on to "Wave. Say, "Give paw wave." Instead of taking his paw, move your hand a little higher so he has to lift his paw up to reach your hand. Don't grab his paw, but praise him for trying to put his paw in your hand. Don't raise your hand too high, or he will stop trying. Repeat. Remember, every time your dog does what he is supposed to, praise him and give him a treat. After a few more repeats, you can drop the "Give paw" part of the command and simply say, "Wave." Practice every day, or nearly every day, for several weeks.

Doesn't your dog look nice when he waves? He's waving like a rock star to his fans, think of the other tricks you can teach him! Just remember to use only positive praise and treats during training, never punishment!

Title, Introduction, and Conclusion

Titles for how-to articles should be straightforward. It is essential for readers to know at a glance what they will learn how to do if they read the article. What are some ways to vary titles of how-to articles? Check the list on page 263, Activity A, for examples of titles.

The introduction of your how-to article should not simply repeat the purpose of the article. It should also emphasize how the reader may benefit from learning the activity, as well as provide any significant background information. You might also try a little humor. In what ways does Miguel's introduction engage his audience?

Your conclusion should accomplish one or more of the following:

- Assure the audience that, by following your steps, they will be successful.

- Offer any special tips or warnings of common mistakes.

- Make a prediction about the impact of your audience's success.

Writer's Tip Keep your directions clear and simple. If one step seems too complicated, break it down into two steps.

Your Turn

Use your list of steps to help you write your first draft.

- Eliminate the numbers from your list of steps.
- Group the steps into paragraphs.
- Use transition words to make the order of the steps clear.
- Write an engaging introduction and a conclusion that sums up what the reader has learned.

Prewriting

Drafting

Content Editing

Revising

Copyediting

Proofreading

Publishing

Content Editing

The content editor reads the draft of a how-to article to see if all the steps have been included and are in the right order. The content editor also checks whether the individual steps are clear. Use the checklist below when editing a how-to article for content.

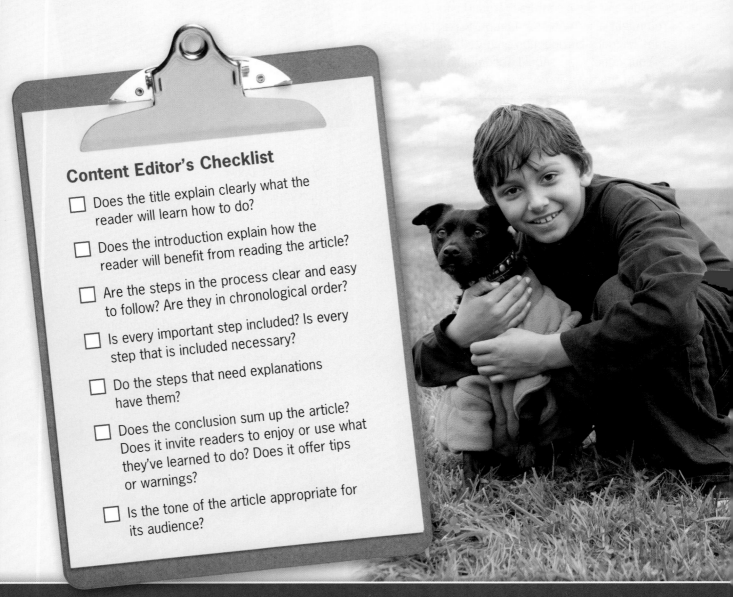

Content Editor's Checklist

☐ Does the title explain clearly what the reader will learn how to do?

☐ Does the introduction explain how the reader will benefit from reading the article?

☐ Are the steps in the process clear and easy to follow? Are they in chronological order?

☐ Is every important step included? Is every step that is included necessary?

☐ Do the steps that need explanations have them?

☐ Does the conclusion sum up the article? Does it invite readers to enjoy or use what they've learned to do? Does it offer tips or warnings?

☐ Is the tone of the article appropriate for its audience?

Miguel read through his draft and used the **Sentence Fluency** Content Editor's Checklist to help him edit his draft. Then he asked his classmate Luis to read it.

Luis took his job seriously. He read the draft twice straight through. Then he used the Content Editor's Checklist as he read the draft a third time. He jotted down some suggestions, and then he and Miguel went over the draft together.

Luis told Miguel he liked his how-to article and he found it well written and easy to understand. He told Miguel that the tone was a good fit for an audience of his classmates. Luis understood how discouraging it can be to hear criticism, even if it is constructive, without hearing any praise. Then he discussed the body of Miguel's article. Here are his comments.

- The phrase *a pretty nice trick* in the introduction doesn't grab me.
- The second paragraph seems to be missing a step. What happens if the dog does the trick right the first time?
- The third paragraph is unclear. Does *next time* mean the next training session? Should the dog sit before the trainer asks him to *Give paw*?
- I think a step is missing in the third paragraph. Should the trainer repeat *Give paw* to the dog to reinforce the lesson?
- In the fourth paragraph, I didn't understand why the trainer shouldn't raise his hand too high or why the trainer should practice every day.

After their conference, Miguel began thinking about how he could use Luis's suggestions as he wrote his next draft.

Prewriting
Drafting
Content Editing
Revising
Copyediting
Proofreading
Publishing

Your Turn

Use the Content Editor's Checklist to help you improve your draft. What are some other ways you can improve it? Then trade how-to articles with a classmate. Again using the checklist as a guide, write comments lightly in pencil on your partner's draft. Or jot down comments on a separate sheet of paper.

When you and your partner have finished content editing each other's articles, discuss them. Be sure to start with overall reactions and positive comments. Next, clarify the written comments and corrections you made. Then you will both be ready to revise your drafts.

Revising

After hearing Luis's comments, Miguel went to work revising his draft. Take a look at the changes he made below.

Teaching Your Dog to Wave

It's not hard to teach your dog to wave, and it's a ~~pretty nice~~ show-stealing trick. ~~As with all dog~~ For this and every trick you train your dog to do, praise him ~~tricks, praise your dog~~ every time he responds correctly and give him a treat ~~every time, or at least most of the time.~~ Is your dog's attention starting to wander? Stop the training session. Begin again when he is rested.

Before you can teach your dog to wave you have to teach the command "Give paw." Have the dog sit. Say "Give paw." Pick up the dog's paw. ~~Feed your dog a treat~~ several times. Be especially enthusiastic if he begins to give you his paw on his own. ~~and praise him.~~ Repeat this, praising him and giving him a treat each time. ~~That's enough training for one day.~~ After a few repetitions, stop the training session for the day.

At the next training session, have the dog sit, ~~Next time,~~ say "Give paw," put your hand out, and see whether the dog remembers to put his paw in it. If he doesnt, take his paw and say "Give paw." to review. Repeat several times.

Once he obeys "Give paw," you can go on to "Wave. Say "Give paw wave." Instead of taking his paw, move your hand a little higher so he has to lift his paw up to reach your hand. Don't grab his paw, but praise him for trying to put his paw in your hand. Don't raise your hand too high, or he will stop trying. Repeat. become discouraged and ~~Remember: every time your dog does what he is supposed to, praise him and give him a treat.~~ After a few more repeats, you can drop the "Give paw" part of the command and simply say "Wave." Practice every day, or nearly every day, for several weeks. to make sure your dog will remember his new trick.

Doesn't your dog look nice when he waves? He's waving like a rock star to his fans, think of ~~the~~ other tricks you can teach him! , like how to speak and bow Just remember to use only positive praise and treats during training, never punishment!

Look at some of the ways Miguel revised

 Word Choice

"Teaching Your Dog to Wave."

- Miguel agreed that *pretty nice* wasn't specific. With what did he replace it?
- He also agreed with Luis that the second paragraph left out what to do if the dog happened to be a quick study. What did Miguel add?
- In what ways did Miguel make the third paragraph clearer?
- What explanations did Miguel add to the fourth paragraph?
- In the last paragraph, Miguel added the name of another trick as an example because he knows that specific details create pictures in readers' minds.

When Miguel revised his draft with the help of the Content Editor's Checklist, he saw that his how-to article repeated the direction of giving the dog a treat too many times. To improve his article, he inserted *For this and every trick you train your dog to do, praise him,* in the second sentence of the first paragraph. He also deleted the repeated reminders in the second and fourth paragraphs.

What are some other changes that Miguel made to his draft? What other changes would you suggest?

Your Turn

Revise your how-to article, using your own ideas and those suggestions of your content-editing partner. After you finish revising, run through the Content Editor's Checklist again. Make sure you remembered all the corrections that you intended to make.

Writer's Tip Do not assume your reader has any prior knowledge or experience with your topic. Explain everything!

Copyediting and Proofreading

Copyediting

Miguel copyedited his piece to make certain that the sentences were constructed correctly and that the piece flowed logically and coherently. He also read it to make certain that he used words and phrases that were both exact and vivid. He used the following checklist to copyedit his draft.

Miguel noticed that the last three sentences in the first paragraph were short and sounded choppy when he read them aloud. How did he improve them? See both the old and new versions below. To improve the flow, he combined them into one longer sentence.

> Is your dog's attention starting to wander? Stop the training session. Begin again when he is rested.

> If your dog's attention starts to wander, stop the training session and begin again when he is rested.

In the second paragraph, Miguel added a transition word and combined two simple sentences.

> Have the dog sit. Say "Give paw." Pick up the dog's paw.

> To begin, have the dog sit. Say "Give paw" and pick up the dog's paw.

Miguel corrected run-on sentences in the last two paragraphs, as well as a few other changes. With what word did he replace the word *nice*? Can you think of another word he could have used?

Copyeditor's Checklist

- ☐ Are there effective transition words in the piece?
- ☐ Do any words seem out of place or awkward?
- ☐ Do the chosen words and phrases convey their intended meaning?
- ☐ Are there any run-on or rambling sentences?
- ☐ Is there a balance of simple, compound, and complex sentences?
- ☐ Is the structure of sentences logical and grammatically correct?

Your Turn

Use the Copyeditor's Checklist to copyedit your draft. Pay particular attention to the rhythm of the sentences, and be on the alert for inexact and overused words. Correct run-on and rambling sentences. Have you repeated an adjective or adverb? Replace repeated adjectives and adverbs with synonyms.

Proofreading

Proofreading is the last step writers take to prepare their draft for publication. They check spelling, punctuation, capitalization, and grammar.

Miguel used this Proofreader's Checklist to catch mistakes in his revised draft.

Proofreader's Checklist

- ☐ Are the paragraphs indented?
- ☐ Have any words been misspelled?
- ☐ Are the beginnings of sentences and proper nouns capitalized?
- ☐ Is the grammar correct?
- ☐ Is the punctuation correct?
- ☐ Were new errors introduced during editing?

Miguel asked his classmate Ana to proofread his how-to article. Ana found several errors in Miguel's article. She noticed a missing apostrophe and a missing quotation mark. Can you find any other mistakes?

Conventions

Your Turn

Here are some tips to sharpen your proofreading skills.

- Use the Proofreader's Checklist to help you proofread your how-to article.
- Be sure to have a dictionary close at hand.
- Place a ruler or blank sheet of paper under each line as you read to help you pay attention to each line.
- Read very slowly and carefully.
- Proofread for one type of error at a time.
- When you have finished proofreading, trade papers with a classmate and proofread each other's work.

Grammar in Action

Make sure you use subject and object pronouns correctly, or else you will confuse your reader. Check each pronoun for agreement with its antecedent.

Writer's Workshop

Publishing

After Miguel corrected the errors he and Ana found as they proofread his how-to article, he used a pen to copy the article neatly on a clean sheet of paper. Then he read it again to make sure he had copied everything correctly. This is Miguel's finished how-to article.

Teaching Your Dog to Wave

It's not hard to teach your dog to wave, and it's a show-stealing trick. For this and every trick you train your dog to do, praise him every time he responds correctly and give him a treat. If your dog's attention starts to wander, stop the training session and begin again when he is rested.

Before you can teach your dog to wave, you have to teach the command "Give paw." To begin, have the dog sit. Say, "Give paw" and pick up the dog's paw. Repeat this several times. Be especially enthusiastic if he begins to give you his paw on his own. After a few repetitions, stop the training session for the day.

At the next training session, have your dog sit, say, "Give paw," put your hand out, and see whether the dog remembers to put his paw in it. If he doesn't, take his paw and say, "Give paw" to review. Repeat several times.

Once your dog obeys "Give paw," you can go on to "Wave." Say, "Give paw wave." Instead of taking his paw, move your hand a little higher so he has to lift his paw up to reach your hand. Don't grab his paw, but praise him for trying to put his paw in your hand. Don't raise your hand too high, or he will become discouraged and stop trying. Repeat. After a few more repeats, you can drop the "Give paw" part of the command and simply say, "Wave." Practice every day, or nearly every day, for several weeks to make sure your dog will remember his new trick.

Doesn't your dog look charming when he waves like a rock star to his fans? Think of other tricks you can teach him, like how to speak and bow! Just remember to use only positive praise and treats during training, never punishment!

After your teacher reviews the class's how-to articles, you can publish them for the students and adults in your school.

There are many ways you can publish your article.

 Create a class book. Work with your classmates to arrange the articles in a meaningful order, numbering the pages, and creating a table of contents that lists the titles, authors, and page numbers. Then make a cover, choosing a snappy title such as "How to Do Just About Anything." Decorate the cover and bind the book in a three-ring binder or a report cover. After everyone in class has had an opportunity to read the articles and to try out a few of them, donate the collection to the school library.

 Post it to an online how-to manual. You may also want to include images of each step. Choose images that may help depict complex steps.

 Create a class book for a younger grade. Some how-to articles such as "How to tie your shoes" may be very useful for younger students.

 Do a PowerPoint presentation. You can make the steps move on-screen in chronological order.

 Post it to your classroom's blog, wiki, or Web site. You can also include images in this medium.

Prewriting

Drafting

Content Editing

Revising

Copyediting

Proofreading

Publishing

Your Turn

You've worked hard to develop, express, and organize your ideas. Why not work just as hard to produce a **Presentation** clean finished copy? To publish your work, follow the steps below.

- Reread your how-to article to make sure you did not insert new mistakes or leave out words when you copied your draft or typed your corrections.

- If you are using a computer, run the spell-checker a final time before printing the article.

- To make the steps in the process even clearer, you may want to include an instructional graphic.

Business Letters

Carl Sandburg Middle School
121 E. Main St. • Greenboro, MA 01864
(617) 555-0403

LiNK

November 7, 20–

Mr. Stephen H. Phillips
Managing Editor
North Fork Daily Journal
1770 Woodlawn Ave.
North Fork, MA 02171

Dear Mr. Phillips:

On behalf of my eighth-grade class, I would like to thank you for leading us on a tour of your newspaper offices. The experience fit in perfectly with our current media unit.

Some of the students were so impressed that they are already talking about joining the high school newspaper staff next year. Please accept the class photo that is enclosed as a token of our gratitude.

As a follow-up, I would like to make a request. Would anyone at your staff be available to speak to our class about life as a journalist? Perhaps you could also provide some information about potential before-school newspaper delivery jobs.

Please contact me at the phone number above to let me know if anyone would be available to speak to our students. Thanks again, and I look forward to hearing from you.

Sincerely yours,

Roberta Andrews

Roberta Andrews
Teacher

Encl: photo
cc: Martin Cohen, principal

Washington Middle School
1433 Glen Road
Glen Falls, Illinois 60025
January 15, 20–

The Honorable George McHenry
City Hall
1500 Central Avenue
Glen Falls, Illinois 60025

Dear Mayor McHenry:

My name is Terrell Taylor. I am a resident of Glen Falls and an eighth-grade student at Washington Middle School. I am also a skateboarder, and I am writing to you in hopes that you will consider making part of the new park land on Cedar Road into a skateboarding park.

Skateboarding is an important and healthy activity for teenagers. It involves physical exercise, concentration, and discipline. It is something fun I can do with my friends that is healthier than going to the mall or hanging out playing video games. Studies have also shown that teens who skateboard get into less trouble with drugs and alcohol than teens who aren't active. The problem is, we have no place to go. We can't use the sidewalks or parking lots because business owners get mad. We can't grind at Riverfront Park because we are told that's "not what the benches or railings are for."

If we had a skate park, kids would no longer bother adults downtown. I think more kids with too much time on their hands would start skateboarding too. Parents would know exactly where their kids are, so they would worry less.

Please consider this proposal. Thank you for your time and consideration.

Sincerely,

Terrell Taylor

Terrell Taylor

What Makes a Good Business Letter?

Have you ever wanted to make a complaint, ask a question, or point something out to a business? If so, it will help to know the basics of writing an effective business letter.

Heading
The writer's address appears on the top left. Following the address there may be a phone number and, if applicable, an e-mail address. The date of the letter appears two lines below the address.

Inside Address
The address of the person receiving the letter appears two lines below the date. If you do not know the person to whom the letter should be addressed, try calling the company to find out. Include a personal title such as *Mr., Ms., Mrs.,* or *Dr.*

Closing
End the letter with a word or phrase such as *Sincerely, Sincerely yours, Cordially, Regards,* or *Best regards.* Leave enough space to sign your name. Then type your name below the signature space.

Carl Sandburg Middle School
121 E. Main St.
Greenboro, MA 01864
(617) 555-0403

November 7, 20—

Mr. Stephen H. Phillips
Managing Editor
North Fork Daily Journal
1770 Woodlawn Ave.
North Fork, MA 02171

Dear Mr. Phillips:

On behalf of my eighth-grade class, I would like to thank you for leading us on a tour of your newspaper offices. The experience fit in perfectly with our current media unit.

Some of the students were so impressed that they are already talking about joining the high school newspaper staff next year. Please accept the class photo enclosed as a token of our gratitude.

As a follow-up, I'd like to make a request. Would anyone at your staff be available to speak to our class about life as a journalist? Perhaps you could also provide some information about potential before-school newspaper delivery jobs.

Please contact me at the phone number above to let me know if anyone would be available to speak to our students. Thanks again, and I look forward to hearing from you.

Sincerely yours,

Roberta Andrews

Roberta Andrews
Teacher

Encl: photo
cc: Martin Cohen, principal

Salutation
The salutation is a greeting. It should read "Dear" (followed by the name of the receiver) or "To whom it may concern" and be followed by a colon.

Body
The body is aligned left, single-spaced with an extra space between paragraphs and an extra line after the last paragraph.

Reference Information
Some letters include reference information at the bottom. "Encl:" indicates what is enclosed with the letter, and "cc:" indicates who else has been sent a copy of the letter.

The Structure of a Business Letter

The best business letters are confident, polite, and concise. A good business letter can be easy to recognize, but challenging to write. Here are some guidelines for writing effective business letters.

- Begin the first paragraph with a professional and polite opening sentence that states the purpose of the letter. Get right to the point and keep it simple.
- In the next paragraph or paragraphs, offer persuasive reasoning, relevant details, statistics, or other information to support your main point. If you are enclosing something with your letter, be sure to explain what it is.
- In the closing paragraph, restate the purpose of the letter. Ask for action if appropriate. If you are making a request, thank the recipient for taking the requested action.

Read over Roberta Andrews's letter. How closely does it follow these guidelines?

ACTIVITY A Create part of a fictitious business letter that you would send from your home to the publisher of a favorite book to request an additional copy. The address can be found at the front of the book. Include the heading, inside address, salutation, closing, and reference information. Write the first paragraph of your letter stating your purpose and leave the rest of the letter blank to finish later.

ACTIVITY B When you write a formal letter to people who hold special positions, you need to use special salutations. Write an opening sentence to the following people, using the salutation given.

1. President: Dear Mr./Madam President
2. U.S. Senator: Dear Senator (surname)
3. Judge: Dear Justice (surname)
4. King/Queen: May it Please Your Majesty
5. Mayor: Sir/Madam (or) Mayor (surname)

WRITER'S CORNER

Write the first three sentences of a letter to a manufacturer or a school supply store, complaining about defective school supplies.

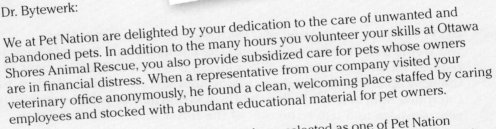

Pet Nation Kibble
103 Crawford Ave.
Skokie, IL 60076
(847) 555-6750

February 17, 20—

Dr. Barbara Bytewerk
Care Plus Animal Hospital
Grand Haven, LA
2723 Jefferson Ave.

Dr. Bytewerk:

We at Pet Nation are delighted by your dedication to the care of unwanted and abandoned pets. In addition to the many hours you volunteer your skills at Ottawa Shores Animal Rescue, you also provide subsidized care for pets whose owners are in financial distress. When a representative from our company visited your veterinary office anonymously, he found a clean, welcoming place staffed by caring employees and stocked with abundant educational material for pet owners.

I am honored to inform you that you have been selected as one of Pet Nation Kibble's Veterinarians of the Year. In recognition of your services, the animal shelter you designate will receive $10,000 and a year's supply of Pet Nation Kibble. We would like to honor you and nine other veterinarians from around the country at a dinner a few weeks from now with overnight accommodations provided by Hospitality House. The food should be delicious. We hope you will be able to attend.

Again, thank you for your service to animals. We are delighted to welcome you to a very special group—Pet Nation Kibble's Veterinarians of the Year.

Best regards,

Mark Morris

Mark Morris
Vice President, Development

cc: R. Andersen, President

1. What mistakes are made in the heading, inside address, and salutation?
2. Why did Mark Morris write the letter?
3. In what paragraph does he explain his purpose? Does he make his point promptly?
4. Are any sentences irrelevant or unnecessary? If so, which ones?
5. Is any important information left out?
6. What should the last paragraph in a business letter do? Does this final paragraph do that?
7. What could Dr. Bytewerk do if she wanted to find out additional information?
8. Is this a well-written business letter? Why or why not?

> **Inside Address and Salutation to a Representative**
>
> The Honorable James Holt
>
> United States House of Representatives
>
> Washington, D.C. 20515
>
> Dear Representative Holt:

ACTIVITY D Rewrite the letter from Activity C. Fix any mistakes in the heading, inside address, and salutation. Make any changes that would make the letter clearer and more concise, such as rearranging sentences, adding important details, or deleting unnecessary sentences.

ACTIVITY E Write a three-paragraph business letter to your principal, proposing an idea for the school to raise money for charity. State the purpose of the letter in the first paragraph. In the second paragraph, offer at least one reason to adopt the idea and restate the purpose in the third paragraph. Use your school address in the heading.

ACTIVITY F Inside addresses for people holding special positions need special titles that are often different from the title used in the salutation. Write imaginary or real inside addresses for the following people. Then match it to the proper salutation from Activity B on page 301.

1. President: The President, The White House
2. Senator/Representative: The Honorable (full name)
3. Mayor: His/Her Honor (full name)

WRITER'S CORNER

Put yourself in Dr. Bytewerk's place. Write a reply to the letter from Mark Morris of Pet Nation Kibble. Thank him for the honor, accept or decline his invitation, and ask for more information about one of the details in the letter.

Purpose and Tone

People are flooded with information every day as letters, e-mails, and phone calls all fight for the recipient's attention. That's why it's important when writing a business letter to get straight to the point, explain the purpose clearly, and support it convincingly with just enough details. Writers must strive to maintain a polite, sincere tone in their letters. The tone should be neither too formal nor (even worse) overly casual and personal.

Stating the Purpose

As noted in Lesson 1, the first and most important step in writing a business letter is to identify the goal or purpose of the letter. Is it to provide information? extend an invitation? request action? Since the rest of the letter supports the purpose, it must be absolutely clear to the writer. After all, if it isn't clear to the writer, how could it possibly be clear to the reader?

Taylor was unhappy with a product she bought, so she wrote a letter to the company that manufactured it. In the first paragraph, she explained the problem. In the second paragraph, she suggested a solution.

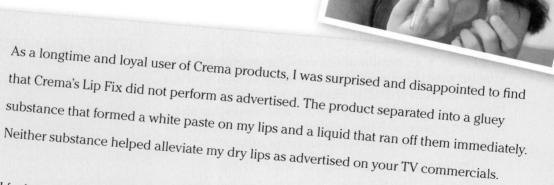

As a longtime and loyal user of Crema products, I was surprised and disappointed to find that Crema's Lip Fix did not perform as advertised. The product separated into a gluey substance that formed a white paste on my lips and a liquid that ran off them immediately. Neither substance helped alleviate my dry lips as advertised on your TV commercials.

I feel sure that your Research and Development Department will be eager to learn of my problems with this product so that they can reformulate it if they have not already done so. I also expect your company to replace the Lip Fix with an improved reformulation if one exists or to refund the purchase price.

Setting the Tone

In her letter Taylor stated the problem immediately, using clear, polite language. She used words such as *surprised* and *disappointed* and the phrase "did not perform as advertised" instead of using angrier words. She did this because she knew that business letters should always be courteous. If Taylor received no response, she could decide to write another polite but more forceful letter.

Not only did Taylor state the problem, but she also gave details and used persuasion. She explained that she is a "longtime and loyal user," a detail she hoped would help persuade the company to pay attention to her problem. Then she gave helpful details such as "The product separated into a gluey substance," which described exactly what the problem was.

ACTIVITY A Imagine that you work in the customer relations department of the Crema Company. You have just read Taylor's letter. What is your reaction to it? Write the first paragraph of a letter responding to her complaint. Pay close attention to the tone of your reply and make sure it is appropriate for the situation.

ACTIVITY B Write the first paragraph of a business letter relating to each of the following situations. Use an appropriate tone. Be sure the readers can easily figure out the purpose of each letter.

1. The clerk at a toy store was rude to your younger brother when he tried to buy a Buzzy Bee with the change in his piggy bank.
2. A student at La Mode Beauty School gave you the best haircut you ever had, and it cost only $5.
3. The photocopier has been malfunctioning, and you're not sure whether or not the new toner you ordered is the problem.

WRITER'S CORNER

Complete the letter you began in Activity A. Support the purpose of the letter with relevant details. Restate the purpose of the letter in the last paragraph.

Revising a Business Letter

Read and evaluate the following business letter. Can you identify the purpose easily? Is the purpose supported by relevant details?

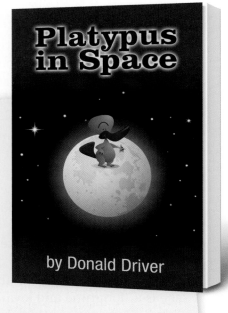

Platypus in Space

by Donald Driver

Pearson School
17 Wright Plaza
Tucson, AZ 85705
(520) 555-0126

March 4, 20—

Mr. Donald Driver
131 Hollyhock Lane
Brunswick, MS 02138

Dear Mr. Driver:

Our class recently read your latest novel, *Platypus in Space,* and just loved it. I especially liked the beginning where the platypus stowed away on the spaceship. I wonder how it got the nerve up to do that. Anyway, the reason I am writing is because I am the president of our class, and I usually write class letters. We would like to invite you to speak at our school. It would be great if we could show you some stories that your novel inspired us to write.

We know you will be on a book tour promoting *Platypus in Space* in our area in May, so we were hoping you would be able to stop by our school to give a talk then. Any time in May would be fine for us, except Memorial Day and May 11, which is Teacher Institute Day, so we won't be having school. Our parent organization has been raising funds to pay for author talks, and most of the students would rather hear you talk than any other author. So we would be able to pay you for your talk. Please let me know how much you charge, and I will find out if we have enough in the book talk fund to pay you. We had a poll last year, and you were voted favorite author. Are you planning to write more platypus books?

Thank you for making us laugh. We hope you can speak to the students at our school in May.

Sincerely,

Seth McCall

President, Mr. Bennett's Class

cc: Mr. Bennett
     Ms. Anthony, Principal

Seth's letter to Mr. Driver is well written. The tone is respectful and polite, he identifies the purpose of his letter, and he includes information Mr. Driver will need to take action. Seth's letter has some problems too.

In the first paragraph, Seth takes too long to get to the point. Does he support the purpose of the letter well? Yes and no. He does give some reasons Mr. Driver might want to visit his school. But he includes quite a few irrelevant details, which might confuse or irritate a busy author.

Remember that the writer of a successful business letter includes just enough information to make his or her point.

ACTIVITY C **Rewrite the body of Seth's letter. Make sure the purpose is in the right place and strengthen the supporting details.**

U.S. President George Washington

ACTIVITY D **Rewrite the three paragraphs you wrote for Activity B. This time write the paragraphs as though no one had responded to your first letter. Modify your tone appropriately.**

ACTIVITY E **Write a short business letter volunteering to assist in your school library. What sort of tone is useful for this letter?**

ACTIVITY F **You have a great idea for a new video game and would like a local company to see your idea. Write to them requesting an interview.**

ACTIVITY G **Write an opening paragraph to one of the following people, using the proper inside address and salutation. (See Activity B and Activity F in Lesson 1.) Make your purpose an appropriate issue, question, or request suitable for your audience.**

1. The President of the United States
2. One of your state senators
3. Your town mayor
4. Your state representative

WRITER'S CORNER

Choose an author to invite to visit your class. Write the first paragraph of a letter of invitation. State clearly why you want this author to visit and what would be expected of him or her.

Adjective and Adverb Clauses

Letter of Submission (Query) for Publication

Dear Agent (or Publisher):

I am requesting permission to submit my manuscript for your evaluation. My manuscript, which is titled "Angry Monkeys of the Rain Forest," is a 30–page double-spaced comedy manuscript with five illustrations. It is about a corporation that encounters hostile monkeys while trying to destroy their habitat for profit.

In business letters, as in all writing, there are many ways to make your sentences more complete or specific. One way is to modify nouns and verbs with adjectives and adverbs. Another way is to add a clause that does the same job as an adjective or an adverb. We call these clauses adjective and adverb clauses.

Adjective Clauses

Just as an adjective is a word that modifies a noun or a pronoun, an adjective clause is a clause (a group of words containing a subject and a predicate) that modifies a noun or a pronoun. An adjective clause usually begins with *whom, who, which,* or *that.* Writers use adjective clauses to shift the emphasis of a sentence, to deepen the meaning of a sentence, or to vary sentence length.

> **The Pueblo live in the Southwest and have a very old culture.**
> **The Pueblo,** *who live in the Southwest,* **have a very old culture.**

In the first sentence, the facts that the Pueblo live in the Southwest and have a very old culture are given equal weight. In the second sentence, emphasis shifts to the age the Pueblo's culture.

Adjective clauses can also deepen the meaning of sentences.

> **Odysseus was a legendary hero of the ancient Greeks.**
> **Odysseus,** *whose adventures are told in an epic poem,* **was a legendary hero of the ancient Greeks.**

The second sentence of this pair includes extra information about Odysseus. Could the same information have been communicated in a separate sentence? Certainly. However,

Statue of ancient Greek mythological hero Odysseus

using adjective clauses allows writers to select how information is communicated. The second sentence lets the writer inform the reader about the epic poem without having to use a separate sentence, which could be too distracting in an essay about famous heroes.

Restrictive and Nonrestrictive Clauses

Adjective clauses are not always optional tools for adding information about a noun. Sometimes writers need to use an adjective clause to identify the noun being modified in a sentence. This is called a restrictive clause. Nonrestrictive clauses are used to add important information that is not necessary to identify the noun in a sentence.

> **The book** *that I bought* **was too difficult.**
> **The book by Leo Tolstoy,** *which I bought*, **was too difficult.**

In the first sentence, the restrictive clause *that I bought* is necessary to identify the book. In the second sentence, the nonrestrictive clause is not necessary because *by Leo Tolstoy* identifies the book.

ACTIVITY A Identify the adjective clause in each sentence. Determine what noun each clause modifies.

1. Wise is the person who keeps silent when ignorant.
2. Benjamin Franklin, who is credited with inventing lightning rods, was a printer as well as a political leader and an inventor.
3. Pam is the person who taught us this technique.
4. That train, which leaves for New York soon, is already full.
5. Our school started a day-care center, which is very popular.
6. Congratulations on winning an award that is quite prestigious.

ACTIVITY B Look at the sentences in Activity A. Identify whether each clause is restrictive or nonrestrictive. Find three sentences that can be modified by changing an adjective clause into a simple adjective.

WRITER'S CORNER

Reread the student's letter on page 299. Identify two adjective clauses. Determine whether they are restrictive or nonrestrictive.

Adverb Clauses

An adverb clause is a clause that does the same job as an adverb. An adverb clause usually modifies a verb, but can also modify an adjective or adverb in a sentence. Adverb clauses are usually introduced by subordinate conjunctions such as *although, while,* or *because.*

An adverb clause can tell when, where, why, or how something happens. It can also make a comparison or set a condition.

> **Colleen spoke** *as if she were confident of the debate's outcome.*
> *After the rain died down,* **the sun broke through the clouds.**
> **You cannot work** *if you don't have a permit.*

Like adjective clauses, adverb clauses let writers create a more vivid picture in the reader's mind or communicate a more complicated thought. A sentence such as "Colleen spoke *confidently*" would not express the same idea as the first example.

ACTIVITY C Identify the adverb clauses in the sentences below. Determine how the clause modifies the verb: by telling *when, where, why,* or *how*; by making a comparison, or by setting a condition.

1. Strike while the iron is hot.
2. Go when you are told.
3. We saw the Mounties when we were in Ottawa.
4. The rabbit ran while the turtle crawled.
5. The plant flowered because it received good care.
6. Pat devotes more time to skiing than she does to swimming.
7. I will get a loan if you need more money.
8. The computer program worked, although some of the commands were wrong.
9. The Saint Bernard played outside all day as if he didn't notice the bitter cold.
10. She saved her money so that she might attend college.

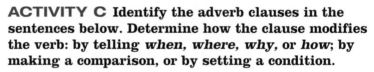

ACTIVITY D Choose five sentences from Activity C. Take out the adverb clause and add one that is introduced by a different subordinate conjunction.

ACTIVITY E Modify the verb in each sentence by inserting an adverb clause.

1. A zookeeper let us watch the lions.
2. The Native Americans decided to fight for their land.
3. Avril is studying harder than ever.
4. You can learn to play the guitar.
5. The Puritans came to America.
6. I applied for the job.
7. The students were fascinated.
8. We will terminate your account in 30 days.
9. Lila danced in the meadow.
10. James sang "The Star-Spangled Banner."
11. Keiko hit the ball.
12. Ping clapped and cheered.

ACTIVITY F Identify whether each clause below is an adjective clause or adverb clause. Then write a sentence using each clause.

1. when the shopping bag broke
2. that we overlooked
3. which was very funny
4. if I could visit any place
5. that I'd never seen before
6. who could help me with this matter
7. as if we'd never met
8. where the weather is cold year-round
9. because he was nervous
10. until it got dark

WRITER'S CORNER

You have been asked to test a new video game or toy. Write a paragraph for the body of a letter describing what you liked, disliked, or would change about the game. Use two adjective clauses and two adverb clauses.

Grammar in Action. Find verbs with adverb clauses in the p. 299 letter.

Compound Words and Clipped Words

Compound Words

Compound words, which are usually adjectives and nouns, are made up of two or more shorter words. The three kinds of compound words are

- closed compounds
  keyboard, makeup, basketball
- hyphenated compounds
  over-the-counter, twenty-five, self-respect
- open compounds
  middle school, post office, attorney general

Pluralizing Compounds

In most cases compound words should be pluralized like any other word, by adding *-s* to the end of the word. This is almost always true for closed compounds, such as *bookmarks* or *checklists*.

Some hyphenated or open compounds are pluralized differently. If the compound includes a noun followed by a word or words that modify it, pluralize the noun being modified. For example, *father-in-law* becomes *fathers-in-law* and *attorney general* becomes *attorneys general*. The words *in-law* modify *father,* while *general* describes *attorney* more specifically. If you are uncertain how to pluralize a compound, consult a dictionary.

Turning Phrases into Compounds

Sometimes it is hard to know whether two words should be written as a phrase or as a compound word. When two or more words modify the noun that follows them, they may be compounded, particularly if they might otherwise cause confusion.

> **We waited anxiously for our grades from the** *second quarter*.
> **We waited anxiously for our** *second-quarter* **grades**.

In the first sentence, the words *second quarter* stand alone, while in the second sentence, they modify the word *grades.*

ACTIVITY A Rewrite the incorrectly spelled compounds on the list. You may consult a dictionary for help.

1. vicepresident
2. sales person
3. stock-broker
4. alright
5. data base
6. X ray
7. yellowfever
8. lightyears
9. alot
10. greatgrandmother
11. African-violet
12. bloodpressure

ACTIVITY B Write the plural of each compound word.

1. anchorwoman
2. secretary of state
3. drive-in
4. bill of fare
5. chief of staff
6. notary public
7. wristwatch
8. also-ran
9. go-between
10. checkbook
11. master sergeant
12. daughter-in-law

ACTIVITY C Combine as many words from the first column with appropriate words from the second column to form compound words. You can use all the words more than once.

sand	storm
thumb	print
hand	stand
news	craft
air	man/woman
cross	bar

Grammar in Action. Find two compound words in the p. 299 letter.

WRITER'S CORNER

Pluralize the following words and use them in sentences. Use a dictionary if you need help.

passerby

teaspoonful

six-year-old

Clipped Words

Many words people use every day, such as *phone* and *exam,* are clipped words, shortened versions of longer words. The word *phone* is a shortened form of *telephone,* and *exam* is short for *examination.*

Writers of business letters must be cautious when using clipped words. Many clipped words, such as *phone,* are too casual for business use. Others, such as *exam,* are so commonly used that they are acceptable in most business letters.

ACTIVITY D Write the longer word from which each clipped word comes. If you're not sure what the longer word is, look up the clipped word in a dictionary. The entry will tell you what the longer word is. Which words would be appropriate to use in a business letter?

1. bike
2. fridge
3. vet
4. photo
5. ref

6. gas
7. taxi
8. fan
9. lunch
10. math

11. sub
12. limo
13. zoo
14. bus
15. flu

16. rep
17. van
18. memo
19. ad
20. pro

ACTIVITY E Choose three clipped words in Activity D. Write three sentences that you might include in an e-mail to a friend. Include a clipped word from Activity D in each sentence. Then write three sentences that you might include in a formal business letter. In each sentence include the longer version of the clipped word. Notice how the word choice affects the tone of each sentence.

ACTIVITY F Rewrite the body of this letter, correcting misspelled compound words and replacing clipped words that are too casual to use in a business letter.

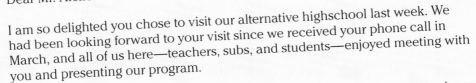

Copper Canyon School
1106 Greentree Ave.
Morrison, CO 80465
(720) 555-2005

May 9, 20—

Mr. Anthony Aiello
6033 Stockton Ave.
Santa Rosa, CA 95406

Dear Mr. Aiello:

I am so delighted you chose to visit our alternative highschool last week. We had been looking forward to your visit since we received your phone call in March, and all of us here—teachers, subs, and students—enjoyed meeting with you and presenting our program.

We will always remember your visit, especially your pleasure at our new science lab, dorms, and gym. The donations from your employees were well spent (and you are quite a base-ball player)! Enclosed with this letter is a note book of letters and photos from our students as a small token of our appreciation.

I look forward to seeing you at the blockparty next fall. Have a wonderful summer, and thanks for the visit.

Best regards,

Mary Cassidy

Mary Cassidy
Freshman Delegate

WRITER'S CORNER

Brainstorm three contemporary, technology-based clipped words. Identify their full word or phrase versions.

Writing Tools

Summarize and Paraphrase

A summary is a condensed version of a text or other source, written in your own words. When you summarize an informational text, you restate only the main points.

- To summarize a story, you restate only important details such as the main characters, the main events, the plot, and theme.
- In a business letter, you may want to summarize only the main points. In the student's letter presented at the beginning of this chapter, the student summarizes the reasons supporting his request for a skate park.

A summary can be as long as one-third the length of the original source. It can also be as short as one sentence.

> **I believe that my experience as a babysitter has prepared me to take on the responsibilities of junior counselor for your camp.**

Reread the personal narrative "Tossed by a Twister" in Chapter 1. A summary of "Tossed by a Twister" should read as follows:

> **This personal narrative is about a boy and his dog getting caught by a tornado. The boy's dog is pulled away from him by the strong winds, but the boy later finds him safely in a hole under a tree branch.**

Paraphrasing is restating individual passages of a work in your own words. It is more detailed than a summary. Researchers, book reviewers, and other writers generally paraphrase a work's supporting details.

Direct Quotation

A direct quotation contains words that are identical to the original text. It must match the original text word for word. A quotation should be enclosed in quotation marks.

Whether you summarize, paraphrase, or quote, your information must be attributed to its original source. Good writers will use all three techniques in their work to avoid plagiarism and to meet the needs of their readers. Be sure to cite others' work no matter what type of medium it comes from, including Web sites, blogs, or films.

ACTIVITY A Read the following excerpt and respond to questions.

There was another noted personage of the sixteenth century who played the part of pirate in the new world, and thereby set a most shining example to the buccaneers of those regions. This was no other than Sir Francis Drake, one of England's greatest naval commanders.

It is probable that Drake, when he started out in life, was a man of very law-abiding and orderly disposition, for he was appointed by Queen Elizabeth a naval chaplain, and, it is said, though there is some doubt about this, that he was subsequently vicar of a parish. But by nature he was a sailor, and nothing else, and after having made several voyages in which he showed himself a good fighter, as well as a good commander, he undertook, in 1572, an expedition against the Spanish settlements in the West Indies, for which he had no legal warrant whatever. . . .

Whether or not Drake's conscience had anything to do with the bungling manner in which he made this first attempt at piracy, we cannot say, but he soon gave his conscience a holiday, and undertook some very successful robbing enterprises. . . .

Whatever this gallant ex-chaplain now thought of himself, he was considered by the Spaniards as an out-and-out pirate, and in this opinion they were quite correct. During his great voyage around the world, which he began in 1577, he came down upon the Spanish-American settlements like a storm from the sea. He attacked towns, carried off treasure, captured merchant-vessels, and in fact showed himself to be a thoroughbred and accomplished pirate of the first class.

1. For what research topics could this excerpt be used as a resource?

2. What is the topic sentence or main idea of this excerpt? Write your answer as a one-sentence summary of this excerpt.

3. Scan the excerpt for important facts and supporting details. Use your own words and phrases to record these facts and details on note cards. You do not need to use complete sentences.

4. Paraphrase the excerpt in complete sentences, using only your note cards.

5. Which sentence would you use as a direct quotation for supporting evidence? Why?

Sir Francis Drake

WRITER'S CORNER

Find a business letter that includes a summary, paraphrasing, and a direct quotation. Share your letter with the class.

With an adult, find a sample business letter online.

Paraphrasing

Paraphrasing contains more detail than a summary and can be used to restate an individual passage or paragraph. Paraphrasing also helps writers avoid too many direct quotations.

To paraphrase, read and then reread the original text until you are sure you understand it. Explain what you have learned in your own words. Follow these tips:

- Highlight or flag important words, phrases, or sentences central to the meaning of the text.
- Use synonyms of phrases and words.
- Do not change concept words, special terms, or proper names.
- Do not "copy-and-paste" from online sources.
- Check your paraphrases against the original to make sure you did not miss any important information.
- Put quotation marks around any phrase you "borrowed" directly from the original source.

Good writers often combine summarizing, paraphrasing, and use of direct quotation. Read the following news article with summaries, direct quotations and paraphrases. Notice how the first sentence summarizes the latest event that has just occurred, while the last sentence summarizes the greater, more general background of the subject being covered:

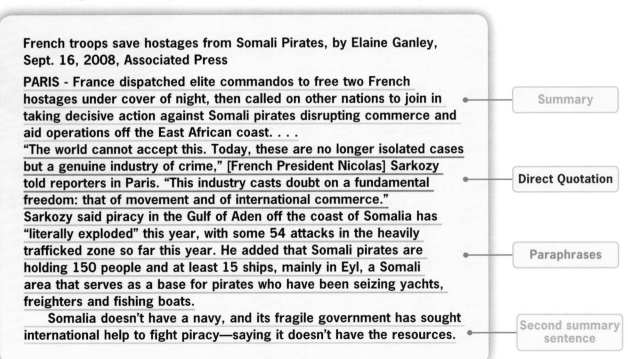

French troops save hostages from Somali Pirates, by Elaine Ganley, Sept. 16, 2008, Associated Press

PARIS - France dispatched elite commandos to free two French hostages under cover of night, then called on other nations to join in taking decisive action against Somali pirates disrupting commerce and aid operations off the East African coast. . . .   — Summary

"The world cannot accept this. Today, these are no longer isolated cases but a genuine industry of crime," [French President Nicolas] Sarkozy told reporters in Paris. "This industry casts doubt on a fundamental freedom: that of movement and of international commerce."   — Direct Quotation

Sarkozy said piracy in the Gulf of Aden off the coast of Somalia has "literally exploded" this year, with some 54 attacks in the heavily trafficked zone so far this year. He added that Somali pirates are holding 150 people and at least 15 ships, mainly in Eyl, a Somali area that serves as a base for pirates who have been seizing yachts, freighters and fishing boats.   — Paraphrases

Somalia doesn't have a navy, and its fragile government has sought international help to fight piracy—saying it doesn't have the resources.   — Second summary sentence

Remember that if you use the original language from a source, it is considered plagiarism. To avoid plagiarizing, follow these steps:

- Use many different sources when conducting research on a topic.
- Set aside your research material.
- Think critically about what you have read. How was the information from different sources similar? How was it different?
- Draw your own conclusions and then start making notes. Find your own words to express your thoughts.
- Go back to your sources to make sure you have not plagiarized.

ACTIVITY B Putting several facts in one complex or compound sentence with adverb and adjective clauses is a good strategy for avoiding plagiarism when paraphrasing. Read the following excerpt. Summarize the main idea of the excerpt in one sentence. Then take notes of important facts and supporting details. Using only the information in your notes, paraphrase the excerpt in one to three compound or complex sentences with adverb and adjective clauses.

If you will find a map of the West Indies in your atlas or geography book, you will also find Puerto Rico. It is one of the four Greater Antilles Islands, and lies east of Haiti and farthest out in the Atlantic Ocean. It is over 400 miles from the east coast of Cuba, a thousand miles from Havana, and about 1,450 miles from New York.

In size it is the smallest of the group. Its area is about 3,550 square miles. Its average length is about 95 miles; its average breadth about 35 miles. In shape it resembles the State of Connecticut, though it is only three-fourths the size of that state. . . .

The surface of Puerto Rico is mountainous. A range of hills traverses the island from east to west. The hills are low and their sides are covered with vegetation. The hills are not rocky and barren, but are cultivated to their very tops. The lower valleys are rich pasture lands or cultivated plantations. The knolls have orchards of coconuts and other trees. Coffee, protected by the shade of other trees, grows to the summits of the green hills. The ground is covered everywhere with a thick carpeting of grass.

The soil is remarkably fertile. This is due partly to the fine climate, partly to abundant moisture. The island has many fast flowing rivers. There are over 1,200 of these. In the mountains are numerous springs and waterfalls, but these are hidden by the overhanging giant ferns and plants.

WRITER'S CORNER

Write a summary of the business letter on page 298.

Tech Tip Post your summary on the class blog.

Business Telephone Calls

Even if you spend every waking minute after school talking on the phone with your friends— except for eating and doing homework, of course—you may not know how to make business telephone calls. Business calls are very different from personal calls, just as business letters are quite different from personal letters.

Suppose that you wrote a letter to Titanic Toys, presenting your idea for a new board game. Mr. Martindale from the company phoned while you were at soccer practice and left a message asking you to call him back. You're so excited that your heart is pounding. After you take a deep breath, follow these guidelines to make sure the telephone call goes smoothly.

Being Professional

- Before you call, take out a sheet of paper and a pencil. Make a few notes of what you'd like to say. During the call, jot down notes to keep track of the conversation and what you need to do as a result.
- Set your tone based on the purpose of your call. If you're pitching an idea or asking for a favor, be extra polite. Ask whether you have called at a convenient time, and if not, find out when you should call back. Show your enthusiasm with an upbeat tone. Thank the person for his or her time and consideration.
- If you're making a complaint, however, be more direct and persistent. If you don't feel your concerns are being addressed, ask to speak to a manager.
  - Listen actively to the person's responses. Prompt the person with responses such as *yes, OK, I understand,* and *great.* Ask follow-up questions that show you have been listening.
  - Above all, be polite to everyone you speak to, whether it is the receptionist or the owner of the company.

Communicating Professionally

- Immediately identify yourself and the purpose of the call. If the person you're trying to reach answers the phone, say something like "Good afternoon, this is Maris Nelson returning your call." If someone else answers, you might say "Good afternoon, this is Maris Nelson. I'm returning Mr. Martindale's call. Is he available?"
- If you're making a follow-up call, remind the person you're calling of the purpose of the call. People get busy at work, and if someone has forgotten why you're calling (or even who you are), don't take it personally.
- Sum up at the end of the conversation to make sure you both share the same understanding of what was said and what you decided to do. Thank the person for talking with you and set a time for your next conversation if one is necessary.
- If you reach someone's voice mail, leave a short message. State your name and telephone number slowly and clearly. Then briefly explain the purpose of your call. At the end of the message, state your name and phone number again so the person does not have to listen to the entire message again for this information.

ACTIVITY A Read the following scenarios. Using the guidelines, jot down notes on what you would say in a business call about each scenario.

1. A repair person fixed your washing machine last week, but it has stopped working again.

2. A famous filmmaker answered your letter. You want to invite her to speak at your school's film society.

3. You've been chosen to find out what happened to the uniforms that your team ordered. The order is now a month overdue.

4. A community foundation gives small grants to kids who have worthwhile projects. You have questions about how to apply.

SPEAKER'S CORNER

Imagine you are Maris Nelson. Practice what you would say if you reached Mr. Martindale's voice mail.

Tech Tip Record your message and review it for improvements.

Listening and Response Tips

Someday you may be on the receiving end of a business call. Here are some tips to help you listen and respond to the caller.

- Keep a notebook and pencil near the phone to jot down notes.
- Pay attention to the speaker's name. Refer to him or her by name.
- Listen actively. To show you are listening, offer occasional feedback or ask follow-up questions.
- If the caller explains anything complicated, repeat it back to the caller to be sure you have understood.
- Tell the caller what action you plan to take in response to the call. If you need to consult with someone else before making a decision, let the caller know.

ACTIVITY B Think of an idea for a new product that you could present over the phone to a company. For each step listed, jot down what you would say as you present your idea.

1. Greet the person.
2. Identify yourself.
3. State the purpose.
4. Describe the product.
5. Request action.
6. Thank the person.

ACTIVITY C Work with a partner to role-play the phone call you planned in Activity B. Take turns being the person making the call and the person receiving it. If you are the recipient of the call, respond as someone who is enthusiastic about the product. Use the Listening and Response Tips above. Critique each other's calls and revise your plan, taking your partner's comments into account.

As you practice your call, ask yourself the following questions:

- Did I greet the person and introduce myself politely?
- Did I concisely explain the purpose of the call?
- Did I describe the product clearly?
- Did I request action of some kind?
- Did I show that I was listening actively?
- Did I thank the person I called?

ACTIVITY D Practice your telephone call with a partner twice more with two different scenarios for the call's recipient. In the first scenario, the person you call is interested but not yet convinced your product will be successful. In the second scenario, the person is not interested in your product. Let your partner critique the content and delivery of your telephone call after you have finished.

ACTIVITY E Think of two more reasons you might call a business. It may be to inform the bank that your statement doesn't match the balance in your checkbook or to complain that the product you purchased doesn't work. Practice making these calls with a partner. Follow the speaking and listening tips outlined in this lesson.

ACTIVITY F Work with a partner to role-play a telephone inquiry call to a high school, magnet school, or college you wish to attend. Use the list below to develop your own set of questions to ask the recipient of your call. The recipient should jot down a list of things you have requested and repeat them back to you. Be sure to speak clearly and to the point. Make a good first impression.

1. Explain who you are and why you are calling: "I am interested in applying to your school . . ."
2. Ask any general questions that may affect your qualifications: "Do you accept applications from eighth graders who have not completed algebra?"
3. Request any information and application forms you need. Ask whether they have an informational Web site.
4. Give your full name and address, and get the full name and address of the proper person to whom you should send your application. If the application is online, make sure you ask for the e-mail address of the recipient. Even if this information is posted online, it is good to double-check to avoid confusion.
5. Ask about any special upcoming events for interested applicants. Meeting people face-to-face can give you an edge.

SPEAKER'S CORNER

Choose one of the telephone calls you practiced with a partner and present it to the class. Use cell phones as props if they are available. Concentrate your attention on the voice of your partner, who is playing the role of the receiver of the call, but turn toward the audience so they can hear you and see your face. Encourage your audience to offer feedback after you finish role-playing the call.

Prewriting and Drafting

Telephone calls and e-mail messages are routine and effective means of business communications. But neither has the authority of business letters. Often a letter is the first contact a businessperson has with the sender, and first impressions stick. That's why learning to write effective business letters and format them properly is so important.

Prewriting

When you write a business letter, prewriting is a time for gathering information and defining your purpose.

Nikki ordered a new pair of boots this winter from Outside Adventures, a company that sells camping equipment and clothing. Boots are an important part of her wardrobe because she trudges through snow for several months every year. These boots looked perfect, tall enough so that snow wouldn't come over the top and furry inside to keep her feet warm. When they arrived, the boots fit, and she liked the way they looked. But Nikki discovered a problem after she wore them for a few hours. The left boot wouldn't stay zipped up. As Nikki got more and more annoyed by having to zip up the boot over and over, she decided to compose a letter of complaint to Outside Adventures.

Gathering Information

Nikki knew that if she sent a letter addressed *To whom it may concern*, the letter might never reach the right person. To find the person or persons to whom she should write, she called the main number for Outside Adventures. A woman in customer relations told her to address her letter to Ethan Jones, the manager of customer service. Nikki also asked for the name of the purchasing director, Barbara Smythe, just to be sure that the person who buys products knows about the defective zipper. Finally, Nikki asked for the full address of Outside Adventures.

Defining the Purpose

Nikki next considered the purpose of her letter, **Ideas** or what she wanted it to accomplish. She used a pros and cons graphic organizer to decide.

PURPOSE	PROS	CONS
Express Anger	Feel better	No refund on boots
Ask for new boots	I like these boots, and will have a new pair.	They may break again.
Refund	Have money to buy new boots	Have to start new search for boots I like

Prewriting

Drafting

Content Editing

Revising

Copyediting

Proofreading

Publishing

Freewriting

After choosing your purpose, freewrite your letter. Jot down words and phrases as quickly as they come to mind. Record details such as date of purchase, guarantees, and any costs including original purchase, shipping, or repairs.

Did Nikki just want to express her irritation? Did she want a refund from Outside Adventures? Did she want the boots replaced, or would a credit be better so she could choose different boots? Since Nikki liked her boots, she decided to ask for another pair and keep her fingers crossed that the zippers on the new boots would stay zipped.

Your Turn

Have you had a complaint about a product you've used recently? Maybe you've thought of a way a product might be improved. Now is your opportunity to vent—or invent. Write a letter of complaint or a letter describing an improvement. Follow these steps:

- Decide on the problem or improvement you want to communicate and the right company to receive your letter.
- Figure out the purpose of the letter, or what action you want taken. Do you want to meet with someone to present your idea? Do you want a refund? Use the pros and cons graphic organizer to help you decide.
- Write a statement of purpose, which you can use when you draft your letter.

Drafting

Read over Nikki's draft. The purpose of the letter is very clear. The letter states the problem and suggests a solution. It includes polite words such as *thanks* and also includes a positive comment. But Nikki's letter does have some flaws. Can you figure out what they are?

December 12, 20—

7 Bailey Road
Clarkfield, MN 56223

Mr. Ethan Jones
Manager, Customer Service
Outside Adventures
1221 Greenview Boulevard
Racine, WI

Dear Mr. Jones:

Thanks for sending me the Outside Adventures catalog. I saw boots I wanted in it and I ordered them on November 3. They arrived promply on November 11 they looked awesome! I was so exited to get them. But they had a problem that I noticed only after I wore them for a few hours.

I was so disapointed to find out that the boots had a problem. I really needed boots and these were just the kind I wanted. I made sure that the zipper really was broken, because otherwise your boots were totally perfect tall enough so snow didn't come over the top and nice and furry to keep my feet warm. Anyway, the zipper on the left boot wouldn't stay up. How can your company make such lousy products?

I made sure the zipper was pulled up firmly. I even put a safety pin through the top of the zipper to see if that would help. It didn't, and why should I have to do this? You should send me new boots. Do you want me to send back these boots? Or do you have another suggestion? You'd better do something about this problem or you'll be sorry!

Thanks for taking care of this problem. I look forward with great anticipation to your resolution of this problem.

Sincerely Yours,

Nikki Van Zandt

Nikki Van Zandt

cc: B. Smythe

Prewriting

Drafting

Content Editing

Revising

Copyediting

Proofreading

Publishing

Nikki glanced at the notes she had made to help her draft a letter of complaint about the boot with the broken zipper. She had written Outside Adventures' address, as well as the name and title of the person to whom the letter was addressed. She had planned what she intended to write in the first, second, and final paragraphs, so she had no trouble getting started. What details did she include in the first paragraph? Why?

Organization

Establishing a Consistent Tone

All business letters should have a courteous, professional, and direct tone. Is the tone of your letter consistent, or does it vary, perhaps by alternating between too formal and too casual, too angry and too friendly?

Try reading aloud your draft. What tone of voice would fit each sentence you have written? If your tone of voice varies quite a bit, perhaps the tone of the draft also varies too much.

Voice

Your Turn

Use the notes you made to draft your letter. Keep your audience in mind and focus on your purpose. Write your letter to try to achieve that purpose.

- In the introductory paragraph, state the purpose.
- In the supporting paragraph or paragraphs, give background information, details, reasons, and so on.
- In the closing paragraph, request action.

Double-space your draft so that you and your editing partner will have enough space to insert corrections and write comments.

Content Editing

A content editor checks ideas for logic, order, and clarity. Nikki knew how important it was that the form of her letter be correct, the tone appropriate, and the content persuasive in order for Outside Adventures to take her letter seriously.

The next day, when she was rested and could look at it with fresh eyes, Nikki turned on the computer and

Sentence Fluency

reread the letter. She tried to put herself in the place of the person who would receive the letter, a revision strategy intended to help strengthen the content and organization. She went over the Content Editor's Checklist that the students in her class use to revise business letters and marked off each item after she checked her letter. Nikki typed questions and comments into the letter in her favorite color, bright orange. That way she could distinguish her comments from the body of the letter.

After Nikki reread the comments she made, she revised the letter. Then she asked her classmate Asha to read it and make suggestions for improvement. She knew that Asha would be able to look at it objectively and notice mistakes and confusing passages more easily than Nikki herself could.

Content Editor's Checklist

- ☐ Does the first paragraph clearly establish the purpose of the letter?
- ☐ Do the next paragraphs give reasons, examples, and details that support the purpose?
- ☐ Does the order in which the information is presented make sense, and is the information tailored to the audience?
- ☐ Do these paragraphs include only relevant information?
- ☐ Does the final paragraph restate the goal and ask for action?
- ☐ Is the tone consistent? Is it courteous and professional?

Asha read Nikki's letter several times. She consulted the Content Editor's Checklist and took a few notes. Then she and Nikki discussed the ways Asha thought the letter might be improved. Here are some of the comments Asha made to Nikki.

- Your letter states its purpose clearly and suggests a solution. I like that, but I think you should state the problem right away in the first paragraph.

- Do you really need to thank the person for sending the catalog? After all, it's routine for companies to send catalogs, hoping to sell things. Also, the person you're going to send the letter to probably didn't send the catalog.

- The tone of the last sentence in your letter is very formal. It seems quite different from the rest of the letter. I'm not sure whether it would be better to make the rest of the letter more formal or this sentence less formal, but I think you should do one or the other.

- In the last two paragraphs, you ask Mr. Jones a question, but you don't suggest whether he should write back or call you. Perhaps you could ask him to call you and add your phone number in the heading.

Asha pointed out several things that Nikki missed, such as the repetition and the inconsistent tone. After her editing conference with Asha, Nikki thought about what she would do to improve her draft.

Your Turn

Use the Content Editor's Checklist to help you revise your draft letter.

- State your purpose as clearly as you can and use details and examples to support your position. If your sentences don't bolster your argument, get rid of them.

- Trade drafts with an editing partner in your class. The two of you should read and comment on each other's letters, again using the Content Editor's Checklist as a guide.

- Begin by talking about some things you liked about the letter. Then discuss with each other your suggestions for improvement.

- Be specific and constructive in your comments. Remember that you are making suggestions. It's the writer's job to decide which comments to accept and which to reject.

Prewriting

Drafting

Content Editing

Revising

Copyediting

Proofreading

Publishing

Revising

This is Nikki's second draft of the letter to Outside Adventures based on her own and Asha's suggestions.

December 12, 20—

7 Bailey Road
Clarkfield, MN 56223
(708) 555-1322
Mr. Ethan Jones
Manager, Customer Service
Outside Adventures
1221 Greenview Boulevard
Racine, WI

Dear Mr. Jones:

I ordered a pair of boots from an Outside Adventures catalog on November 3.
~~Thanks for sending me the Outside Adventures catalog. I saw boots I wanted in it and~~
~~I ordered them on November 3.~~ They arrived promply on November 11 *and* they looked

But I was disappointed to find that the left boot had a faulty zipper, which
awesome! ~~I was so exited to get them. But they had a problem that~~ I noticed only

after I wore them for a few hours.

~~I was so disapointed to find out that the boots had a problem. I really needed boots~~
~~and these were just the kind I wanted.~~ I made sure that the zipper really was broken,

for our deep winter snow
because otherwise your boots were totally perfect tall enough so snow didn't come

over the top and nice and furry to keep my feet warm. ~~Anyway, the zipper on the left~~
~~boot wouldn't stay up. How can your company make such lousy products?~~

pulled

I ~~made sure~~ the zipper ~~was pulled~~ up firmly. I even put a safety pin through the top of the zipper to see if that would help. It didn't, and why should I have to do this? You

a pair of   If you are planning to send new boots,

should send me new boots. Do you want me to send back these boots? Or do you have another suggestion? ~~You'd better do something about this problem or you'll be sorry!~~

resolving the problem with the defective zipper. Please call me at the number

Thanks for ~~taking care of this problem. I look forward with great anticipation to your~~ above to address this issue. I look forward to hearing from you as soon as possible. ~~resolution of this problem.~~

Sincerely Yours,

Nikki Van Zandt

Nikki Van Zandt

cc: B. Smythe

Notice how Nikki improved her letter. She took out some sentences such as "How can

Word Choice

your company make such lousy products?" and "You'd better do something about this problem or you'll be sorry!" How did these deletions affect the tone of her letter? In the last paragraph, she changed the tone to make it less formal. What did she add?

Compare Nikki's second draft with the first draft. In what other ways has Nikki improved her letter? In what other ways might she make her letter better?

Your Turn

- Using your own ideas and the suggestions from your editing partner, revise your letter.
- Review the Content Editor's Checklist again to make sure that you can answer yes to each question.

Copyediting and Proofreading

Copyediting

After Nikki used the Content Editor's Checklist and Asha's suggestions to help her revise her letter, she was confident that it made sense and had a clear purpose and supporting details. Because she wanted to make sure that every word was appropriate, she reviewed her letter for accuracy in word meaning, sentence structure, and logic, using the Copyeditor's Checklist.

Nikki asked Asha to read aloud the letter while Nikki listened. In that way Nikki would notice whether any words she used were too casual or whether her sentences were unclear.

Asha was uneasy with her description of the boots as *awesome*. She suspected that some people reading the letter might think that the slang word *awesome* was too casual to use in a business letter. Nikki changed *awesome* to *wonderful*. Nikki made two other word changes. She took out the word *totally* because it seemed both too casual and unnecessary. She deleted the words *nice and* from the phrase *nice and furry* for the same reason.

Nikki made sentence changes too. For example, she moved the question "Or do you have another suggestion?" and combined it with the first sentence of the paragraph.

Copyeditor's Checklist

☐ Are any sentences awkward or confusing?

☐ Is every sentence and every word in the letter needed?

☐ Is there a variety in sentence length?

☐ Is the structure of each sentence logical and grammatically correct?

☐ Is the letter written in the format of a business letter?

☐ Is the language appropriate for business communications?

Your Turn

Ask your editing partner to read aloud your revised letter or read it aloud yourself. Pay close attention to the words in each sentence. Use the Copyeditor's Checklist to help you.

Prewriting

Drafting

Content Editing

Revising

Copyediting

Proofreading

Publishing

Proofreading

Nikki input all the revisions that she found when copyediting her letter. Next, she used the

Conventions grammar-checker and spell-checker on her computer. After that, she read over the letter herself.

Nikki carefully checked the format of the letter. She also used the Proofreader's Checklist.

Nikki asked another friend, Kay, to help her proofread the letter. They both checked the format, spelling, grammar, and punctuation. When they were finished, they compared the errors they found.

Proofreader's Checklist

☐ Is there a line of space before each new paragraph?

☐ Have any words been misspelled?

☐ Are there any errors in grammar?

☐ Are capitalization and punctuation correct?

☐ Were new errors introduced during editing?

Your Turn

Use the Proofreader's Checklist to proofread your letter carefully. To avoid missing mistakes, go through your letter once for each item on the list.

- Check the entire letter to make sure it has all the parts of a business letter
- Check the format.
- Make sure you have used capital letters correctly.
- Continue with the rest of the items on the list, checking your letter item by item.
- If your letter is on a computer, use the spell-checker.

After you proofread your letter, exchange letters with a classmate.

- Proofread your classmate's letter and ask your classmate to proofread yours, again using the Proofreader's Checklist.
- Use a dictionary to check the spelling of compound words and any other words for which you are not entirely certain of the spelling or meaning.

Writer's Tip When writing a business letter on a computer, use a readable, professional font such as Times New Roman, size 12. Arial, Helvetica, and Verdana are also acceptable fonts.

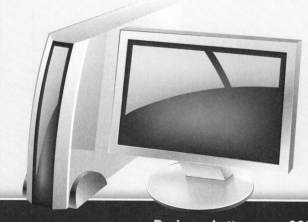

Publishing

This is Nikki's edited and proofread letter to Outside Adventures.

7 Bailey Road
Clarkfield, MN 56223
(708) 555-1322

December 12, 20—

Mr. Ethan Jones
Manager, Customer Service
Outside Adventures
1221 Greenview Boulevard
Racine, WI 53407

Dear Mr. Jones:
I ordered a pair of boots from an Outside Adventures catalog on November 3. They arrived promptly on November 11, and they looked wonderful! But I was disappointed to find that the left boot had a faulty zipper, which I noticed only after I wore the boots for a few hours.

I made sure that the zipper really was broken, because otherwise the boots are perfect for our deep winter snow—tall enough so snow doesn't come over the top and furry enough to keep my feet warm. I pulled the zipper up firmly. I even put a safety pin through the top of the zipper to see if that would help. It didn't, and why should I have to do this?

I think you should send me a new pair of boots, unless you have a better suggestion. If you are planning to send new boots, do you want me to send back this pair?

Thanks for resolving the problem with the defective zipper. Please call me at the number above to address this issue. I look forward to hearing from you as soon as possible.

Sincerely yours,
Nikki Van Zandt
Nikki Van Zandt

cc: B. Smythe

You have put a lot of hard work into creating a clear business letter. Here are a few ways you can share your work with others.

 Put your letter in a portfolio to refer to as a model in the future. It will also serve as a record if you need to refer to it later.

 Mail or e-mail your letter, but don't forget to sign it. You can add a signature insert through most word-processing programs.

 Make a classroom newsletter. Include your letter with your classmates' letters in a "Letters to the Editor" section.

 Post your letter on your class wiki or blog for peer review. Ask your classmates for feedback on your word choice and tone.

Your Turn

To produce a final copy of your letter, make your last corrections and read it over. Make **Presentation** sure all the parts of the letter are included and don't forget the date or your signature. Finally, make sure no spelling or punctuation errors crept in when you copied or input your final draft.

When you are sure that your letter is ready to be published, print it out and sign your name below the closing. Then fold your letter into thirds. Begin by folding the bottom third of the paper up. Next, fold the top third of the paper down. Last, press the folds firmly so that the letter is flat.

Address a business-sized envelope to the company, copying the inside address exactly. Put the return address in the upper left-hand corner of the envelope.

When you have finished, put the letter in the classroom mailbox. Then take one of your classmates' letters from the mailbox and open it. Read the letter and provide feedback. If you had received this letter, how would you respond to it?

Prewriting
Drafting
Content Editing
Revising
Copyediting
Proofreading
Publishing

7 Bailey Road
Clarkfield, MN 56223

Mr. Ethan Jones
Manager, Customer Service
Outside Adventures
1221 Greenview Boulevard
Racine, WI 53407

Descriptions

LiNK ## The King of the Golden River

by John Ruskin

In a secluded and mountainous part of Stiria there was, in old time, a valley of the most surprising and luxuriant fertility. It was surrounded, on all sides, by steep and rocky mountains, rising into peaks, which were always covered with snow, and from which a number of torrents descended in constant cataracts. One of these fell westward, over the face of a crag so high, that, when the sun had set to everything else, and all below was darkness, his beams still shone full upon this waterfall, so that it looked like a shower of gold. It was, therefore, called by the people of the neighborhood, the Golden River. . . . In time of drought and heat, when all the country round was burnt up, there was still rain in the little valley; and its crops were so heavy, and its hay so high, and its apples so red, and its grapes so blue, and its wine so rich, and its honey so sweet that it was a marvel to everyone who beheld it, and was commonly called the Treasure Valley.

> This is an example of good descriptive writing. Ruskin uses words that create memorable sensory images for the reader.

Noah Greene
Room Number 278

Dazzled by the Teeming City

From the moment you step off the train and into the cavernous main concourse of Grand Central Terminal, you know that you are in New York City. Perhaps no other building in Manhattan more thoroughly embodies the broad diversity of this city's inhabitants. They shuttle this way and that, like a sea of humanity of which you are just a tiny drop.

When you leave the terminal, the city overwhelms you. Though you might want to hurry, the torrent of sensations stops you short. First, there is the noise: the chattering of voices, the rumbling of cars, and the honking of horns all merge into one chaotic symphony. Then there are the smells. Far from the pastoral scent of nature so familiar to the countryside, New York offers a potpourri of contrasting odors, from exhaust fumes and garbage to the sweet smell of hot, steaming peanuts from nearby street vendors.

What really strikes you, though, are the sights. You'll have to crane your neck to find the top of the buildings that tower above you. To your right and left you see an endless line of cars, trucks, and taxis inching down East 42nd Street. On the sidewalk, people hurry by—dressed in suit coats or T-shirts, wearing smiles or scowls, and speaking in languages you never knew existed. The pace of it all seems frantic, but keeping up is possible. Just take a breath, step onto the sidewalk, and get ready to take a bite out of the Big Apple.

What Makes a Good Description?

Descriptive writing uses vivid language to bring to life a person, a place, a thing, or an idea. Descriptions can be objective, such as describing a baby spreading cereal and bananas on her face. Descriptions also can be subjective, such as describing your feelings as you awaited your turn in the final round of the National Spelling Bee.

Word Choice

Good descriptive writing sketches its subject in words so vivid, precise, and concrete that a detailed picture forms in readers' minds. Writers choose sensory words, which evoke the senses. Metaphors, similes, and other figures of speech can create memorable word pictures.

The writer of "Dazzled by the Teeming City" chooses vivid adjectives such as *cavernous, chaotic,* and *pastoral.* He also chooses verbs that create a strong image, such as *shuttle, chattering, rumbling,* and *tower.* Finally, the writer uses similes and metaphors to create images. A symphony is a metaphor for the city sounds, the crowds are compared to a sea, and taking a bite out of an apple is a metaphor for exploring New York City.

Purpose and Mood

Mood is the overall impression or emotion expressed in a piece of writing. The careful use of vivid words is one way to set a mood for the subject of a description. The writer of "Dazzled by the Teeming City" does not describe the train he got off or the suitcase he carries. Instead, he focuses on the sights, sounds, and odors of the city because he is eager to begin his tour.

You know the writer's mood is eager anticipation when he calls the city sounds a symphony, implying that the sounds are wonderful despite the chaos. Even potentially offensive odors, such as exhaust fumes, are mingled with the mouth-watering smell of hot, steaming peanuts. How else does the writer convey mood?

ACTIVITY A Rewrite the sentences below to make them more interesting. Add descriptive words or substitute vivid, concrete words for vague, overused ones.

1. We went into the ballroom.
2. The happy child ran to his mother, who was waiting for him.
3. The queen placed the crown on her head and looked out at the people.
4. In the distance we saw a mountain outlined against the sky.
5. The horse ran along the track.
6. Stanley works in a small office without windows.
7. I couldn't solve a difficult puzzle like that one.
8. Seagulls flew back and forth as the waves came onto the beach.
9. My mother criticized me for staying out too late.
10. Our teacher likes to tell us about the things her dogs do.

ACTIVITY B From the topics below, choose five that interest you most. For each topic write a descriptive sentence that might appear in a paragraph describing the topic.

1. Times Square in New York City on New Year's Eve
2. the Battle of Gettysburg
3. a 100-year-old house
4. the big blizzard
5. the electricity suddenly going out
6. Wilbur in *Charlotte's Web*
7. making chocolate fudge
8. an expert juggler at work
9. the tallest building in the world
10. shopping on the day after Thanksgiving

ACTIVITY C Rewrite the following phrases. Change the nondescript verbs to vivid verbs that create more memorable word pictures and stronger moods.

1. Jesse said . . .
2. Lucy ran . . .
3. Xavier ate . . .
4. Shoshona looked . . .

WRITER'S CORNER

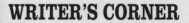

Choose two phrases you changed in Activity C and make them complete sentences with additional descriptive words.

ACTIVITY D Read these paragraphs from two descriptions, both of which describe the same event. Then answer the questions that follow.

A. From the moment I arrived at the gazebo that stood in the center of the park on a deep green carpet of grass, I knew the concert would be a smashing success. My red-and-white band uniform was dry-cleaned and freshly pressed, and I had my saxophone and the new reeds I had bought the night before. Most of the school band had already arrived, and I could hear the scraps of music coming from them as they were warming up. My stomach filled with butterflies at the sight of all 60 of us in uniform for the first time that autumn. Mr. Bretzloft, the conductor, was there too, dressed in his white three-piece suit with a maroon-colored shirt and white tie. He sat on a small, wooden folding chair, studying some notes, with a furrowed brow that created a deep crease across his forehead.

B. From the moment that I arrived at the dilapidated gazebo that squatted on the park grounds like a mangy dog, a sinking sensation stole into my belly and told me the concert would not go well. The muggy, humid evening air blanketed the park and set everyone on edge. Only half of the band members had bothered to show up, and of that number, only a third were in uniform. My own red-and-white uniform still bore the mustard stain from last week's hot dog on its white tunic. Mr. Bretzloft, the conductor, was there, dressed in a gray wool suit. He was pacing back and forth, ordering the wayward players back to their assigned seats. Tired notes wheezed here and there as some members in the band warmed up.

1. What are some details that are included in both paragraphs?

2. How are the details shown differently in each paragraph?

3. Which details are sensory details? To which senses do the details appeal?

4. How would you compare the mood of the two paragraphs?

5. What are some words that helped you figure out the mood?

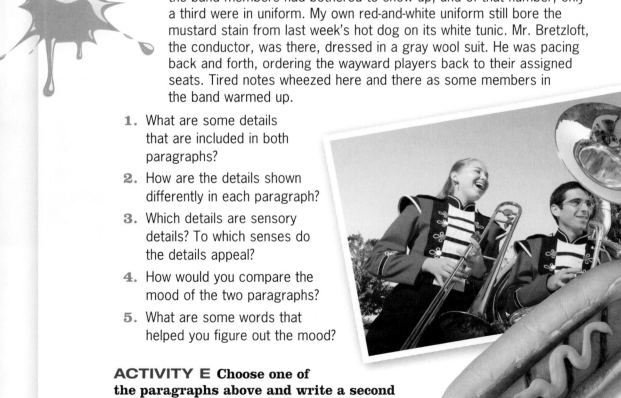

ACTIVITY E Choose one of the paragraphs above and write a second paragraph to the story. Use vivid words and sensory details to convey the same mood as the original paragraph.

ACTIVITY F Rewrite the sentences below, using different verbs and adjectives to set a new mood.

1. Ray straightened his starched collar and marched into the bustling office for his job interview.
2. A driving rain battered the creaky house.
3. Hanging from a nearly invisible thread, the rust-colored spider labored to spin its web.
4. Her many layers of clothing made the woman on the park bench look like an overstuffed easy chair.
5. As we crept down the rickety cellar stairs, a damp, musty smell enveloped us.
6. Alicia's joyous squeal echoed through the hall.
7. The blazing sun beat down mercilessly on the exhausted hiker.
8. As I woke up, I breathed in the smell of bacon coming from the kitchen downstairs.

ACTIVITY G Rewrite the sentences to include additional sensory details such as sights, sounds, or smells that are not mentioned in the original sentence.

1. The office building is around the corner.
2. Yolanda hung the painting on the wall.
3. Three mules stood outside the barn.
4. I can hear the concert from my apartment.
5. Isa opened the door and looked into the basement.
6. The fireworks lit up the sky.
7. We spent the summer day at the beach.
8. The mountain stood behind the valley.
9. The cat chased after the mouse.
10. Dinner simmered on the stove.

WRITER'S CORNER

Choose one of the sentences you wrote in Activity F or G and expand it into a short description.

Organization

Good descriptive writing never lists details at random. Writers organize the details they observe in a meaningful way to create the mood and to build important ideas or themes. Writers commonly organize descriptive writing in the following ways. Sometimes these methods are combined, and sometimes sentences depart from an overall organization for emphasis, particularly in introductions and conclusions.

Chronological Order

Descriptive writing that follows chronological order describes a scene in the order that it unfolds. This organization may be useful in describing an elaborate dance routine or telling how the sky changes colors as the sun peeks over the horizon.

Spatial Order

In spatial order, details are described in the order they appear in a given space. For example, you might describe a building from left to right, from top to bottom, or from the inside out. Can you think of any other ways that things might be described using spatial order?

Order of Importance

Another way to organize details is by order of importance, either from least to most important or from most to least important. A description of a new bike can move from the least impressive to the most impressive features, while a description of your feelings can list the strongest feelings last.

Comparison and Contrast

When writers compare and contrast, they state likenesses and differences, particularly when they describe two or more people, places, things, or ideas. Effective comparative descriptions give equal weight to the subjects being compared.

ACTIVITY A Read the descriptive paragraphs below and identify their method of organization.

Mies van der Rohe's Farnsworth House in Plano, Illinois

1. Mies van der Rohe's Farnsworth House is an elegant example of the International Style of architecture. The house consists of two rectangular blocks, each supported by white-painted steel columns. The façade is glass, forming a transparent cube that seems to float above the ground, bracketed by the columns. From the inside, one realizes that in a glass box, the distinction between inside and outside almost disappears.

2. As I envision the qualities of an ideal class president, the essential one is integrity. Our president must be honest and trustworthy in dealing with the student body, the administration, and the community at large. The president must also be a people person, because he or she must communicate and work with all the different interest groups at school. Finally, the president must be a good communicator, able to articulate a vision and draw us all together.

3. The twins' personalities couldn't be more different. Jason is shy, quiet, thoughtful, and smart. He is clueless about the music the rest of us listen to and the TV shows we watch. If I were in a jam, though, Jason would be the sibling I'd ask for help. Jenna, on the other hand, is a total social butterfly. She works just hard enough to get decent grades so she can spend the rest of her time hanging out at the mall or talking on the phone. Want to know about the supposedly private lives of pop stars? Ask Jenna.

4. To create a PowerPoint presentation, you must begin by creating your own slides from scratch or using the template given. The first slide is the title slide. Add text to this slide. Next, click on the "Next Slide" button to create a new slide. Once again start by adding the text. After this you can add movement, such as bulleted items of text that slide in from offscreen. You can also add images. When you have completed this slide, click on "Next Slide" again. If you think your slides should be placed in a different order, go to "outline" and rearrange them.

WRITER'S CORNER

Write five sentences describing someone famous you admire. Organize the details in your writing by order of importance.

Tech Tip Post your description on the class blog.

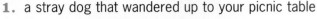

ACTIVITY B List four details you might include in writing about each of the following topics. Tell which form of organization you would use in writing a paragraph on each topic. Explain why.

1. a stray dog that wandered up to your picnic table
2. an energy-efficient home office
3. the kitchen in your home after you have made dinner
4. a perfect summer day
5. an invention that changed history
6. a fashionable shopping area of a big city
7. the most amazing person you ever met
8. the network of highways surrounding a city

ACTIVITY C Kayla wanted to describe the Independence Day fireworks celebration in chronological order. However, some events are out of sequence. Rewrite the paragraph, putting all the events Kayla described in chronological order.

An hour later, in complete darkness, the fireworks show began. After we spread out the blanket, we amused ourselves by racing out along the beach and dipping our feet in the water. The best part was the finale, a barrage of reds and yellows exploding on top of each other and lighting up the sky. Next, we dried off our feet and munched on the light snack of fruit, crackers, and cheese that we brought in our picnic basket. When the sun had finally set, but before darkness enveloped the beach, two boys nearby waved sparklers, writing their names and creating intricate patterns in the twilight air. The sun had not yet set, but had expanded into a wide, orange disk that hung close to the horizon when my mother, sister, and I arrived at the beach to wait for the show to begin. During the show, bouquets of pyrotechnics popped gracefully outward and faded just as quickly.

ACTIVITY D With a small group, read the excerpt from *The Reptile Room* on page 345 and discuss the following questions.

1. How is the excerpt organized?
2. What is the mood of the excerpt? What descriptions helped you decide the mood?
3. What sensory details does the excerpt include?

ACTIVITY E James wanted to describe his house from the outside to the inside, using spatial order. But his description is confusing because the sentences are out of order. Rewrite the paragraph to describe the house from the outside to inside the writer's bedroom.

My bed is located against the far wall of my bedroom, under the window that faces the street. The house itself is made of red bricks and has a mahogany front door. A wood-paneled corridor on the left of the entry hall leads to the bedrooms. My house is easy to spot from the street because it has shrubs lining the concrete walkway to the front door. My bedroom is the first door on the left in the corridor, just past the picture of my great-grandmother. Stepping into the tiled, rectangular entry hall from the front door bathes the visitor in warm sunlight that comes from the skylight above.

ACTIVITY F Write a paragraph describing one of the following situations. Use order of importance, chronological order, comparison and contrast, or spatial order.

1. You are a sports reporter for your school newspaper and have just finished watching a game where the school record for points scored by a single player was broken. Describe the game.

2. Describe the new bike you just received. How is it different from your old bike?

3. Your birthday party must have been a success. Just look at the mess. Describe the family room and kitchen after the party.

4. You come back from Disney World just as the builders are finishing your $12 million house. You had no idea it would look like this. Describe your new mansion.

5. After years of pleading, your parents have finally agreed to let you have the pet you've always wanted. Describe the pet of your dreams.

WRITER'S CORNER

With a partner choose a situation from Activity F that neither of you wrote about. Write a description together. After you have finished, discuss the effectiveness of its organization.

Graphic Organizers

When you have decided how to organize a description, the right graphic organizer can help you map it out in more detail. As you learned in Chapter 1, a time line can help organize writing in chronological order. A Venn diagram is useful when comparing and contrasting two items or ideas, while a word web can help organize details in a variety of ways.

Venn Diagrams

Maya is writing about the former library in her town, which is now a Boys and Girls Club, and the new library, which was completed last year. She thinks the new library is beautiful, but she loved the comfortable, old library too. To explore her ideas and feelings about the buildings, she compares and contrasts them.

Maya begins by making a Venn diagram, which will help her sort out the differences and similarities between the two buildings. She writes the similarities between the buildings in the overlapping part of the circles and the differences in the parts of the circles that do not overlap.

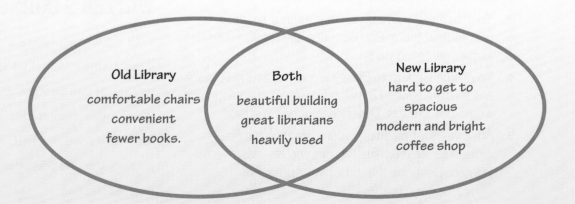

Old Library
comfortable chairs
convenient
fewer books.

Both
beautiful building
great librarians
heavily used

New Library
hard to get to
spacious
modern and bright
coffee shop

ACTIVITY A Answer the following questions about Maya's Venn diagram.

1. Which library is cozy?
2. Which library is modern?
3. Which library is more beautiful?
4. Write a summary sentence of Maya's thoughts on the libraries.

ACTIVITY B Make a Venn diagram to compare and contrast two familiar buildings. You might choose two houses in which you have lived, two schools you attended, two department stores you like, or any other buildings you know well. Write at least three differences and three similarities for each building.

ACTIVITY C Using the information from the Venn diagram on page 346, write pairs of sentences that compare and contrast the following details of the two libraries.

1. convenience
2. appearance
3. librarians
4. other features

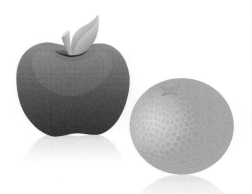

ACTIVITY D Make a Venn diagram to compare and contrast one of the following pairs. Then write a sentence that tells the reader what the description is about.

1. spring and autumn
2. apples and oranges
3. dogs as pets and cats as pets
4. baseball and tennis

WRITER'S CORNER

Make a Venn diagram comparing two of your favorite leisure activities. How are the two activities alike? How are they different? Write your answers in a descriptive paragraph.

Word Webs

A word web is a graphic organizer that can help you organize your ideas in a variety of ways, such as spatial order or order of importance.

Ellen is writing a description of the city's new museum. Because the museum deals with so many aspects of the city, she used a word web to organize her thoughts about what she saw.

A word web is a useful tool for organizing a description of a place. The floor plan of a museum divides the subjects it covers into separate areas within the building. Ellen created a word web based on the separate areas of the museum.

After you finish your word web, look at it and decide if you have too much information. If so, eliminate some of the least important details from your subtopics.

This is how Ellen developed her word web for the Mayville Historical Museum.

1. Ellen started her word web with the central topic and drew a box around it. In this case the main topic is Mayville Historical Museum.
2. Next, she wrote four subtopics that are dealt with at the museum. She then drew an oval around each subtopic. The subtopics are arranged so that they stem from the main topic like spokes on a wheel.
3. Around each subtopic she wrote details relating to that particular subtopic. These are the details that will most likely fill out her description.

Study Ellen's word web on page 348. How many paragraphs do you think she will include in the body of her description? Why do you think so?

ACTIVITY E Make word webs for three of the following topics. Use a textbook, an encyclopedia, or the Internet to help you.

1. wind instruments in the orchestra
2. the parts of a flower
3. the branches of the federal government
4. types of clouds
5. Olympic Games
6. attending a ball game
7. World War II battles in Europe

ACTIVITY F With a partner make a word web for your city or town. Then write separate paragraphs in either spatial order or order of importance, using different details from the word web. Read your paragraphs to the class. Listen to your classmates' paragraphs. How similar are their paragraphs to yours? What did your classmates include that you did not?

WRITER'S CORNER

Select one of the word webs you made for Activity E. Write a paragraph using the details in your word web.

Thesaurus

One of a writer's most useful tools is a thesaurus, a book of synonyms and related words. A thesaurus can help you choose precise and vivid words and avoid repeating words in your writing.

Dictionary Thesaurus

In a dictionary thesaurus, you simply look up the word that you want to replace. The book is organized alphabetically, and the writer chooses from a list of synonyms and related words that accompany each entry. The dictionary style is easy to use, but thesauruses organized this way take up more pages and are more repetitious than those that follow the index style.

Index Thesaurus

The entries of an index thesaurus are organized under classes of ideas. Under each class is a list of more specific words that make up that class. Finally, under each word is the full numbered entry that lists all the synonyms.

Using an index thesaurus takes a couple of steps. First, turn to the index at the back of the book and find the word that you want to replace. When you find that word, you will see a list of possible uses of that word, each followed by a number. Flip through the thesaurus, using the guide numbers at the top of the pages to find the number listed in the index.

Suppose you wanted to find a word to replace *prize,* which you

prize

> *noun:* desire 100.11
> award 646.2
> leverage 906.1

646.2
award, reward, prize, first prize, second prize, etc;
blue ribbon; consolation prize; Nobel prize

used too often in a description of prize-winning architecture. After *prize* in the index, you note the number 646.2, which matches the meaning of the word *prize* as it relates to *award*. Using the guide numbers at the top of the pages, you quickly locate 646.2 under *HONOR*.

You will find a list of words such as *award, reward,* and *blue ribbon* to choose from. Any of these words might be a good replacement for *prize*. The advantage of using an index thesaurus is that it gives you a broader range of possible word choices.

Online Thesauruses

You can also use the Internet for help with words. You can choose from dozens of online thesauruses, and most are easy to use. Usually, you type the word for which you would like to find a synonym, click on the search button, and choose a suitable word from the list of suggestions that pop up.

ACTIVITY A Read the following paragraph about writer and explorer John Wesley Powell's expedition through the American West. Use a thesaurus to replace the italicized words with more exact ones.

John Wesley Powell enjoyed naming many of the places he saw. At one point on the Colorado River, one boat was *broken* on the rocks. Powell named the site "Disaster Falls." Later he called a *part* of the river that was thick with mud "Dirty Devil." When things got very *bad* for his expedition, Powell stopped to pray for *help* by a *pretty* stream. He named the stream "Bright Angel."

Grand Canyon expedition of John Wesley Powell

ACTIVITY B Using a dictionary thesaurus, an index thesaurus, or an online thesaurus, find three synonyms to replace each word below. Then write sentences using one of the synonyms.

1. pay
2. joke
3. ruin
4. vacation
5. charm
6. manage

WRITER'S CORNER

Choose two words from the description you wrote for the Writer's Corner on page 347. Then, using a thesaurus, find two vivid synonyms for each word.

Tech Tip With an adult, find vivid words in an online thesaurus.

Hamlet

To sleep, perchance to dream.
Ay, there's the rub,
For in that sleep of death what
dreams may come
When we have shuffled off this
mortal coil . . .
For who would bear the whips
and scorns of time . . .

William Shakespeare

Denotation and Connotation

When you use a thesaurus, remember that words have both denotations, or literal meanings, and connotations, or implied meanings. Be careful when using a thesaurus to replace a word with a synonym whose meaning isn't clear to you. You may choose a word whose connotation was not what you intended. The best rule to follow is this: If you don't know the meaning of a word, look it up in a dictionary.

Here's an example of what can happen if you ignore this rule. Suppose you were describing someone with whom you liked to pass the time and whom you trusted. You might describe this person as a *friend* or *pal,* but would you want to describe that person as an *acquaintance* or a *colleague*? Obviously you would not. An acquaintance is someone you may merely nod to in the hallway, and a colleague is someone you work with.

ACTIVITY C Read each sentence and the words that follow it. Use a thesaurus and a dictionary to choose the best word to replace the italicized word in each sentence. Make sure you choose a word with the same connotation.

1. Though the building sits on marshy land, underground supports will keep the city's newest skyscraper *stable.*

   indestructible   immobile   secure   established   permanent

2. The *populace* of cities come from varied backgrounds.

   inhabitants   natives   pioneers   lodgers   occupiers

3. Some kids like wearing *hand-me-downs* from older brothers or sisters, but most don't.

   duds   tatters   clothing   rags   castoffs

4. I've never heard *yells* like the ones that erupted when our team finally won.

   cheers   screams   shouts   hooplas   hurrahs

5. Union and management hammered out an *agreement* so that the renovation of city hall could continue.

   adjustment   contract   regulation   assimilation   reconciliation

ACTIVITY D Use a dictionary to find the denotation of each word below. Then use a thesaurus to find three synonyms with different connotations for each word.

1. thought
2. weak
3. rare
4. shake
5. follow
6. mass

ACTIVITY E Choose two words below. Find each word in a thesaurus. Write a descriptive sentence for two synonyms of each word that you chose.

1. fake
2. eerie
3. sloppy
4. slow

ACTIVITY F Explain the differences in connotation among the words in each group. Use a dictionary if you need to check the exact meaning of any words.

1. sleepless, watchful, aware
2. gluttony, overeating, piggishness
3. solitude, loneliness, isolation
4. sociable, talkative, jolly
5. trendy, up-to-date, fashionable
6. servant, drudge, custodian
7. gab, speak up, talk
8. beast, critter, creature
9. nuke, destroy, ravage
10. camouflage, eclipse, hide

WRITER'S CORNER

Write a paragraph to follow the descriptive paragraph you wrote for the Writer's Corner on page 349. Use a thesaurus to choose words with connotations that convey the same tone as your first paragraph.

Grammar in Action. Find the two infinitives that are direct objects in the p. 337 description.

Figurative Language

Like the connotations of words, figurative language goes beyond the literal meanings of words. Figures of speech such as similes, metaphors, personification, and hyperbole are examples of figurative language that can create vivid pictures in readers' minds. That's why these and other figures of speech are so useful in descriptive writing.

A **simile** uses the words *like* or *as* to compare two unrelated things.

> **That high-rise looks like a glass arrow aimed at the sky.**
> **My pink velvet dress is as soft as a whisper.**

Many similes, such as *like a ton of bricks* or *as quiet as a mouse,* are **clichés.** Clichés are similes that have become overused and worn-out. Try to avoid using clichés in your writing.

A **metaphor** is an implied comparison between two different things. It's almost like a simile except that *like* and *as* are not used.

> **Max's poems are caravans of the imagination.**
> **Shanti's eyes are bottomless pools of feeling.**

Personification is a figure of speech that allows an idea, inanimate object, or animal to take on the qualities of a person.

> **Outside, the wind shrieked through the eaves of the house.**
> **The dog's constant barking mocked Tim's attempts to silence it.**

Hyperbole is deliberate exaggeration. The exaggeration reveals the truth about something in order to emphasize an idea.

> **Ana can talk until your ears fall off.**
> **My old dog's breath could curdle milk.**

Woof! Woof!

ACTIVITY A Identify which two things are being compared in each of the following similes. Write the quality or idea that the things share.

EXAMPLE **My brother Sam's *brain* works like a *computer*.**
A brain is compared to a computer.

1. Wind shook the branches as a mother dog shakes her pups.
2. After a demanding performance, the ballet dancer collapsed like a discarded marionette.
3. That poodle's teeth were as sharp as needles.
4. If you use the wrong ingredients for the recipe, the muffins will taste like sand.
5. That deed is as phony as a rubber chicken.
6. When he saw the scratch on the car, my father was as mad as a hornet.

ACTIVITY B Complete each cliché. Then work with a classmate to rewrite the clichés to make them fresh and vivid.

1. as busy as a _____
2. slept like a _____
3. as happy as a _____
4. green with _____
5. as hungry as a _____
6. works like a _____
7. fits like a _____
8. eats like a _____
9. cry like a _____
10. as smart as a _____
11. stick out like a _____
12. as slow as a _____

WRITER'S CORNER

Choose a pet or favorite animal. Use figurative language to write four sentences describing the animal.

ACTIVITY C Explain the meaning of the metaphors in the following sentences.

> EXAMPLE   Those *bad grades* are a *stain* on my transcript.
> *Bad grades make a transcript look less worthy.*

1. Computers are the on-ramps to the information superhighway.
2. Dan's thoughts are pebbles rattling inside a can.
3. The day before summer vacation, classrooms are three-ring circuses.
4. The governor's speech was a torpedo that sank any chance the bill had to pass the legislature.
5. Mr. Sanchez's face was stone when the workers presented their demands.

ACTIVITY D Use hyperbole to complete each sentence.

1. That bug is so ugly _____.
2. I'll be your best friend until _____.
3. It's so hot this summer _____.
4. The smell of the crowded room _____.
5. I'm hungry enough to eat _____.
6. Frank talks on the phone so long _____.
7. Uncle Hugo is such a slow driver _____.
8. Glenna has such a cheerful smile _____.
9. That cat is as old as _____.
10. The plains are so flat _____.
11. That newborn is as tiny as _____.
12. Dad bellows like _____.

ACTIVITY E Create a simile to complete each of the following sentences. Avoid using clichés.

1. The football player ran down the field _____.
2. Birds flew through the air _____.
3. The love she felt for her new baby brother _____.
4. The thunder clap sounded _____.

ACTIVITY F Identify the noun that is personified in each sentence. Identify the words that give human qualities to that noun.

1. Two huge Tudor houses stand sentry at the end of the block.
2. Just when Alan recovered, a second injury robbed him of his chance to play football.
3. I'm afraid a colony of termites has gained a foothold in our basement.
4. Autumn, brightly dressed, danced through the park.
5. The shy sun peeped out from behind a cloud.
6. The clouds grew dark and cried rain upon the baseball game.
7. After a few well-placed kicks, the machine spit out our candy bars.
8. The engine is starting to cough when the car comes to a stop.
9. A tiny train crawled to the top of Mount Baldy.
10. The fields sleep under a blanket of snow.

ACTIVITY G Use personification, hyperbole, simile, or metaphor to write a descriptive sentence for each topic.

1. a pitcher who regularly throws over 90 m.p.h.
2. a bridge being demolished
3. a broken water main
4. a singer who hits high C
5. a day when 36 inches of snow falls
6. an approaching storm
7. a gymnast who performs a perfect routine on the uneven bars.

The Rubáiyát

Wake! For the Sun, who scatter'd into flight/The stars before him from the Field of Night./Drives Night along with them from Heav'n, and strikes The Sultan's Turret with a Shaft of Light.

Omar Khayyám

Nastia Liukin, 2008 Olympic gold medalist

WRITER'S CORNER

Write a paragraph or poem comparing yourself to an animal or an element of nature. Use a metaphor or a simile.

Oral Description

Have you ever told friends about a favorite restaurant? What about an amusement park? You've probably described places like these to your friends many times. Presenting a talk that describes a place to an audience is not that different from describing it to your friends.

Choose the Right Topic

You are going to describe a place that genuinely made an impression on you, either positively or negatively. It might be a creepy abandoned house, an elegant hotel built in the 19th century, or a new baseball stadium with old-fashioned charm and high-tech features.

List some possible places you might talk about. Which ones interest you most? Of those places which one is clearest in your mind? Which one do you have the most to say about? Which one will intrigue your audience most? Consider these questions as you choose the topic of your talk.

Do Your Research

If you want to add factual information to bolster your description, it must be accurate. Do the necessary research in books or online to make sure you've got the facts right.

Let Your Words Express Mood

How did you feel about the place? Was it beautiful, exciting, scary, or astonishing? Make sure the emotions you associate with the place are expressed in the details you include.

Select Your Words Carefully

Make sure your description is lively and detailed. Appeal to all the senses by using vivid and specific words to explain what you saw, heard, smelled, felt, and tasted. Figures of speech will strengthen your description. Avoid clichés.

Read the following paragraph written by a visitor to Wrigley Field in Chicago who takes the opportunity to imagine that she witnessed Babe Ruth's famous home run. The writer will share this oral description with her drama class.

I emerged from the darkened stairwell and stepped into the brilliance of the sunlit ballpark. Standing in a sea of empty green seats, I took in the eerie silence. In the distance a lone groundskeeper pushed a wheelbarrow along the famed ivied wall that bounded the outfield. Though the stadium was empty and quiet, my mind's eye and ear took in the history that had been lived here. The roar of the crowd filled my head as I looked down at the white lines of the batter's box and imagined Babe Ruth on that fateful date when it was believed that he "called the shot." I could almost see him point toward the outfield at the place where his next home run would fly.

ACTIVITY A Choose a topic for your talk. Let the place's image flood your mind. Jot down sensory details on a list like the one below. You do not have to include all five senses on the list, but try to include as many as you can.

My Place:

What I see:

What I smell:

What I taste:

What I hear:

What I touch:

SPEAKER'S CORNER

Consult the chart you made in Activity A. Write notes for your talk. Include descriptive details that support the desired impression of the place.

Grammar in Action. Find the participial phrases in the p. 336 excerpt.

Organize

Make sure that the introduction of your talk hooks the audience and that the conclusion leaves them with an idea or insight that's worth remembering.

Listeners will quickly lose interest if you present them with a disorganized mass of details. In the body of your talk, keep in mind both the overall impression and the important details you would like your audience to remember. Organize your talk by following one of the forms of organization you studied in this chapter: chronological order, spatial order, order of importance, comparison and contrast, or a combination of these.

Rehearse

Try out your talk on a classmate. He or she might notice parts that are boring or confusing. Ask your partner to make suggestions to improve the content of your talk. Ask for comments on the delivery too. Did you speak too quickly or too slowly? Could your partner understand all your words?

After you revise your talk, practice it often so that you almost know it by heart. Remember, everyone gets nervous when speaking to a group. The more you practice, the less nervous you will most likely be.

Present

Before and during your talk, remember the following points.

- Check your appearance in a mirror before you begin your talk.
- Stand up straight and breathe calmly. Avoid fidgeting or shifting from foot to foot.
- Make eye contact. Don't look only at one person or one part of the room. Glance around the entire audience.
- Be enthusiastic. Your enthusiasm will transfer to your audience.
- Use gestures for emphasis. Don't overdo it, though, or you will distract the audience from the impact of your words.
- Control your voice. Use your tone of voice to emphasize the meaning of your words. For example, prior to a dramatic moment, try slowing down and lowering your voice.

Display Visual Aids

If you have posters, drawings, postcards, slides, or photographs of the place, use them to illustrate your talk. Visual aids will present your audience with lots of information, leaving you free to focus on details and discuss your feelings and impressions.

Be an Effective Listener

Just as speaking before an audience is a skill that gets better with practice, listening to speakers is a skill that you can also improve. Here are some suggestions.

- Listen actively. Picture the place that the speaker is describing. Add new details to the picture in your mind as the speaker presents them. Think critically. Ask yourself if the details add up to a coherent picture.
- Listen for important ideas. Identify the mood the speaker creates for the subject.
- Do not interrupt, even if you are confused or have a question. Save questions and comments for the end of the talk.

ACTIVITY B Get used to speaking in front of an audience. Find a descriptive passage from an essay or a story. Read it aloud to a small group of classmates. Practice speaking at an appropriate pace and volume. Make sure to pronounce all the words clearly.

Grammar in Action, Find the gerund in the Iroquois Constitution excerpt.

LiNK

The Iroquois Constitution

The thickness of your skin shall be seven spans—which is to say that you shall be proof against anger, offensive action, and criticism. Your heart shall be filled with peace and good will and your mind filled with a yearning for the welfare of the people of the confederacy.

The Iroquois Nation

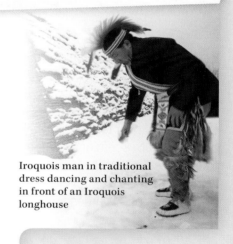

Iroquois man in traditional dress dancing and chanting in front of an Iroquois longhouse

SPEAKER'S CORNER

Present your oral description to the class. After your talk, ask for feedback from your audience. Write the helpful suggestions in a notebook or journal to review before you give another speech.

Prewriting and Drafting

Well-written descriptions can make people, places, and events come alive on the page. You have learned about how to organize and express descriptive details through graphic organizers and by using figurative language. Now you will use what you have learned to write a comparative description.

Prewriting

Before you write a comparative description, take some time to brainstorm, choose a topic, and organize your ideas. Prewriting is also the time to develop a plan for how you will structure your description. Descriptions require vivid language to be effective. Yet the details of the description need to be organized for the reader to understand them. A comparative description requires even more thought.

Choosing a Topic

The first step in writing a description that compares and contrasts is to choose two related subjects. The two subjects should have something in common, such as both being places to visit, something to do, or something to buy.

Lydia, an eighth grader, brainstormed a list of ideas that she might write about in a comparative description. Her list included ideas from restaurants to roller coasters, from buildings to baseball players.

From her list Lydia selected the topic that seemed most appealing to describe. Lydia had recently visited Chicago on a trip with her family and was fascinated by two of the city's skyscrapers—the John Hancock Center and Willis Tower.

For her freewriting exercise, Lydia drew a line down the center of a sheet of paper and wrote the name of a building on each side of the line. Under each name she wrote all the details she recalled relating to the building.

Your Turn

Use the following steps to develop your ideas:

- Write *Two Kinds of* _____ at the top of a sheet of paper and list details of your two subjects, as Lydia did.
- When you have finished, look over your paper and note which side has more details. This can serve as a guide for gathering more information.

Gathering Information

Lydia was able to remember quite a few details in her freewriting session. However, she didn't want to rely solely on the memories of her trip and felt she needed to learn more about both skyscrapers. So she gathered more information from the library and online and added it to her lists.

Organizing Your Ideas

 Organization

Once writers choose a pair of subjects to compare or contrast in a description, they plan what they want to say. Lydia thought a Venn diagram would be a helpful way to organize the details she wanted to compare and contrast. Here is what she wrote.

Your Turn

Create a Venn diagram for your pair of subjects. Decide how you will organize your description. Then create an outline to show which details will go in each paragraph.

Two Tall Buildings

John Hancock Center

Called "Big John" by Chicagoans

Building tapers as it goes up

X-bars mean no inside supports

44th floor has America's highest indoor swimming pool

Lights at the top change color for holidays

Both

look impressive in skyline

topped by antennae

designed by architect Bruce Graham

observatories with nice views

Willis Tower

tallest building in Chicago and the United States

High-tech telescopes

Building goes up to different heights

nine tubes of various heights

fast elevator—1,600 feet per minute

When her Venn diagram was complete, Lydia made an outline to arrange her details logically. She decided to arrange her description in spatial order. Study Lydia's outline. What information did she transfer from the Venn diagram to the outline? Look at the subheads (A, B, and C) of the second main head (Body). What themes did Lydia choose for comparison and contrast in her description?

I. Introduction

II. Body

  A. Far

    1. both towers over 1,000 feet tall

    2. both have two large antennae

  B. Near

    1. Hancock has X-bars

    2. Willis Tower made up of nine tubes

    3. both needed less material

  C. Inside

    1. both towers have express elevators and observatories

    2. Willis Tower has elevator that goes 1,600 feet per minute

    3. Hancock has open-air skydeck

III. Conclusion

Drafting

Lydia developed her Venn diagram and outline into a coherent comparative description. She had to give enough details to help readers visualize and compare and contrast the buildings. Read Lydia's draft.

Two Tall Buildings

Chicago has many tall buildings, and two of the tallest are the John Hancock Center and Willis Tower. On a recent trip to downtown Chicago with my family, I decide to visit these impressive buildings.

The similarities of the two buildings is obvious. They both go up more than 1,000 feet and architect Bruce Graham designed both buildings. On top of each, two large antennae go up into the clouds.

On closer inspection, I noticed several differences between the towers. The sides of the John Hancock Center are covered with huge X-shaped bars and they become narrower as they go up. Willis Tower has several levels of different heights, and is made up of nine tubes. Graham's designs mean less material was needed to build both buildings.

We went inside each building, we waited in similar long lines before taking an elevator that went quickly to the top. The observation areas were different. Willis Tower's elevator took us to a room with windows, while the Hancock's observatory includes an open-air skydeck that let you feel the sun and the wind blowing. While I was on the Hancock's skydeck, I learned that the building had America's highest indoor swimming pool on the 44th floor.

Prewriting

Drafting

Content Editing

Revising

Copyediting

Proofreading

Publishing

Looking down from either building gives you a similar breath-taking view. You see everything from up there. For that reason, both Willis Tower and John Hancock Center are worth visiting. Whichever building you decide to visit, you will feel exhilarated when you are on top of the city.

Figurative Language

Figurative language is useful for descriptions. As you write, you might sometimes think of several similes or metaphors before you hit upon the one that best expresses the image you want to create. Remember, however, that a cliché is figurative language that has been so overused that it shows the reader nothing new and doesn't contribute anything to your description.

Voice

Writer's Tip Use a thesaurus to help you choose precise and vivid words for your description.

Your Turn

Follow these steps to write your draft:

- Use your Venn diagram and outline to write your draft.
- Double-space it to make your draft easier to revise.
- Don't feel compelled to use everything in the Venn diagram or outline.

Content Editing

Lydia knew that editing the content of a comparative description meant revising for the logic, order, and clarity of its comparisons and its contrasts. She also knew that a content editor makes sure that the things being compared and contrasted are given equal weight.

Lydia revised her draft, referring to the Content Editor's Checklist. Then she asked her friend Sam to read it. She chose Sam because he had not visited either building. In this way she might find out if he could actually visualize the details of what she had written.

Sam read through Lydia's draft carefully and then reread it, checking it against the Content Editor's Checklist. Then he had a conference with Lydia.

Sam began the conference by telling Lydia what he liked about her description. Here are Sam's comments.

- I like your topic choice. You give a pretty good sense of what these buildings look like and what they would be like to visit. You use some great words, like *breathtaking* and *exhilarated*. The description also seems to be well organized.

- You might start off with a more interesting introduction. In the opening paragraph, you should also say that you will be comparing and contrasting the two buildings.

- You seem to cover both buildings with an equal amount of detail. I don't feel as if one building is being shortchanged.

- In the second and third paragraphs, you might add more detail. I know the buildings are tall, but it's not very clear. And *Willis Tower has several levels of different heights* is kind of confusing.

Content Editor's Checklist

☐ Does the introduction engage the reader and tell what is being compared and contrasted?

☐ Does the description give equal weight to the things that are being compared and contrasted?

☐ Does the body provide enough details for the reader to form an accurate picture of the subject?

☐ Are there unnecessary details that keep the description from flowing well?

☐ Is the description organized logically?

☐ Are figurative and sensory language used?

☐ Does the conclusion sum up the comparison and leave the reader something to think about?

- In the third and fourth paragraphs, you identify what type of details you will be describing by using *On closer inspection* and *We went inside each building*. Can you do the same for your second paragraph?
- Instead of writing *You can see everything from up there* in the last paragraph, can you describe what you would see?

Lydia considered Sam's comments and decided to revise her draft.

Your Turn

Use the following steps to edit your draft:

- Before giving your draft to a classmate to read, review it on your own by checking it against each question in the Content Editor's Checklist.
- Trade drafts with a classmate. Refer to the Content Editor's Checklist as you read your classmate's description a few times.
- When you have finished reading your partner's draft, give your partner constructive criticism. Tell him or her the strong points of the piece before suggesting ways it might be improved. Your partner should do the same for you.

Grammar in Action

Use participial phrases to add description and sentence variety.

Prewriting

Drafting

Content Editing

Revising

Copyediting

Proofreading

Publishing

Revising

This is how Lydia revised her description based on her and Sam's suggestions.

Two Tall Buildings

Chicago's skyline boasts many majestic buildings, but two skyscrapers loom larger than the rest: ~~Chicago has many tall buildings, and two of the tallest are~~ the John Hancock Center and Willis Tower. On a recent trip to downtown Chicago with my family, I decide to visit these impressive *structures. I hoped to see what similarities and differences I could find.* ~~buildings.~~

From a distance The similarities of the two buildings is obvious. They ~~both go up~~ *rise confidently into the sky* more than 1,000 feet ~~and~~ *, and both stand over the city's other buildings like parents watching their children.* architect Bruce Graham designed both buildings. On top of each, two large antennae ~~go up~~ *dart* into the clouds.

Up close ~~On closer inspection,~~ I noticed several differences between the towers. The sides of the John Hancock Center ~~are covered with huge X-shaped bars~~ *, which are covered with huge X-shaped braces, taper* and they become narrower as they go up. Willis Tower *, on the other hand,* has several levels of different heights *that make the tower look like a stack* ~~, and is~~ *of building blocks. The building is made up of nine support tubes of various heights.* ~~made up of nine tubes.~~ Graham's designs mean less material was needed to build both buildings.

When We went inside each building, we waited in similar long lines before taking an elevator that ~~went quickly to the top.~~ *blasted to the top like a rocket* The observation areas *, however,* were different. Willis Tower's elevator took us to a room with windows, while the Hancock's observatory includes an open-air skywalk that let you feel the sun and the wind blowing. ~~While I was on the Hancock's skywalk, I learned that the building had America's highest indoor swimming pool on the 44th floor.~~

Looking down from either building gives you a similar breath-taking view. You
see everything from up there. For that reason, both Willis Tower and John Hancock

distant buildings, tiny cars, and people who look like ants

Center are worth visiting. Whichever building you decide to visit, you will feel

exhilarated when you are on top of the city.

Notice how Lydia improved her draft. She
changed the introduction to make it draw the
reader in with vivid words and images. She added

👀 **Sentence Fluency**

a sentence at the end
of the first paragraph to state that her description
would compare and contrast the buildings.

- What did Lydia add to the second paragraph,
  and what effect did these additions have on her
  description?
- Lydia agreed that the third paragraph was
  unclear. How did she clarify it? What
  did she add to the fourth
  paragraph to help her
  readers visualize more
  clearly?
- Lydia agreed that in the
  last paragraph, saying
  that *you see everything*
  doesn't say much. How
  did she fix this?
- Lydia noted that
  Sam did not find
  any unnecessary
  details. However,
  she disagreed. What
  unnecessary details
  did Lydia delete
  from her draft?

Your Turn

Use your ideas and the ideas you got from
your content editor to revise your draft.

- Don't feel obliged to use every suggestion
  your editor makes. Choose the ideas that
  you agree will make your draft stronger.
- When you have finished, go over the
  Content Editor's Checklist again. Have you
  addressed all the points on the checklist?

Writer's Tip Use your outline as an additional
checklist to make sure you addressed all your
points of comparison.

Prewriting

Drafting

Content Editing

Revising

Copyediting

Proofreading

Publishing

Copyediting and Proofreading

Copyediting

When Lydia finished revising her draft for content, her next step was to copyedit her description. At this stage Lydia focused on making sure each sentence was clear, logical, and grammatically correct. She used the Copyeditor's Checklist to edit her draft.

When she looked it over, Lydia thought some sentences and word choices still needed work.

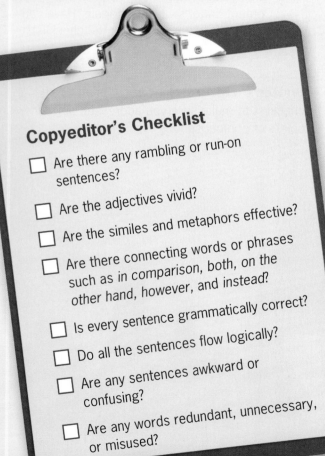

Copyeditor's Checklist

- ☐ Are there any rambling or run-on sentences?
- ☐ Are the adjectives vivid?
- ☐ Are the similes and metaphors effective?
- ☐ Are there connecting words or phrases such as in comparison, both, on the other hand, however, and instead?
- ☐ Is every sentence grammatically correct?
- ☐ Do all the sentences flow logically?
- ☐ Are any sentences awkward or confusing?
- ☐ Are any words redundant, unnecessary, or misused?

In the second paragraph, she found that the second sentence was a run-on sentence, so she turned the second clause into a separate sentence. She also revised the first sentence of the fourth paragraph, which was also a run-on sentence.

Lydia noticed that throughout the description  she overused the word *tall*. With what synonym can she replace this word?

The description also needed more comparison words such as *however* and *on the other hand*. Lydia looked for places where they might be useful.

Lydia also noticed that the last sentence in the fourth paragraph referred to feeling "the sun and the wind blowing." Why doesn't this phrase make sense, and how did Lydia fix it?

Your Turn

Use the Copyeditor's Checklist to review your revised draft.

- Check that your sentences are grammatically correct. In particular look for any rambling sentences, run-on sentences, or sentence fragments.
- Make sure every sentence is clear and logical.
- Read over your draft one more time. Make sure that no words are redundant, unnecessary, or misused.

Proofreading

Before writing the finished copy of a description, a good writer proofreads the draft to check for spelling, punctuation, capitalization, and grammar. A checklist like this one helps a writer proofread.

Conventions

Proofreader's Checklist

- ☐ Are the paragraphs indented?
- ☐ Have any words been misspelled?
- ☐ Are capitalization and punctuation correct?
- ☐ Is the grammar accurate?
- ☐ Were new errors introduced during the editing step?

Good writers ask a proofreader to check their work for errors in grammar, mechanics, and punctuation. A proofreader will often catch errors that the writer missed.

Lydia asked Jennifer, a classmate, to proofread her report. Jennifer looked it over, using the Proofreader's Checklist, and made proofreading marks on Lydia's draft. Because Lydia did a thorough job of copyediting, Jennifer found only a few errors. She noticed that the verb *is* in the second paragraph should be changed to *are,* and in the fourth paragraph, *let* should be changed to *lets* to agree with the subject of the clause. What other errors can you find?

Your Turn

- Use the Proofreader's Checklist as you read your description.
- Read it once for each item on the list. When you have gone through the list, trade papers with a partner.
- Review your partner's draft in the same way. Be sure to use a dictionary if you are unsure of a spelling.

Publishing

Lydia read her description again to see if it was error-free. Then she carefully typed it and added her own byline. While she read the finished draft, she realized that the title might be more interesting, so she revised it.

Chicago's Steel Giants

by Lydia Romero

Chicago's skyline boasts many majestic buildings, but two skyscrapers loom larger than the rest: the John Hancock Center and Willis Tower. On a recent trip to downtown Chicago with my family, I decided to visit these impressive structures. I hoped to see what similarities and differences I could find.

From a distance the similarities of the two buildings are obvious. They rise confidently into the sky more than 1,000 feet, and both stand over the city's other buildings like parents watching their children. Architect Bruce Graham designed both buildings. On top of each, two large antennae dart up into the clouds.

Up close, I noticed several differences between the towers. The sides of the John Hancock Center, which are covered with huge X-shaped braces, taper as they go up. Willis Tower, on the other hand, has several levels of different heights that make the tower look like a stack of building blocks. The building is made up of nine support tubes of various heights. Graham's designs mean less material was needed to build both buildings.

When we went inside each building, we waited in similar long lines before taking an elevator that blasted to the top like a rocket. The observation areas were different, however. Willis Tower's elevator took us to a room with windows, while the Hancock's observatory includes an open-air skywalk that lets you feel the sun shining and the wind blowing.

Looking down from either building, gives you a similar breathtaking view. You see distant buildings, tiny cars, and people who look like ants. For that reason, both Willis Tower and John Hancock Center are worth visiting. Whichever building you decide to visit, you will feel exhilarated when you are on top of the city.

There are many ways to share your comparative description with your class, your friends and family, and even the public.

 Create a classroom book. Your classmates may have photographs, illustrations, or other souvenirs of their experience. These are interesting items to attach to the descriptions.

 Post it to a Web site that publishes student writing. Work with an adult to find one for which your description is appropriate. Lydia posted hers on a student travel Web site.

 Post it on a bulletin board or on your classroom wiki. Since Lydia's description is informational, she linked it to other student entries on the class wiki about architecture and Chicago.

 Make a pop-up book. Lydia's pop-up book was educational and very popular with her younger brother's class.

Whenever you publish your work, your goal is to share your thoughts and experiences with other people.

Your Turn

Once your draft has been proofread, it should be ready to publish. Before you publish your finished description, it's always a good idea to check it over one more time. Follow these steps:

- Check the content of your description to make sure you have not left out anything important or left in anything unnecessary.

- Proofread for correct spelling, grammar, capitalization, and punctuation. If your computer has a spell-checker, it can alert you to misspelled words. Make sure that when you made your corrections, you did not make any new mistakes.

- Make sure any proper names or titles are spelled correctly. People don't like seeing their names misspelled in print.

The way your description looks is important too. Be sure to use a font that is easy to read or use your best handwriting. Consider **Presentation** adding an image to your description. You can insert an image from clipart or from a free online Web site. You might even create a small caption to place below the image.

After your description has been published, be willing to receive feedback from your peers. They will want to receive your feedback on their descriptions as well.

Prewriting

Drafting

Content Editing

Revising

Copyediting

Proofreading

Publishing

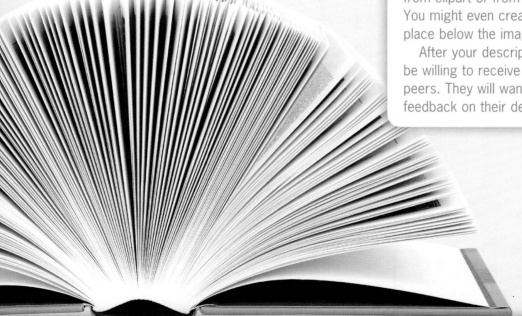

Expository Writing

LiNK ## The Story of the Greeks
by H.A. Guerber

Although Greece (or Hel´las) is only half as large as the State of New York, it holds a very important place in the history of the world. It is situated in the southern part of Europe, cut off from the rest of the continent by a chain of high mountains which form a great wall on the north. It is surrounded on nearly all sides by the blue waters of the Med-it-er-ra´ne-an Sea, which stretch so far inland that it is said no part of the country is forty miles from the sea, or ten miles from the hills. Thus shut in by sea and mountains, it forms a little territory by itself, and it was the home of a noted people.

The
Story Of The Greeks
(1896)

H. A. Guerber

> This is a good example of an expository essay. The topic is stated in the first sentence, and supporting information is organized according to order of importance.

Fats for Health

by Juan Martinez

Fat can be good for you. Surprised? You have probably heard that Americans eat far too much fat, especially saturated fat. This is the kind of fat that is solid at room temperature. It's also the type of fat that contributes to obesity, diabetes, heart problems, and cancer. Many Americans' diets comprise more than the recommended maximum of 30 percent fat. But the right kinds, the right amounts, and the right proportions of fats are necessary for good health. The fats known as essential fatty acids (EFAs) are just that—essential, especially for strong hearts and alert brains.

Sharp minds require what's known as EFA omega-3, which is found in fish such as salmon, tuna, and cod, and plants such as flax, pumpkin seeds, and walnuts. Omega-3 fats maintain the health of the outer membrane of brain cells through which signals from the nerves pass. Omega-3 fats also form the membrane necessary for learning and memory and may help battle the bad effects of stress and combat mental disorders such as depression. How many omega-3 fats should people eat each day? No one knows precisely, but scientists currently recommend one to three grams, about as much as in a three-ounce serving of salmon.

Some EFAs, such as the polyunsaturated oils found in corn, safflowers, and sunflowers, have hardly any omega-3 fats. Instead, they contain omega-6 fats. A balance of omega-3 and omega-6 fats in the diet keeps both the brain and the heart functioning at their best. Again, the exact ratio is unknown, but without a doubt the typical diet has far too few omega-3 fats. The best guess currently of an ideal ratio of omega-3 to omega-6 fats is about 1 to 4. Most people eat a ratio of about 1 to 10.

Clearly then, not all fats are created equal. Overall fat should comprise no more than about 30 percent of your diet, and saturated fats should be kept to an absolute minimum. Most of the fat you do eat should be EFAs in the proper ratio.

What Makes a Good Expository Essay?

Yo Ho! Treasure

No one knew how to drill terror into sailors' hearts like the dreaded pirate Blackbeard, who ruled the Caribbean Sea and the Atlantic Coast from 1716 to 1718. Among the legends of his cruelty: he fired randomly at his crew, and he once forced a captive to eat his own ears.

TimeforKids.com

The purpose of expository writing is to inform. Good expository writers provide relevant information about a specific topic, often answering these six questions: *who?, what?, where?, when?, why?,* and *how?* Expository writing is written in a neutral tone and takes many forms, including reports, articles, and essays. Expository essays often appear in magazines and academic journals.

Topic and Organization

The topic of an expository essay is clearly stated in a topic sentence, which appears in the introduction. The main idea, or what the writer wants to say about the topic, is often included in the topic sentence or elsewhere in the introduction.

Effective essays are well organized. Some ways of organization that can be applied to expository writing include order of importance, chronological order, and comparison and contrast. Another way to organize expository writing is to explain cause-and-effect relationships. An expository essay organized by cause and effect explains *why* something happens.

Supporting Paragraphs

Supporting paragraphs provide information that supports the main idea stated in the introduction. Each paragraph focuses on a different aspect of the topic, and all the sentences in the paragraph relate to that aspect. The support might include factual examples, statistics, or quotations.

Conclusion

The conclusion summarizes the main idea of the essay. It leaves the reader with food for thought—a new way of looking at or thinking about the topic. This effect can be accomplished in many ways, such as through a unique insight or a thought-provoking statement.

ACTIVITY A **Read the expository essay and answer the questions.**

Pasta Through Time and Space

Since its origin thousands of years ago, pasta of many shapes and sizes has appeared in all kinds of dishes worldwide. *Pasta,* the Italian word for dough, is most closely identified with Italy. But pasta was discovered by the Chinese as long ago as 5000 BC.

No other country has such an astonishing variety of pasta as Italy, and the names of the different kinds describe their shapes or their uses. The pasta Americans know best is spaghetti, which means "strings" in Italian. Some other kinds include flat, wide strands of fettuccine, or "little ribbons"; lasagna, long, ripple-edged strips, whose name means "cooking pot"; narrow and flat linguine, "little tongues"; and mostaccioli, diagonally cut tubes whose name means "little mustaches." Other kinds of descriptively named pasta are radiatore, or "radiators"; vermicelli, "worms"; lumache, "snails"; and farfalle, "butterflies."

Pasta, which is made up mostly of carbohydrates, can form an important part of people's diets. Ingredients besides flour and water vary slightly, but flat strands of Italian pasta are usually made with eggs, and tube-shaped pasta is not. Many different kinds of pasta are available in grocery stores. Some are colored red or green. Some are flavored with basil or made from whole wheat. When you eat your next bowl of spaghetti, think of the long and varied history of pasta.

1. What is the topic of this essay?
2. What is the main idea?
3. What important idea is introduced in the second paragraph? the third?
4. What are some details in the second and third paragraphs?
5. Which concluding sentence sums up the main idea?

WRITER'S CORNER

Choose an original topic related to diet, health, or exercise. Write a topic sentence to introduce the idea.

ACTIVITY B Write a separate topic sentence for each main idea. Be sure the sentences are informational, not persuasive or entertaining.

1. team sports
2. backpacking
3. computer games
4. allowances
5. gymnastics
6. restaurants
7. museums
8. amusement parks
9. pets
10. vacations

ACTIVITY C Write a thought-provoking statement that might be included in the conclusion of an expository essay that begins with each topic sentence.

1. Smoking is bad for your health.
2. Experts agree that Jupiter is the oldest planet in the solar system.
3. A good baseball player must be able to get on base consistently.
4. Skipping breakfast is never a good idea for anyone, especially children and teenagers.
5. An essential companion to eating right is getting enough exercise.
6. Even small changes in eating habits can eventually produce big results.
7. Portion sizes at restaurants are much larger than they used to be.
8. Increasingly, Americans are exchanging their fuel-oil furnaces for gas-fired ones.
9. Discount retail stores are an enormous and growing market for value-priced consumer goods.
10. Learning to play a musical instrument can help children sharpen their math skills.

ACTIVITY D Write a topic sentence and three supporting sentences on a topic of your choice. How would you organize the information?

ACTIVITY E Read the topic sentences. Identify which way of organizing an expository essay would work best for each topic: chronological order, order of importance, comparison and contrast, or cause and effect. Explain your answers.

1. A popular type of house for pioneers living in the Great Plains was a sod house, or "soddie."

2. A base on the moon offers many advantages for space exploration.

3. Let's examine the features of the Tracker and the Forager SUVs side by side.

4. If you ask whether there is a simple way to get the proper nutrition, I respond with an emphatic yes.

5. Photosynthesis turns sunlight energy into chemical energy for plants.

6. A comparison of the typical American diet with the traditional Japanese diet reveals stark differences.

7. On casual examination a knockoff, or copy, looks much like the designer original that inspired it, but if you look closer, you'll find many differences.

8. The American Revolution and the French Revolution, while inspired by similar ideas, were very different.

9. Teaching adults to read is both different from and similar to teaching reading to children.

10. The Black Eagles of the 99th Pursuit Squadron fought Germans as well as discrimination within the U.S. Army during World War II.

11. Astronomers use the Hubble Telescope to estimate the age of the universe.

12. The type of soil in a garden determines what plants will thrive there.

LiNK

A Weighty Issue

"What's the right weight for my height?" is one of the most common questions girls and guys have. It seems like a simple question. But, for teens, it's not always an easy one to answer. Why not? People have different body types, so there's no single number that's the right weight for everyone.

KidsHealth.org

WRITER'S CORNER

Make a list of places you might find information for the topic you chose for the Writer's Corner on page 377. Then determine the type of organization you would use for an essay on your topic.

Grammar in Action. Identify the adverbs in the excerpt above.

Fact and Opinion

Women's History Week

In 1978, a California school district started Women's History Week to promote the teaching of women's history. It was so popular that in 1981, Congress passed a resolution making the week a celebration for the entire country!

TimeforKids.com

Facts are statements that can be verified or proved true by objective means such as checking public records or reading reference sources. Opinions are statements of judgment. Their credibility depends on the qualifications of the speaker. Most expository pieces are free of opinion or include very few opinions.

> **Fact:** Membership at the Petoskey YMCA went up in 2009.
>
> **Opinion:** The Petoskey YMCA has the best gym in the city.

The first statement is a fact because someone could check the records of the Petoskey YMCA to verify whether membership increased in 2009. The second statement is an opinion because there is no way to check it objectively. One person might think that the Petoskey YMCA is the best gym; someone else might disagree.

Some opinions are more credible than others, and good writers use credible opinions. What if a world-famous bodybuilder visited the Petoskey YMCA, as well as other gyms in the city, and said it was the best gym? The bodybuilder's opinion would be more credible than an average individual's opinion because of the bodybuilder's extensive knowledge of gyms. Keep in mind, however, that the bodybuilder's opinion would still be just an opinion, most likely not appropriate to include in an expository piece of writing. The "best" gym for an Olympic swimmer may be one with a longer pool.

A statement of fact may be proved untrue. If the person checking the Petoskey YMCA records discovered that membership in 2008 was higher than 2009, the factual statement would have been proved to be incorrect.

Use Relevant Facts

The world is full of facts. Anytime you research a topic, you are bombarded with them. When researching for an expository essay, it is important to use only the facts that are relevant to the topic. An essay describing how the Civil War began, for example, does not need to mention the fact that President Lincoln once ran a general store in New Salem, Illinois. Your job as a writer is to sort through facts and use the ones that directly support your topic's main idea.

ACTIVITY A Identify the sentences as facts or opinions. Explain why you think each sentence is either a fact or an opinion.

1. Neil Armstrong was the first human to set foot on the moon.
2. Global warming is the most important problem we face.
3. The prettiest color for bridesmaids' dresses this year is lavender.
4. The USDA recommendations for healthful eating have changed.
5. Without a doubt, math classes are the ones that students complain about loudest and most frequently.
6. Wearing seat belts and lowering speed limits to 55 m.p.h. decreases traffic fatalities.
7. That serving of granola cereal contains five grams of sugar.
8. Aerobic exercise is more important for optimum health than anaerobic exercise.
9. The golden retriever is the best dog for people with large families.
10. This year's football team is sure to uphold our winning tradition.

ACTIVITY B Change the facts to opinions. Change the opinions to facts.

1. Eleanor Roosevelt traveled the world in support of social causes.
2. Nancy Reagan probably loved Ronald more than any other president's wife loved her husband.
3. Jackie Kennedy Onassis promoted American fashion designers through her choice of clothing.
4. Hillary Clinton was the first president's wife to seek an independent political career of her own.
5. Mary Todd Lincoln had the most tragic life of all the presidential wives.
6. Abigail Adams wrote, "No man ever prospered in the world without the consent and cooperation of his wife."

Neil Armstrong

Abigail Adams

WRITER'S CORNER

In random order write five facts and five positive opinions about your school. Meet with a partner and trade papers. Identify each of your partner's sentences as a fact or an opinion. Tell why you identified each statement as you did.

The Scoop on Cereal

In 1894, one of the foods they prepared was a wheatmeal. What emerged on the other end of the rollers was to change the world forever. Instead of a unified flat sheet, the wheat came out as flakes, one for each wheat berry. They roasted the flakes and served them to their patients. They had an immediate success on their hands.

Mr.Breakfast.com

Opinion Signal Words

Clue words or phrases such as *probably, perhaps, usually, often, sometimes, I believe, I think, it's evident, obviously, everyone knows,* and *certainly* might help you identify opinions at a glance. Value words such as *pretty, creative, wonderful, good, ugly, boring, horrible, dangerous, mean,* and *unattractive* can also signal opinions.

ACTIVITY C **Read the excerpt from *The Scoop on Cereal*. Identify two facts, one opinion, and one signal word or phrase.**

ACTIVITY D **Read each topic sentence and the set of facts that accompanies it. Determine which fact is irrelevant to the main idea of the topic and explain why.**

1. Building the Panama Canal was a long and difficult engineering project.
   a. The Canal took seven years to build.
   b. Panama was once a province of Colombia.
   c. More than 232 million cubic yards of earth were moved to build the Canal.
   d. Nearly 6,000 workers died during the Canal's construction.

2. The Roman Empire grew by conquering many different lands.
   a. Rome faced the Carthaginian general Hannibal in the Second Punic War.
   b. Greece fell to Rome in 147 BC.
   c. The Roman poet Horace lived in the Augustan age.
   d. The Battle of Actium brought Egypt under Roman control.

3. Simón Bolívar helped liberate parts of South America from Spanish rule.
   a. Simón Bolívar was born in Caracas, Venezuela, on July 24, 1783.
   b. He was called the "George Washington of South America."
   c. Simón Bolívar was the first president of Colombia.
   d. Bananas are a major product of Venezuela.

Simón Bolivar

ACTIVITY E Rewrite the persuasive essay to make it an expository essay. Take out or revise opinions so that the purpose of the essay is to inform. Include only relevant facts. Be sure to include a topic sentence and summarize the topic in the conclusion.

Breakfast in England

If you think that English breakfasts are just like American breakfasts, you couldn't be more wrong. Imagine that you are sitting down to an American breakfast on a leisurely weekend. Perhaps you will have eggs, pancakes or waffles, bacon or sausage, and, of course, orange juice. Yum! But breakfasts in England are tastier and much more interesting.

In its full traditional glory, the English breakfast has at least three courses. The first is generally eggs and bacon or ham, along with grilled tomato. You might see deviled kidneys (yech!) or mixed grill, which is a lamb chop, sausage, liver, and half a tomato. Second is a course of fruit or cereal. Third comes the fish course. It may be kippers, which are salted, dried, smoked herring, or kedgeree, an Indian dish of curried rice and lentils that may have fish, hard-boiled eggs, and cream sauce. There may be a final cold course too. Oh, and crumpets, oat cakes, and toast are on the table throughout the meal.

Now don't you think this breakfast is better than the one you usually eat? We're not sure about an American breakfast, but if you eat the English breakfast described above, you are sure to push yourself away from the table stuffed to the max.

ACTIVITY F Read the expository essay that you wrote for Activity E. Answer the following questions about your writing.

1. What is your topic?
2. What is your topic sentence?
3. What organizational pattern did you use?
4. What is one example of an opinion that you changed into a fact?
5. How did you sum up the topic in your conclusion?

WRITER'S CORNER

Read an expository news article. Record at least five facts from the article. Record any opinions you find.

Tech Tip Share an expository news article on the class blog.

Evaluating Web Sites

The Internet is full of information, but only some of it is reliable enough to use in an expository piece. An important part of your work as a researcher is to determine if information from the Internet is credible and accurate. Following are some ideas for conducting good Internet research.

Determining Web Site Credibility

One main challenge in conducting research on the Internet is that almost anyone can develop a professional-looking Web site. Therefore, many Web sites contain wrong or biased information. Relying solely on the "look" of a Web site can lead a researcher to inaccurate information. Useful and reliable online Web sites include online libraries, periodicals, reputable university sites, almanacs, and encyclopedias. Fortunately, search engines often place credible sites at the top of their listings.

Once you link to a Web site, navigate it to find information. The more information you read from the Web site, the better able you will be to determine if the information is reliable. Here is a checklist of some questions to ask when evaluating Web sites.

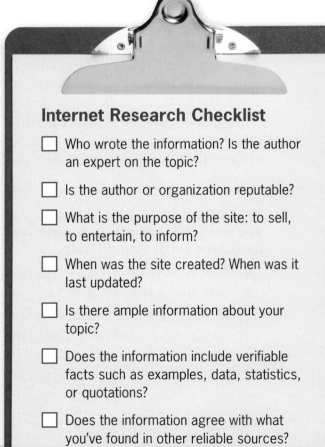

Internet Research Checklist

☐ Who wrote the information? Is the author an expert on the topic?

☐ Is the author or organization reputable?

☐ What is the purpose of the site: to sell, to entertain, to inform?

☐ When was the site created? When was it last updated?

☐ Is there ample information about your topic?

☐ Does the information include verifiable facts such as examples, data, statistics, or quotations?

☐ Does the information agree with what you've found in other reliable sources?

Practicing online safety is important when searching Web sites, especially if you are not sure of a site's credibility. Never reveal personal information over the Internet, either through a Web site or a chat room, without first asking a parent or guardian.

Conducting Research

When doing research on the Internet, begin with a keyword search on a favorite search engine. Use words from your topic as keywords. Carefully study the Web site addresses and descriptions that come up. Link only to sites that seem professional. The three-letter extension at the end of a Web site address can help you quickly determine the site's origin. The following are some common extensions:

.com	commercial sites
.edu	sites developed by schools, from elementary schools to universities
.gov	government sites
.mil	military sites
.org	sites developed by organizations

Recording Internet Research

There are several ways to record Internet research, such as printing the Web page and highlighting the information you will use, copying and pasting the information into a word-processing file and printing it, or taking notes as you read the information on the screen. Whichever way you choose, be sure to document your sources and include the date on which you visited the site because it may be altered in the future.

ACTIVITY A Work in small groups to develop a list of guidelines to follow for online safety. Consider your safety and the safety of others.

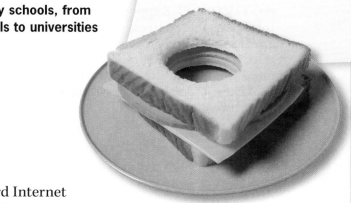

LiNK

Fighting Chronic Malnutrition

According to UNICEF data from 2007, Guatemala has the highest percentage of chronically malnourished girls and boys in Latin America, and the fourth highest in the world.

Unicef.org

WRITER'S CORNER

Use a search engine to find five credible Web sites with information about the topic you chose in the Writer's Corner on page 377.

ACTIVITY B Find the UNICEF Web site and answer the following questions.

1. Does the Web site seem credible to you? Explain why or why not.
2. What is the purpose of the Web site?
3. What audience does the Web site address?
4. What information does the Web site offer?
5. In what format is the information presented to the visitor? Does the Web site use examples, statistics, surveys, expert opinions, or a combination of formats?
6. What multimedia formats (such as video, audio, or interactive documents) are offered to the visitor?
7. Does the information seem to be up-to-date? Explain why.

ACTIVITY C Suppose you were writing about international projects to immunize children against childhood diseases such as measles. Which of the following Web sites would probably have the most reliable information? Which would probably have the least reliable information? Explain your answers.

1. A pbs.org site with information about a public television show on a UNICEF immunization project
2. An .edu site publishing a report written by a fifth grader at Morningside Elementary School
3. The .com site of a large pharmaceutical company that makes vaccines
4. An .edu site on communicable diseases sponsored by a university science department
5. The .com site of a health magazine that publishes a monthly column on children's health
6. The .com site titled "Plague!" whose sponsor is not identified
7. A .gov site sponsored by the U.S. Department of Health and Human Services
8. The .org site of Citizens Against Immunizations

ACTIVITY D Type the following topics into a search engine of your choice. Link to a Web site for each topic. Evaluate the site based on the questions in Activity B on page 386. How credible is the site? How credible is the information on the site? Record one credible fact from each Web site. Compare your results with those of your classmates.

1. global warming
2. the Peace Corps
3. extreme sports
4. cartoons

ACTIVITY E Imagine that you will write an expository essay about the Boston Massacre. Find a reliable Web site about the topic. Document your source, using the Internet Research Checklist on page 384.

The Boston Massacre by Paul Revere

ACTIVITY F Do Internet research for three of the following topics. Record three facts for each topic from a reliable Web site. Document each Web site source.

1. the importance of rain forests
2. the effects of sunbathing
3. nurses in the Civil War
4. most popular dog breeds in the United States
5. biographical information about the author of the Lemony Snicket book series
6. everyday lives of pioneer women
7. the education system in Japan
8. the volcanic disaster in ancient Pompeii
9. the life cycle of a monarch butterfly
10. the best kind of dog for a person with allergies

WRITER'S CORNER

Choose one reliable Web site that you found in the Writer's Corner on page 385. Do research, using the Web site. Record at least 10 facts about your chosen topic. Document your source.

Noun Clauses

The Death of Socrates

This led to [Socrates'] prosecution on the double charge of blasphemy and of corrupting the Athenian youth. The fact that Alcibiades had been his pupil was used to prove the demoralizing tendency of his teachings. He was condemned to drink the fatal hemlock. The night before his death he spent with his disciples, discoursing on the immortality of the soul.

P. V. N. Myers

Socrates on trial

Noun clauses can make your writing more interesting by allowing you to communicate relationships concisely, to describe something poetically, or to place the emphasis of a sentence more precisely.

A noun clause is a dependent clause used as a noun. Noun clauses are usually introduced by introductory words such as *how, whether, what, why,* and *that.* Here are some ways that a noun clause can be used in a sentence.

As a subject

> *That the polio vaccine benefits many people* **has been proved.**

As a direct object

> **We know** *that the polio vaccine benefits many people.*

As the object of a preposition

> **He spoke of** *how the polio vaccine benefits many people.*

As a subject complement

> **The fact is** *that the polio vaccine benefits many people.*

As an appositive

> **The fact** *that the polio vaccine benefits many people* **cannot be denied.**

Using Noun Clauses

A writer might use a noun clause in a sentence to show relationships between ideas, to give emphasis to an idea, or to achieve sentence variety. Read these two sentences, paying close attention to each subject.

> **Bryan's** *defeat* **was unfortunate.** (noun)
>
> *That Bryan was defeated* **was unfortunate.** (noun clause)

In the first sentence, Bryan's defeat is described as an unfortunate event. In the second sentence, the emphasis shifts away from the event itself to the effect of the event. It was not the defeat that was unfortunate; it was the idea of the defeat that was unfortunate.

A noun clause reveals the relationship between things. Read the following sentences:

Henry did not know the answer to the question.
Henry did not know Sasha's response.
Henry did not know that Sasha's response answered the question.

The first sentence tells that Henry did not know the answer to the question. The second sentence tells that Henry did not know Sasha's response. The third sentence, however, links all three things to Henry: the question, the answer, and Sasha's response.

ACTIVITY A Identify the noun clause in each sentence. Tell whether it is used as a subject, a direct object, an object of a preposition, a subject complement, or an appositive.

1. What we should do next was the question.
2. Howard insisted that Andy eat the peas.
3. Whether they would pay attention to the magician was uncertain.
4. The man addressed the crowd from where he stood.
5. Why she did not call to explain her lateness disturbed us.
6. The textbook explains how the kidneys purify the blood.
7. Janet told the truth, that she had not accepted a bribe.
8. My hope is that we finish this work soon.
9. That our guests are enjoying the performance is obvious.
10. The truth is that the person who made the decision did not have all the facts.

WRITER'S CORNER

Use the following noun clauses in five sentences. Tell how each clause is used.

1. that she was creative
2. how the team played the game
3. what he prized most
4. that the tourists arrived
5. that the flights were canceled

Varying Sentences with Noun Clauses

Effective writers vary the lengths of their sentences. Noun clauses can be useful tools to accomplish this. A well-placed noun clause can energize writing by breaking up monotonous sentences.

In the following example from the Gettysburg Address, Abraham Lincoln uses two parallel noun clauses to draw attention to the sacrifices made by the soldiers who fought in the Battle of Gettysburg. The noun clauses are italicized.

> **The world will little note, nor long remember** *what we say here*, **but it can never forget** *what they did here*.

A writer may also shorten a sentence with a well-placed noun clause. The second sentence is less wordy and communicates the same idea as the first.

> **This skateboard belongs to someone, and I think you know to whom it belongs.**
>
> **I think you know who owns this skateboard.**

A noun clause will not always improve a sentence. Sometimes noun clauses just add clutter. In the example below, eliminating the noun clause improves the sentence.

> **A metronome is what pianists often use to mark time.**
> **Pianists often use metronomes to mark time.**

ACTIVITY B Complete each sentence with an appropriate noun clause.

1. _____ was long remembered.

2. The greatest attribute of the team is _____.

3. _____ was soon discovered.

4. Have you heard the news _____?

5. It was Colette's hope _____.

6. Do you believe the report _____?

7. Dan's dream, _____, seemed a possible reality.

8. What Candice wondered was _____.

9. _____ has always interested me.

10. Earl did _____.

11. Julie said _____.

12. I do not know _____.

13. Her favorite saying is _____.

14. _____ is an important piece of information.

15. It cannot be denied _____.

16. The teacher's suggestion was _____.

ACTIVITY C Use noun clauses to combine each pair of sentences into one sentence. The new sentence can reveal a relationship between things or emphasize something.

1. Kyle's fear seemed unreasonable. The air conditioner could fall out the window.

2. How might such a thing happen? It was not clear to us.

3. The air conditioner had not been securely installed. That is a fact.

4. The air conditioner shook loose and fell on the car. We were stunned.

5. The screws were in the wrong places. Kyle showed us.

6. The accident had occurred. The car owner was angry.

7. The man was not hurt. He did not change his complaint.

8. He spoke to the police. People should be careful about how they install air conditioners.

9. We would not have to pay for the repair. The driver decided.

10. The insurance will pay for the repair. He hoped.

11. He had another question. How we will pay for a new air conditioner?

12. Kyle insisted. He will install it this time.

13. The police officer made a suggestion. We should use window fans instead.

14. The insurance would cover all damages. We were delighted.

ACTIVITY D Write five sentences that demonstrate the five ways noun clauses can be used: as a subject, a direct object, an object of a preposition, a subject complement, and an appositive.

WRITER'S CORNER

Using your research from the Writer's Corner on page 387, write three supporting sentences for your topic. Include a noun clause in each sentence.

Prefixes

A prefix is a syllable or syllables placed at the beginning of a word to change its meaning or to make another word. Most prefixes come from other languages, such as Latin or Greek. Some prefixes change the meaning of words to make antonyms. For example, adding the prefix *il-* to the root word *legal* makes the word *illegal,* which means "not legal." This chart shows some common prefixes, their meanings, and example words. Learning the meaning of prefixes can help you figure out the meaning of the words in which you find them. Learning prefixes is a great way to increase your spoken and written vocabulary.

COMMON PREFIXES

PREFIX	MEANING	EXAMPLES
anti-	against	antiestablishment, antisocial, antiwar
dis-	not, opposite of	disagree, disarm, discontinue
il-, in-, ir-	not	illegible, inactive, irregular
inter-	between, among	interaction, interstellar, international
mis-	bad, wrong	misconduct, misfortune, misprint
mono-	one	monoculture, monorail, monotone
multi-	many, much	multipurpose, multiword, multipart
out-	surpassing	outbid, outdo, outnumber
pre-	earlier, before	prewar, preview, prehistoric
re-	again, back	recall, reappear, rewrite
under-	below, less than	underground, underpass, underage
poly-	many, more than one	polygon, polymer, polyglot

ACTIVITY A Choose five prefixes from the chart on page 392. Provide another example word for each prefix.

ACTIVITY B Add a prefix from the chart on page 392 to each word below. Give the meaning of each new word and write a narrative using four the words.

1. gram
2. pass
3. task
4. climax
5. game
6. election
7. change
8. democratic

ACTIVITY C Look up the following words in a dictionary. Identify each prefix and give its meaning. Then define the word. How does the meaning of the prefix help you understand the meaning of the word?

1. paramedic
2. superwoman
3. circumnavigate
4. hyperactive
5. enslave
6. postscript
7. unpatriotic
8. malnutrition
9. reword
10. interstate
11. ambidextrous
12. intramural
13. immature
14. polyethnic

ACTIVITY D Reread the excerpt on page 375. In the second and third paragraphs, there are several words that begin with prefixes. Identify the words and their prefixes. Use a dictionary to find the definition of each word. If you use an online dictionary, be sure to use a reliable site.

WRITER'S CORNER

Choose one prefix from the chart on page 392. Work with a partner to write a list of at least five words with that prefix. Then use at least three of the words in a short expository piece about prefixes.

ACTIVITY E Using what you know about prefixes, make an educated guess about the meaning of the following words. Consult the chart on page 392 as you work and record your ideas. Check your answers in a dictionary.

1. multilateral
2. outwit
3. monofilament
4. preorbital
5. overblown
6. misconduct
7. illogical
8. antislavery
9. aerodynamics
10. recharge

ACTIVITY F Think of the word that would best complete each sentence. The prefix of the word is given for you.

1. When Paul first wakes up, he speaks in mono_____.
2. Sara doesn't go to parties on school nights because her parents would dis_____.
3. The Intra_____ Waterways are great for boating and fishing.
4. The United Nations was established to help solve inter_____ problems.
5. The multi_____ banner attracted plenty of attention.
6. Sometimes a semi_____ divides a compound sentence.
7. The basketball team made it to the semi_____.
8. A poly_____ is commonly called a lie detector.
9. Chewing gum loudly or wearing your hat at the dinner table is considered to be im_____.
10. The school talent show is not happening this year but next year because it is a bi_____ event.

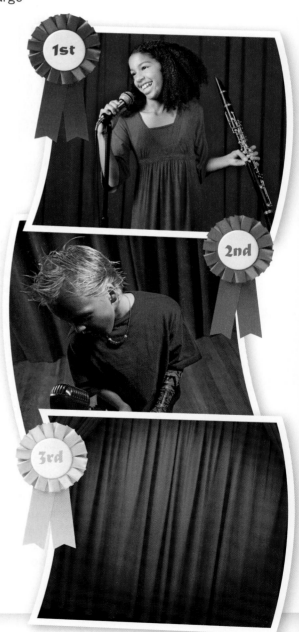

ACTIVITY G Fill in the blanks on the chart below. Use a dictionary to check your answers.

PREFIX	LANGUAGE OF ORIGIN	MEANING	EXAMPLE
deca-	_____	ten	_____
fore-	_____	_____	forefather
sub-	Latin	_____	
aero-	_____	air	_____
mega-	Greek	_____	
_____	Latin	_____	extraordinary
_____	_____	excessive	hypersensitive
im-	_____	_____	impure
_____	_____	not	nonperson
_____	Latin	_____	supersonic
tele-	Greek	_____	_____
trans-	Latin	_____	_____
_____	Greek	_____	nanosecond

Jacques Cousteau, an oceanographer

ACTIVITY H Use each example word from the chart above in a sentence.

ACTIVITY I In the library or online, find an article, Web site, or informational text about a topic below. Identify three words with prefixes in your source. Using a dictionary, define the prefixes and the words. Then write the topic sentence for an expository essay on the topic.

1. oceanography
2. forms of government
3. prehistoric invertebrates
4. volcanoes

A trilobite, a prehistoric invertebrate

WRITER'S CORNER

Write another example word for three prefixes in the chart above. Using the new words, write an expository paragraph about a topic of your choice.

Self-Help Presentations

An excellent way to share information about a topic that interests you is to tell people about it. An expository presentation might share the history of an everyday object, the scope of new technology, or the culture of a distant land. One popular type of expository talk is a self-help presentation—one in which the speaker explains how the audience might live better, more healthfully, or with fewer problems. Here are some guidelines to help you prepare and deliver an effective self-help presentation.

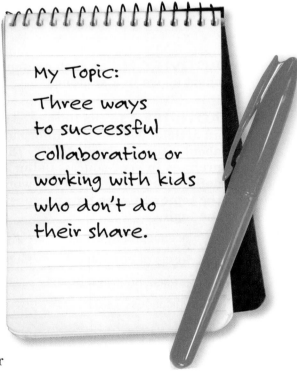

My Topic:

Three ways to successful collaboration or working with kids who don't do their share.

Selecting a Topic

Self-help information offers new ways to solve old problems or to improve common situations. Unlike a how-to article, a self-help presentation offers approaches toward fixing something, rather than a step-by-step plan. You might start by thinking about things that you have fixed or wish you could fix.

Choose a problem, a situation, or a pet peeve you have already fixed or one that many people, including you, wish they could fix. If it is a problem you have solved, consider whether your solution would work for other people. If it is a problem that needs a solution, consider how and where you might find strategies that will serve both you and your audience. Either way, choose a topic of interest to you and your audience. Remember to narrow your topic to allow yourself time to offer examples of simple, safe, and effective self-help solutions.

Audience

Know your audience and tailor your talk to their needs. A self-help presentation is meant to offer information your listeners can use on their own to solve a problem. Ask yourself these questions:

- What does the audience already know?
- What do they wish they knew?
- What strategies will help them most help themselves?

For example, imagine how your approach to getting students to work together successfully might differ if you were talking to a group of teachers, a group of teenagers, or a group of attendance officers. Think about the way your audience looks at the topic and match your ideas, organization, and language to their needs.

ACTIVITY A **Read each expository topic below. Write a narrower version of the same topic that would make an effective self-help presentation.**

1. nutrition for people of all ages
2. traveling safely
3. studying
4. career education
5. repairing cars
6. running or jogging
7. lifting weights
8. potatoes and you
9. music
10. Internet safety

SPEAKER'S CORNER

Make a list of five topics for a self-help talk. Trade lists with a partner and write the problem you think each topic would address and what you would hope to learn. Discuss your responses with your partner.

Grammar in Action. Identify the prepositional phrases that function as adverbs in the last paragraph on the p. 375 model.

Research and Organization

A self-help presentation is organized around the problem or situation that needs to be fixed and the strategies for fixing it. The audience will be looking to you, as a self-help speaker, for information. For just those few minutes, you are the expert, so help yourself to know what really works. Research the strategies that help people fix the problem and try out the strategies to learn the benefits (and pitfalls) of each. Check out print and online sources, especially interviews, to find firsthand information to add human interest.

Plan your talk, using a brief outline or note cards. As always, identify what will be the main ideas of your introduction, body, and conclusion.

Introduce your topic, the problem or situation, in a way your audience can immediately identify. You might describe a common scenario gone wrong or relate an actual event in heartbreaking detail.

In the body, offer three strategies your audience can use right away and support each with anecdotes that show the strategy in action. Include bits of data, statistics, and definitions where you can to support your ideas and to encourage the audience to have confidence in your advice.

End your talk with a quick summary of the benefits that your audience will soon be enjoying. And then, as always, practice, practice, practice.

Main Idea:

Three ideas for dressing up for a costume party when you don't want to dress up.

Wear Groucho Marx glasses or glasses with fake eyeballs.

Wear a T-shirt with glow-in-the-dark lettering or logos.

Muss up your hair with styling gel or mousse.

Actively Listening

When listening to a self-help presentation, follow these guidelines.

- Identify the organizational structure of the talk to increase your understanding and to help you predict what might come next.
- Try to form a picture in your mind of what the speaker is saying. Ask yourself questions such as *Does this make sense?* and *Would that strategy work for me?*
- Pay attention to any visual aids. They often allow you to see what the speaker is saying in a new way.
- At the end, limit your questions to strategies and advice you want to understand more clearly.

ACTIVITY B Discuss with a partner what resources you would use to research each topic below. Then, on your own, choose one self-help topic and write a brief outline telling what kind of information you would offer in the introduction, the body, and the conclusion of a presentation.

1. six ideas for letting go of stress
2. strategies for running a faster marathon
3. grooming a poodle at home for a fraction of the cost
4. eating in public without embarrassing yourself
5. raising your personal television viewing standards
6. a star sumo wrestler's best advice on competition
7. the benefits of learning to play a musical instrument
8. using what you know about dogs to meet people
9. finding meaning in life through nursery rhymes
10. three win-win conflict resolution techniques

SPEAKER'S CORNER

Practice your talk with a partner, varying your tone of voice and emphasizing important words. When you are the listener, describe your reaction to the speech.

 Tech Tip Record a podcast of your talk for review.

Prewriting and Drafting

Everyone is curious or knowledgeable about something, from Civil War battles to current tennis players. What topic do you know a lot about? What topic do you want to know more about? Any of these ideas might be an excellent topic for an expository essay. Now you will write an expository essay, using what you have discussed in this chapter.

Prewriting

The prewriting stage for writing an expository essay includes choosing a topic, gathering ideas from research, and planning the piece. Of course before you research, you need to find out what you already know.

Choosing a Topic

Denver, an eighth grader, is writing an essay for health class. He brainstormed a list of health-related topics that interested him, using a list of ideas.

I was amazed to learn _____ about health.

One healthy habit is _____.

One unhealthy habit is _____.

It's important to teach children about _____.

I'd rather _____ than do any other exercise.

I just love to eat _____.

My favorite sport is _____.

I can't believe that the human body can _____.

After reviewing his list, Denver chose to write about the DARE (Drug Abuse Resistance Education) program at his old school. Denver knew he could find additional information about it through research. The topic was narrow enough to maintain a clear focus in an essay.

Your Turn

Brainstorm ideas for an expository essay. Choose a topic that interests you, that you already know something about, that you can find additional information about, and that is narrow enough to maintain a clear focus. Use Denver's list if you need help.

Gathering Ideas

Denver knew that before he could make a plan for writing, he should explore his topic and do research to find important information. Denver decided to use a KWL chart to explore his topic and to record research.

Ideas Denver filled in the Know and Want to Know columns before doing his research. Then he did some Internet research to fill in the Learned column. He checked his completed chart to be sure it answered the questions *who, what, where, when, why,* and *how.*

Writer's Tip The prewriting process includes choosing a topic, gathering ideas from research, and planning the piece.

Prewriting

Drafting

Content Editing

Revising

Copyediting

Proofreading

Publishing

What I KNOW	What I WANT to Know	What I LEARNED
• team effort by police, teachers, and parents • teaches kids ways to keep from drinking and taking drugs • first few lessons teach about harm • next lessons teach about resisting drugs • at the end kids pledge to be drug-free • is in schools across America	• What does DARE stand for? • Which grades participate? • What do expert adults think of DARE? • What else can you learn?	• stands for Drug Abuse Resistance Education • There is a DARE program for every grade. • Ms. Giovanni, my former principal, says, "I've seen the effects of DARE. This is one program that really works." • how to find role models, and the influence of media

Planning an Expository Essay

Denver studied the information on his KWL chart and started to think about how he might use the information in an expository essay. He knew that he had to consider his audience, his purpose, and the organizational structure. Here is Denver's plan.

Topic: the DARE program at my old school

Audience: my health teacher

Organization Structure:

Introduction: Define program and its goals

Body: Explain program in chronological order

Conclusion: Summarize the program and its goals

Your Turn

Make a KWL chart about your topic and do your research to complete the chart. Then make an organizational plan for your

 Organization

expository essay.

Record your topic, your audience, and an organizational structure, including what you will most likely place in the introduction, the body, and the conclusion.

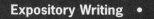

Drafting

Denver was ready to follow his writing plan and incorporate his KWL notes to create a draft of an expository essay. He kept in mind that he did not have to use all the information from his KWL chart. He also knew that he could add information not on the chart. Denver wrote a double-spaced draft so he would have room for revisions.

Take a DARE!

DARE is a program people have heard about but not everyone knows what it is exactly and I think they should because I participated in DARE in my last school, so I can explain it to you. Drug and alcohol abuse can cause kids problems all their lives so DARE tries to help them stay off drugs. DARE stands for Drug Abuse Resistance Education. The program is a team effort by the police department, teachers, and parents to have an educational program that teaches kids ways to keep from drinking and taking drugs.

The oficial DARE program has 17 lessons. DARE at all grades. They are about an hour long but in my old school sometimes we were having such good discussions that my teacher let us keep talking a lot longer. The first few lessons are about drugs and alcohol and the harm that they can do. Then come lessons that teach kids how to resist drugs those lessons can be fun, especially if you like to act because you do a lot of role-playing. You learn better ways to build self-esteme and manage stress than taking drugs. You also learn about the influence of the media and how to find better role models, and form a support system. At the end of the program students take a pledge to be drug-free. The last lesson is graduation, with a party and certificites.

DARE is not a perfect program but overall the students I talked to like it because it gives them a chance to get to know officers and get information and ask questions they might have been afraid to ask and another good thing about the program is it teaches teachers and principals and parents too. DARE is one way to help keep kids from ruining their lives. As Ms. Eileen Giovanni, principal of Disney Middle School, says "I've seen the effects of DARE. This is one program that really works."

Prewriting

Drafting

Content Editing

Revising

Copyediting

Proofreading

Publishing

Cause and Effect

Cause explains why something happens. Effect explains what happens as a result. Some expository essays use cause-and-effect relationships as their organizational structure. For example, an introduction might define an effect, such as global warming. Then the body of the essay might explain several causes of the effect, such as pollution, aerosol use, and deforestation. The conclusion might then sum up the significance of the cause-and-effect relationships. Writers use words such as the following when writing an expository essay organized using cause-and-effect relationships: *as a result of, because, consequently, due to,* and *so.* Before you begin writing, determine if your expository essay topic lends itself to being structured around cause-and-effect relationships. If so, you might want to use this organizational structure for your essay.

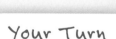

Your Turn

Use your KWL chart and writing plan as you draft an expository essay. Feel free to change your plan if you think of information you want to add or delete.

Concentrate on getting down the important points, using the organizational structure you selected. Remember to leave extra space between the lines to leave room for revisions.

Editor's Workshop

Content Editing

When Denver finished his draft, he thought he had written a good expository essay. But he also knew that the points the essay raised about DARE would need to be edited for logic, order, and clarity.

Denver gave his essay to Chandra, a classmate who had participated in the DARE program. He thought that her knowledge of the program would make her an ideal content editor and that she would best notice how well his ideas were expressed. He also thought she would know what information would be necessary and what would not be necessary.

Chandra used the following Content Editor's Checklist to edit Denver's draft. Chandra read Denver's draft twice, first to understand its overall purpose and to notice major problems and the second time to focus on details.

Content Editor's Checklist

- [ ] Does the essay have an identifiable topic sentence?
- [ ] Is the essay well organized? Is the organization of the essay logical?
- [ ] Are there opinions presented as facts?
- [ ] Are all the facts presented relevant to the main idea?
- [ ] Do the paragraphs in the body contain facts that support the essay's main idea?
- [ ] Are all the ideas easy to understand?
- [ ] Is all the information stated as concisely as possible?
- [ ] Does the conclusion sum up the main idea and provide additional insights?

Chandra complimented Denver on his draft and said she understood clearly the points he made. Chandra told Denver she thought most people would understand his essay and find it interesting, especially if they had heard of the DARE program but didn't know much about it.

As with all first drafts, Chandra knew Denver would revise it. Here are her suggestions.

- The topic sentence is unclear to me. I think you should explain right away in the first paragraph what DARE stands for and what the program does.

- The essay seems to be well organized by order of importance. You begin with what DARE is, proceed to how it's organized, and end with why it's a good program.

- Although no facts are presented as opinions, the first paragraph has too much opinion for an expository essay. It's not necessary to tell the readers that you think they should participate in the program.

- Most of the facts seem to be relevant, but the fact that you participated in the program is not relevant. I would delete that part.

- The paragraphs in the essay contain sufficient information to support your main idea.

- The ideas you present are easy to understand.

- Generally, I think you should tighten up your writing. You can cut quite a bit without losing any important information. In the second paragraph, is it important to tell readers that discussions often lasted longer than required?

Denver considered Chandra's suggestions carefully. He respected her opinion and agreed with many of her suggestions. He took out unnecessary information and tightened up his writing until he was satisfied that he had improved his draft.

Prewriting

Drafting

Content Editing

Revising

Copyediting

Proofreading

Publishing

Your Turn

Revise your first draft, using the Content Editor's Checklist as a guide. Have you

 **Voice** presented the important points as concisely and clearly as you possibly can?

Next, trade drafts with a partner. You and your partner should read each other's drafts and suggest improvements, if necessary, in each area on the checklist. Finally, talk over the suggestions and accept the ones that seem sensible to you.

Writer's Tip Since the purpose of an expository essay is to inform readers about a topic, the writer's voice should be confident.

Revising

This is Denver's draft, which shows the revisions he plans to make.

Take a DARE!

~~DARE is a program people have heard about but not everyone knows what it is exactly and I think they should because I participated in DARE in my last school, so I can explain it to you.~~ Drug and alcohol abuse can cause kids problems all their lives so ~~DARE tries to help them stay off drugs.~~ that's why DARE was organized. DARE stands for Drug Abuse Resistance Education. The program is a team effort by the police department, teachers, and parents to have an educational program that teaches kids ways to keep from drinking and taking drugs.

The oficial DARE program has 17 lessons. ~~DARE at all grades.~~ , which is taught at all the grades, They are about an hour long ~~but in my old school sometimes we were having such good discussions that my teacher let us keep talking a lot longer.~~ The first few lessons are about drugs and alcohol and the harm that they can do. Then come lessons that teach kids how to resist drugs those lessons can be fun, especially if you like to act because you do a lot of role-playing. You learn better ways to build self-esteme and manage stress than taking drugs. You also learn about the influence of the media and how to find better role models, and form a support system. At the end of the program students take a pledge to be drug-free. The last lesson is graduation, with a party and certificites.

Prewriting

Drafting

Content Editing

Revising

Copyediting

Proofreading

Publishing

DARE is not a perfect program but overall ~~the students I talked to~~ like it because it gives them a chance to get to know officers and get information and ask questions they might have been afraid to ask and another good thing about the program is it teaches teachers and principals and parents too. DARE is one way to help keep kids from ~~ruining their lives.~~ _abusing alcohol and drugs_ As Ms. Eileen Giovanni, principal of Disney Middle School, says "I've seen the effects of DARE. This is one program that really works."

Examine how Denver revised his draft.

- First, Denver agreed that the introduction was unclear. Fortunately, he found that he had a

Sentence Fluency

strong topic sentence in his first paragraph. How did he clarify his introduction?
- Second, he deleted the unnecessary opinion in the first paragraph. What irrelevant fact did he delete?
- Third, he tightened up his writing and revised the second paragraph. What unnecessary information did he eliminate?
- Finally, Denver noticed that Chandra did not comment about his conclusion. Though he thought he summed up his main idea, the conclusion seemed a little vague. How did he make his conclusion more clear?

Your Turn

Revise your draft, using the Content Editor's Checklist and your editing partner's suggestions. Reread your revised draft. Can you think of any other ways to make it better?

Grammar in Action

Add noun clauses to your essay to make your writing more concise. Review noun clauses in Lesson 4 of this chapter if you need help.

Copyediting and Proofreading

Copyediting

Denver revised his essay, using his own and Chandra's suggestions. When he was confident that the ideas of his essay were clear and logical, he read his essay again. This time he read it for
_____ word meaning,
👓 Word Choice word choice,
_____
sentence structure, and the overall logic of his expository essay.

Denver used the following Copyeditor's Checklist for this task.

Copyeditor's Checklist

☐ Do the sentences flow smoothly?

☐ Are any sentences awkward or confusing?

☐ Are words with prefixes used correctly?

☐ Are any words repeated too often?

☐ Do transition words support the pattern of organization?

☐ Does the structure of the sentences vary?

☐ Are noun clauses used correctly?

☐ Is the structure of each sentence logical and grammatically correct?

Denver read his essay aloud so that he could hear how it sounded. He knew that the parts he stumbled over when he read it might trip up readers too. He took out extra words to fix those sentences.

He also corrected two run-on sentences and a rambling sentence he found in the last two paragraphs. In correcting these sentences, Denver added small details such as clearly stating the goal of the DARE strategies and describing the kind of certificates the participants receive.

Denver decided that the word *kids* was too informal to use in his essay, so he changed *kids* to *students* and *children*. He also revised the sentences that started with *you* because he wanted to keep the tone of his essay objective. He made a few other language changes.

Your Turn

Reread your revised draft, concentrating on the sound and meaning of each sentence and each word. Read the draft aloud at least once to hear how the words sound and how the sentences flow. Use the Copyeditor's Checklist to help you improve your draft.

Proofreading

Denver now needed to have his essay proofread to make sure the spelling, grammar, punctuation,

and usage were correct. He asked another classmate, Steven, to proofread his piece. Having another person proofread your work is a good way to get a fresh perspective on your writing. Because Steven hadn't read Denver's essay before, he might spot mistakes in spelling, grammar, punctuation, and usage that Denver and Chandra missed.

Steven checked each item on the checklist in order. He circled the errors. When he wasn't sure about the spelling of a word, he looked it up in a dictionary. Steven found a paragraph that was not indented. He also found five punctuation mistakes and three spelling errors. How many mistakes can you find?

Conventions

Prewriting

Drafting

Content Editing

Revising

Copyediting

Proofreading

Publishing

Your Turn

- Work with a partner to proofread both of your expository essays.
- Make photocopies of the essays. Then, as one person reads one of the papers aloud, the other follows along and marks the mistakes.
- Say the name of the punctuation as you read too. That helps the proofreader know that the punctuation has been included and that it is correct.
- Using the Proofreader's Checklist as a guide, check for one type of error at a time.

Proofreader's Checklist

- ☐ Are the paragraphs indented?
- ☐ Have any words been misspelled?
- ☐ Are the sentences capitalized and punctuated correctly?
- ☐ Is the grammar accurate?
- ☐ Were any new errors introduced during editing?

Publishing

Denver edited and revised his draft several times until he felt it was good enough to publish. He made a finished version to submit to his health teacher. When he finished, he knew it was his best work, so he felt ready to share it.

Take a DARE!

DARE stands for Drug Abuse Resistance Education. The program is a team effort by the police department, teachers, and parents to teach students strategies to avoid drinking and taking drugs. Drug and alcohol abuse are serious issues that can cause lifelong problems, so that's why DARE was developed.

The official DARE program, which is taught at all the grades, has 17 lessons. Each lesson is about an hour long. The first few lessons teach about drugs and alcohol and the harm that they can do. Then come lessons that teach children strategies for resisting drugs. These lessons can be fun for students, especially students who enjoy acting because the lessons involve role-playing. The goal is to teach children better ways to build self-esteem and manage stress than taking drugs and drinking. Subsequent lessons teach about the influence of the media, ways to find good role models, and how to form a support system. At the end of the program, students take a pledge to be drug-free. The last lesson is a graduation and celebration at which certificates of completion are awarded to students who completed the program.

DARE is not a perfect program, but overall, students like the program because it gives them a chance to get to know police officers, get information, and ask questions they might have been afraid to ask previously. Another strength of the program is that it involves teachers, principals, and parents. DARE is one way to help keep children from abusing alcohol and drugs. As Ms. Eileen Giovanni, principal of Disney Middle School, says, "I've seen the effects of DARE. This is one program that really works."

Publishing is a way for you to share your thoughts and experiences with other people. Here are a few ways to publish your expository writing.

 Post it on your class Web site. You may want to add photographs, diagrams, or clipart. These are interesting items to attach to an expository essay. You might include a feedback questionnaire for reader comments.

 Create a classroom book. Ask your school librarian if your class's book could be a checkout book for a limited time.

 Make a classroom newsletter. Your expository essay will be a valuable resource for other students in your school who share the same interest in your topic.

 Read your essay aloud for Parents' Night. You might wish to record it with a video recorder.

Whenever you publish, make sure the message is clear and neatly presented.

Your Turn

Before you publish your expository essay, carefully make any needed revisions from the proofreading stage. If

Presentation

you write your essay by hand, use your best handwriting and copy your corrections accurately. If you type your essay on a computer, don't forget to do a thorough spell-check and grammar-check before printing your essay. Proofread your essay one last time, just to be sure you didn't add new mistakes or leave out any parts.

After you do a final check of your essay, you might want to add a diagram or an illustration to explain a key idea visually. You might attach this visual to the front of a folder that acts as a cover for your published piece.

Prewriting

Drafting

Content Editing

Revising

Copyediting

Proofreading

Publishing

Persuasive Writing

LiNK

The American Forests

by John Muir

All sorts of local laws and regulations have been tried and found wanting, and the costly lessons of our own experience, as well as that of every civilized nation, show conclusively that the fate of the remnant of our forests is in the hands of the federal government, and that if the remnant is to be saved at all, it must be saved quickly. . . .

Any fool can destroy trees. They cannot run away; and if they could, they would still be destroyed—chased and hunted down as long as fun or a dollar could be got out of their bark hides, branching horns, or magnificent bole backbones. Few that fell trees plant them; nor would planting avail much towards getting back anything like the noble primeval forests. . . .

> Persuasive essays, like this one by naturalist John Muir, appeal to the public's logic and emotions to support the main topic. Muir's essay also works to convince others to share his viewpoint about preserving nature.

Rain Forests in Danger

by Amy Garcia
Room 213

Our planet is at a critical point. Our environment is threatened from many sides. I want to talk about our disappearing rain forests and what we can do to protect them.

Deforestation, the act of cutting back rain forests for commercial purposes, has increased at an alarming rate over the past few decades. Not long ago, rain forests covered 14 percent of the earth's land surface. Today they take up only about 5 percent. Every second we lose another acre. In half a century, the rain forests may be completely gone.

One effect of this loss is an increase in global warming. Scientists believe that this may cause the earth's climate to become more extreme, resulting in more air pollution, creating changes in food and water supplies, and increasing the occurrences of floods and droughts. We cannot risk the impact these things would have on human health.

Another grave result would be the loss of hundreds of thousands of plant and animal species that the rain forests nurture. Who knows what knowledge will be lost when the last tropical tree is cut down? What medicines will go undiscovered? What wondrous creatures will disappear forever? We would certainly lose much more than we stand to gain.

What can we do to help? One way to take action is to stop buying things made of mahogany, teak, rosewood, and other woods that come from rain forests. Another way, surprisingly enough, is to stop eating so many hamburgers. For every hamburger you eat, 55 square feet of rain forest must be chopped down to provide grazing land for cattle. Finally, write to your senators and members of Congress, urging them to pay less attention to commercial special interests and more attention to the interests of our grandchildren.

We must be stewards of the world's natural resources, not exploiters; and we must start today.

Save the Rain Forests!

What Makes Good Persuasive Writing?

Good persuasive writing focuses on one topic that can be viewed in different or opposing ways. The writer of a good persuasive essay clearly takes a position on the topic and states it. All the ideas in good persuasive writing appeal to either logic or emotion and work toward convincing readers to share the writer's viewpoint.

Persuasive writing can take many forms, including advertisements, letters to the editor, book and movie reviews, and campaign speeches. These are some of the things you should keep in mind when you write a persuasive essay.

Position Statement

A persuasive essay should begin with a position statement. This statement appears in the introduction and should tell exactly where the writer stands on the issue in question.

Supporting the Position

The body of a persuasive essay often provides readers with logical reasons to agree with the position statement. These reasons are then supported by examples or explanations, which are often opinions and statements of fact. For example, consider the model on page 413.

Position Statement: We must combat deforestation of the rain forests.

Reason: If we don't, there will be an increase in global warming.

Example (fact): Global warming causes an increase in air pollution.

Explanation (opinion): We cannot risk the impact on human health.

Writers might organize the body of a persuasive essay by developing a paragraph for each reason to agree with the position statement. The topic sentence of each supporting paragraph states the reason. The sentences that follow provide relevant examples and explanations that appeal to either logic or emotion.

Conclusion

A good persuasive essay ends with a conclusion that summarizes the position statement and leaves an impact on the readers. The conclusion should not add any new reasons, but should restate the position in a convincing manner. A good persuasive conclusion might also summarize the strongest evidence supporting the position or even call on readers to take action. Any way that it is expressed, a good persuasive conclusion leaves readers thinking about the topic, even after they have finished reading the piece.

ACTIVITY A Read the body of this letter to the editor. Then answer the questions.

Everyone eligible to vote in the United States should cast a ballot on Election Day. As it stands now, when the turnout for a national election is over 50 percent, news reports comment on the high percentage of participation. That's only about half the registered voters. Many people have been discouraged from voting and encouraged to believe they are powerless. As long as they don't vote, the truth is they are powerless. They are invisible. If we want to be governed fairly, we have to make ourselves visible by voting—every one of us.

1. What is the position statement?

2. What is the general tone of the letter's body? Is the author angry, sad, concerned, or hopeful? Why do you think so?

3. What sections of the letter's body try to convince the reader through factual explanations?

4. What sections of the letter's body give opinions?

5. What are the reasons that support the position statement?

6. What is the conclusion of this essay? Does it leave an impact on the readers? Why or why not?

WRITER'S CORNER

Make a list of changes you'd like to see at home or at school, in your city or state, in our country, or in the world. Circle five ideas that are of particular interest to you and write a position statement for each.

ACTIVITY B Read this paragraph from a newspaper editorial about the need for a community recreation center. Write another paragraph that features a different reason for its construction. Include explanations or examples to support your reason.

One reason that our community must build a recreation center is so teenagers will have something to do rather than get in trouble. Statistics show that teenagers are most likely to exhibit dangerous behaviors in the hours just after school. Teenagers of working parents will no longer have to go home to an empty house or to friends' houses that might also have no adults present. Teenagers will have a safe, fun place to go.

ACTIVITY C Read the following topics about which people have different opinions. Make a two-column chart for each topic. List all the reasons you can think of for and against the topic. Do you have more reasons for the topic or against the topic? Where do you stand on the topic? Write a position statement for each topic based on the conclusions you drew from your chart.

1. nuclear power
2. U.S. involvement in the politics of developing countries
3. professional athletes' salaries
4. eating meat
5. hunting

TOPIC:

For	Against

ACTIVITY D Read the following paragraphs from the conclusions of persuasive essays. Replace each of the italicized sentences with one or more powerful statements or questions that you think will lead the reader to agree with the writer.

1. Developing energy alternatives to those derived from fossil fuel makes sense financially, environmentally, and globally. *It's not too late to make a change.*

2. Lengthening the school day will disrupt extracurricular activities and increase the dangers facing students returning home at the end of each day. *These concerns are too great to ignore.*

ACTIVITY E Write two radio commercials to sell two of the items listed below. Remember to appeal to both the consumers' logic and emotions.

1. tickets to your band's rock concert
2. sandwiches for a team's fund-raising campaign
3. tickets for a school's neighborhood car wash
4. greeting cards made by your park district's photo club
5. your dog's six puppies
6. fruits and vegetables at your local farmer's market

ACTIVITY F Work with a partner. Choose a popular commercial that you have seen on television. Prepare a short speech to present to the class. Include the following:

- What product the commercial advertises
- How the commercial is presented
- How the commercial appeals to the logic of the viewer
- How the commercial appeals to the emotions of the viewer

WRITER'S CORNER

Work with a partner. Find two newspaper or magazine advertisements that appeal to both logic and emotion. Write two imperative sentences that would enhance the advertisements.

Voice and Audience

Voice

The tone of voice in a persuasive essay sets the mood. The mood that is created can work to the writer's advantage and effectively convey a message to readers. If a writer isn't careful, however, the mood can annoy readers and perhaps even anger them.

Persuasive writers often use tone of voice to set one or more of the following moods in a piece:

uplifting	hopeful	enthusiastic
tense	concerned	warning
frank	confident	caring

To use a specific kind of voice to create a mood, writers carefully choose verbs, adjectives, and adverbs. These verbs, adjectives, and adverbs are vivid, have punch, and help bring out emotion in the reader.

The writer of this paragraph about the potential opening of a Boys and Girls Club used an upbeat and enthusiastic tone to encourage people to approve the club.

The prospect of opening a Boys and Girls Club in Riverglen is exciting for another reason. Kids get to develop important skills that they may not experience at school. Imagine a gym filled with enthusiastic volleyball players, gymnasts, and wrestlers; activity rooms brimming with happy, young people dancing, singing, building, and sewing; and a play yard alive with the sounds of jump ropes and bouncing basketballs. The possibilities for a child's personal growth are endless.

ACTIVITY A A second writer wrote this paragraph about the opening of the Boys and Girls Club. How is the mood different from that of the first paragraph? What words, phrases, sentence style, and punctuation did each writer use to set the mood?

To deny the youth of Riverglen a Boys and Girls Club is a shameful crime! Where are kids supposed to go to develop important skills that they don't experience at school? Because so many schools have cut fine arts, applied arts, and athletics, many young people are left out in the cold. The boys and girls of Riverglen cannot and will not develop to their full potential unless something is done now!

ACTIVITY B Rewrite the following paragraph. Change the mood from angry to warning.

Anyone who does not think we should spend the money that our class has raised to go on a class trip to the art museum is just foolish and not thinking right. A trip to the art museum will make everybody happy and more familiar with art, which is certainly more important and valuable than the other ideas.

ACTIVITY C Rewrite the following paragraph. Change its mood from angry to hopeful.

One reason that I can't believe my parents won't let me have a sleepover is because I always do all my chores. Responsible kids should be rewarded. My parents are so unfair! Even when my brother ignores our chore chart, I still do what I'm supposed to. I take out the stinky trash, wash the filthy dog, and set the dinner table. This worker deserves a reward!

WRITER'S CORNER

Read a letter to the editor in your local newspaper. Identify the mood that is set, using the list on the preceding page. Write the words or phrases the writer uses to create the mood.

With an adult, find letters to the editor responses online.

I Wanna Iguana

Dear Mom,
I know you don't think I should have Mikey Gulligan's baby iguana when he moves, but here's why I should. If I don't take it, he goes to Stinky and Stinky's dog, Lurch, will eat it.

You don't want that to happen, do you?
Signed,
Your sensitive son, Alex

Karen Kaufman Orloff

Audience

A writer often chooses a particular voice or mood for a piece of writing depending on the audience. For example, a person who is trying to persuade the city council to provide money for a new park would probably use a different voice or tone from a person who is trying to persuade a group of neighbors to have a block party. Students who are trying to persuade their teachers to assign less homework would use a different tone from students who are trying to persuade their classmates to come to a pep rally.

To whom do you think the paragraphs about the Boys and Girls Club on pages 418 and 419 were addressed? Which tone do you think would work best with that particular audience?

What effect do you think the paragraph about the sleepover on page 419 had on its intended audience?

ACTIVITY D Rewrite the following paragraph. Change its mood from uplifting to concerned.

A recycling program at our school is needed for another reason. It would bring the students closer together and give us a sense of community. I just know that we can work for a common cause that bridges the gaps between all student groups at school, while at the same time reduces the amount of waste we create. Recycling is the perfect way to build a better environment, both in and out of school.

ACTIVITY E Read each position statement. Write one sentence that an active listener might argue if he or she disagreed with the statement.

1. Recycling is a waste of time and energy.
2. All students should attend college.
3. Eating three meals a day is important to your health.
4. Screaming will damage your vocal cords.
5. Drinking milk gives you strong bones.
6. Students should be required to attend physical education classes daily.

ACTIVITY F Choose one of these topics and audiences. Select a voice or tone that you think would convince that audience. Then write an introduction to a persuasive essay. Use your selected topic, audience, and voice.

A. You are applying for a part-time job as a babysitter. Write the introduction of a persuasive letter of application. Give your qualifications and tell why you would be good for the job.

B. You are the editor of the school newspaper. Write the introduction for a persuasive editorial addressed to the school board. Give reasons why summer vacation should be eliminated.

C. You are a citizen who strongly believes that your community should have a recycling plan. Write the introduction for a letter to the mayor, explaining your position.

D. Your class is planning its eighth-grade party. Some students want to go horseback riding. Others want to go bowling. You don't like either activity. Write the introduction for a persuasive essay that explains why the class should choose your favorite activity.

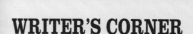

E. Your class has been asked to help build the set and gather props for the third-grade play. Many of your classmates do not want to give up their time to help the third graders. Others feel that the third graders do not need any help. Write the introduction of a persuasive speech to be presented to your class. Give reasons why your classmates should be willing to help.

F. Your parents have given you a curfew a half hour earlier than your friends. They agreed to discuss the matter tomorrow night. Prepare by writing three reasons you believe your curfew should be extended. What voice would you use to persuade your parents?

G. You are running for class treasurer in the upcoming election. Your persuasive essay will be printed in the school paper with the other candidates' essays. Your classmates will vote based on the persuasive essays. Write your essay to convince your classmates that you are best candidate for the job.

WRITER'S CORNER

You are going to write a piece based on one of the position statements you wrote for Activity C on page 416. What mood will your piece convey? List some adjectives or adjective phrases that you will use to set the mood.

Grammar in Action, Identify the adverb clause in the fourth paragraph in the student model on p. 413.

Advertisements

The purpose of an advertisement is to persuade you to buy or do something. Drawing conclusions from and making decisions about advertisements is an important part of independent thinking.

Advertisements can be found almost everywhere. Sometimes advertisements can be obvious. Other times they can be subtle, such as placing a product in a movie or having the hero drive a certain car.

LiNK

LINCOLN said
"With malice toward none; with charity for all;······ let us strive on to finish the work we are in;····to bind up the nation's wounds;···· to do all which may achieve and cherish a just and lasting peace."

America's food pledge 20 million tons

Save food for world relief

UNITED STATES FOOD ADMINISTRATION

Propaganda

Following are specific propaganda devices that advertisers use to persuade their audience. Knowing about these devices can help consumers make wise decisions about advertisements.

Bandwagon—This device tells you to do something or buy something because many other people do it or buy it.

> **Everyone eats at Schemale's Pizza Parlor.**

Loaded words—This device uses words that will provoke an emotional response.

> **Governor Stanton's new fees are a burden on small businesses.**

Here the writer uses *burden* to describe the fees; however, the bill may be a small fee that small businesses could afford but do not want to pay.

Testimonial—This device uses the opinion of a well-known expert or celebrity. Many ads for sporting goods use testimonials.

> **Famous figure skater Shoshana Peebles says, "Mercury skates help me fly across the rink!"**

Vague or sweeping generality—This device uses absolute words to describe a product or service in terms so broad that they can't possibly be proven wrong.

Herrmann's serves the best Polish sausage in the city!

Analyzing Advertisements

Advertising is designed to appeal to the desires of its audience. For example, many older people want to be young or appear youthful. Pick up your favorite magazine and examine the ads inside. Pay close attention to the ads that try to create a youthful identity. They might create a perception of action or fun, or use mascots, slang, bright colors, or misleading visuals.

Use the Advertising Analysis Checklist to analyze ads.

Advertising Analysis Checklist

☐ Is the purpose of the writing to persuade or give information?

☐ What is the claim? Is the claim provable?

☐ What evidence is given, if any, to support the claim?

☐ Does just one person make the claim?

☐ Why is the claim being made?

☐ Who is making this statement? What are the qualifications of this person? Is he or she worthy of my attention?

ACTIVITY A Read each statement and identify the propaganda device or devices used.

1. Blast-O-Pod bubble gum is the best!
2. The Boomer baseball bat will help you hit the ball out of the park every time.
3. Nine out of ten dentists agree that Whitex toothpaste is effective in removing plaque from your teeth.
4. Senator Rose Dearborne is soft on crime!
5. Have a NutriBar, the snack loved by millions!
6. Where does stock car driver Miles Neff put his trust in motor oil? Under the hood of his car.
7. The Forest Bill will provide much-needed relief for our state's parks.
8. Pitcher Miguel Estrada says he never takes the mound without his Blanchard glove.

WRITER'S CORNER

Find an ad in a favorite magazine and analyze it, using the checklist. Write five sentences describing the persuasive devices used in the ad.

Writing Advertisements

Advertisements are a form of persuasive writing. For that reason knowing how to write an advertisement is just as important as knowing how to read one. It's also a useful skill to have if you want to place an ad on a bulletin board, in a newspaper, or online.

Any time you write a short statement trying to persuade someone to do something, you are probably writing an advertisement. For example, you might write notices for lost pets or other items, or campaign posters for student elections. Consider these suggestions when writing advertisements.

Sales Ads

Print and online sales ads need to have a clever, concise title; contain a clear description of the item; and use a persuasive tone of voice. Because online ads don't require any paper, you will probably have more space to describe your item than in a print ad. Take this opportunity to include a vivid description of the item, using what you discussed in Chapter 4. For online ads, you will probably want to provide a digital image of the item you want to sell.

Lost-and-Found Ads

Lost-and-found ads, like sales ads, need a concise and vivid description. If you can afford it, consider offering a reward for the lost item or pet. Few words can be more persuasive than *reward offered.*

Campaign Posters

Campaign posters need an eye-catching visual, such as the slogan of the candidate or graphics that bring the candidate to life on the poster. Use your imagination to think of clever slogans that help people remember the candidate's name. It's not necessary to provide details for why people should vote for your candidate. The candidate should do that in speeches and debates. The posters are there to generate positive associations with the candidate's name. If possible, the candidate's photo should appear on larger posters.

ACTIVITY B Use the checklist on page 423 to analyze the following ad. Examine the claims made by the ad and tell if they are credible.

Hey, kids! Come on over to the hip place to be—the Green Zone Game Palace. We've got all the hot video games, like Quester, Maw, Firelight, and the award-winning Yonk! Our prizes are the best in town! And that's not all! When you get hungry, just stop at our mouth-watering pizza bar and grab a slice that's loaded with all your favorite toppings! Everybody's in the Green Zone, so why aren't you?

ACTIVITY C Write an online sales ad. The object should be something that someone would want to own after you've owned it, such as a bike, a tennis racket, or a violin.

ACTIVITY D Write a lost-and-found ad for a lost pet. Be sure to include a vivid description and the name of the pet. If possible, design a handbill for your ad and include a picture of the pet.

ACTIVITY E Design a campaign poster for yourself for student body president. The poster should include some version of your name and a slogan by which you want your candidacy to be remembered.

ACTIVITY F Work with a partner. Write an advertisement of your choice, using some of the propaganda techniques described on pages 422–423: bandwagon, loaded words, testimonial, and vague or sweeping generality. Read aloud your advertisement and challenge your classmates to identify each technique you used.

WRITER'S CORNER

Work with a partner and analyze the ad you wrote in Activity C. Use the checklist on page 423 to guide your discussion.

Transition Words

Effective writers use transition words or phrases to connect one idea to the next. These connections help writing flow and make it easier to understand. They show relationships between ideas. Here are some common transition words and phrases.

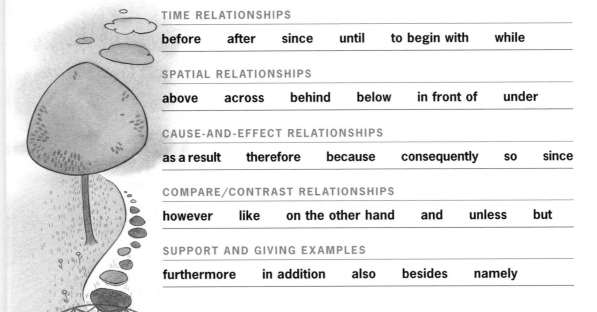

TIME RELATIONSHIPS

before	after	since	until	to begin with	while

SPATIAL RELATIONSHIPS

above	across	behind	below	in front of	under

CAUSE-AND-EFFECT RELATIONSHIPS

as a result	therefore	because	consequently	so	since

COMPARE/CONTRAST RELATIONSHIPS

however	like	on the other hand	and	unless	but

SUPPORT AND GIVING EXAMPLES

furthermore	in addition	also	besides	namely

ACTIVITY A Add as many transition words or phrases as you can to each of the lists above. Share your list with a partner. Did each of you think of words or phrases that the other didn't? Add your partner's words or phrases to your list.

ACTIVITY B Write a sentence for each relationship group listed above. Use a transition word or phrase in each sentence.

ACTIVITY C Choose the correct transition word or phrase in parentheses to complete each sentence.

1. Our nation's energy grids used to be sufficient. With today's needs, (however unlike), they are not.

2. All students should respect their teachers, (since yet) many do not.

3. Families spend less money when children wear school uniforms. (Furthermore Unlike), children are less likely to compare themselves to others based on looks.

4. (While Therefore), our town council should allow local businesses to host live entertainment on weekends.

5. Our students deserve an all-school dance (because as a result) we have shown respect and maturity throughout the year.

ACTIVITY D Complete each sentence so that the ending fits the italicized transition word.

1. Treating local sewers helps control the mosquito population, *so* _____.

2. *Although* our lakes and rivers are not polluted, _____.

3. We did not go to the movie *until* _____.

4. Auto accidents among teens will rise *unless* _____.

5. Flooding is nearly out of control *across* _____.

6. *In addition* to needing the money, I have to get a summer job _____.

7. I want a new computer *so* _____.

8. *Furthermore*, I want to practice at the batting cages _____.

9. Books about pollution are easily available, *therefore* _____.

10. Going to the theater can be fun *since* _____.

11. Famous leaders of our nation are quoted *as a result* _____.

12. On the plains of Africa, elephants roam freely *but* _____.

WRITER'S CORNER

Work with a partner. Choose a relationship group from the chart on page 426. Write a persuasive paragraph, using three of the words from your chosen group.

ACTIVITY E Revise the following paragraphs. Use transition words or phrases to connect the ideas and make the paragraphs flow.

1. Students need more time to exercise or visit with friends. They need to relax and refresh their minds and bodies. They will go back to class relaxed and ready to work. They will be better prepared to think and learn. Recess should be extended from 15 to 20 minutes.

2. It's not difficult to set up an aquarium. Place the aquarium on a sturdy stand. Put the underwater filter on the bottom. Cover the filter with 2 or 3 inches of gravel. Make the gravel slope from the back of the aquarium to the front. Install the heater. Add some rocks to cover the heater and make the aquarium look natural. Carefully pour in the water. Plant some plants to provide hiding places. Add your fish. Enjoy many entertaining hours watching them.

Austrian commemorative stamp of Franz Ferdinand

3. Swimming and hiking are both good forms of exercise. Swimming benefits your whole body. Hiking mainly exercises your legs. A body of water is necessary for swimming. Hiking requires a pair of good shoes or boots. Hiking can be done in any weather. Swimming outdoors is possible only when the weather is nice. Both swimming and hiking can be done alone. Both sports are more fun when enjoyed with friends.

4. Driving a car with an automatic transmission is not that difficult. Look around the car for any obstructions. Step into the car. Adjust the seat and mirrors to see clearly around you. Insert the key into the ignition. Start the car. Release the emergency brake. Put the car into Drive or Reverse. Depress the accelerator lightly. Always look in the direction the car is moving. Be aware of your surroundings at all times.

Front page of a newspaper showing the assassination of Archduke Franz Ferdinand

5. World War I had many causes. The Great Powers of Europe formed alliances to protect one another. Archduke Franz Ferdinand was assassinated on June 28, 1914, in Sarajevo, Bosnia. Austria-Hungary blamed Serbia for the assassination and declared war on Serbia. Russia helped Serbia. Germany declared war on Russia and France. German troops invaded France through Belgium. Great Britain declared war on Germany.

ACTIVITY F Write a persuasive sentence about each topic, using emotional appeal. Use the transition word or phrase in parentheses.

1. filling potholes on local streets (before)
2. allowing a class field trip to a museum (after)
3. eliminating soft drinks in school vending machines (unless)
4. hiring a full-time art teacher for school (to begin with)
5. ending poaching of animals in Africa (consequently)
6. convincing parents to raise your allowance (so)
7. convincing a teacher to raise a grade (unlike)
8. reducing water usage in the home (on the other hand)
9. recycling (as a result)
10. reinstating a school's music program (because)

ACTIVITY G The following sentences each contain a transition word or phrase. Write a sentence that you think could have come before each one.

1. While the milk was warming up, I chopped the chocolate.
2. As a result, I had to remove my muddy shoes.
3. We could not wash until the plumber was finished.
4. Furthermore, I think big cars are hard to park.
5. On the other hand, I like to ski in the winter.
6. Behind the counter, a clerk was refolding shirts.
7. In addition, the soldier was honored at the assembly.
8. Because we were excited, we decided to celebrate early.
9. Since the temperature was too high, the ice was not frozen.
10. While the dog was barking, the owner asked me to call the police.
11. However, she was still able to drive confidently.
12. Therefore, the campers were able to fall asleep.

WRITER'S CORNER

Reread a persuasive piece that you've written. Consider each paragraph. Are there any sentences that need to be connected with transition words or phrases? Revise your writing by adding them.

Suffixes

LiNK

Gettysburg Address

The world will little note nor long remember what we say here, but it can never forget what they did here. It is for us the living rather to be dedicated here to the unfinished work which they who fought here have thus far so nobly advanced.

Abraham Lincoln

A suffix is a syllable or syllables added to the end of a word to change its meaning or to make another word. The word to which the suffix is added is called the base word.

Suffixes can be added to base words to change their parts of speech. When you write, be sure to use the correct suffix for each base word. Remember that the suffix can change the meaning of a word and that the wrong suffix can send the wrong message.

Study the suffix charts. Notice how a suffix can change a word's part of speech. Look for base words that change their spelling when a suffix is added.

VERB SUFFIXES

Suffix	Base Word	Example
-ize	legal	legalize
-ate	necessity	necessitate
-ify	identity	identify
-en	deep	deepen

NOUN SUFFIXES

Suffix	Base Word	Example
-or	act	actor
-er	teach	teacher
-ity	responsible	responsibility
-ment	agree	agreement
-ance	appear	appearance
-ness	happy	happiness

ADJECTIVE SUFFIXES

Suffix	Base Word	Example
-ful	care	careful
-less	help	helpless
-y	thirst	thirsty
-able	enjoy	enjoyable

ADVERB SUFFIX

Suffix	Base Word	Example
-ly	quick	quickly

ACTIVITY A Use an example from each chart in a separate sentence. Underline the suffixes. Trade your paper with a partner. Tell the meaning of each word with an underlined suffix.

ACTIVITY B Identify the words that contain suffixes in the following paragraph. Then give a definition for each word.

One reason that my math teacher deserves the Teacher of the Year Award is because she takes her job seriously and she treats us very kindly. She is helpful when explaining new concepts and selfless in giving her time. My math teacher makes algebra more than tolerable—she makes it interesting and fun.

ACTIVITY C Brainstorm additional base words and examples for each suffix in the suffix charts. Then choose one suffix and make a list of as many example words as you can with that suffix. Discuss the meaning of each word on your list with a partner.

WRITER'S CORNER

Write five sentences that use words with suffixes. Include at least two infinitive phrases. Underline the words with suffixes.

ACTIVITY D Complete a chart like the one below by writing the word, its meaning, and other words that end with the same suffix. Use the example to get started. Use a dictionary if you need help with spelling.

SUFFIX	BASE WORD	NEW WORD	MEANING	OTHER WORDS
-ize	real	realize	to come to understand	dramatize emphasize
-er	bake			
-ful	neglect			
-ly	quiet			
-ate	motive			
-hood	neighbor			
-less	friend			
-able	comfort			
-y	hand			
-ance	attend			

ACTIVITY E Complete each sentence with a word from the chart in Activity D.

1. That teacher is able to _____ her students to do well.

2. It's important to wear _____ shoes while jogging.

3. My uncle is so _____ that he can fix anything.

4. If you weren't so _____, you wouldn't lose things.

5. Please walk _____ so you won't wake the baby.

6. We are organizing a block party in my _____ for the Fourth of July.

7. Most people do not _____ how physically challenging dance class really is.

8. The teacher took _____ to determine who was missing from our class.

9. The _____ vigorously kneaded the dough.

10. He cared for the child who was alone and _____.

ACTIVITY F Add an appropriate suffix to each word. Then give the meaning of the new word and use it in a sentence.

1. social
2. father
3. sad
4. drive
5. rely
6. profess

7. greed
8. time
9. wonder
10. enlighten
11. slow
12. grace

ACTIVITY G Add the correct suffix to the word in parentheses to complete each sentence.

1. The (cold) of the lake makes swimming unpleasant.
2. We all felt the winner's (enjoy).
3. The boy's older sister acted very (mother) toward him.
4. Will that toothpaste (white) your teeth?
5. That (harm) old dog won't hurt you.
6. The (sincere) of the speaker helped convince everyone.
7. Please be (care) when you take the bread out of the oven.
8. I hope it's not (cloud) on the day of our picnic.
9. The fact that she told a (false) shocked us all.
10. You need some (bend) wire to form the ornaments.
11. It is (help) to label each file.
12. The woman (kind) helped my mother.
13. That room is (mess) and disorganized.
14. You will not find the review session (use) unless you study.
15. We approached the car (slow).
16. He went to the hospital to receive (treat).
17. It is (doubt) that she will be on time.
18. When the sun comes out, it always (bright) my day.

WRITER'S CORNER

Choose a page in a novel. Find all the suffixes on the page and write them. Also, find two noun clauses and write them.

Persuasive Speeches

One of the most important reasons that speeches are made is to persuade an audience. In fact, it's no exaggeration to say that persuasive speeches have sometimes changed the course of history. Think of the impact of Martin Luther King Jr.'s "I Have a Dream" speech or Franklin Roosevelt's fireside chats.

What these speeches have in common is that they persuaded people to change the way something had been done in the past. They pointed out a problem and persuaded their audience to adopt the speaker's solution. These speeches made appeals to logic and emotion, and they supported their positions with factual evidence. Here are some guidelines to help you prepare a speech that advocates change.

Taking a Position on a Topic

To plan a speech that advocates change, first identify a problem and create a position statement that proposes a possible solution.

> **Problem: Some public school students cannot play sports because they cannot afford the extra fees.**
>
> **Position Statement (Solution): Extra fees to play sports should be eliminated for public school students.**

To choose a topic, brainstorm problems that you have encountered and select one problem from the list. Form a position statement by proposing a solution.

Like the self-help talk you gave in Chapter 5, a persuasive speech needs facts to support the position. Whether you use the Internet or other sources, it is important to research the position you take.

Audience

Keep your audience in mind when you plan your speech and use a tone that will appeal to it. Speeches that propose change need to discuss the problem in terms that are familiar to the audience.

Think about these questions when you plan your speech:

- What do my listeners know about this problem?
- What do they wish they knew?
- How can they become involved in the solution?

Imagine you are proposing that all pets should be leashed. Consider what parents might think about the problem. How might such a speech differ if you were speaking to your fellow students? How might it differ if you were speaking to people who don't own pets?

Introduction, Body, and Conclusion

The introduction of a persuasive speech should include a position statement that tells exactly where you stand on the issue.

The body of your speech should include both practical and persuasive reasons to agree with your position. As you offer explanations of your reasons, use strong opinion words that appeal to logic and emotion. Arrange your ideas in a logical order that creates a strong impression on the audience.

End your speech by rephrasing your position statement and giving your listeners a sense of closure. Ask your listeners to think about or act upon what you've said.

Visuals and Gestures

Think about sharing a visual, such as a thought-provoking photograph or a graphic that includes relevant statistics. Make eye contact with your audience. Consider using gestures such as nodding or shaking your head, or moving your hands to make important points.

ACTIVITY A Reread the essay on page 413 and turn it into a persuasive speech. Make note cards for your position statement, reasons and explanations, and conclusion. Ask a classmate to listen to you present your speech.

ACTIVITY A Reread the essay on page 413

SPEAKER'S CORNER

Choose a topic for a persuasive speech to present to your class. Write a position statement and make notes that give supporting reasons and explanations.

Tech Tip Post your statement on your class blog for peer review.

Practice

The more you prepare and practice, the more comfortable you'll feel on the day of your speech. Have your note cards ready. Obtain or prepare any visuals you plan to use. When everything is ready, practice in front of a mirror or a friend or family member. As you practice, ask yourself the following questions:

- Does my introduction clearly state my position on the topic?
- Do I present both practical and emotional reasons?
- Are my reasons supported by relevant facts?
- Does my visual support my position, helping bring out favorable feelings or thoughts from the audience?
- Do I speak with emotion or emphasis so listeners believe me?
- Do I end so the audience will agree and feel a need to act?

Listening Tips

Follow these guidelines when listening to a persuasive speech:

- Listen carefully to the speaker's reasons for his or her position. Ask yourself: *Do I agree with this?*
- Listen for persuasive language. Are the speaker's emotional appeals effective? Use your own knowledge and common sense when deciding whether or not to agree with the speaker.
- Save your questions for after the speech.
- Evaluate the persuasiveness of the speech no matter your opinion. Limit your feedback to the appeals that the speaker used to persuade the audience.

ACTIVITY B Read each broad topic and determine a specific problem that relates to it. Write each problem as a complete sentence. Then develop and write a position statement that offers a solution for each problem.

1. airport security
2. the cost of auto insurance
3. genetically engineered food
4. oil drilling
5. being healthy
6. taxes
7. seatbelt laws
8. illiteracy
9. speed limits
10. women in "men's" sports
11. the space program
12. global warming

ACTIVITY C Select four position statements you wrote for Activity B. For each position statement, write three reasons to agree with it. For each reason write an explanation. Record each set of ideas on note cards.

ACTIVITY D On a sheet of paper, copy the following chart, filling in a position statement that you wrote in Activity B (but not Activity C) and three reasons that support it. Under the column *Disagree*, write three reasons that an active listener might think of to disagree with the position statement.

POSITION STATEMENT:

_____

Agree	Disagree
1. _____	1. _____
2. _____	2. _____
3. _____	3. _____

I disagree because . . .

SPEAKER'S CORNER

Present your persuasive speech, following the guidelines in this lesson. Remember that you want to convince your listeners to agree with you, so make sure your reasons and explanations are clear.

Prewriting and Drafting

Have you ever heard the expression "The pen is mightier than the sword"? It means that using words to persuade others is more effective than using force. Now you can use what you have discussed in this chapter to write a persuasive essay.

Prewriting

Maya, an eighth grader, wants to enter an essay contest sponsored by her local city council. The prewriting stage for her persuasive essay was a time for brainstorming, choosing a topic, and planning the piece. She also thought about the audience for her essay and the right tone that would appeal to it.

Choosing a Topic

Maya brainstormed a list of possible topic ideas for her persuasive essay. When choosing a topic, Maya wanted to identify an issue about which she felt strongly. She knew that the more passionately she feels about an issue, the better and more persuasive her writing will be.

After brainstorming a list of possible topics, she settled on persuading the Grandview city council to build a new community center. After deciding her position, she wrote her position statement at the top of a graphic organizer called a persuasion rake. Then she put her persuasive reasons on the rake as shown.

Writing for an Audience

Voice The position statement of a persuasive essay should be written with the audience in mind. What tone of voice is most likely to convince the Grandview city council to adopt Maya's position on the community center? Should the piece encourage or warn? Should the tone be upbeat or pessimistic?

Maya decided that a reasonable and fair tone of voice would be most effective for her essay.

Your Turn

Brainstorm a list of at least five issues about which you have strong feelings one way or another. Choose one topic and identify the audience you would address about that topic. Use a persuasion rake to map your reasons. Write a strong position statement that clearly shows which side of the issue you are on and sets the tone of voice you will use in a persuasive essay.

Planning a Persuasive Essay

👓 Organization   Maya composed her position statement and used her persuasion rake to plan the rest of her essay.

Maya knew that a persuasive essay consists of three main parts: the introduction, the body, and the conclusion. The introduction includes the position statement. The body includes paragraphs that give the logical and emotional reasons for readers to agree with the position statement. The conclusion rephrases the position statement and calls on the reader to think or act.

A plan is an excellent way to organize a persuasive essay. Read Maya's plan, paying attention to how she follows every reason she gives with an explanation.

We want a new COMMUNITY CENTER

Position Statement: *Grandview needs a community recreation center.*

Reason: *help community members get to know one another*

Explanation: *Kids from different schools find common interests and create bonds. Adults from across the community gain better understanding of one another.*

Reason: *keeps teenagers busy and out of trouble*

Explanation: *Kids with nothing to do find trouble. (Cite recent study.)*

Reason: *provides after-school care for kids*

Explanation: *Parents who work have a safe place to put their kids.*

Conclusion: *Citizens will be healthier and happier with a community center.*

Your Turn

Study the plan Maya wrote. Create a plan of your own that gives reasons to support your position statement. Be sure to include explanations for your reasons, supported with research if necessary.

Drafting

Maya knew that she had to give valid reasons for asking the city council to allocate money for such a huge project. Maya reviewed her plan and wrote a first draft, adding information and details as she went. She organized her paragraphs based on her plan.

Grandview Needs a Recreation Center

Many cities have recreation centers, but Grandview doesn't. Maybe it needs one.

Children from different schools will find common interests and create lasting bonds. As a result, there will be less school rivalrie. in addition, adults from across the community will gain a better understanding of one another and see how their neighborhoods and families are alike. Furthermore, a recreation center will keep teenagers busy and out of trouble. Recent studies show that most dangerous and riskful teenage behavior occurs between the time school is out and when parents get home from work.

A recreation center would provide after-school care for children of working parents. Parents will have a safe place to send their first through sixth graders as they finish up their workday.

As I've stated, Grandview needs a community recreation center. Citizens will be healthier and happier and Grandview will be an even better place for both adults and children.

Supporting Opinions with Reasons

Opinions by themselves are not very convincing. To persuade others, writers must give solid reasons to back up their opinions. Read the following opinion and reasons. Which reason is the least convincing to you? Why?

Opinion: Everyone who is able should know how to swim.
Reason: Swimming is good exercise.
Reason: Swimming cools you off on hot days.
Reason: Swimming could save your life.

As you write your draft, be sure that you give your readers good reasons for agreeing with you. One way to do this is to list all the reasons that support your opinion and then choose the ones that will be most convincing to your audience.

Look at Maya's first draft. It starts with her position statement. The body gives reasons for wanting a recreation center, which appeal to both logic and emotion. Maya closes her speech by rephrasing her position statement.

Your Turn

Follow your plan as you write your draft. Keep in mind that you will probably rewrite your paper several times. Double-space between lines to make room for revisions.

 Word Choice Keep your audience in mind as you write. Be sure your writing uses strong opinion words.

Writer's Tip Be sure to vary sentence length and style so that your writing remains interesting to your reader.

Content Editing

Maya read over her first draft. She thought it was a good persuasive essay, but she knew that its ideas could be improved. She asked Ty, a fellow eighth grader who also lived in Grandview, to edit her draft. She wanted him to edit the essay to make sure her appeals to logic and emotion were reasonable, her essay was organized in logical order, and her ideas were clearly expressed.

Ty used the following Content Editor's checklist to edit Maya's draft.

Ty read Maya's draft a few times and checked it against the Content Editor's checklist. Then he and Maya had a conference.

First, Ty told Maya about the things that he liked. Ty thought the writing was very convincing, especially because her reasons appealed to both logic and emotion.

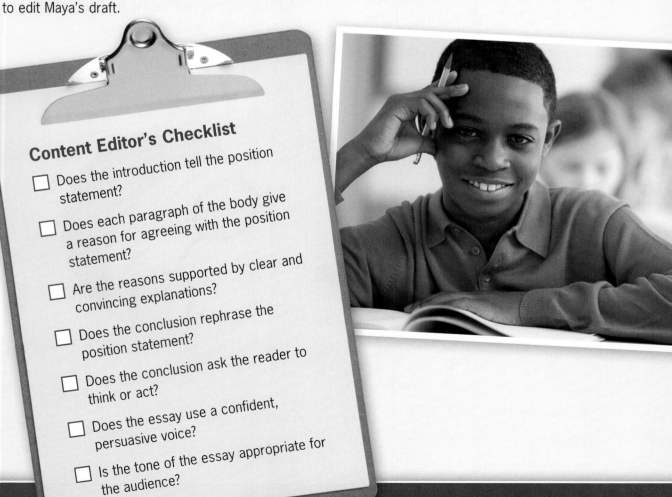

Content Editor's Checklist

☐ Does the introduction tell the position statement?

☐ Does each paragraph of the body give a reason for agreeing with the position statement?

☐ Are the reasons supported by clear and convincing explanations?

☐ Does the conclusion rephrase the position statement?

☐ Does the conclusion ask the reader to think or act?

☐ Does the essay use a confident, persuasive voice?

☐ Is the tone of the essay appropriate for the audience?

However, there were some things in her piece that could be improved. Here are Ty's comments.

- The second paragraph doesn't tell how a recreation center relates to the recent studies. I think you should end the paragraph by linking its two main ideas.
- Some cities are thinking about having their recreation centers open all night to keep teenagers off the streets. Maybe you could mention this idea.
- Your conclusion restates your position statement but doesn't challenge the reader to think or act. Consider adding something to your conclusion.
- The essay is very confident and persuasive. You strongly believe Grandview should have a community center.
- The tone was reasonable and fair. A city council would take this essay seriously.

Maya thought that Ty's ideas were good ones, so she made most of the changes he suggested. She decided not to add his idea about the all-night center because she thought it was too controversial. She saw that Ty missed the first item of the checklist that asked about the position statement. She added a stronger position statement in the introduction.

Prewriting

Drafting

Content Editing

Revising

Copyediting

Proofreading

Publishing

Your Turn

Look for ways to improve your first draft by asking yourself these questions:

- Does the introduction clearly state your position?
- Does the body give good reasons that are supported by convincing explanations?
- Does the conclusion both restate your position and challenge the reader to think or act?

Trade drafts with a classmate. Read your classmate's draft several times and go over the Content Editor's Checklist. Give your honest opinion of how you think the piece could be improved and comment on the strong points too.

Revising

Revising is the time for Maya to choose which edits she wants to put in her essay. This includes the changes Ty suggested as well as those that she wants to make.

Grandview Needs a Recreation Center

Let me explain why I believe Grandview needs a recreation center. Grandview is now a good place to live. A recreation center would make it a great place to live.

~~Many cities have recreation centers, but Grandview doesn't. Maybe it needs one.~~ To begin with, a recreation center will help community members get to know one another. Children from different schools will find common interests and create lasting bonds. As a result, there will be less school rivalrie. in addition, adults from across the community will gain a better understanding of one another and see how their neighborhoods and families are alike. Furthermore, a recreation center will keep teenagers busy and out of trouble. Recent studies show that most dangerous and riskful teenage behavior occurs between the time school is out and when parents get home from work. A recreation center would fill that void and give teenagers a healthy place to spend time.

A recreation center would provide after-school care for children of working parents. Parents will have a safe place to send their first through sixth graders as they finish up their workday.

As I've stated, Grandview needs a community recreation center. Citizens will be healthier and happier and Grandview will be an even better place for both adults and children. Please vote for it, plan for it, and build it. You'll be glad you did.

Look at what Maya did to improve her essay.

- How did Maya strengthen her position statement?
- How did Maya link the two ideas in the third paragraph?
- How did Maya strengthen the conclusion?

To make her essay easy to follow and less choppy, Maya could incorporate transition words. Transition words and phrases help connect Maya's ideas in her essay.

Grammar in Action

Use adjective and adverb phrases to add detail to your persuasive essay.

Your Turn

Use your ideas and the ideas you got from your content-editor classmate to revise your draft. When you have finished, go over the Content Editor's Checklist again.

Editing for Good Transitions

Use these transition words and phrases to show these relationships between events, objects, and ideas.

When?

before, after, since, until, while, to begin with

Where?

above, across, behind, below, under, in front of

Why?

because, since, as a result, therefore, so, consequently

Why not?

however, like, on the other hand, yet, unless, but

What else?

furthermore, in addition, also, besides, namely

Prewriting

Drafting

Content Editing

Revising

Copyediting

Proofreading

Publishing

Copyediting and Proofreading

Copyediting

Maya revised her essay, using her own and Ty's suggestions. When she felt certain that her reasons and explanations were logical and clear, she was ready to begin copyediting her persuasive essay. Maya wanted to edit her essay for overall logic, word choice, and sentence structure. She also read her essay to make sure she used transition words and phrases properly.

Maya used the following Copyeditor's Checklist to edit her draft.

Copyeditor's Checklist

☐ Are any sentences awkward or confusing?

☐ Are suffixes used correctly?

☐ Are transition words and phrases used effectively to link reasons and explanations?

☐ Are all words used correctly?

☐ Is the structure of each sentence logical and grammatically correct?

Maya knew that she would submit her essay to members of the city council for the essay contest. She wanted her essay to be as good as she could make it.

When Maya read her essay aloud, she noticed ◉◉ **Sentence Fluency** that she jumped into the second paragraph too quickly. She added a sentence to her second paragraph to make a smoother transition from one paragraph to another.

Maya also saw that the fourth paragraph needed a transition. She added another sentence that made the third and fourth paragraphs less choppy.

Your Turn

Look over your revised draft. Be sure that you've used transition words and phrases to help your writing flow. One way to do this is to ask yourself the questions *when*, *where*, *why* or *why not*, and *what else*, as you get to each new idea or topic. This will help you check that the ideas are correctly connected to one another.

Proofreading

Maya wanted to have her essay proofread to make sure spelling, grammar, punctuation, and usage were correct. She asked Jessica, another classmate, to proofread her essay. Jessica hadn't read Maya's essay, so Jessica could read it with fresh eyes and catch errors that Maya might otherwise miss.

Jessica used the following Proofreader's Checklist to edit Maya's draft.

Jessica read the essay carefully and checked each item on the checklist in order. She looked up unfamiliar words in a dictionary.

Jessica found a paragraph that wasn't indented, an incorrect suffix, a word that hadn't been capitalized, a misspelled word, and a missing comma. Can you find all these errors in Maya's draft on page 444?

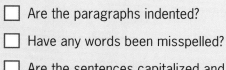

Proofreader's Checklist

- ☐ Are the paragraphs indented?

- ☐ Have any words been misspelled?

- ☐ Are the sentences capitalized and punctuated correctly?

- ☐ Is the grammar accurate?

- ☐ Were any new errors introduced during the editing stage?

Your Turn

- Read your draft carefully against the Proofreader's Checklist. A good idea is to read it once for each item on the list. First, check for indentation, then check for misspelled words, and so on. Be sure to use a dictionary if you are at all unsure of the spelling of a word.

- When you have gone through the checklist, trade drafts with a partner. Go through your partner's draft in the same way.

Publishing

Maya corrected the errors Jessica found and printed out her finished draft.

Grandview Needs a Recreation Center

Let me explain why I believe Grandview needs a recreation center. Grandview is now a good place to live. A recreation center would make it a great place to live.

To begin with, a recreation center will help community members get to know one another. Children from different schools will find common interests and create lasting bonds. As a result, there will be less school rivalry. In addition, adults from across the community will gain a better understanding of one another and see how their neighborhoods and families are alike.

Furthermore, a recreation center will keep teenagers busy and out of trouble. Recent studies show that most dangerous and risky teenage behavior occurs between the time school is out and when parents get home from work. A recreation center would fill that void and give teenagers a healthy place to spend time.

Besides, a recreation center would provide after-school care for children with working parents. Parents will have a safe place to send their first through sixth graders as they finish up their workday.

As I've stated, Grandview needs a community recreation center. Citizens will be healthier and happier, and Grandview will be an even better place for both adults and children. Please vote for it, plan for it, and build it. You'll be glad that you did!

Maya edited her persuasive piece again, making it even better. When she felt that her piece was ready, she printed it out. She was now ready to submit it to the contest.

There are many ways you can publish your persuasive essay.

 Make a classroom newsletter. Share your ideas with others. Refine your argument by publishing your ideas for your peers to review and even disagree with. Disagreement will help you understand the opposition you hope to persuade.

 Post your essay on a bulletin board or class blog for feedback. Your classmates may have additional experiences or views that will strengthen your argument.

 Send your essay to the editor of your local newspaper. If your persuasive essay is something of local importance, be heard! Often it takes practice before a letter to the editor is finally published, so don't get discouraged. Read the letters of others, and keep trying.

Whenever you publish your work, your goal is to share your thoughts and experiences with other people.

Grandview Needs a Recreation Center

Let me explain why I believe Grandview needs a recreation center. Grandview is now a good place to live. A recreation center would make it a great place to live.

To begin with, a recreation center will help community members get to know one another. Children from different schools will find common interests and create lasting bonds. As a result, there will be less school rivalry. In addition, adults from across the community will gain a better understanding of one another and see how their neighborhoods and families are alike.

Furthermore, a recreation center will keep teenagers busy and out of trouble. Recent studies show that most dangerous and risky teenage behavior occurs between the time school is out and when parents get home from work. A recreation center would fill that void and give teenagers a healthy place to spend time.

Your Turn

Persuasive writing often takes the form of a letter to the editor, a magazine article, or a

 Presentation newspaper editorial.

Once a piece is sent to a newspaper or magazine, it can't be taken back. If it is poorly written or full of mistakes, the editor of the magazine or newspaper will probably reject it.

You may not be sending your essay in for publication, but you will be submitting it to your teacher. Be sure that you are happy with your writing before you publish it by turning it in.

To publish, follow these steps:

1. Make sure your position statement clearly tells where you stand on the issue.
2. Make sure each reason that supports your position statement is backed up by a solid, convincing explanation.
3. Check to see that you have made appeals to both logic and emotion.
4. Use your neatest handwriting or a computer to make a finished copy of your revised draft.
5. Proofread your essay one more time for correct spelling, grammar, capitalization, and punctuation. If you can, use your computer's spell-checker.

Creative Writing

LiNK ## Midas the King

by Freddie Green, Magic Parrot Productions

Enter King Midas, then wife, daughter and fiancé strolling in the garden.

Enter four children, playing with a ball.

MIDAS: Stop right there! What are you doing in my garden?

CHILD 1: Oh, nothing, sir. We were just admiring your lovely garden!

CHILD 2: You must be very clever and wise to make a garden as good as this. Are you the gardener?

MIDAS: Gardener? I'm no gardener! I'm the King! You must be thieves, stealing my apples! I ought to have your heads chopped off right now!

DAUGHTER: Oh, father. They're not thieves! They're only children!

CHILD 4: We just wanted our ball back! That's all! It's getting late. We must be going home!

MIDAS: This is my garden! And trespassers should be executed.

WIFE: (*sternly*) Midas! If you want to please me, let them go! They are doing no harm!

> Plays, also called dramas, are performed writing pieces. King Midas is brought to life by the elements of playwriting: plot, theme, characters, setting, dialogue, and stage directions.

CHAPTER 7

Chris Hoffm
Room 623

The Empty Pocket Blues

CHARACTERS
CASEY   ANGELA

SETTING
A comfortable living room with a table center stage left
and a couch center stage right.

SCENE 1

(CASEY walks in with a shopping bag and sees ANGELA at the table with a piggy bank, counting money.)

ANGELA: *(to herself)* One hundred and sixty-six, one hundred and sixty-seven, one hundred and sixty-eight. *(She stacks the money and updates her records.)* Only $32 to go!

CASEY: *(interested)* Cool! Let's go to the mall and buy some clothes, a new video game, and some of those trendy shoes everyone is wearing. *(He reaches over to grab the stack of money, but Angela pushes him away.)* What? You have enough to spare.

ANGELA: That's because I've been keeping track and limiting my unnecessary spending so that I can save for a new bicycle. I'm going to get the Road Rasher 3000 this summer.

CASEY: Saving isn't fun. Money is meant to be spent. I'm going to the mall.

(CASEY leaves the room. End of scene.)

SCENE 2

(ANGELA enters wearing a bike helmet. CASEY is digging in the couch cushions.)

ANGELA: I just had the best ride. The Road Rasher 3000 is the best purchase I've ever made. *(Notices CASEY)* What are you doing?

CASEY: I want to go on vacation with my friends; however, I'm broke. *(Exasperated)* Where did all my money go, anyway?

ANGELA: A penny saved is a penny earned.

451

What Makes Good Playwriting?

Playwriting is a unique form of writing. Unlike narrative short stories and novels, which are meant to be read, plays, also called dramas, are meant to be performed.

All plays share the same elements: plot, theme, characters, setting, dialogue, and stage directions. Here are some points to keep in mind about plays.

Plot

An effective drama is composed of a series of dramatic actions that connect the story. Plots have a beginning, a middle, and an end, no matter how many scenes the play has.

- Playwrights almost always put exposition in the beginning of a play. Through dialogue, action, and setting, exposition provides the background information about the characters and what they do. A playwright then creates an inciting incident, an event that creates a problem for a main character to solve.
- Once the problem is established, a playwright continues with action-filled events, building tension and further heightening dramatic conflict. These events are called the rising action. A playwright then leads us from the rising action to the climax, an exciting, defining moment or turning point.
- The problem is solved in the events that follow. These events, called the falling action, drive the plot to its resolution. The resolution answers remaining questions and concludes the play.

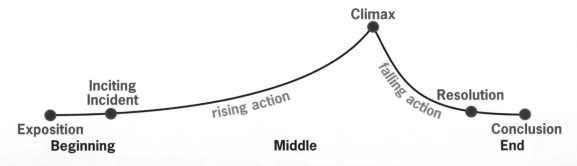

Theme

All plays have at least one theme. A theme is the central idea, usually a generalization about human nature that the writer wants to show the audience. Effective themes can be subtle, or they can exhibit obvious lessons. Directors and designers use their interpretations of the play's theme or themes to develop their productions.

ACTIVITY A Choose one of the following inciting incidents. Act out the incident with a partner and create your own dialogue. Write a list of at least three steps that might show the rising action that follows.

A. Your best friend suddenly stops speaking to you.

B. You arrive at the music store just in time to see your friend grab the last copy of the new CD you wanted.

C. You meet someone you knew when you were younger.

D. You and a sibling break some of your parents' expensive china.

ACTIVITY B Look at the diagram on page 452 that shows the progress of a plot. Read the model on page 451. Then answer the questions.

1. What background information is provided about Angela?

2. Name two events that are part of the rising action.

3. What is the climax?

4. Name two events that are part of the falling action.

5. What is the resolution?

6. What is the theme of this play?

ACTIVITY C With a partner choose one of the following themes. Brainstorm ideas for a play, using your chosen theme.

1. Honesty is the best policy.

2. Slow but steady wins the race.

3. Things are not always what they seem.

4. Sticks and stones may break my bones, but names will never hurt me.

5. A stitch in time saves nine.

WRITER'S CORNER

Summarize a simple plot for a play from the scenario you acted out in Activity A. Introduce a conflict, briefly describe the rising action and climax, and finish with the falling action and resolution.

Graph your plot as a PowerPoint presentation.

Character

All plays must have at least one character, but they usually have several. In a play the central character is often called the protagonist. The character or force that opposes the main character is often called the antagonist. Opposition between the protagonist and antagonist creates the conflict of the drama, which drives the main action.

A playwright can reveal a character in a variety of ways. First, the playwright often provides a physical and social description of each main character at the beginning of a script. Then the playwright reveals what he or she wants the audience to know through the character's words and actions in the play. A playwright also reveals a character through what the other characters say about him or her.

The following tips can help you develop your characters:

- Always remember that each character must have a reason for being in the play.
- Each character must have a goal to achieve throughout the play.
- Specific physical traits can help reveal character. Brainstorm many possibilities.
- In the beginning of the play, remember to establish background information for each character.
- Each character should be interesting and believable.

Setting

Time and place in a play are just as important as the play's characters. Plays can be set in outer space, in medieval times, in fantasy worlds, or in the present—just about any place and time imaginable. Think about your daily surroundings and how they influence your everyday actions. You may act differently depending on whether you're at home, in school, or spending time with your friends. As you write a play, always have a good reason for including a specific year or location.

The same is true for the time period. Playwrights usually have a specific reason for the time and place they choose to set their story. For example, Lorraine Hansberry set her play *A Raisin in the Sun* in the South Side of Chicago during the 1950s. She wanted to show that discrimination affected African Americans who lived in Northern cities, as well as those who lived in the South.

ACTIVITY D Look back at the plot summary you wrote for the Writer's Corner on page 453. Choose a setting in which your plot will take place. Briefly describe the place, atmosphere, and time period. Think about interesting surroundings for your story and how the surroundings will affect your characters and their behavior.

ACTIVITY E Read the model on page 451. Then answer the questions about character and setting.

1. What is the setting for the play?
2. What clues in the text inform you about the goal, appearance, and personality of Angela? of Casey?
3. Who is the protagonist?
4. Who is the antagonist?
5. What is Angela's objective?

ACTIVITY F Think about the plot you developed for the Writer's Corner on page 453. Choose two characters that would likely be a part of your play. Using the questions below, write a character sketch for each character.

1. Where is your character from? How would your character speak?
2. What does your character look like? What does this say about the character?
3. What mannerisms or behaviors do your characters use?
4. How does your character relate to the other characters? to the setting?
5. What is your character doing when he or she is not talking?

LiNK

The Importance of Being Earnest

Morning-room in Algernon's flat in Half-Moon Street. The room is luxuriously and artistically furnished. The sound of a piano is heard in the adjoining room. Lane is arranging afternoon tea on the table, and after the music has ceased, Algernon enters.

Oscar Wilde

WRITER'S CORNER

Costume is also a part of the setting and character. Think about the characters you developed for Activity F. Write a paragraph describing the clothes and props your characters would wear or use.

Play Structure and Format

Plays are usually divided into acts, each of which may contain separate scenes. Many plays have more than one act, but one-act plays are also common. A one-act play generally takes place in a shorter time than a multi-act play, and has a simpler plot and fewer characters. One-act plays share the essential elements of all plays: plot, theme, characters, setting, dialogue, and stage directions. All play scripts follow similar formats.

Character and Setting Description

Most scripts include an opening section that describes the characters and the setting. The character list provides information about each character, such as age, gender, and relationships with other characters. Characters' names are printed in all capital letters throughout the script, unless the name is used in dialogue. This is done so that actors can easily locate their lines.

Setting descriptions provide brief information for the director, actors, and designers regarding time and place.

The setting description at the opening of a scene is generally more detailed than the initial statement of time and place. Terms such as *downstage left* and *upstage center* tell where things are located and where actors move on the stage. Stage locations are always given from the perspective of the actor facing the audience.

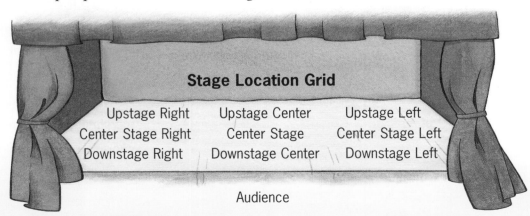

Stage Location Grid

Upstage Right	Upstage Center	Upstage Left
Center Stage Right	Center Stage	Center Stage Left
Downstage Right	Downstage Center	Downstage Left

Audience

CHARACTERS

JET: An 18-year-old female who is very ambitious and outspoken but quite naïve. She has been raised by HAROLD, her grandfather, and she will do anything to make her dreams of becoming a singer in the big city come true.

HAROLD: A stern, older man with strong values and strict views. Protective of JET.

PLACE

The action all takes place in HAROLD's New York City apartment.

TIME

A winter day sometime around 2010.

Setting is described in further detail at the beginning of each scene.

SCENE ONE

(Lights come up on the living room of a small apartment. Upstage right, a window shows the New York City skyline. Snow is visible outside. Upstage left are a door and a coat rack. Everything is neat and in place with a warm, comfortable feel. Center stage is a large sofa with a large chair downstage right of sofa.)

ACTIVITY A Look back at the character sketches you wrote for Activity F. Using the model above as a guide, rewrite your character sketches in the format found in the opening section of a play.

ACTIVITY B Draw a blank stage location grid. Read the Stage Location Grid on page 456 and the description of the apartment for Scene One above. Write letters in your blank grid to show where the following items would be found on the stage.

A. sofa

B. chair

C. window

D. door

WRITER'S CORNER

Use the setting description you wrote for Activity D on page 455. Rewrite it to fit the format described in this lesson. Include at least two stage locations.

Dialogue and Stage Directions

Dialogue is formatted so that it can be read aloud easily. Character names are set apart from their dialogue with a colon. The dialogue is the only text in the script that is spoken.

Stage directions are italicized and set off by parentheses. They tell actors where and how to move onstage. They can prompt stage activity or suggest ways in which a character speaks or feels. Playwrights often avoid specific description in stage directions, letting the actors decide the best way to speak the lines. Read the following example of dialogue and stage directions.

All directions, actions, and descriptions are in italics and separated by parentheses.

Character names
Character names are in boldface and all capital letters.

Dialogue
Dialogue is in a regular font. These are the only words in the script that are spoken.

Dashes indicate interruption or overlapping of dialogue.

(HAROLD enters the apartment and locks the door behind him. Slowly and deliberately, he makes his way to the chair and sits down. He sighs and puts his face in his hands.)

JET: *(From offstage)* Harold! Harold! *(There is a loud knock.)* Let me in, please!

HAROLD: *(Getting up and walking toward the door)* OK! Hold your horses. I'm coming. *(He opens the door and JET bursts in. She runs to the sofa and sits down with her legs propped up on the side.)* Make yourself comfortable. *(He shakes his head.)* Some people might think it disrespectful to call your grandfather by his first name.

JET: I've always called you Harold. Now why won't you listen to me? You know how important—

HAROLD: Enough, Jet! I will not hear another word.

JET: *(Jumping up from the sofa)* But Harold, it's the biggest—

HAROLD: Stop. The discussion is over.

ACTIVITY C Read the dialogue from page 458 and answer these questions.

1. Who are the characters in this scene?
2. How can the actors quickly find their lines?
3. Which actor is supposed to knock on the door? How do you know?
4. After Harold says, "Stop. The discussion is over," what might Jet say? Write your answer in correct dialogue format.

ACTIVITY D Tell how you would retype each dialogue or stage direction correctly. Not all items have errors.

1. Harold: I am too old to worry about you.
2. JET: *You just don't realize that this is my dream!*
3. **HAROLD walks into the kitchen and begins to look very busy preparing dinner. JET slowly follows him.**
4. **JET:** Wait! Let me help you with that, Grandpa.
5. **HAROLD;** (Let's both just sit down and talk about this at dinner.)

ACTIVITY E Read the dialogue. Add four or five stage directions that you think might happen in this scenario.

JET: Will you please listen to me? I just want to talk to you.

HAROLD: There is nothing to discuss, young lady.

JET: But Harold, this is all I've ever wanted. You know I can sing. You've always said I had a pretty voice.

HAROLD: You are not going to go running around the country with a bunch of long-haired musicians!

ACTIVITY F Study a play script that you find in your classroom, in the library, or on the Internet. Compare and contrast the script to the examples in this lesson. What has the playwright done the same and differently concerning structure and format? Make a list of at least three ways that format and structure are the same and three ways that format and structure are different.

WRITER'S CORNER

Find four to six lines of dialogue from a favorite novel or story written in narrative form. Convert the lines into a short scene in script format. Use the examples in Activity E as a model. Add stage directions to show action.

Dialogue, Monologue, and Asides

Dialogue

Just like in other writing, dialogue in plays is the spoken words of the characters. Playwrights carefully construct dialogue to engage the audience, provide them with important information, and advance the story. In other words, dialogue reveals exposition and plot.

Dialogue is usually intended to sound like the natural speech of a specific time and place. To achieve this, many playwrights do research. Playwrights might gather writings and recordings depicting speech patterns from a specific era. The grammar, word use, style, and even cultural accent of a character are all clues that help tell the story.

Playwrights also read aloud and revise the dialogue in their scripts. If the dialogue is awkward or seems unnatural, the audience will not believe the world created on the stage.

In our everyday lives, we usually speak in complete sentences. But many times we also speak in fragments and unfinished sentences, or are interrupted by someone else. For natural-sounding dialogue, playwrights incorporate this type of speech.

> **JACKSON:** I just wanted to tell you that I—
>
> **KIANA:** It's very important to me that we get this house ready for the party.
>
> **JACKSON:** But Kiana—
>
> **KIANA:** Jackson, I don't have time to listen to you. We have a lot to get done and I just . . . I need to get to work.

ACTIVITY A With a partner read aloud the dialogue above. Then answer the questions.

1. What do you know about Kiana from reading the dialogue?

2. What do you know about Jackson?

3. What do you think Jackson might say next?

ACTIVITY B Read the excerpt from a play. Then answer the questions.

SCENE ONE

(Curtain comes up on a community center meeting hall, a large room with folding chairs in which an audience of 12 to 15 people sits. SPEAKER at the podium is interrupted abruptly by young woman who rises from audience.)

SPEAKER: *(getting louder)* As I was—

GRETA: Enough! We've heard enough. MacMaster is the biggest polluter in seven states. We've tried endless discussions. Now we've got to do something they won't forget! *(Crowd murmurs in agreement.)*

SPEAKER: But our committee has a meeting scheduled with MacMaster's lead attorney for next—

GRETA: How many meetings have we had? Ten? Twenty? Forget meetings! Let's march! *(Crowd cheers.)*

1. Which character is probably the protagonist?
2. What sort of person does Greta seem to be? How would you describe her mood?
3. What have you discovered about the plot?
4. Whom do you think the antagonist might be?
5. What is likely to happen next?
6. Does the dialogue seem natural? Why or why not?

ACTIVITY C Read the stage directions. Then write a brief dialogue between the two characters mentioned in the stage directions.

SCENE ONE

(Lights come up in the kitchen of a suburban home. A 14-year-old female is babysitting her 5-year-old brother. She has just discovered that the boy has made a mess. Flour, sugar, eggs, and milk are all over the counters, walls, floor, and the boy. Knowing her parents will be home soon, the girl is quick to react.)

LiNK

On the High Road

FEDYA: Are you from far off?

SAVVA: From Vologda. The town itself . . . . I live there.

FEDYA: And where is this Vologda?

TIHON: The other side of Moscow. . . .

FEDYA: Well, well, well. . . . You have come a long way, old man! On foot?

Anton Chekov

Anton Chekov, Russian writer and dramatist (1860–1904)

WRITER'S CORNER

As accurately as you can, write interesting excerpts of conversations that you hear in public places. Be sure to include pauses, interruptions, and fragments.

Monologue

A monologue is a long speech given by one character. A monologue is always delivered within the action of the play. A monologue can be spoken to the audience or to another character. A soliloquy is similar to a monologue. It is also a long speech given by one character. In a soliloquy the speaker is always talking to himself or herself, not to others. Both monologues and soliloquies aid in character development.

Asides

An aside is dialogue in which an actor stops the play action and directly addresses the audience. During an aside it is assumed that the other characters in the play cannot hear or see it. Playwrights might use this tool to have a character seek the sympathy of the audience, to show how much smarter or more clever a character is than the others, or to give a brief commentary on what is happening on the stage. For example,

FELICIA: *(aside to audience)* I don't look that foolish, do I?

ACTIVITY D Expand the dialogue on page 460 by adding a monologue for one of the characters. Be sure the monologue consists of at least four sentences and conforms to the character's traits as you understand them.

ACTIVITY E Rewrite the following dialogue. Add two asides, one for each character. The asides can be inserted anywhere within the dialogue. Use the asides to reveal information to the audience that the other character should not know or to give some commentary about an event onstage.

JONATHA: *(turns, sees SUNHEE)* What are you doing, Sunhee?

SUNHEE: Setting the table, silly!

JONATHA: At midnight?

SUNHEE: I like to be prepared, that's all.

ACTIVITY F Choose two inciting incidents. Create at least six lines of dialogue for each incident. Include a monologue and an aside in each section of dialogue.

A. Gina, age 4, has just hit her whiny little brother Peter, 3, over the head with a toy truck. Their dad has witnessed the incident and is running over as quickly as he can.

B. Suddenly, odd plants that look like furry, little animals are sprouting all over town. When Carl tries to dig one up by the roots, he hears a faint noise that sounds like "Ouch!"

C. Mrs. Chen is very fond of Logan, a bright boy of 11, but his ceaseless talking constantly disrupts the class. She asks Logan to stay after class to discuss the problem.

D. Jordan's parents constantly warn him about communicating with people he doesn't know on the Internet. But he feels that he does know Paige, a friend from a chat room, so he arranges to meet her at the mall.

E. Corinne has won a scholarship to the Academy of Math and Science, a very selective boarding school. Corinne is excited, but she wonders how she will tell her best friend, Blaine, the news, especially since Blaine was not accepted.

F. Grace is forbidden to go into her sister Faith's bedroom, so of course that's where she goes every chance she gets. One day Grace is in Faith's room, trying on her sister's prom dress, when Faith, who has gotten off work early, walks in.

G. Something must have gone wrong with the science experiment Charles and Martin are conducting. They followed the steps precisely, but glowing foam has bubbled up over the beakers and is flowing all over the room.

H. Hannah wants to help, but she doesn't think it's fair that she has to take care of her brother and sister and make dinner every day that her mother works. She has a phone conversation with her father about the situation.

WRITER'S CORNER

Reread the dialogue you created for Activity E. Write a brief paragraph telling how the meaning of the play changed when you added the asides.

Idioms, Slang, and Jargon

Idioms

An idiom, also called an idiomatic expression, is a phrase whose literal meaning differs from the actual meaning. Unless the implied meaning of the expression is evident, the words may not make sense. For that reason people often learn the meanings of idioms by hearing them used in proper context. The following are a few common idioms:

- *a piece of cake*
- *break the ice*
- *down in the dumps*
- *ants in her pants*

A simple task is often referred to as *a piece of cake. Break the ice* is an appropriate idiom for starting a conversation in awkward social settings that can seem frozen when nobody is speaking. *Down in the dumps* suggests that someone is in a rut or having a hard time. *Ants in her pants* suggests that someone is restless or jittery, as if she had ants crawling inside her pants. It is not meant to be taken literally.

Idioms enter our language from many sources. Idioms can tell us something about our history. The idiom *face the music,* which means "coming to terms with unpleasant consequences," may have come from the military. When a soldier was court-martialed, drum music was often played.

LiNK

The Tempest

TRINCULO: I have been in such a pickle since I saw you last that, I fear me, will never out of my bones: I shall not fear fly-blowing.

SEBASTIAN: Why, how now, Stephano!

William Shakespeare

Playwrights often include idioms in dialogue to create characters that seem realistic and believable. They carefully choose idioms for their characters, matching idioms to the characters' genders, ages, cultures, and personalities.

ACTIVITY A Use each of these idioms in a sentence. If you don't know a meaning, look up the most important word in a dictionary. You may be able to find the meaning of the idiom in the part of the entry that follows the definition of the word.

1. turn over a new leaf
2. eat your words
3. see eye to eye
4. right up my alley
5. in the same boat
6. know the ropes
7. fat chance
8. half-baked idea
9. for the birds
10. mend fences
11. all ears
12. cut corners
13. take the cake
14. see red
15. give a hand
16. lend an ear
17. keep an eye on
18. ran him ragged
19. in over your head
20. sit tight

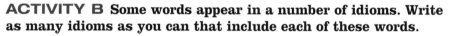

ACTIVITY B Some words appear in a number of idioms. Write as many idioms as you can that include each of these words.

1. make
2. give
3. turn
4. take
5. get
6. run
7. pull
8. break
9. have
10. play
11. go
12. throw

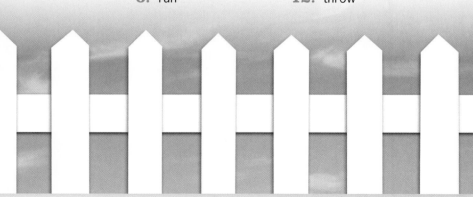

WRITER'S CORNER

Look back at one or more pieces of your writing and identify at least two idioms. Which ones would be easy to replace with words or phrases that are not idioms?

Slang

Playwrights use slang carefully in their work. Slang is nonstandard, informal language. Writers must keep in mind that slang can become outdated. For example, many people in the 1950s used *swell* to describe things they liked. In the 1960s *groovy* was often used for the same meaning. Do you hear *swell* and *groovy* very often today? What adjectives do you use to describe things you like? What adjectives do your parents use?

Jargon

Another type of speech playwrights use is jargon, the special vocabulary of a particular profession or hobby. Snowboarders, computer programmers, and doctors all use jargon when they talk to others in the same profession. A playwright's task is to use enough jargon so that such characters seem real but not in a way that the audience cannot understand what the characters are saying. A playwright's goal is for all of his or her characters to speak appropriately for their age, family background, profession, and personality. All language should reflect the historical time in which a play takes place.

ACTIVITY C Write a short definition of what you think each word or phrase means. Using a dictionary or online resource, find each example and compare it to your definition.

1. best boy
2. gnarly
3. grind the rail
4. chill out
5. a four top
6. wet behind the ears
7. far out
8. cut and paste
9. with bells on
10. ASAP
11. lost his marbles
12. rain on my parade
13. LOL
14. way groovy
15. hit the hay
16. back up the hard drive

ACTIVITY D Browse through online and print newspapers and magazines to collect 20 terms of slang or jargon. For each item cite the source and provide a definition based on the context. If the definition is not clear from the source you found, research it further. (Hint: Type the word or phrase into a search engine and examine the results.)

ACTIVITY E Write a few lines of dialogue for each set of characters. Include idioms, slang, and jargon where they make sense.

1. a pioneer family heading west in a covered wagon
2. high school students at cheerleading camp
3. surgeons during an operation
4. a couple who draw cartoons for a living
5. architects and engineers at a construction site
6. two caterers getting ready for a big party
7. a boy and girl on a first date, eating at a fancy restaurant
8. a boy hopping a freight train during the Great Depression
9. twin surfers, age 13, at the beach
10. two signers of the Declaration of Independence
11. the first earthlings to land on Mars
12. two audience members watching a rodeo

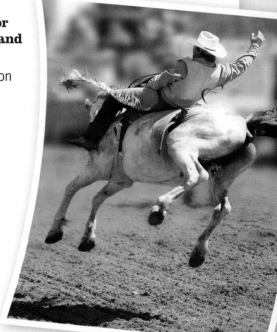

ACTIVITY F Identify in each sentence whether the language used is an example of an idiom, slang, or jargon.

1. "I need a CT scan, stat!" cried the doctor on call.
2. The cowboy said, "Howdy, partner! Y'all from these parts?"
3. "Cat got your tongue?" he teased.
4. Claire's new dress is totally awesome and way cool.
5. "Well, pin a rose on your nose," Tommy grumbled.
6. "I ain't done nothin' wrong by speaking to the gentleman," cried Eliza.
7. "The suspect had a rap sheet with several priors," Officer Suarez told the chief.

WRITER'S CORNER

With a partner act out the dialogue you wrote for one item in Activity E. Does the dialogue sound realistic and believable? Explain why or why not. Revise your dialogue based on your partner's suggestions. Act it out again. Was it better the second time?

With your classmates, videotape your dialogue.

Free Verse

Free verse is a form of poetry that does not follow conventional rules of rhyme and rhythm. The purpose of free verse is to evoke emotions and images. To do this, free verse can use all the conventional tools of poetry, such as rhyme, rhythm, and meter, as well as figurative language such as metaphor and similes.

Here is an example of a free verse poem written in 1918 by the American poet Carl Sandburg. We can identify it as free verse because the pattern of feet in each line varies and the meter is irregular.

River Roads
Let the crows go by hawking their caw and caw.
They have been swimming in midnights of coal mines somewhere.
Let 'em hawk their caw and caw.

Let the woodpecker drum and drum on a hickory stump.
He has been swimming in red and blue pools somewhere hundreds of years
And the blue has gone to his wings and the red has gone to his head.
Let his red head drum and drum.

Let the dark pools hold the birds in a looking-glass.
And if the pool wishes, let it shiver to the blur of many wings, old swimmers from old places.

Let the redwing streak a line of vermilion on the green wood lines.
And the mist along the river fix its purple in lines of a woman's shawl on lazy shoulders.

Line length in free verse may vary according to what sounds and looks right, and what makes sense to the poet. The number of lines in each stanza, or group of lines separated by an extra space, also varies.

Free Verse Versus Prose

Free verse may sometimes sound like prose, or ordinary, unadorned writing, but it is not. In some ways free verse can be more difficult to write than rhymed poetry. To demonstrate the difference between free verse and prose, read the following passage:

> Crows belong to the family Corvidae, along with jays, nutcrackers, and magpies. Although crows are classified as songbirds, their usual call is a harsh caw.
>
> An adult crow is 15–18 inches long and weighs about 20 ounces. Its wingspan can be up to three feet. The beak is large, about 2½ inches long, and quite sturdy. Both males and females are entirely black.
>
> Crows flock in groups ranging from family units to several hundred—or even several thousand—birds. They fly at speeds of 25–30 miles an hour and range for food as far as 30 miles a day. Crows are omnivorous; they eat insects, grain, fruit, eggs, organic garbage, and just about anything else they can find or kill.

ACTIVITY A **Reread "River Roads" and the prose passage above. Then answer the questions.**

1. How does Sandburg tell the reader what sounds crows make? How does he describe their color?

2. How does the prose passage give this information? How is this different from the poem?

3. Which passage sounds like a person speaking? Why?

4. Which passage seems to be informative, and which seems to be imaginary? Why? Give examples.

5. What pictures come into your mind when you read the poem and the passage? Which are more vivid? Why?

6. What do you think is Sandburg's purpose in writing this poem?

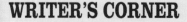

WRITER'S CORNER

Choose a topic. Freewrite 10 ideas that evoke strong sensory images and emotions for you.

The Poetic Process

The following are some tools that poets can use to write free verse.

Sensory Language

Free verse uses sensory language to create vivid pictures of its subject.

Read this passage from Robert Penn Warren's "Mediterranean Beach, Day After Storm." Warren uses sensory words to let the reader see and hear the waves crashing against the shore. Words such as *whang, clang,* and *fling* sound like what they mean. This is called onomatopoeia.

> How instant joy, how clang
> And whang the sun, how
> Whoop the sea, and oh,
> Sun, sing, as whiter than
> Rage of snow, let sea the spume
> Fling.

Rhythm, Rhyme, and Repetition

The mood, or attitude, of a poem can be determined by the rhythm of its language. A light, quick-moving rhythm usually conveys a whimsical thought and creates a joyous mood. Slower rhythm generally suggests a more thoughtful or sad mood.

The rhythm of a poem can often be determined by reading it aloud. Your voice will automatically stress the accented syllables. In many types of poetry, the stress falls on a regular beat. Listen for the accented syllables as you read aloud these lines from one of Shakespeare's sonnets:

> So are you to my thoughts as food to life,
> Or as sweet-seasoned showers are to the ground;

When lines of poetry have a repeated rhythm as the lines above do, they are said to have regular meter. Meter is how the words are arranged in poetry to achieve its rhythm.

Free verse does not usually follow regular meter; however, rhymes do sometimes appear in free verse poetry. Read this line of "River Roads" aloud: *And the blue has gone to his wings and the red has gone to his head.* Note the rhyme *red* and *head.* Sandburg uses a singsong rhythm to describe the woodpecker.

"River Roads" achieves its rhythm by varying its meter and repeating *Let* and the phrases *caw and caw* and *drum and drum.* Sandburg also selected words that have similar vowel sounds, such as *hawk, hawking,* and *caw.* This is called assonance. Alliteration, using words that start with the same consonant sound, is another way to build a poem's rhythm. "Mediterranean Beach" uses alliteration when it repeats the *"s"* sound in *sun, sea, snow,* and *spume.* The *"wh"* sound is repeated in *whang* and *whoop.*

Figurative Language

Free verse poetry relies heavily on metaphors, similes, and hyperbole to paint vivid images in the reader's mind. By using figurative language in poetry, two ideas that seem to make no sense can be put together. Read this line of "River Roads": *They have been swimming in midnights of coal mines somewhere.* Though it seems absurd to think of swimming in midnights, the metaphor communicates the essential blackness of the crow's feathers.

ACTIVITY B Read each abstract word. Then write several images that the word suggests to you. Use the first image that comes to mind, even if it does not make sense. Choose words that paint a picture in the reader's mind.

EXAMPLE: boredom—a drippy, wet sponge

1. sadness
2. freedom
3. honesty
4. pain
5. trust
6. bravery
7. dreams
8. justice
9. relaxation
10. beauty

ACTIVITY C Choose an image that you wrote in Activity B and write a short poem that uses that image. Use the techniques discussed in this lesson—such as rhythm, rhyme, and repetition—to write your poem. Use a rhyming dictionary or online source to help you find similar-sounding words.

WRITER'S CORNER

Write a free verse poem, using the ideas you wrote for the Writer's Corner on page 469. Add to, pare down, and alter your lines until they sound and look like poetry to you.

Reader's Theater

Reader's theater is a convenient and enjoyable way to present favorite stories in dramatic form. The scripts for reader's theater performances are generally adaptations of stories. The stories are rewritten with parts for narrators and characters so the stories can be performed for an audience. Reader's theater is a blend of reading aloud and putting on a play.

Choose a Story

Pick a story that you think performers will like and one that is suitable for the intended audience. Consider the number of parts to be read and the number of readers. Sometimes it might be necessary to combine or divide a few parts to match the number of readers. If necessary, brainstorm ideas to revise the original story to make it livelier or easier to understand or perform in script form. After you have chosen a story and revised it, you can write the script.

Create a Script

The script for reader's theater is taken from the story on which it is based. When you write the dialogue, be sure it reveals everything the audience should know about the characters and the setting. Most importantly, write dialogue to reveal the plot, including the rising action, the climax, and the resolution. Spoken dialogue in the story is assigned to characters, while descriptive and narrative prose is assigned to the narrator.

When the script is done, assign parts, and have each reader use a colored marker on a photocopied script to highlight the lines that he or she will read. Generally, if the narrator's part is the longest, consider dividing the narrator's role into smaller parts, each to be read by a different reader.

Setting the Stage

Setting a stage for reader's theater is simple. Because the audience relies on the narrator to paint a mental picture of the setting, there is very little need for physical props or sets. Often, the setting for reader's theater is made up of stools or chairs for the readers to sit on while another actor is speaking. You can use cardboard boxes, blocks, chairs, and other simple props to stand for just about anything the script calls for. If you like, experiment with simple lighting, sound effects, and music.

In reader's theater, the readers don't exit the performance area, but they might do simple actions such as step back or turn away from the audience to indicate that they are "offstage." Readers who move around should hold their scripts in one hand rather than resting them on a stand.

ACTIVITY A Find and read one or two of the following short stories. Determine if they would be good choices for reader's theater. Explain why or why not.

1. "Why I Live at the P.O."—Eudora Welty
2. "The Monkey's Paw"—W. W. Jacobs
3. "Dreamworld"—Isaac Asimov
4. "The Lottery"—Shirley Jackson
5. "Masque of the Red Death"—Edgar Allen Poe
6. "The Ransom of Red Chief"—O. Henry

ACTIVITY B Write character descriptions for the characters you read about in one of the short stories from Activity A. Include information about the characters' personalities that you think the actors needs to know in order to play each part. Then write a brief dialogue between two of these characters based on an event that happens in the short story.

SPEAKER'S CORNER

Choose a few lines of dialogue from a short story. Read the dialogue several different ways, in different tones of voice and emphasizing different words. Express different emotions as you read.

Rehearse

After choosing a story and developing the script, rehearse the performance. Practice several times, having the readers experiment with different voices and gestures. Consider switching roles among readers to experiment with dialogue styles and to keep the rehearsals interesting.

Perform

Though the scripts do not need to be memorized, the more familiar the readers are with the script, the more smoothly and expressively they will be able to read the dialogue.

Readers may want to read over the scripts both silently and aloud, making notations to remind themselves of how they want to read. They might, for example, underline words they want to emphasize or mark places where they need to make a movement.

Readers should keep these tips in mind:

- Stand or sit up straight.
- Project your voice. Speak louder, more clearly, and slower than seems natural.
- Do not let the script block your face.
- Read with feeling. Let your face show a lot of expression.
- Face the audience as much as possible, even when miming an action.
- When not reading, stay still.

Audience Tips

As the audience of reader's theater, try to imagine the world that the narrator creates in reciting the words of the script.

- Listen carefully and use your imagination to picture the setting. Figure out as quickly as you can who the characters are, what they are doing, and why they are doing it.
- Be polite. Interrupting the readers can cause them to lose their place and disrupt the performance.
- Enjoy yourself and let the readers know that you enjoyed their performance.

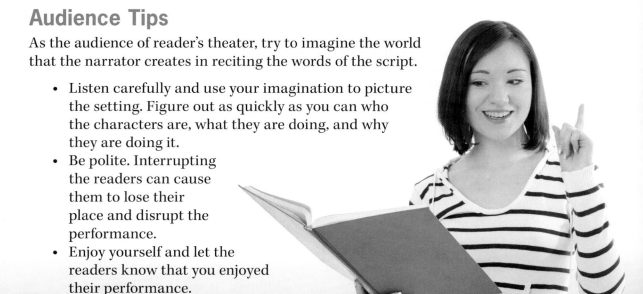

ACTIVITY C Read the following paragraph and determine what props are necessary for the scene.

Michael returns from school and sits down to start his homework. The phone rings. As he gets up to answer it, he trips over his little brother's toys and stubs his toe. Michael jumps out in pain and knocks into his mother's favorite lamp. Michael reaches out to grab the lamp before it falls and luckily makes the catch. He sets the lamp back on the side table and wipes his brow in relief. As he returns to his homework, the phone rings. Michael pulls headphones out of his backpack, puts them on, and goes back to work.

ACTIVITY D Using the example on page 456 as a template, create a picture of what the stage would look like with props for the paragraph in Activity C.

ACTIVITY E Read the line below, using the following characters. You can improvise the words to reflect the voice and gestures the character would use.

"Hello, how are you doing today? I'm feeling well."

1. a cowboy or cowgirl in the South
2. a British professor to his students
3. a hippie or flower child in the '70s
4. a mad scientist after making a breakthrough
5. an elderly woman to her grandchildren
6. a six-year-old boy playing with his toys

ACTIVITY F Select a favorite short story or novel that has more than one character and plenty of dialogue. Record the various roles that appear in the story. Then write a plot summary in paragraph form.

ACTIVITY G Write a reader's theater script based on the passage you selected in Activity F. Use the conventions of playwriting discussed in Lessons 1, 2, and 3 for writing your script.

SPEAKER'S CORNER

Work with classmates to perform the script from Activity G. Follow the suggestions in this lesson to make your performance a success.

Prewriting and Drafting

Playwriting can be a fun way to share a story. Through a script of dialogue and stage direction, you can craft a work that brings a story to life. Now you will use what you have discussed in this chapter to write a one-act play.

Jamal, an eighth grader, looked forward to writing a play. He liked listening to people talk, and the idea of writing the way people speak sounded exciting.

Prewriting

Before you sit down to write your play, take time to think about what you want to write. The prewriting stage for playwriting involves brainstorming and freewriting to develop characters and themes. It's also a time for developing the play's plot.

Brainstorming

Some playwrights begin to think of ideas for plays by brainstorming different characters and the conflicts that can be sparked between them. Characters might consist of people that playwrights know, have read or heard about, or have made up in their imaginations. Playwrights may brainstorm various themes they want to write about.

Jamal brainstormed some incidents that involved conflict from his life and his friends' lives. When he was finished, Jamal chose a conflict between himself and his mother, one in which his mother made him babysit his sister during the day for a week.

Freewriting

When Jamal decided on a conflict, he used freewriting to explore and expand his idea. To help guide his freewriting session, he asked himself the following questions:

1. Who is the protagonist? Micah
2. Who or what is the antagonist? What is the relationship to the protagonist? Mrs. Johnson. They are son and mother.
3. What is the main conflict of the play? Mrs. Johnson wants Micah to take care of the baby every afternoon while she is at work. Micah wants to hang out with his friends and look cool and thinks the baby will ruin everything.
4. What is the inciting incident? Micah and his mother get into a shouting match. Mrs. Johnson threatens to take away Micah's cell phone for a month. Micah angrily gives in.
5. How is the conflict resolved? Micah discovers that the baby attracts girls' attention. Suddenly, he is very popular, so he is pleased with his babysitting job.
6. What is the theme of the play? Good things can come from unpromising beginnings.

Your Turn

Brainstorm a list of possible play ideas. When you have finished, choose one and freewrite to explore and expand the idea. Then ask yourself the same six questions Jamal asked. Is your idea clear?

Planning the Play

Next, Jamal decided which characters he would include in his play and what they would be like. He had already identified his two main characters. He decided to use a doll for the baby. He also planned to include a few friends for Micah and three girls who would be attracted by the baby.

Then Jamal figured out how many scenes his

Organization play required. He decided that for his one-act play, he would need three scenes. To help organize his thinking, he constructed a plot outline that shows what happens at each point in the plot.

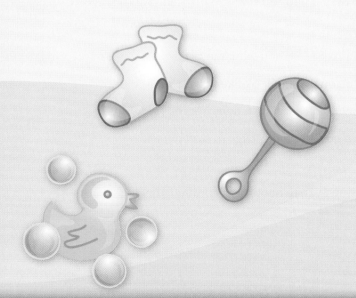

Beginning:
Setting: Family apartment, this year
Micah and his mother argue about who will take care of the baby.

Middle:
Setting: City park, next day
Micah's friends tease him about getting stuck with the babysitting chore. Then three girls stroll by and notice Micah's baby sister. They swoon over the baby and compliment Micah for being so thoughtful to watch his sister. Micah is surprised and overwhelmed by the attention.

Ending:
Setting: Family apartment, later that day
Conflict is resolved by Micah eagerly volunteering to watch the baby every day that summer. The play ends with Micah thinking to himself out loud of all the parks and beaches he can take the baby to.

Your Turn

- Figure out how many characters your play requires and who they will be.
- Write a character list that briefly describes each character.
- Write a plot outline. Write one or two sentences or phrases that describe what happens in each scene, how the plot builds tension, and how the tension is resolved.

Drafting

Jamal reviewed his planning notes, plot outline, and character list. Then he wrote a first draft. Here is the first scene in his script.

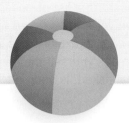

Baby Blues

SCENE 1

(Inside of apartment. Mrs. Johnson jigles baby who is fussing and paces as she argues with son. TV in background)

MRS. JOHNSON: *(calmly)* It will be just be for a few months until school is out. And you know you love Naomi. Besides I don't have anyone else I trust.

MICAH: *(yells)* Mom, no, I can't! Please don't make me. You just don't understand!

MRS. JOHNSON: You can, Micah and you will. I just don't have anyone else I trust. What is the big deal? It will be just for a few hours you'll have plenty of time to do homework after I get home.

MICAH: Homework I am not worried about homework! I'll look like a dweeb even stupider than I do now. Nobody else has to drag a baby around. No boys, anyway. I'll just have to stay inside and suffocate.

MRS. JOHNSON: Please do not say anything else. Do you want me to take away the cell phone? You are my hansome son so you will not look like a dweeb and I absolutely forbid you to stay inside. You need fresh air and so does Naomi. *(glares at Micah in a way that ends the argument) I am going to the kitchen to start dinner. (walks away)*

MICAH: *(to her back)* OK, fine, You win. I hope you're happy you're ruining my life! *(micah exits.)*

Writing Natural-Sounding Dialogue

Listen carefully to the way people speak. Notice the frequent sentence fragments, interjections, and interruptions. Use such natural-sounding speech patterns in the dialogue you write.

Read aloud the following dialogue to help you figure out where contractions would naturally appear. Choosing to use or not to use contractions can help you place the emphasis where you want it to be.

Compare the following sentences:

- You'll do what I tell you, no matter what, Missy said.
- You will do what I tell you, no matter what, Missy said.

Interruptions make for natural-sounding speech. Use dashes to indicate interrupted sentences.

Remember, though, that dialogue must sound natural to the character speaking. Think of a character type who usually speaks clearly and enunciates words fully, such as a butler who

Voice

takes pride in being a perfectionist. Would slang or contractions sound natural coming from that character? Probably not.

Grammar in Action

Identify the conjunctive adverb in Jamal's first draft on p. 478.

Identify the conjunctive adverb in Jamal's first draft on p. 478.

Your Turn

Gather your planning notes, plot outline, and character list and prepare to write your first draft. Unlike Jamal's excerpt, your play draft will need to include a beginning, a middle, and an end.

What sounds natural?

Editor's Workshop

Content Editing

Jamal read his first draft and thought it was a good scene. He also knew that his play would have to be edited for content. Like expository and persuasive essays, the ideas behind creative writing need to be edited for logic

 Sentence Fluency

and clarity. Events within a play must follow a logical order that the audience can understand. He asked Evan, a classmate, to read *Baby Blues* and edit the play.

Evan used the following Content Editor's Checklist to edit Jamal's draft.

Content Editor's Checklist

☐ Does the play have a protagonist and an antagonist?

☐ Are the characters well developed?

☐ Is the inciting incident for the main conflict included?

☐ Does the conflict make sense?

☐ Is enough exposition provided so that the audience can figure out what is going on?

☐ Do the characters have something to do onstage?

☐ Are the stage directions a good blueprint for someone to direct the play?

☐ Can a theme be inferred from the play?

☐ Does the play have a plot that has a rising action and a climax?

☐ Does the ending resolve the conflict?

Evan read Jamal's draft and jotted down some questions and suggestions. Then he and Jamal got together for an editing conference. Here is what Evan had to say about Jamal's draft.

- I like your script a lot. The characters seem like real people. Mrs. Johnson and Micah both had understandable motivations that didn't feel forced.

- The conflict was very realistic. I can imagine how it would feel having to babysit every day. That would be a real problem that most kids could relate to.

- I couldn't figure out what Micah and his mother were arguing about until nearly the end of the scene. I think you should explain the conflict sooner. The audience will want to know what's going on right away.

- You repeated Mrs. Johnson's line about not having anyone to trust. Maybe you should take out the repeated words or change them.

- We learned that people often interrupt each other when they speak. Since they appear to be arguing, should your characters do this, too?

- This is only the first scene, so I don't know whether the action rises to a climax and I don't know if the conflict is resolved. But I can't wait to see how the rest of the play turns out!

Your Turn

Trade your draft script with a partner. Review each other's scripts, using the Content Editor's Checklist as a guide. Then have an editing conference.

- What did you like about your partner's script?
- Ask questions about the parts that confused you.
- Make suggestions for improvements. Be specific!
- Refer to the script as you give reasons for your opinions.

Writer's Tip You may find that reading your partner's script aloud will help both of you notice things that you missed when you read it silently.

Prewriting

Drafting

Content Editing

Revising

Copyediting

Proofreading

Publishing

Revising

To revise his play, Jamal carefully read his own and Evan's suggestions and selected the ones he would put into his draft. This is how he revised his scene.

Baby Blues

SCENE 1

~~Lights come up on the living room of a modest~~ →A couch can be seen center stage.
(~~Inside of~~ apartment. Mrs. Johnson jigles baby who is fussing and paces as she argues
with son. A plays TV in background)

MRS. JOHNSON: *(calmly)* It will be just ~~be~~ for a few months until school is out. And
you know you love Naomi. Besides ~~I don't have anyone else I trust.~~

MICAH: *(yells)* Mom, no, I can't! ~~Please don't make me.~~ You just don't understand! *(kicks leg of couch)*

MRS. JOHNSON: You can, Micah and you will. I just don't have anyone else I trust. to babysit Naomi
What is the big deal? It will be just for a few hours you'll have plenty of time to do
homework after I get home.

MICAH: Homework I am not worried about homework! I'll look like a dweeb even
stupider than I do now. Nobody else has to drag a baby around. No boys, anyway. I'll
just have to stay inside and ~~suffocate.~~

MRS. JOHNSON: ~~Please do not say anything else.~~ That's it! Do you want me to take away
the cell phone? You are my hansome son so you will not look like a dweeb and I
absolutely forbid you to stay inside. You need fresh air and so does Naomi. *(glares at
Micah in a way that ends the argument)* I am going to the kitchen to start dinner.
(~~walks away~~) Mrs. Johnson turns and starts walking offstage left.

MICAH: *(to her back)* retreating OK, fine, You win. I hope you're happy you're ruining my life!
(micah exits) center stage right. Sound of door slamming is heard.

Jamal could see the point of Evan's comments. He went back to his draft and made some changes, which he felt improved his script quite a bit.

- Jamal explained earlier what the argument was about. What did Jamal do so that the audience would immediately know why Micah and Mrs. Johnson were arguing?

- Jamal agreed with Evan that he needlessly repeated the line about Mrs. Johnson not having anyone to trust. How can Jamal make his script more concise?

- What did Jamal do to make the dialogue  sound more realistic? Does the use of slang, idioms, and jargon work with the way Jamal's characters speak?

- Jamal noticed that Evan didn't mention what the characters were doing while they were speaking or where they were onstage. What did Jamal add so that the reader could understand what was going on?

Your Turn

Using the Content Editor's Checklist, consider your own ideas and your editor's suggestions to revise your draft script. Then read the script aloud to make sure the characters' dialogue sounds natural.

Prewriting
Drafting
Content Editing
Revising
Copyediting
Proofreading
Publishing

Copyediting and Proofreading

Copyediting

Jamal was happy with the changes he made in his script. He was confident that they would help an audience understand the conflict and the reasons for Micah's and Mrs. Johnson's behavior more clearly than they would have before he improved his script.

Now he needed to copyedit his script. Copyediting a play is similar to copyediting other types of writing. You edit your draft for accuracy in word choice and sentence structure, as well as for the overall logic of the draft.

Jamal used the following Copyeditor's Checklist to edit his draft.

Jamal was still not sure about some of the words the characters said and wondered whether they sounded right. So he read the dialogue aloud. He decided that replacing some of the words with contractions would make the characters' speech sound more natural. Other dialogue lines seemed too long, so Jamal punctuated them to make them sound more like natural speech.

Your Turn

Look over your revised draft. Use the Copyeditor's Checklist to edit your draft. Be sure the sentence structure of the stage directions is logical and grammatically correct.

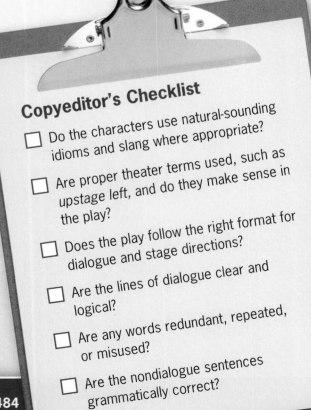

Copyeditor's Checklist

☐ Do the characters use natural-sounding idioms and slang where appropriate?

☐ Are proper theater terms used, such as upstage left, and do they make sense in the play?

☐ Does the play follow the right format for dialogue and stage directions?

☐ Are the lines of dialogue clear and logical?

☐ Are any words redundant, repeated, or misused?

☐ Are the nondialogue sentences grammatically correct?

Proofreading

 Conventions   Playwrights proofread their drafts to find mistakes in spelling, capitalization, punctuation, and grammar. They also check to make certain that no new errors have been introduced during the revising stage.

Most people find it difficult to catch all the mistakes when they proofread their own work. That is because they are very familiar with it, having written and revised it several times. Their eyes tend to skip over mistakes. That's why it is a good idea to ask someone else to proofread your draft. Jamal asked Rosa, another classmate, to proofread his draft.

Rosa used the following Proofreader's Checklist to proofread Jamal's play.

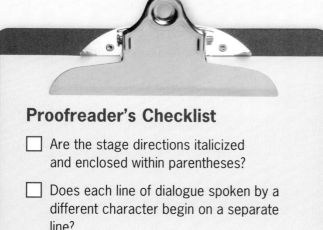

Proofreader's Checklist

☐ Are the stage directions italicized and enclosed within parentheses?

☐ Does each line of dialogue spoken by a different character begin on a separate line?

☐ Are the characters' names at the beginning of their lines in all capital letters, boldface, and followed by a colon?

☐ Does a line of space precede and follow each character's lines to make the script easy to read?

☐ Is the grammar correct?

☐ Is every word spelled correctly?

☐ Are capitalization and punctuation correct?

Rosa proofread the draft carefully word by word, consulting a dictionary when she wasn't sure about spelling. She checked off each item on the Proofreader's Checklist. Rosa found a few mistakes in Jamal's script. She found a missing colon, three examples of missing end punctuation, three missing commas, two sentences that were not capitalized, and two misspelled words. She also found characters' names that should have been capitalized and directions that should have been in italics. How many mistakes can you find in Jamal's script?

Writer's Tip It is a good idea to ask someone else to proofread your draft to find mistakes in spelling, capitalization, punctuation, and grammar.

Prewriting

Drafting

Content Editing

Revising

Copyediting

Proofreading

Publishing

Publishing

Jamal corrected the mistakes he and Rosa had found in his script. He made a few final editing changes too. Then he looked at his revisions again because he wanted to avoid having any errors creep into his script at the last minute. Now that his first scene looked professional, Jamal finished the play.

Baby Blues

SCENE 1

(Lights come up on the living room of a modest apartment. A sofa can be seen center stage. MRS. JOHNSON *jiggles baby who is fussing and paces as she argues with son. TV plays in the background.)*

MRS. JOHNSON: *(calmly)* It will be just for a few months until school is out. And you know you love Naomi. Besides—

MICAH: *(yells)* Mom, no, I can't! You just don't understand! *(kicks leg of sofa)*

MRS. JOHNSON: You can, Micah, and you will. I just don't have anyone else I trust to babysit Naomi. What is the big deal? It will be just for a few hours. You'll have plenty of time to do homework after I get home.

MICAH: Homework! I'm not worried about homework! I'll look like a dweeb, even stupider than I do now. Nobody else has to drag a baby around. No boys, anyway. I'll just have to stay inside and—

MRS. JOHNSON: That's it! Do you want me to take away the cell phone? You are my handsome son, so you won't look like a dweeb. And I absolutely forbid you to stay inside. You need fresh air and so does Naomi. *(She glares at Micah in a way that ends the argument.)* I'm going to the kitchen to start dinner.

(MRS. JOHNSON turns and starts walking offstage left.)

MICAH: *(to her retreating back)* Okay, fine. You win. I hope you're happy you're ruining my life!

(MICAH exits center stage right. Sound of door slamming is heard.)

Whenever you publish your work, your goal

 Presentation is to share your thoughts and experiences with other people. Here are a few ways you can publish your play.

 Collect the plays the class wrote and bind them together in a book. Keep the book in the school library or classroom reference section for later use.

 Host a one-act play festival. Each student or group writes and directs their own one-act play. Cast fellow classmates as the actors.

 Videotape each one-act play and share it with your friends and family.

 Have your class perform your play for Parents' Night.

However you decide to publish, make sure the message is clear.

Your Turn

After your teacher reviews your script, you can produce your play with props or as reader's theater. See Lesson 6 for tips on producing reader's theater.

- Collect or make costumes and very simple props. If possible, find CDs and noisemakers for special effects.
- Make enough photocopies of the script so that each actor has one.
- Choose a director and actors for all the parts. The director should figure out how much and what kinds of movement will happen in the production and what each character will do at every moment.
- Rehearse. The actors should become familiar with their lines so they can speak naturally.
- Go through the script several times, first by reading it, then by acting it.
- Perform the play before an audience.

Research Reports

LiNK

History of the Samurai
by Stephen Phillips

Though the samurai were tightly controlled by their masters, they exerted great power over the commoners and peasants under them. During the Tokugawa era (1603–1868), the samurai held the power of life or death over peasants and merchants (Morrow). This meant the samurai could murder on the spot any peasant who showed the slightest sign of disrespect.

The code by which the samurai lived was called *bushido,* or the way of the warrior. Much of the code derived from Buddhism and Confucianism, but the central tenet of the code was service to the master above all else, including their own lives (Gore 24). Because wealth was tightly controlled within Japan, frugality was a prized virtue within the code. Other virtues of *bushido* were politeness, courage, charity, and showing no fear or pain in the face of suffering. Any violation of the code or any slight sign of disrespect to a samurai's master required the samurai to pay with his life (Reynolds 50). This was called *seppuku,* and it often restored a samurai family's honor.

> A research report, like this excerpt from "History of the Samurai," is expository writing that thoroughly develops a topic and is supported with factual information and credible source material.

CHAPTER 8

Nora M., Room 117
March 12, 20—

Thomas L. Jennings

Have you ever wondered how, why, or who invented dry cleaners? The answer is Thomas L. Jennings. He was born in 1791 and died in 1856. He was a tailor and dry cleaner in New York City. On March 3, 1821, Thomas L. Jennings was the first African American to receive a patent. He invented dry cleaners, which was then called "dry scouring" (Haskins 31).

Jennings had many major accomplishments. He worked as a tailor in New York City, and after he invented the dry scouring process, he became a prominent leader in many clubs, including a leading member of the First Annual Convention of the People of Color. Thomas L. Jennings was also a member of the first African American club, called the African Society for Mutual Relief. The first meeting was held on March 23, 1810 (Haskins 33).

Jennings wasn't just an abolitionist and an inventor; he was also a family man. Jennings had a wife and several children. They all lived on 167 Church Street and attended Abyssinian Baptist Church. Jennings wasn't the only successful one in his family. His son, Thomas L. Jennings Jr., studied dentistry in Boston and opened a business in New Orleans. Matilda Jennings, his daughter, was a dressmaker; she married and lived in San Francisco (Haskins 34).

Thomas L. Jennings's sister, Elizabeth, was also a big part of his life. In 1854 his sister filed suit against Third Avenue Railway Company for discrimination. Chester A. Arthur was her lawyer. Elizabeth won her case in 1855, four years before Thomas L. Jennings died. After the case was won, Chester A. Arthur eventually became the president of the United States (Haskins 35).

Thomas L. Jennings was a great person and inventor. Generous and helpful to everyone, Jennings aided his family and his community. One of the amazing things he did was buy his family out of slavery. Thomas L. Jennings was a great person and helped many people (Bellis and Haskin 31–35).

What Makes a Good Research Report?

A research report is a comprehensive piece of expository writing that has a clear focus on one topic. This focus, expressed as the thesis statement, is supported by factual information gathered from research. Research reports are written in a confident voice that uses formal language. The conclusion to a research report summarizes the report's thesis and the important ideas raised in the body of the report.

The following are some points to keep in mind when writing your research report. How closely did the writer of the report on page 489 follow these points?

Topic

A good topic for a research report is one that interests the writer and that is neither too broad nor too narrow. Often, writers of research reports select topics that are too broad to cover adequately within a limited number of pages, such as "crime in the United States." On the other hand, a topic should not be too narrow, or a writer will not find enough information, such as "crime on my block."

The topic of a research report should also be focused and appropriate for its audience.

Thesis

A thesis statement should be clearly stated in the introduction of a research report. The rest of the paper develops the thesis.

Before settling on a thesis statement, however, many writers ask themselves preliminary questions to guide their research and maintain their focus on the topic. For example, the writer of "History of the Samurai" may have known about the samurai from watching TV or movies and was interested in discovering what role the samurai played in Japanese culture. The writer then asked questions such as "Why did the samurai act a certain way?" or "What role did the samurai have in Japanese society?"

After exploring some library sources about the samurai, the writer learned that they were guided by a strong warrior code and that the samurai played a greater role than mere foot soldiers. By learning this new information about the samurai, the writer could better focus the report's thesis on a specific idea that is convincing and informative: the role of the samurai warrior evolved into one of the most influential features of Japanese culture.

Organization

Because research reports rely on multiple sources to support a focused thesis, good organization is especially important. Some ways of organizing research papers include cause and effect, comparison, chronological order, and order of importance.

ACTIVITY A Practice focusing topics for research reports. Suggest ways to narrow the following topics. Write the questions you would ask to focus your topic.

1. literary prizes
2. history of flight
3. energy sources
4. U.S. immigration
5. volunteer opportunities
6. the age of the dinosaurs
7. world hunger
8. women in the workforce

Memorial to aviation pioneers Orville and Wilbur Wright in Kill Devil Hill, North Carolina

Tech Tip With an adult, search online to begin your topic search.

Documentation

Research reports cite and document their sources. The bibliography that accompanies a research paper, often called the Works Cited page, lists every source the writer used in the paper. The Works Cited page is helpful to readers who want to learn more about your topic.

Documenting your sources also guards against plagiarism. Writers must avoid plagiarizing, presenting another writer's words or ideas as one's own. Plagiarizing is the theft of words and ideas and is unethical.

ACTIVITY B Choose three topics that you narrowed in Activity A. Write a preliminary thesis statement for each topic.

EXAMPLE: **Topic:** energy sources

Focused topic: alternative energy sources for electric power plants

Thesis: Solar power and wind power are two alternative energy sources for our nation's power plants.

ACTIVITY C Which way would you organize a research paper about each of these topics? Would you use cause and effect, comparison, chronological order, or order of importance? Explain why that structure would be most logical.

1. elementary education in the United States and Japan
2. solving world hunger
3. gun control laws around the world
4. environmentally friendly homes
5. homeland security in an open society
6. homelessness in American cities
7. destruction of the rain forests
8. animal rights
9. history of the U.S. census
10. global climate change

ACTIVITY D Choose one of the following topics. Then fill in a chart like the one below.

1. origin of movies
2. evolution of video games
3. high-tech kites
4. physical education in schools
5. computer viruses
6. professional women's soccer
7. exploring Mars
8. fighting wildfires
9. safe schools
10. bicycle racing
11. conquering Mount Everest
12. endangered species

TOPIC	WHAT I KNOW	WHAT I WANT TO KNOW

ACTIVITY E Briefly research the topic you chose in Activity D and find three separate sources of information about it.

ACTIVITY F Based on the information you wrote about a topic in the chart in Activity D, and the research you did in Activity E, write an introduction for a research report on the topic.

Grammar in Action. Diagram the last sentence in the p. 489 excerpt.

WRITER'S CORNER

Practice writing thesis statements or research questions for the topics you suggested in the Writer's Corner on page 491.

Research and Organization

An important part of prewriting a research report is taking notes. Notes are gathered from reading the various sources that you find in the course of your research.

Taking Notes

A useful way of taking notes is to write them on note cards. This is a good way to summarize important information from your source. Summarizing will help you become familiar with what the source is saying and determine whether the information will be helpful to your research report.

When you find an important detail that relates to your topic, write it on a note card. The detail can restate a fact or an idea in your own words, or it can be a direct quotation. Then write the source's name and the page number of the source at the bottom of the card. If you quote a source, include quotation marks to remind you that you are using the source's words and not your own.

Be sure always to write just one fact on each note card. This will make it easier to rearrange your facts when you organize your notes.

Here are two note cards used by the author of the report on page 488.

Write the reference information for each source on a separate set of note cards. Be sure to list all the required information that will appear on your Works Cited page, which is discussed in Lesson 3.

Samurai pay kept low

The daimyo paid the samurai only in cash or rice.

Bresson p. 89

Samurai family wealth

Samurai family pay was set at a fixed rate. If a samurai had more children, there was less money to divide.

Travers p. 243

ACTIVITY A **Read these sources and follow the directions.**

A. From page 234 of the book *The Forgotten War* by Thomas Sommes

Tensions between the United States and two European powers, Great Britain and France, led to embargoes against all foreign trade and precipitated the War of 1812. Some Americans wanted war with France, some with Britain. However, seizures of men and ships on the high seas by Britain were too humiliating for the Americans to let stand. Negotiations to prevent war failed when Congress declared war on Britain two days after Britain agreed to stop seizing ships.

The U.S.S. *Constitution* defeats the H.M.S. *Guerriere* in a naval battle on August 19, 1812.

B. From the article "Naval Warfare in the War of 1812," by Kimberly Crick, found on the Web site www.livinghistory.org

The War of 1812 was fought in a series of almost isolated sea and land battles. Naval battles were fought off the coast of Africa, as well as on the Great Lakes. A victory by the Americans in the Battle of Lake Erie on September 10, 1813, allowed the Americans to move west. However, the British blockade off the Eastern seaboard kept many ships in their harbors.

C. From the article "The Myth of Unity" by Nelson Rooker in the magazine *Politics Today,* Summer 2005, page 45

Throughout the War of 1812, there were political divisions between the New England states and the Southern and Western states. New England shipbuilders hated the war because they wanted trade with Great Britain and France, and the embargoes prevented that. On the other hand, Southerners, known as War-hawks, believed British Canada could be easily conquered.

1. Write two note cards for a report about ships and shipping in the War of 1812.

2. Write five note cards, including one from each source, for a report on the War of 1812.

3. Write three note cards for a report for this thesis statement: "The War of 1812 was caused by trade embargoes."

4. Write one note card about the role of the Great Lakes in the War of 1812.

WRITER'S CORNER

Choose a topic that interests you and find four sources on the topic. Write three note cards from each source.

Organizing Your Notes

When you have completed your research and notes, gather your notes together and organize them into a preliminary outline. Follow these steps as you organize your notes:

- Separate your cards into groups of main ideas that support your thesis statement.
- Read each note card in each group. Do the notes support your thesis statement? If not, consider altering the thesis statement or taking more notes.
- Once you have decided on a thesis statement, remove any note cards that do not fit your thesis.
- Arrange the groups of note cards into a preliminary outline that best supports your thesis.
- Review your preliminary outline to see if it is in logical order according to the note cards you have organized. If not, rearrange your stacks into a more logical order.
- To help visualize your report, create a revised detailed outline from your note cards. Give a heading to each subtopic and list the related details under each subtopic.

Outlines

Using an outline lets you take all the information and sort it into smaller pieces of data that can be more easily handled. An outline can also give direction to your writing.

An outline follows a specific format. Main ideas are divided into subtopics, which are supported with details. Study this outline of a research report about how plants, animals, and humans survive in the desert.

I. Introduction
II. Plant life
   A. Roots
   B. Stems
   C. Flowers
III. Animal life
   A. Carnivores
   B. Herbivores
IV. Human life
   A. Oases
      1. Springs
      2. Wells
   B. Pipelines
V. Conclusion

ACTIVITY B Organize the following notes about the Ghanaian civilization of West Africa into the following three subtopics: government, trade, agriculture. Eliminate any notes that do not fit into subtopics. Then think of a thesis statement that fits the subtopics.

- Ghana's actual name was Wagadugu
- earliest known West African kingdom
- Ghanaian kingdom was founded on gold and salt mining
- Ghana grew crops of kola nuts
- Ghanaian king assisted by a council
- Ghana made advances in iron-working
- trade caravans could have up to 12,000 camels
- Muslims to the north of Ghana were called Almoravids
- the Niger River Valley provided agricultural support to Ghana
- droughts in the area rivers helped bring about Ghana's decline
- traded copper, salt, and gold with other kingdoms
- Ghanaian kings created a way to tax gold

Women carrying goods to market near Elmina west of Accra in Ghana

ACTIVITY C Create an outline from the subtopics and details in Activity B. The outline should identify subtopics, and the details should be listed under each subtopic.

ACTIVITY D Reread the student model on page 489. Put the items below into an outline. Remember to add an introduction and conclusion.

1. Thomas L. Jennings's accomplishments
2. Inventor
3. Sister (Elizabeth)
4. Tailor
5. Family
6. Children (Thomas, Matilda)

WRITER'S CORNER

Sort into subtopics the notes you made on note cards from the previous Writer's Corner. Then create an outline from the groups of note cards.

Citing Sources

Whenever you use a source in a research report, you must tell the reader where you got your information at the point in the report where the source is used. This is called citing sources.

Works Cited Page

The Works Cited page lists every source used in the research report alphabetically according to the author's last name, when available. Use a "hanging indent" format when listing all sources so that the author's name stands away from the text of the notation. This lets the reader find the source easily. Sources that you disregarded when taking notes are not listed.

This page goes at the end of your report on a separate sheet of paper. Type the words *Works Cited* at the top of the page, centered, then begin listing the sources. Notations are written differently for different sources, but all of them follow a similar and logical pattern: first, the author's name; second, the title of the work itself; and, finally, the publisher's information. Pay close attention to the formats that follow and be sure to reproduce them in your research report.

Books

Book titles normally appear in italics but in Works Cited pages, book titles are underlined. Following the title are the city and state where the publisher is located, a colon, then the name of the publisher and the year of publication. Most of this information can usually be found on the title page of the book.

> **Works Cited**
>
> Grimaldi, Helen. <u>Global Climate Change</u>. New York, NY: Wordsmith, 2001.
>
> Sperling, Arthur, and Jenny Anderson. <u>Eat Your Way to Health</u>. Emmaus, PA: Green Acres Press, 2004.

If a book has more than one author, it is alphabetized by the last name of the first author listed on the title page. If a book has more than three authors, list the first author, last name first, and then add *et al* (Latin for "and others") after the name.

Periodicals

Magazines, newspapers, and journals are called periodicals because they appear at regular intervals, or periods of time.

The titles of magazine and newspaper articles are enclosed within quotation marks. The full date of publication is included after the italics or underlined title of the publication. The pages on which the article appears follow a colon after the date. If an article begins on one page and ends on a nonsequential page, simply place a plus (+) sign after the first page on which the article appears.

> Furtado, Nellie. "Your Place in the World." *Wild Life Magazine* 15 Nov. 2005: 20–22.
>
> Groark, Virginia. "Speed Limit Cut Near Toll Plazas." *Chicago Tribune* 4 Aug. 2004, Metro, 1+.

ACTIVITY A **Answer the questions that follow this Works Cited page.**

Barker, Mary, and Alan Marshall. *Genetic Modification: The Triumph of Science.* Hagerstown, MD: Scientific Press, 2002.

Herbert, Kinasha. *What You See Is What You Get.* New York: Cooper Village Publishing, 2000.

Walker, Stanley, and Allison Walker. *Three Easy Steps to Growing Perfect Vegetables.* Boston: Nature's Way Publishing, 2000.

Brennan, Susan. "Take Two Zucchinis and Call Me Tomorrow." *Newsworthy* 18 Feb. 2001: 66–68.

1. What is the difference between titles that are italicized and titles that are enclosed within quotation marks?
2. Why are some names listed last name first and others in the reverse order?
3. What information is included for each item?
4. What might be the topic of the research report?
5. In what order should the entries above be listed?

WRITER'S CORNER

Go to your school or local library and find five books and five articles from magazines about your topic. Write a citation for each source.

Tech Tip Type your Works Cited in a word processing program.

Citing Other Sources

Books, newspapers, and magazines are not the only sources of information available to you for a research report. The following are other sources of information and how they should be presented on your Works Cited page.

Radio and Television Programs

> "Teenagers at Risk." PBS. WGVU, Grand Rapids, Michigan. 3 October 2005.

Sound Recordings

Like other citations, begin with the name of the artist, the title of the song, the title of the album, the publisher, and the date of release.

> The Beatles. "Help!" *Love.* Capitol Records, 2006.

Interviews

If you speak with an expert on your research topic, make sure that you record the date of the interview. If you want to use a tape recorder, be sure to ask permission from your subject first.

> Diener, Teri. Personal interview. 17 January 2005.

Online Documents

Review Chapter 5, Lesson 3, Evaluating Web Sites, before conducting research on the Internet. The notation format for online publications is similar to books and periodicals: author's name, title of the document or article, the date you accessed the Web site, and the Web site's address within angle brackets. If the Web site address is too long or cumbersome, provide the address to the Web site's home page.

> Green, Robert Lane. "Abroad Appeal" *New Republic Online* 4 August 2004, <www.tnr.com>.

Encyclopedia Articles

Encyclopedia articles are often unsigned. In this case begin the notation with the title of the article. Since encyclopedias are often organized alphabetically, page or volume numbers are not necessary.

> "Digestion." *World Book.* 2005 ed.

Indonesian coral garden

Parenthetical Notations

One way to credit a source is to use parenthetical notations. To note a source parenthetically, paraphrase or directly quote from the source in your report. Place the author's last name and the page number of the source you used within parentheses at the end of the sentence, before the period. See the report on page 488 for examples of parenthetical notations.

Paraphrasing

When you rewrite someone else's ideas, using your own words, you are paraphrasing. Paraphrasing lets you use your own words to inform the reader what you have learned. However, because you learned your information from another source, you must note your source, just as you do for direct quotations. Effective paraphrasing requires excellent knowledge of your source material.

Study the following examples:

$$e = mc^2$$

Original Text
Einstein often hid his fierce intellect in a bumbling, self-effacing shell. The mussed-up mop of white hair, the not-too-clean cardigan, the absent-minded-professor demeanor: all were masks.

Incomplete Paraphrase
Einstein hid his intellect behind a modest, absent-minded shell to which his hairstyle and clothing contributed.

Good Paraphrase
Einstein's messy hair and clothes, as well as his awkwardness and forgetfulness, were ways he invented to conceal his genius.

ACTIVITY B Write an expository paragraph on a topic of your choice. Consult at least two sources and use one or more quotations in your paragraph. Use parenthetical notations.

WRITER'S CORNER

Practice paraphrasing. Choose a few sentences from a nonfiction book and then write a paraphrase of them. Include a parenthetical notation. Trade papers with a classmate. Compare the paraphrase to the original. Does the original meaning remain?

Reference Tools

You can learn just about anything from reference books. Encyclopedias, almanacs, atlases, and the *Reader's Guide to Periodical Literature* are some of the most useful reference books.

REFERENCE	TYPE OF INFORMATION
almanac	annual facts, statistics, year's events
atlas	maps and other geographic information
biographical reference	information on famous people
encyclopedia	articles on specific topics
periodicals	periodic publications such as magazines
Reader's Guide to Periodical Literature	index of magazine articles

Almanacs

Almanacs are published every year, and they can cover almost any subject. Farmers were the traditional readers of almanacs. Farmers used the books to plan their crops for the coming year. Almanacs contained information about yearly weather patterns, as well as "commonsense" advice. Today there are specialized almanacs for a wide variety of topics, everything from sports to religion. General-information almanacs cover population statistics, significant events of the year, and much more. These almanacs include *The World Almanac and Book of Facts, TIME Almanac,* and *Farmers' Almanac.*

Atlases

An atlas is a book of maps, but it is also much more. The maps in an atlas cover political boundaries, regional climates, highways and train lines, and rivers and lakes. Atlases can also provide demographic and economic information, such as where most people in a given country live and what goods that country produces.

Biographical References

A biographical reference is a book or set of books that gives short biographies of notable people. Some popular biographical reference books include *American Men and Women of Science, Contemporary Authors, Current Biography Yearbook,* and *Who's Who in America.*

1992 Nobel Peace Prize winner

ACTIVITY A Use a current general-information almanac to answer these questions.

1. What were two top news stories of last year?
2. What was the population of the United States in 2000?
3. Who won the Nobel Peace Prize in 1992?
4. What is the origin of the name of the state of Colorado?
5. What are the highest and lowest places in the world?
6. Where were the Summer Olympic Games held in 1932?
7. Who was the National Basketball Association's Rookie of the Year in 1985?
8. What will be a good night to search the sky for meteor showers next summer?
9. What is the population of the Federated States of Micronesia?

ACTIVITY B Identify which reference tool you could use to find out the information below.

1. The political boundaries of Bolivia
2. The average rainfall of your area
3. The year Thomas Edison was born
4. The winning teams of the Super Bowl for the last 10 years
5. The birthplace of Oscar Wilde
6. Urban population growth of Atlanta
7. The temperature in Australia in July

WRITER'S CORNER

Look up these people in a biographical reference book. Explain in paragraph form why each one is famous.

1. Steven Spielberg
2. Mahatma Gandhi
3. Louise Nevelson
4. Kofi Annan

Grammar in Action. Diagram the last sentence in the model on p. 488.

Information Sources

No search tool is totally comprehensive, so it is important to use and cite a variety of sources. A good place to begin your research may be an online search engine. There are general search engines that require a simple keyword to begin the search. Many search engines exist to help narrow the broad range of information and limit the results to guidelines you set. Visit your local or school library for a variety of search-engine options. A librarian can assist you in using specific search engines and help you find the most pertinent, helpful research for your topic.

The library will also have several reference guides that gather information and make it available to you for easy use. For your research report, you might be interested in only recent articles regarding your topic. The *Reader's Guide to Periodical Literature* is an index of articles found in popular magazines, such as *Time, Newsweek, Ebony,* and *Popular Mechanics.* This subject-and-author guide to articles from popular magazines is published twice every month, so it is a good source of up-to-date information.

When you find the article titles that you are looking for, a librarian can help you find the magazines. You might find back issues either online or in print. Often, back issues will be stored on microfilm or microfiche, an electronic machine for reading archived printed materials. If you are unfamiliar with how to use the equipment, ask a librarian to help you. Some microfilm and microfiche readers are equipped with a photocopier to make copies of the pages you need.

LiNK

Works Cited

Arendt, Hannah. 2010. *The Human Condition.* Chicago, IL: University of Chicago Press.

Aries, Philippe. 2009. *Centuries of Childhood: A Social History of Family Life.* New York: Random House.

Danah Boyd

Plagiarism

Failure to cite the source of information or ideas gathered through research is called plagiarism. Plagiarism is stealing another person's ideas or information and pretending that it is your own. Always use and cite credible sources, both online and in printed materials, and paraphrase the text in your own words and thoughts. Online search engines will help get you started, but it is your own research and diligence that will help make your research report accurate and engaging.

ACTIVITY C Consult an atlas to answer these questions.

1. In which state is most of Yellowstone National Park?
2. What mountain range is in New Hampshire?
3. How many countries border Germany?
4. Through which states would you travel to get from Illinois to Florida the most direct way?
5. What is the principal use of the land around Dubuque, Iowa?

ACTIVITY D Which of these magazines would you use to find information on the topics that follow?

Consumer Reports   National Geographic   Rolling Stone
Architecture Digest   Newsweek

1. building design in New Orleans, Louisiana
2. latest political and cultural news
3. the aboriginal tribes of Australia
4. profile of a popular musical group
5. comparisons of new digital cameras on the market

ACTIVITY E After an initial online search, identify which reference tools you could use to find the following information. Review and apply only the tools learned in this lesson. Some items may have more than one answer.

1. the topography of Italy
2. last year's weather in the Midwest region
3. major accomplishments of Charles Lindbergh
4. latest trends in corporations "going green"
5. the number of Web sites devoted to the TV series *Star Trek*
6. a photo of the front page of the local newspaper from 50 years ago
7. the volcanoes of the Pacific Islands

Aboriginal vases depicting Australian animals

WRITER'S CORNER

Use the *Reader's Guide to Periodical Literature* to look for articles on a possible research report topic. Then read at least two of the articles. Do you still think this topic would be suitable for a four- or five-page report?

Multiple-Meaning Words

As you know, a word can have both literal and implied meanings. In addition, some words have more than one literal meaning. Think of the word *bridge.* One meaning of *bridge* is a structure that spans a river or other body of water. Other meanings include the area of a ship that houses the controls, a part of a musical instrument, and a part of a person's nose. Words like *bridge* are called multiple-meaning words.

Readers usually know which meaning of a word is correct by the context in which it is used. When you hear someone say "The captain has left the bridge," you assume that the captain has walked out of the ship's control room, not off a river-spanning structure.

ACTIVITY A Choose the correct meaning of the italicized word in each sentence.

1. The Reptile's second *number* was a blues tune called "Come into My Kitchen."
   a. one of a set of positive integers
   b. one of the separate offerings in a musical program
   c. a numeral used for identification

2. They played an *arrangement* for guitar and flute.
   a. an adaptation of a composition for other instruments
   b. an agreement
   c. the process of arranging

3. To gain weight, drink a *shake* instead of a glass of milk.
   a. to cause to move with jerky movements
   b. a foamy drink of milk and ice cream
   c. to disturb or agitate

4. Mike has *radical* political views.
   a. the root of a quantity
   b. advocating basic changes in current practices
   c. favoring extreme changes

5. Watching Westerns, you would assume everyone in the Old West *packed* a pistol.
   a. had available for action
   b. filled up with items
   c. crowded to capacity

6. The new library is in an *ideal* location.
   a. a goal
   b. an honorable principle
   c. excellent

7. Don't *gather* mushrooms unless you are positive they are edible.
   a. to cause to come together
   b. to pick up and enfold
   c. to harvest or pick

8. Unchecked gossip can certainly *smear* someone's name.
   a. to spread with a sticky substance
   b. to stain the reputation of
   c. to apply by spreading

ACTIVITY B The italicized words in the sentences below have more than one meaning. Write a new sentence for each word that reflects another meaning of that word.

1. Every time Emma's brother doesn't get his way, he throws a *fit*.

2. How far did stocks *fall* this week compared to last?

3. A sudden *jar* in their sleep first warned most people of the earthquake.

4. Who can *break* a dollar so Arnetta can put money in the meter?

5. The teacher described the behavior of her class as a *disgrace*.

6. After Katia sent in the *grant* application, all she could do was wait.

7. I need more *quarters* if I want to continue playing the video game.

8. The raccoons made such a *racket* last night that I couldn't sleep.

Amanita muscaria, commonly known as the fly agaric, is a poisonous fungus.

WRITER'S CORNER

Work with a partner to explore words with multiple meanings. Choose a few words from one of your papers. Think of as many meanings of the words as you can. Check a dictionary to see whether you thought of all the definitions.

Homographs

The word *bridge* meaning a card game has a separate entry in a dictionary from the word *bridge* referred to on page 506 because it has a different word origin. *Bridge* and *bridge* are homographs—words that are spelled the same but have different etymologies and meanings. In a dictionary a homograph is followed by a superscript number to show that it is a separate entry.

Many homographs are pronounced the same. One word *bat,* for example, means "a small, flying mammal." A second word *bat* means "a stick used to hit a ball." As a verb, this word also means "to swat or hit." You can have fun with homographs by using more than one in the same sentence.

Pedro will *bat* **at the** *bat* **with a** *bat.*
Can the platform *bear* **the weight of the** *bear*?

Some homographs that are used as different parts of speech have distinct pronunciations. This is because they are derived from separate word origins.

Teresa waited a *minute* **before she stepped onto the stage.**
Oscar found *minute* **flaws in the antique vase.**

In the first sentence, the noun meaning "60 seconds of time" has the stress on the first syllable. In the second sentence, the adjective meaning "tiny" has the stress on the second syllable.

ACTIVITY C Each of these words is a homograph of at least one other word. For each item, write a sentence that uses at least two of the homographs of the word. Look up the words in a dictionary if you need help. Be creative!

EXAMPLE **A sow cannot sow corn.**

1. ear
2. fine
3. nag
4. converse
5. can
6. stall
7. long
8. peaked
9. sewer
10. baste
11. lime
12. pad
13. lumber
14. boil
15. impress

ACTIVITY D The words defined by each pair of meanings are homographs. Write the homograph for each pair. If the homographs are pronounced differently, underline the stressed syllable in each.

1. a. a tale
   b. a building floor

2. a. to make angry
   b. a fragrant substance to burn

3. a. a piercing tool
   b. to hit

4. a. to drill a hole
   b. a dull person

5. a. place of entry
   b. to delight

6. a. an agreement
   b. to crush

7. a. to climb on a horse
   b. _____ St. Helens

8. a. to avoid
   b. to feel the loss of

9. a. to waste
   b. a small cake

10. a. a wise person
    b. an herb

11. a. item used with a hammer
    b. part of a finger or toe

12. a. helpful or friendly
    b. a type of something

13. a. a part of a drill
    b. a small piece

14. a. a control panel
    b. to comfort

ACTIVITY E Each of these words is the homograph of at least one other word. Look up the words in a dictionary. Write a sentence that shows the meaning of each homograph.

1. school
2. bowl
3. lap
4. pod

5. bank
6. wake
7. light
8. case

9. elder
10. hatch
11. bail
12. mint

WRITER'S CORNER

Use a dictionary to find five other homographs that have not been discussed in this lesson. Write a sentence for each homograph that shows one of its meanings.

Oral History Report

An oral history report is a researched talk about something that occurred in the past. This can include a historical person, a significant invention, or a historical event or era. Like the research report, an oral history report must be researched, logically organized, and appropriate to its audience.

Keep these points in mind as you prepare your oral history report.

Choosing a Topic

To find a topic for your oral history report, think about historical topics that you would like to know more about. History is full of strange and fascinating stories that would appeal to you and almost any audience. Use the following tips to find a topic for your report:

- Recall ideas from your social studies or history classes that interested you. Take a few minutes to jot them down on a sheet of paper.
- Use a search engine on the Internet to look up historical people and events. Reading what others have written on a general historical topic, such as the Great Depression, can give you ideas of what you want to talk about.
- View movies that are based on historical events or time periods, such as *Apollo 13, Gone With the Wind,* or *Glory.* Consider focusing your report on the background of these events and why they became significant.
- Browse through historical almanacs. These books summarize historical events that happened on certain days of the year.

It is important to narrow your topic choices to the item you believe to have enough sources from which to draw. Remember the topic should be broad enough to cover a range of points but narrow enough to have sufficient source material.

Research the Topic

Recall what you discussed in Lesson 2 for tips on researching your report. Begin your research by locating sources from the library or the Internet.

Once you have your sources, take notes on what you read and create a set of note cards. On each card be sure to document the source, using the styles discussed in Lesson 3.

Organizing Your Report

First, think of subtopics that your notes can easily fall into. Next, organize your note cards, creating a separate pile for each subtopic. Discard any note cards that don't fall into any subtopic.

When you have organized your report, think of a thesis statement that fits your notes. Ideally, your thesis statement should summarize your topic in one sentence, such as "The American civil rights movement captured the nation's attention in the early 1960s."

Audience

Since your audience will be your classmates, make sure that everyone will be able to understand your historical report. If you learned some new terms or ideas that are critical to understanding your topic, be sure to define them for your audience.

ACTIVITY A Listed in pairs are some topics that could be assigned for an oral history report. Choose one topic from each pair and explain why that topic interests you more than the other.

1. the Great Depression or the New Deal
2. submarines in World War I or submarines in World War II
3. the Emancipation Proclamation or women's suffrage
4. the United Nations or the League of Nations
5. the Lewis and Clark expedition or the Zebulon Pike expedition
6. Anne Hutchinson's trial or the Salem trials
7. César Chávez or Mother Jones
8. The Underground Railroad or the Great Migration
9. building the Great Pyramids or building the Golden Gate Bridge
10. the cotton gin or the printing press

SPEAKER'S CORNER

Choose a topic for an oral history report to present to your class. Write a thesis statement and take notes that give supporting details and explanations.

Engaging with Media

Using visual and audio aids can bring your oral history report alive by letting the audience see or hear the people who made history. An oral report on the history of jazz in America, for example, could include bits of music from different jazz eras and styles. A painting of the British Army's surrender at Yorktown can help your audience imagine the event for themselves.

While you research your report, look through your sources for ideas that could be illustrated through audio or visual materials. The audio or visual aids you choose should not take away from the integrity of your report. The focus of the report should be on your presentation and what you say. Avoid using lengthy audio and video clips. Use the following suggestions to help you,

Video or Film Clips

If your topic is an event from recent history, there might be useful video or film clips that can illustrate the event. Most libraries have a broad selection of documentaries and newsreel clips.

Audio Clips

Sometimes an audience wants to hear what you're talking about. Historical events that include famous speeches are good opportunities to use audio clips in your report. If your report is on the panic caused by Orson Welles's "War of the Worlds" radio broadcast, it would probably need to include a short excerpt of the program.

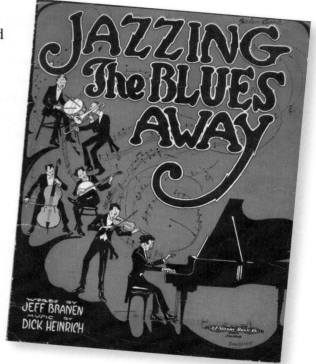

Jazz sheet music approximately 1918

Practice and Present Your Report

After you finish writing your oral history report, practice presenting it. Read it aloud to a classmate. Ask yourself these questions:

- Have I used my own words?
- Is the report clear and understandable?
- Is my tone of voice calm and objective?

Ask your classmate to critique your presentation. He or she should comment on the following:

- The main idea
- The supporting ideas
- The appropriateness of the vocabulary
- The ease of your delivery
- Your posture, gestures, the volume of your voice, and eye contact

Based on the comments from your classmate, rewrite any parts of your report that are confusing and take out any parts that are repetitive. When you have finished revising your report, write key phrases from it on a series of note cards. That way you can maintain eye contact with your audience, and your presentation will be much more interesting.

Present your report to a group of classmates or to the entire class. Remember to stand up straight, make eye contact with the audience, and speak at an appropriate volume and pace. After you finish, ask your audience whether they have any questions.

Listening Tips

- Have a mental conversation with the speaker to stay engaged in what he or she is saying. Ask yourself questions such as *Does this report make sense?* and *Is it informative?*
- Identify the key idea or ideas in the report.
- Do not interrupt the speaker. Ask questions or make comments after the speaker has finished the presentation.
- Make at least one positive comment before offering constructive criticism about the content or presentation of the report. Ask questions about things that genuinely interest you.

ACTIVITY B Prepare your oral history report, following the guidelines in this lesson. Remember that you want to inform your listeners, so make sure your research and ideas are solid.

SPEAKER'S CORNER

Practice and present your oral history report. Remember to speak clearly, particularly when you are explaining complicated concepts. At the end of your report, invite your audience to ask questions. Answer them if you can.

Prewriting and Drafting

Throughout this chapter you have discussed what makes a good research report. You have also discussed ways to take notes and document sources. It's now time to use what you have learned in this chapter to develop, organize, and write a research report.

Prewriting

Prewriting is the time to brainstorm, choose a topic, take notes, and do research. It is also the time to explore what you already know about a topic, because your knowledge will help guide your research. Once you decide on your topic and research it, you will have an opportunity to organize and plan your research report.

Choosing a Topic

Dillon, an eighth grader, is writing a research report for science class. She brainstormed a list of possible topics that interested her. To help get herself started, she browsed the encyclopedia in her school's library and researched possible  science topics on the Internet. After she finished browsing, she summarized her thoughts and listed them on a sheet of paper.

After reviewing her list of science-related topics, she chose to write about global warming. Dillon remembered watching a documentary film on the topic. From the film she learned that some scientists believe global warming does not exist. She disagreed with that view, so she decided the thesis of her report would be that global warming is harmful and that governments and businesses should do something about it.

Your Turn

Brainstorm a list of research topics. If you need help thinking of possible research topics, browse an encyclopedia or the Internet. Recall Activity A on page 491 and use your work to help narrow possible research topics.

Researching

Dillon knew that before she could make a plan for writing, she needed to research her topic to find important information. To help guide her research, she made a KWL chart to explore her topic. Next, she took her questions with her when she went to the library to do her research. As she gathered her sources, she jotted down her notes on cards.

Is global warming real?

Polar ice caps are melting at an increased rate.
Greater than 20% of polar ice caps have melted
since 1979.

Bowles <u>Global Climate Change</u>
New York: University Press, 1999, p. 64

Planning a Research Report

Dillon studied her note cards to decide how to plan her research report. She sorted her cards into separate piles that she thought would be good subtopics for her report. When she finished, she **Organization** had a good idea about how her report should be organized. Then Dillon wrote the following outline.

Global Warming

I. Introduction: What is global warming?

  A. Definition of global warming

  B. Relation to greenhouse effect

  C. Relation to ozone layer

II. What causes global warming?

  A. Natural variation in temperatures

  B. Emissions

    1. Fossil fuels

      a. Gasoline

      b. Coal

      c. Oil and natural gas

      d. Chlorofluorocarbons

    2. Deforestation

Your Turn

Make a KWL chart about your topic and then research your topic. Use the library's resources, such as the _Reader's Guide to Periodical Literature_ and other reference materials, to gather information. Write facts and information on note cards and then organize the cards into main ideas and subtopics. Write your outline on a sheet of paper.

Here are some points to keep in mind when you take notes.

- Take notes on the aspects of your topic that you will be writing about.
- Take notes on interesting ideas, strong opinions, and unique points of view. (Remember to give the author credit in your report.)
- When you find words and sentences that you want to quote directly, be sure to write them exactly as they appear in the source and enclose them within quotation marks.
- Use separate note cards for information from different sources.

STOP GLOBAL WARMING

Drafting

Drafting is Dillon's first chance to develop and organize her notes and outline into a written research report.

Using her prewriting notes, Dillon followed her outline to write the first draft of her report. The following are the first page and the conclusion of Dillon's research report.

The Threat of Global Warming

This report will examine the strengths of the arguments for and against the existence of global warming and the seriousness of the threat it will also examine who is making the arguments (and who they work for and which organizations they belong to) and examine the issue of preponderance of evidence versus absolute proof. If you live in a cold climat global warming might not seem like such a bad idea. Global warming is no joke. It is a real threat to our environment and it has already begun! What is global warming? It is an increase in the average temperature of the Earth's surface, caused mostly by an increase in greenhouse gases.

Experts agree that global warming is mostly caused by burning fossil fuels, such as gasoline, coal, fuel oil and natural gas (Teeter 47). Burning hydro-carbons makes two compounds, water and carbon dioxide or CO_2 and carbon dioxide is a real heat-trapping gas. If it did not trap heat, said Dan Yarlow, "life could not exist on earth because the sun's heat would bounce off the planet" (45). Yikes! That's really scary! This process is called the "green house effect" because carbon dioxide acts like a glass roof of green house, which traps the sun's heat inside.

In conclusion, its obvious that global warming is a growing problem. And that's too bad, because we just don't want to do anything about it. The solutions to global warming, however, will not be easy to put into place. Global warming may be a difficult problem, but the solutions are within reach.

Counterarguments

When you research your topic, you will sometimes find that certain researchers disagree with others. The work of some research may support your thesis, while the work of others does not. Points of view that run against your thesis are called counterarguments. To make your report stronger, be sure to include counterarguments when you present your research in the body of the report. Presenting counterarguments shows a reader that you have considered all points of view. Because you have done this, it makes your thesis sound more convincing.

How can I make my report stronger?

Your Turn

Follow your outline to write a first draft of your report. Be sure to note your sources properly and include a Works Cited page with your first draft.

Prewriting
Drafting
Content Editing
Revising
Copyediting
Proofreading
Publishing

Content Editing

Dillon was proud of the draft that she had written. By organizing her notes into an outline and planning her report, Dillon found writing a draft of the research report to be far less stressful.

Dillon gave her draft to Eileen, a classmate who had also learned how to take notes and use library reference materials. Because Eileen knew what a research report should include and leave out, Dillon thought Eileen would be able to read and edit her research report effectively.

When you content edit, you edit ideas of your draft for logic, order, and clarity. Eileen read Dillon's draft to see how well Dillon's ideas were expressed. In addition, Eileen read the report to make sure all the necessary information was included. Eileen used the Content Editor's Checklist to edit Dillon's draft.

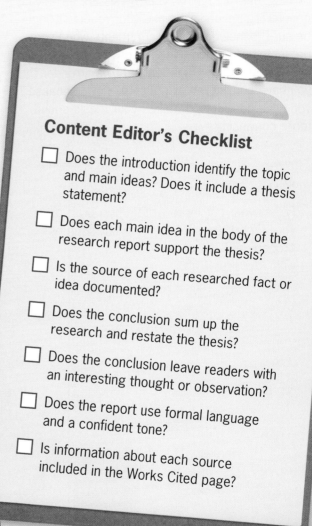

Content Editor's Checklist

- [ ] Does the introduction identify the topic and main ideas? Does it include a thesis statement?

- [ ] Does each main idea in the body of the research report support the thesis?

- [ ] Is the source of each researched fact or idea documented?

- [ ] Does the conclusion sum up the research and restate the thesis?

- [ ] Does the conclusion leave readers with an interesting thought or observation?

- [ ] Does the report use formal language and a confident tone?

- [ ] Is information about each source included in the Works Cited page?

Eileen enjoyed reading Dillon's report. She hadn't known very much about the topic, but the report changed that because it was well stocked with relevant information and expert opinions. Still, Eileen spotted areas that needed improvement. Here are Eileen's suggestions to Dillon for revising her research report.

- The first paragraph seems a little unclear to me. I think you should explain what your thesis is in the first or second sentence. I also had trouble understanding which main ideas you wanted to cover in the report.

- The conclusion doesn't really sum up the research. Maybe you should insert a sentence or two that covers some of the main ideas in the report.

- I think the conclusion should restate the observation that the CO_2 content seems to be approaching the limit of what's acceptable sooner than most experts thought. That was something that really caught my attention, and I think the reader should be left with that thought.

- Your tone seems to be confident, but in one  or two places, your tone is a little too informal and preachy. Your report is backed up by facts, which is enough to convince readers.

- The Works Cited page has all the sources that you document in the report.

Writer's Tip Make sure all necessary information is included and that it supports your thesis statement.

Prewriting

Drafting

Content Editing

Revising

Copyediting

Proofreading

Publishing

Your Turn

- Revise your draft, using the Content Editor's Checklist as a guide. If necessary, focus on specific parts of your report with corresponding questions in mind.
- Trade drafts with a partner. You and your partner should read each other's drafts and suggest changes.
- As discussed in previous Writer's Workshops, be sure to include positive comments and constructive criticism.

Revising

Dillon took Eileen's suggestions seriously and worked in those that she thought were most effective. Dillon knew that revision was the time to incorporate both Eileen's suggestions and her own changes. The following is Dillon's draft, which shows the revisions that she plans to make.

The Threat of Global Warming
(Problem inserted above "Threat")

This report will ~~examine the strengths of the arguments for and against the~~ argue that global warming is harmful and discuss what governments, individuals, and businesses can do to slow the affects of the problem. ~~existence of global warming and the seriousness of the threat it will also examine who is making the arguments (and who they work for and which organizations they belong to) and examine the issue of preponderance of evidence versus absolute proof.~~ If you live in a cold climat global warming might not seem like such a bad idea. But Global warming is no joke. ~~It is a real threat to our environment and it has already begun! What is global warming? It~~ Global warming is an increase in the average temperature of the Earth's surface, caused mostly by an increase in greenhouse gases.

Experts agree that global warming is mostly caused by burning fossil fuels, such as gasoline, coal, fuel oil and natural gas (Teeter 47). Burning hydro-carbons makes two compounds, water and carbon dioxide or CO_2 and carbon dioxide is a real heat-trapping gas. (Laslow 345) If it did not trap heat, said Dan Yarlow, "life could not exist on earth because the sun's heat would bounce off the planet" (45). ~~Yikes! That's really scary!~~ This process is called the "green house effect" because carbon dioxide acts like a glass roof of green house, which traps the sun's heat inside.

Prewriting

Drafting

Content Editing

Revising

Copyediting

Proofreading

Publishing

Yarlow's research about rising levels of CO_2 in the atmosphere makes this clear. In conclusion, its obvious that global warming is a growing problem. ~~And that's too bad, because we just don't want to do anything about it.~~ The solutions to global

They will require industrialized nations to significantly cut back their use of fossil fuels. The warming, however, will not be easy to put into place. Global warming may be a solutions will also mean that these nations must develop new technologies.

difficult problem, but the solutions are within reach.

Examine how Dillon revised her draft.

- Dillon reorganized the introductory paragraph **Word Choice** so that it made more sense. What did she add so that the reader would understand her argument more clearly?
- How did she finish the first paragraph?
- Dillon agreed that the conclusion needed to be more developed. How did she strengthen her conclusion?
- She also agreed with Eileen that an insightful observation could improve her conclusion. What fact did she repeat?
- Dillon agreed that her tone was too informal. How did she polish the tone of her report?
- She did notice that Eileen didn't check to see if all the facts were documented. Dillon quickly saw one sentence that needed documentation. Where did Dillon add her documentation?

Your Turn

Revise your draft, using the Content Editor's Checklist and your editing partner's suggestions. Reread your revised draft. What other ways can you improve your report?

Editor's Workshop

Copyediting and Proofreading

Copyediting

Dillon wanted to be sure that every sentence in her report was as smooth as it could be and that it used the most accurate words to support her main ideas. When Dillon copyedited her report, she read it for accuracy in word meaning, word choice, sentence structure, and overall logic.

She used the following Copyeditor's Checklist to edit her draft.

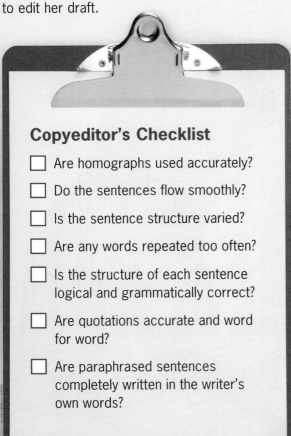

Copyeditor's Checklist

- [ ] Are homographs used accurately?
- [ ] Do the sentences flow smoothly?
- [ ] Is the sentence structure varied?
- [ ] Are any words repeated too often?
- [ ] Is the structure of each sentence logical and grammatically correct?
- [ ] Are quotations accurate and word for word?
- [ ] Are paraphrased sentences completely written in the writer's own words?

 Sentence Fluency Dillon read her essay aloud so that she could hear how it sounded.

She revised a run-on sentence in the second paragraph. Dillon also noticed that she confused *affect* with *effect,* so she corrected it.

Dillon replaced the word *real* in the second paragraph with *proven,* which was a more accurate word.

Dillon saw that she used the word *increase* too often. She read each sentence that used that word and consulted a thesaurus to see if a better word or phrase could be used. In one instance she found an alternative.

Your Turn

Reread your revised draft. Pay particular attention to the sound and meaning of each sentence and each word. Read your draft aloud at least once to make sure the sentences flow smoothly and the sentence length varies. Use the Copyeditor's Checklist to help you improve your draft.

Proofreading

Dillon now needed to have her draft proofread  to find any mistakes in spelling, capitalization, punctuation, and grammar. She also needed to have her report checked to make certain that no new errors had been introduced during the revising stage.

Dillon asked another classmate, Jacques, to proofread her draft. Because he hadn't read her report before, Dillon knew he would be able to read it with a fresh pair of eyes. That way Jacques was in a better position to catch any mistakes that Dillon and Eileen might have missed.

Jacques used the following Proofreader's Checklist to edit Dillon's draft.

Proofreader's Checklist

- ☐ Is the documentation format followed consistently? (For example, have book and periodical titles been underlined? Is the Works Cited page in alphabetical order?)

- ☐ Is each word spelled correctly?

- ☐ Are the sentences capitalized and punctuated correctly?

- ☐ Is the grammar accurate?

- ☐ Were any new errors introduced during the revision process?

Jacques checked each item on the checklist in order. He circled the errors he found. He also consulted a dictionary to check the spelling of any word he didn't know. Jacques found two punctuation mistakes and one spelling error. How many mistakes can you find?

Your Turn

Pair up with a classmate and proofread each other's research reports. Read the report carefully, at least one time for each item on the list, and look for that particular error. Recall the proofreading marks you discussed in Chapter 1 and use them when you proofread your classmate's report.

Writer's Tip Read your draft aloud at least once to make sure sentences flow smoothly and sentence length varies.

Prewriting
Drafting
Content Editing
Revising
Copyediting
Proofreading
Publishing

Publishing

Dillon edited and revised her report several times until she was
comfortable with it. She made a finished copy.

The Problem of Global Warming

If you live in a cold climate, global warming might not seem like such a bad
idea. However, global warming is no joke. Global warming is a rising in the average
temperature of the earth's surface caused primarily by an increase in greenhouse
gases. This report will argue that global warming is harmful and will discuss what
governments, individuals, and businesses can do to slow the effects of the problem.

Experts agree that global warming is mostly caused by burning fossil fuels, such
as gasoline, coal, fuel oil, and natural gas (Teeter 17). These fuels are also called
hydrocarbons because they are made up of carbon and hydrogen atoms. Burning
these hydrocarbons makes two compounds, water and carbon dioxide, or CO_2.
Carbon dioxide is a proven heat-trapping gas (Laslow 345). If it did not trap heat,
said Dan Yarlow, "life could not exist on earth because the sun's heat would bounce
off the planet" (45). This process is called the "greenhouse effect" because carbon
dioxide acts like a glass roof of a greenhouse, which traps the sun's heat inside.

In conclusion, it is obvious that global warming is a growing problem. Yarlow's
research about rising levels of CO_2 in the atmosphere makes this clear. The solutions
to global warming, however, will not be easy to put into place. They will require
industrialized nations to significantly cut back their use of fossil fuels. The solutions
will also mean that these nations must develop new technologies. Global warming
may be a difficult problem, but the solutions are within reach.

Works Cited

Laslow, Meredith. The Uncertain Future of Mother Earth. St. Louis, MO: American
    Science Press Inc., 2008.

Teeter, Jonas. "Our Burning Earth." NewsSource Magazine. 11 July 2007: 16–21.

Yarlow, Dan. Global Warming and the Greenhouse Effect. Eugene, OR: Arcadia Press,
    2009.

There are many ways you can publish your report to make it accessible for others.

 Submit your report to a magazine or newspaper that publishes student work. Add relevant photos or illustrations that support your topic.

 With permission from your teacher, stage a formal debate between opposing sides of the same issue. Research rules of debate beforehand with help from an adult or online.

 Make a documentary film of your research report. Film footage that relates to your report and present it to the class.

 Start an online discussion about your topic on the class blog. See what other people think about your issue.

Whenever you publish your work, your goal is to share your thoughts and experiences with other people.

Your Turn

- Carefully make revisions to your report and publish it. If you write your report by Presentation hand, use your best handwriting and copy the corrections accurately. If you type your report on a computer, don't forget to run the spell-checker before printing it.

- When you have written or printed your report, read it again to make sure no new errors were introduced.

- Collect the class's research reports and create a classroom encyclopedia. Organize the reports alphabetically according to the subject of the report. Bind them into a folder and use dividers to separate the reports.

Grammar in Action

Diagram the last sentence in the conclusion on p. 524.

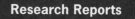

Common Proofreading Marks

Use these proofreading marks to mark changes when you proofread. Remember to use a colored pencil to make your changes.

Symbol	Meaning	Example
¶	begin new paragraph	over. ¶Begin a new
‿	close up space	close u p space
∧	insert	students ^{should} think
ℓ	delete, omit	that the ~~the~~ book
/	lowercase letter	/Mathematics
∼	letters are reversed	letters are reve(sr)ed
≡	capitalize	washington
⌄ ⌄	quotation	ˇI am, I said.ˇ
⊙	add period	Marta drank tea⊙

Not Too Scary

or equinaphobia
I have no idea where my fear of horses came from. Fear of horses is called equinophobia. Maybe a horse thought I was a bucket of oats when I was a baby! Just kidding. Since I live in the suburbs of Philadelphia, this fear wasn't really a big problem, at least not during the school year, but in the summer I usuall~~...~~... really ....cle Henry's farm, and that's when my equinophobi... ...about my problem. I couldn't go on trail ...n't go anywhere

Grammar and Mechanics Handbook

Grammar

Adjectives

An adjective points out or describes a noun.

> **That** dog is **hungry**.

Adjective Clauses

An adjective clause is a dependent clause used as an adjective. See CLAUSES.

Adjective Phrases

An infinitive phrase can be used as an adjective. See INFINITIVES.

A participial phrase can be used as an adjective. See PARTICIPLES.

A prepositional phrase can be used as an adjective. See PREPOSITIONS.

Articles

An article points out a noun. See ARTICLES.

Common Adjectives

A common adjective expresses an ordinary quality of a noun or a pronoun: *tall* ship, *majestic* mountains.

Comparison of Adjectives

Most adjectives have three degrees of comparison: positive, comparative, and superlative.

The positive degree of an adjective shows a quality of a noun or a pronoun.

> My grandmother is a **tall** woman.
> The dancer is **famous**.
> LaTonya is a **careful** worker.

The comparative degree is used to compare two items or two sets of items. This form is often followed by *than*.

> My grandfather is **taller** than my grandmother.
> The singer is **more famous** than the actor.
> James is a **less careful** worker than LaTonya.

The superlative degree is used to compare three or more items or sets of items.

> My uncle Jack is the **tallest** member of the family.
> The singer is the **most famous** person here.
> Gloria is the **least careful** worker of them all.

The adjectives *few, fewer,* and *fewest* are used to compare concrete nouns. Note that the nouns are plural in form.

> Lorna made **few** free throws.
> Gail made **fewer** free throws than Lorna.
> Mary Pat made the **fewest** free throws of all.

The adjectives *little, less,* and *least* are used to compare abstract nouns. Note that the nouns are singular in form.

> I have **little** time to practice free throws.
> My brother has **less** time to practice than I do.
> Of us all, my sister has the **least** time to practice.

Comparison with *as . . . as, so . . . as,* and *equally*

Comparisons with *as . . . as* may be made in positive or negative sentences. Comparisons with *so . . . as* may be made only in negative sentences. Never use *as* with *equally* in a comparison.

> The brown horse is **as swift as** the white horse.
> The brown horse is not **as swift as** the black horse.
> The brown horse is not **so swift as** the black horse.
> The two gray horses are **equally swift**.

Demonstrative Adjectives

A demonstrative adjective points out a definite person, place, thing, or idea. The demonstrative adjectives are *this, that, these,* and *those. This* and *that* are singular; *these* and *those* are plural. *This* and *these* refer to things or people that are near; *that* and *those* refer to things or people that are farther away.

> **This** dog is very friendly. (singular and near)
> **Those** cats are more skittish. (plural and far)

Descriptive Adjectives

A descriptive adjective gives information about a noun or pronoun. It tells about age, size, shape, color, origin, or another quality.

> I have a **sweet**, **little**, **gray**, **Persian** kitten.

Indefinite Adjectives

An indefinite adjective refers to all or any of a group of people, places, or things. Some of the most common indefinite adjectives are *all, another, any, both, each, either, every, few, many, more, most, neither, no, one, other, several,* and *some.* Note that *another, each, every, either, neither, no, one,* and *other* are always singular, and the others are plural.

> **Each** player has a glove.
> **Several** players have bats.

Interrogative Adjectives

An interrogative adjective is used in asking a question. The interrogative adjectives are *what, which,* and *whose.*

Which is usually used to ask about one or more of a specific set of people or things. *What* is used to ask about people or things but is not limited to a specific group or set. *Whose* asks about possession.

> **Which** position do you play?
> **What** time is the game?
> **Whose** equipment will you borrow?

Numerical Adjectives

A numerical adjective tells an exact number: *twenty-five children, eighth grade.*

Participial Adjectives

A participle is a verb form that is used as an adjective. A participial adjective stands alone before or after the word it modifies. See PARTICIPLES.

Position of Adjectives

Most adjectives go before the words they describe.

> **Mexican** pottery comes in many shapes.

Adjectives may also directly follow nouns.

> The vase, **ancient** and **cracked**, was found nearby.

An adjective can follow a linking verb (as a subject complement), or it can follow a direct object (as an object complement).

> The archaeologist was **excited**.
> She considered the vase **extraordinary**.

Possessive Adjectives

A possessive adjective shows possession or ownership. Possessive adjectives have antecedents. A possessive adjective must agree with its antecedent in person, number, and gender.

> John has a skateboard. **His** skateboard is silver.
> Jo and Luis have bikes. **Their** bikes are new.

Possessive adjectives change form depending on person and number. Third person singular possessive adjectives change form depending on gender.

	Singular	**Plural**
First Person	my	our
Second Person	your	your
Third Person	his, her, its	their

Proper Adjectives

A proper adjective is formed from a proper noun: *Brazilian* rain forest, *Chinese* emperors.

Subject Complements

An adjective may be used as a subject complement. See SUBJECT COMPLEMENTS.

Adverbs

An adverb is a word that modifies a verb, an adjective, or another adverb. Adverbs indicate *time, place, manner, degree, affirmation,* or *negation*.

> **Sometimes** my family goes to the zoo. (time)
> We like to watch the animals **there**. (place)
> We stroll **slowly** along the paths. (manner)
> Watching the animals can be **quite** entertaining. (degree)
> We'll **undoubtedly** go to the zoo next week. (affirmation)
> We **never** miss an opportunity to see the animals. (negation)

Adverb Clauses

A dependent clause can be used as an adverb. See CLAUSES.

Adverb Phrases

A prepositional phrase can be used as an adverb. See PREPOSITIONS.

Adverbial Nouns

An adverbial noun is a noun that acts as an adverb. Adverbial nouns usually express *time, distance, measure, value,* or *direction.*

> The trip took a few **hours**. (time)
> We traveled about a hundred **miles**. (distance)
> The temperature was about 70 **degrees**. (measure)
> The bus fare was 30 **dollars**. (value)
> It was the farthest **north** I've ever been. (direction)

Comparison of Adverbs

Most adverbs have three degrees of comparison: positive, comparative, and superlative.

> Grace works **carefully**.
> Zach works **less carefully** than Grace.
> Meagen works **most carefully** of anyone in class.
>
> Wiley ate **rapidly**.
> David ate **less rapidly** than Wiley.
> Matt ate **least rapidly** of all.
>
> Carly walks **fast**.
> Maggie walks **faster** than Carly.
> Ryoko walks **fastest** of us all.

Comparison with *as . . . as, so . . . as,* and *equally*

Comparisons with *as . . . as* may be made in positive or negative sentences. Comparisons with *so . . . as* may be made only in negative sentences. Never use *as* with *equally* in a comparison.

> Isabelle sings **as well as** Lupe.
> She does not sing **as well as** Jorge.
> She does not sing **so well as** Jorge.
> Isabelle and Lupe sing **equally well**.

Conjunctive Adverbs

A conjunctive adverb connects independent clauses. A semicolon is used before a conjunctive adverb, and a comma is used after it. Common conjunctive adverbs include *also, besides, consequently, finally, furthermore, hence, however, indeed, instead, later, likewise, moreover, nevertheless, nonetheless, otherwise, still, therefore,* and *thus.*

> Ryoko walked fastest; **therefore**, he arrived first.

Interrogative Adverbs

An interrogative adverb is used to ask a question. The interrogative adverbs are *how, when, where,* and *why.*

> **When** did Ryoko arrive?

Antecedents

The noun to which a pronoun or a possessive adjective refers is its antecedent. A pronoun or a possessive adjective must agree with its antecedent in person and number. Third person singular personal, possessive, intensive, and reflexive pronouns and possessive adjectives must also agree in gender. See GENDER, NUMBER, PERSON.

Appositives

An appositive is a word (or words) that follows a noun and helps identify it or adds more information about it. An appositive names the same person, place, thing, or idea as the noun it explains. An appositive phrase is an appositive and its modifiers.

An appositive is restrictive if it is necessary to understand the sentence. It is nonrestrictive if it is not necessary. A nonrestrictive appositive is set off by commas.

> The Italian sailor **John Cabot** explored Canada.
> Magellan, **a Spanish navigator**, sailed around the world.

Articles

An article points out a noun. *The* is the definite article. It refers to a specific item or specific items in a group. *The* may be used with either singular or plural concrete nouns and with abstract nouns.

> We went to **the** park yesterday.
> **The** parks in our area are very well kept.
> **The** grass is always mowed.

A and *an* are the indefinite articles. Each is used to refer to a single member of a general group. *A* and *an* are used only with singular concrete nouns. The article *an* is used before a vowel sound. The article *a* is used before a consonant sound.

> I ate **a** sandwich and **an** apple.

Clauses

A clause is a group of words that has a subject and a predicate. An independent clause expresses a complete thought and can stand alone as a sentence. A dependent clause does not express a complete thought and cannot stand alone as a sentence.

Adjective Clauses

A dependent clause can describe a noun or a pronoun. An adjective clause usually begins with a relative pronoun *(who, whom, whose, which, that)* or a subordinate conjunction *(when, where)*. These words connect the dependent clause to the noun it modifies.

> I read a book **that was fascinating**.
> I'll never forget the place **where we met**.

A restrictive adjective clause is necessary to the meaning of the sentence. A nonrestrictive adjective clause is not necessary to the meaning. Nonrestrictive clauses are set off by commas. As a general rule, the relative pronoun *that* is used in restrictive clauses and *which* in nonrestrictive clauses.

> Chicago, **which has many tourist attractions**, is located on Lake Michigan.
> The attraction **that we liked most** was Navy Pier.

Adverb Clauses

A dependent clause can describe or give information about a verb, an adjective, or other adverb. An adverb clause can tell *where, when, why, in what way, to what extent (degree)*, or *under what condition*. An adverb clause begins with a subordinate conjunction.

> We'll go **wherever you'd like**.
> We can leave **after you finish your homework**.
> **Because it's late**, we'll take a taxi.

Noun Clauses

Dependent clauses can be used as nouns. These clauses can function as subjects, complements, appositives, direct objects, indirect objects, and objects of prepositions. Most noun clauses begin with one of these introductory words: *that, who, whom, whoever, whomever, how, why, when, whether, what, where*, and *whatever*.

> **That rabbits make good pets** was a surprise to me. (subject)
> The fact is **that chinchillas make good pets too**. (subject complement)

The idea **that I could like a ferret** seems strange. (appositive)
My parents will buy me **whatever I choose**. (direct object)
I am interested in **how guinea pigs are raised**. (object of preposition)

Conjunctions

A conjunction is a word used to join two words or groups of words in a sentence.

Coordinating Conjunctions

A coordinating conjunction joins words or groups of words that are similar. The coordinating conjunctions are *and, but, nor, or, so,* and *yet.*

The boys **and** girls ran into the park. (nouns)
They played on the swings **or** in the sandbox. (prepositional phrases)
They sailed boats, **but** they didn't go swimming. (independent clauses)

Correlative Conjunctions

Correlative conjunctions are used in pairs to connect words or groups of words that have equal importance in a sentence. The most common correlative conjunctions are *both . . . and, either . . . or, neither . . . nor, not only . . . but also,* and *whether . . . or.*

Each correlative conjunction appears immediately in front of one of the words or groups of words that are connected. In sentences with *neither . . . nor,* the verb agrees with the subject closest to it.

Both my mother **and** my father like dogs.
Neither my brothers **nor** my sister likes cats.

Subordinate Conjunctions

A subordinate conjunction is used to join a dependent and an independent clause. Common subordinate conjunctions include *after, although, as, as if, as long as, because, before, even though, if, in order that, since, so that, than, though, unless, until, when, whenever, where, wherever,* and *while.*

Unless you help me, I won't finish this today.
I can't help you **until** I've completed my own project.

Direct Objects

The direct object of a sentence answers the question *whom* or *what* after the verb. A noun or an object pronoun can be used as a direct object.

Consuela made **cookies**.
The children ate **them**.

Gender

Third person singular personal, possessive, intensive, and reflexive pronouns and possessive adjectives change form depending on gender—whether the antecedent is masculine *(he, him, his, himself)*, feminine *(she, her, hers, herself)*, or neuter *(it, its, itself)*.

Gerunds

A gerund is a verb form ending in *ing* that is used as a noun. A gerund can be used in a sentence as a subject, an object, a subject complement, or an appositive.

Reading is his favorite pastime. (subject)
People from many cultures enjoy **dancing**. (direct object)
My dad likes to relax by **cooking**. (object of a preposition)
My favorite hobby is **skateboarding**. (subject complement)
Her hobby, **hiking**, requires little equipment. (appositive)

A gerund phrase consists of a gerund, its object or complement, and any descriptive words or phrases. The entire phrase acts as a noun.

Reading mysteries is a relaxing form of recreation. (subject)
Linda's hobby is **riding her bike**. (subject complement)
People around the world enjoy **watching fireworks**. (direct object)
Americans celebrate the Fourth of July by **attending firework shows**.
   (object of a preposition)
His job, **creating fireworks displays**, can be very dangerous.
   (appositive)

Indirect Objects

An indirect object tells *to whom* or *for whom*, or *to what* or *for what*, an action is done. A noun or an object pronoun can be used as an indirect object

I gave **Sven** a present.
I gave **him** a birthday card too.

Infinitives

An infinitive is a verb form, usually preceded by *to,* that is used as a noun, an adjective, or an adverb.

To study is your present job. (noun)
I have a history report **to do**. (adjective)
I went **to study** in the library. (adverb)

An infinitive phrase consists of an infinitive, its object or complement, and any descriptive words or phrases.

To finish the science report was my goal. (noun)
I made a decision **to write about bears**. (adjective)
I arrived too late **to finish it today**. (adverb)

Hidden Infinitives

A hidden infinitive is an infinitive without *to.* Hidden infinitives occur after verbs of perception such as *hear, see, know,* and *feel* and after verbs such as *let, make, dare, need,* and *help.*

I heard the birds **sing** this morning.
I'll help **build** a birdhouse.

The word *to* is also omitted after the prepositions *but* and *except* and the conjunction *than.*

I'll do anything but **mow** the lawn.
I'd rather help out than **do** nothing.

Split Infinitives

An adverb placed between *to* and the verb results in a split infinitive. Good writers try to avoid split infinitives.

Subjects of Infinitives

An infinitive used as a direct object can have a subject. The subject tells the doer of the infinitive. If the subject is a pronoun, it is always in the object form.

> We wanted **her** to clean the garage.

Interjections

An interjection is a word or phrase that expresses a strong or sudden emotion, such as happiness, delight, anger, disgust, surprise, impatience, pain, or wonder.

> **Ouch!** I stubbed my toe.
> **Wow**, that's amazing!

Mood

Mood shows the manner in which the action or state of being of a verb is expressed.

Indicative Mood

The indicative mood is used to state a fact or ask a question. The simple tenses, the progressive tenses, and the perfect tenses are all part of the indicative mood.

> I **bought** a new cell phone.
> **Have** you ever **sent** pictures with a cell phone?
> The pictures **are** amazing!

Imperative Mood

The imperative mood is used to express a command or a request. The imperative mood uses the base form of a verb. The subject of an imperative sentence is usually understood to be the second person pronoun, *you.*

> Follow the directions carefully.
> Watch out!

A command can be given in the first person by using *let's* before the base form of a verb.

> Let's go.

Emphatic Mood

The emphatic mood gives special force to a simple present or past tense verb. To make an emphatic mood, use *do, does,* or *did* before the base form of the verb.

> I **do like** to use cell phones.
> I **did use** my cell phone last night.

Subjunctive Mood

The subjunctive mood is used to express a wish or a desire; to express a command, a recommendation, or a necessity after *that;* or to express something that is contrary to fact.

The past tense of a verb is used to state present wishes or desires or contrary-to-fact conditions. *Were* is used instead of *was,* and *would* is used instead of *will.*

> I wish you **were** here. (a wish or desire)
> If we **had** enough money, we **would** go to the movies.
> (a contrary-to-fact condition)

The base form of a verb is used in a clause after *that.*

> The coach insisted that Laura **be** on time. (command after *that*)
> It's imperative that she **call** him tonight. (necessity after *that*)

Nouns

A noun is a name word. A singular noun names one person, place, thing, or idea: *girl, park, ball, memory.* A plural noun names more than one person, place, thing, or idea: *girls, parks, balls, memories.*

Abstract Nouns

An abstract noun names something that cannot be seen or touched. It expresses a quality or a condition: *morality, sadness, idea, duration.*

Appositives

An appositive is a word (or words) that follows a noun and helps identify it or adds more information about it. See APPOSITIVES.

Collective Nouns

A collective noun names a group of people, animals, or things considered as one: *team, herd, bunch.*

Common Nouns

A common noun names any one of a class of people, places, or things: *reader, province, star.*

Concrete Nouns

A concrete noun names something that can be seen or touched: *table, hammer, artist, Ohio River.*

Gerunds

A gerund is a verb form ending in *ing* that is used as a noun. A gerund or a gerund phrase can be a subject, an object, a subject complement, or an appositive. See GERUNDS.

Infinitives Used as Nouns

An infinitive is a verb form, usually preceded by *to.* An infinitive or infinitive phrase used as a noun can be a subject, a subject complement, an object, or an appositive. See INFINITIVES.

Noun Clauses

A dependent clause can be used as a noun. See CLAUSES.

Noun Phrases

A gerund phrase can be used as a noun. See GERUNDS.

A prepositional phrase can be used as a noun. See PREPOSITIONS.

Possessive Nouns

A possessive noun expresses possession or ownership.

To form the singular possessive, add -*'s* to the singular form of the noun.

| student | student**'s** | Heather | Heather**'s** |

To form the possessive of a plural noun ending in *s,* add the apostrophe only. If the plural form of a noun does not end in *s,* add -*'s.*

| cowboys | cowboys**'** | children | children**'s** |

The singular possessive of a proper name ending in *s* is usually formed by adding -*'s.*

| James | James**'s** | Mrs. Williams | Mrs. Williams**'s** |

The plural possessive of a proper name is formed by adding an apostrophe to the plural of the name.

Mr. and Mrs. Adams   the Adamses' children

The possessive of compound nouns is formed by adding *-'s* to the end of the term.

commander in chief   commander in chief**'s**
brothers-in-law   brothers-in-law**'s**

Separate possession occurs when two or more people own things independently of one another. To show separate possession, use *-'s* after each noun.

Diane**'s** and Peter**'s** murals are colorful.

Joint possession occurs when two or more people own something together. To show joint possession, use *-'s* after the last noun only.

Marta and Ryan**'s** mural is colorful.

Proper Nouns

A proper noun names a particular person, place, or thing: *Meryl Streep, Hollywood, Academy Award.*

Number

The number of a noun or pronoun indicates whether it refers to one person, place, thing, or idea (singular) or more than one person, place, thing, or idea (plural).

Object Complements

An object complement follows the direct object of a sentence. A noun used as an object complement follows the direct object and renames it. An adjective used as an object complement follows the direct object and describes it.

We elected Yoko **president**.
We found her leadership **inspiring**.

Participles

A participle is a verb form that is used as an adjective. A present participle always ends in *ing*. A past participle generally ends in *ed*.

Participial Adjectives

A participial adjective stands alone before or after the word it modifies.

The **sobbing** child clung to her mother.
The child, **sobbing**, clung to her mother.

A participle has voice and tense. The present participle shows a relationship between the time of the action of the participle and of the main verb. Past and perfect forms show action that was completed at some time before the action indicated by the main verb.

The project **being started** now is supposed to end today.
(present passive)
The project **started** yesterday is important. (past passive)
Their group, **having started** late, rushed to finish.
(present perfect active)
Having been delayed twice, the project is behind schedule.
(present perfect passive)

A participle that is essential to the meaning of a sentence is restrictive and is not set off by commas. A participle that is not essential to the meaning of the sentence is nonrestrictive and is set off by commas.

The project **started on Monday** ran into terrible snags.
The other project, **started a day later**, finished first.

Dangling Participles

A dangling participle is a participial phrase that does not modify a noun or pronoun. Dangling participles should be corrected.

Working hard, the doghouse was soon finished. (incorrect)
Working hard, the girls soon finished the doghouse. (correct)

Participial Phrases

A participial phrase consists of the participle and an object or a complement and any descriptive words or phrases. A participial phrase can come before or after the word it modifies.

Kissing the child gently, the mother tried to soothe him.
The child, **sobbing loudly**, refused to quiet down.

Person

Personal, possessive, intensive, and reflexive pronouns and possessive adjectives change form according to person—whether the antecedent is the person speaking (first person), being spoken to (second person), or being spoken about (third person).

Phrases

A phrase is a group of words that is used as a single part of speech.

Gerund Phrases

A gerund phrase consists of a gerund, its object or complement, and any descriptive words or phrases. See GERUNDS.

Infinitive Phrases

An infinitive phrase consists of an infinitive, its object or complement, and any descriptive words or phrases. See INFINITIVES.

Participial Phrases

A participial phrase consists of the participle, its object or complement, and any descriptive words or phrases. See PARTICIPLES.

Prepositional Phrases

A prepositional phrase is made up of a preposition, the object of the preposition, and any modifiers of the object. See PREPOSITIONS.

Verb Phrases

A verb phrase is two or more verbs that work together as a unit. A verb phrase may have one or more auxiliary verbs and a main verb.

> The boy **is studying**.
> He **has been studying** for an hour.

Predicates

The predicate of a sentence names an action or a state of being.

> The horses **jumped**.
> They **were** beautiful.

Complete Predicates

The complete predicate is the verb with all its modifiers and objects or complements.

The horses **jumped all the hurdles well**.

Compound Predicates

A compound predicate contains more than one verb joined by a coordinating conjunction.

The horses **ran swiftly and jumped** over the fence.

Simple Predicates

The simple predicate is the verb or verb phrase.

The horses **have been running** for a long time.

Prepositions

A preposition is a word that shows the relationship between a noun or pronoun (the object of the preposition) and some other word in a sentence.

Prepositional Phrases

A prepositional phrase is made up of a preposition, the object of the preposition, and any modifiers of the object. A prepositional phrase may be used as an adjective, an adverb, or a noun.

She was the winner **of the game**. (adjective)
She threw her hat **into the air**. (adverb)
On the podium is where she stood. (noun)

Pronouns

A pronoun is a word used in place of a noun. The noun to which a pronoun refers is its antecedent. A pronoun must agree with its antecedent in person and number. Third person personal, possessive, intensive, and reflexive pronouns must also agree in gender. See GENDER, NUMBER, PERSON.

Demonstrative Pronouns

A demonstrative pronoun points out a particular person, place, or thing. The demonstrative pronouns are *this, that, these,* and *those. This* and *that* are singular; *these* and *those* are plural. *This* and *these* point out things that are near; *that* and *those* point out things that are farther away.

> **This** is my bike. (singular and near)
> **Those** are my skates. (plural and far)

Indefinite Pronouns

An indefinite pronoun refers to any or all of a group of people, places, or things. Indefinite pronouns can be used as subjects or objects.

> **Many** had heard about the strange old house.
> The loud noises were heard by **everyone**.

Most indefinite pronouns are singular, but some are plural. Singular indefinite pronouns include *another, anybody, anyone, anything, each, either, everybody, everyone, everything, much, neither, nobody, no one, nothing, one, other, somebody, someone,* and *something.* Plural indefinite pronouns include *both, few, many, others,* and *several.*

> **Everyone** is busy.
> **Nobody** wants to make a mistake.
> **Several** are drawing posters.
> **Others** want to use the computer.

The indefinite pronouns *all, any, more, most, none,* and *some* can be singular or plural, depending on how each is used in a sentence. These pronouns are singular and take a singular verb when they are followed by a phrase with a singular noun or an abstract noun. They are plural and take a plural verb when they are followed by a phrase with a plural noun.

> **Most** of the work was completed.
> **Most** of the projects were completed.

The indefinite pronouns *no one, nobody, none,* and *nothing* are negative words. They should never be used in sentences with other negative words such as *no, not,* or *never.*

Intensive Pronouns

Intensive pronouns end in *self* or *selves*. An intensive pronoun emphasizes a preceding noun or pronoun. It must agree with its antecedent in person, number, and gender.

> My sister paid for the car **herself**.
> I **myself** can't afford to buy a car.

Intensive pronouns change form depending on person and number. Third person singular intensive pronouns change form depending on gender.

	Singular	**Plural**
First Person	myself	ourselves
Second Person	yourself	yourselves
Third Person	himself	themselves
	herself	
	itself	

Interrogative Pronouns

An interrogative pronoun is used to ask a question. The interrogative pronouns are *who, whom, whose, which,* and *what.*

Who refers to people. It is often the subject of a question. *Whom* also refers to people. It is the object of a verb or a preposition.

> **Who** is the captain of the hockey team?
> **Whom** did he meet at the rink?
> To **whom** will they sell their old skates?

Whose is used to ask about possession. *Which* is used when asking about a group or class. *What* is used for asking about things or seeking information.

> **Whose** are those skates?
> **Which** of the teams will be the toughest opponent?
> **What** did you buy at the refreshment counter?
> **What** is the date of the first game?

Object Pronouns

An object pronoun can be used as a direct or an indirect object of a verb or as the object of a preposition. The object pronouns are *me, you, him, her, it, us,* and *them.*

> Tom met **her** at the video store. (direct object)
> Gina wrote **him** an e-mail. (indirect object)
> Martha received messages from **them**. (object of a preposition)

Personal Pronouns

Personal pronouns change form depending on person and number. Third person singular pronouns change form to reflect gender.

	Singular	**Plural**
First Person	I, me	we, us
Second Person	you	you
Third Person	he, she, it, him, her	they, them

Personal pronouns also change form depending on whether they are used as subjects *(I, you, he, she, it, we, they)* or objects *(me, you, him, her, it, us, them)*.

Possessive Pronouns

A possessive pronoun shows possession or ownership. It takes the place of a possessive noun. Possessive pronouns must agree with their antecedents in person, number, and gender.

> The green bike is **mine**.
> Jill left **hers** near the fence.
> Joe, where is **yours**?

Possessive pronouns change form depending on person and number. Third person singular possessive pronouns change form to reflect gender.

	Singular	**Plural**
First Person	mine	ours
Second Person	yours	yours
Third Person	his, hers, its	theirs

Reflexive Pronouns

Reflexive pronouns end in *self* or *selves*. A reflexive pronoun can be the direct or indirect object of a verb or the object of a preposition. A reflexive pronoun generally refers to the subject of the sentence. Reflexive pronouns must agree with their antecedents in person, number, and gender.

> I consider **myself** lucky to have won. (direct object)
> He gave **himself** a pat on the back. (indirect object)
> They did it by **themselves**. (object of a preposition)

Reflexive pronouns change form depending on person and number. Third person singular reflexive pronouns change form depending on gender.

	Singular	Plural
First Person	myself	ourselves
Second Person	yourself	yourselves
Third Person	himself	themselves
	herself	
	itself	

Relative Pronouns

A relative pronoun connects an adjective clause to the noun it modifies. The relative pronouns are *who, whom, whose, which,* and *that.*

Who and *whom* refer to people. *Who* is used as the subject of an adjective clause. *Whom* is used as the object of an adjective clause.

> George Washington, **who** was a famous general, was the first president of the United States.
> George Washington, **whom** we call the father of our country, started out as a surveyor.

Which refers to animals, places, or things, *That* refers to people, animals, places, or things. *Whose* often refers to people but can also refer to animals, places, or things.

> Mount Vernon, **which** was Washington's home, is in Virginia.
> It's a place **that** many tourists visit.
> They learn about Washington, **whose** possessions are displayed in the house.

Subject Pronouns

A subject pronoun can be used as the subject or the subject complement in a sentence. The subject pronouns are *I, you, he, she, it, we,* and *they.*

> **We** went to the mall on Saturday. (subject)
> The clerk we talked to was **she**. (subject complement)

Sentences

A sentence is a group of words that expresses a complete thought.

Complex Sentences

A complex sentence has one independent clause and at least one dependent clause, which may function as a noun, an adjective, or an adverb.

> He claimed that he was the fastest runner.
> The race that would decide the championship began at noon.
> Because he tripped and fell, he lost the race.

Compound Sentences

A compound sentence contains two or more independent clauses.

> The boys ran a race, and Hassan won.
> Chris was leading at the halfway mark, but he tripped and fell.
> Will they run the race again, or will Hassan get the prize?

Declarative Sentences

A declarative sentence makes a statement. It ends with a period.

> I have a new cell phone.

Exclamatory Sentences

An exclamatory sentence expresses a strong emotion. It ends with an exclamation point.

> It's so cool!

Imperative Sentences

An imperative sentence gives a command. It usually ends with a period but may end with an exclamation point. In imperative sentences the subject *you* is understood.

> Call me tomorrow.

Interrogative Sentences

An interrogative sentence asks a question. It ends with a question mark.

> Will you take my picture?

Inverted Order in Sentences

A sentence is in inverted order when the main verb or an auxiliary verb comes before the subject.

Around the chimney curled the wispy smoke.
When did you light the fireplace?
There were many birds atop the chimney.

Natural Order in Sentences

A sentence is in natural order when the verb follows the subject.

The wispy smoke curled around the chimney.

Simple Sentences

A simple sentence is one independent clause. It has a subject and a predicate, either or both of which may be compound.

Milwaukee is the largest city in Wisconsin.
Milwaukee and Green Bay have professional sports teams.
Many people in Wisconsin fish and boat in the summer.

Subject Complements

A subject complement follows a linking verb such as the forms of *be*. A noun or pronoun used as a subject complement renames the subject of the sentence; it refers to the same person, place, thing, or idea. An adjective used as a subject complement describes the subject of the sentence.

My uncle is a **police officer**.
The officer who won the medal was **he**.
His job can be **dangerous**.

Subjects

The subject names the person, place, or thing a sentence is about.

Complete Subjects

The complete subject is the simple subject plus all the words that describe it.

The tiny lamb with the black face trotted across the field.

Compound Subjects

A compound subject contains more than one noun or pronoun joined by a coordinating conjunction.

The **lamb** and its **mother** trotted across the field.

Simple Subjects

The simple subject is the noun or pronoun that a sentence is about.

The **lamb** trotted across the field.

Tenses

The tense of a verb expresses the time of the action or state of being.

Perfect Tenses

Perfect tenses consist of a form of the auxiliary verb *have* and the past participle of the main verb. The present perfect tense tells about an action that took place at an indefinite time in the past or that started in the past and continued into the present. The past perfect tense tells about an action that was completed before another action was begun or completed. The future perfect tense tells about an action that will be completed before a specific time in the future.

Present Perfect Active	He **has finished** his homework.
Past Perfect Active	He **had finished** it before dinner.
Future Perfect Active	He **will have finished** dinner by six o'clock.

The passive voice of perfect tenses is formed by inserting *been* between the auxiliary of a form of *have* and the main verb.

Present Perfect Passive	The car **has been washed**.
Past Perfect Passive	The car **had been washed** before it started to rain.
Future Perfect Passive	**The car will have been washed** by the time Dad gets home.

Progressive Tenses

Progressive tense consist of a form of the auxiliary verb *be* and the present participle of the main verb. These tenses show ongoing action.

Present Progressive	I **am reading** my math book now.
Past Progressive	I **was reading** my math book when the phone rang.
Future Progressive	I **will be reading** my math book until dinner time.

Simple Tenses

The simple present tense indicates an action that is repeated or always true. The simple past and future tenses indicate action in the past or in the future.

Simple Present	I *eat* a lot of fruit.
Simple Past	I *ate* some melon for lunch today.
Simple Future	I *am going to eat* some cherries as a snack.
	I *will eat* them after school.

Verbals

Verbals are words made from verbs. There are three kinds of verbals: participles, gerunds, and infinitives.

A participle is a verb form that is used as an adjective. A gerund is a verb form ending in *ing* that is used as a noun. An infinitive is a verb phrase, usually preceded by *to*, that is used as a noun, an adjective, or an adverb. See GERUNDS, INFINITIVES, PARTICIPLES.

The **frightened** cat ran and hid under the porch. (participle)
Getting the dog into the house was my priority. (gerund)
My hope is **to establish** a level of tolerance between Coco and Buster. (infinitive)

Verbs

A verb shows action or state of being. See MOOD, TENSES, VOICE.

Lupe **opened** her mailbox. (action)
She **was** excited to find an e-mail from Carla. (state of being)

Auxiliary Verbs

An auxiliary verb is a verb that combines with a main verb to form a verb phrase. Auxiliary verbs help show voice, mood, and tense. Some common auxiliary verbs are the forms of *be, have,* and *did.* Other auxiliary verbs are *can, could, may, might, should,* and *will.*

Intransitive Verbs

An intransitive verb does not have a receiver of its action. It does not have a direct object.

Danny **relaxed** under the big oak tree.

Some verbs can be transitive or intransitive, depending on their use in the sentence.

Danny **plays** baseball in the summer. (transitive)
He usually **plays** in Gresham Park. (intransitive)

Irregular Verbs

The past and past participle of irregular verbs are not formed by adding -*d* or -*ed*.

Present	Past	Past Participle
sing	sang	sung
write	wrote	written
put	put	put

Linking Verbs

A linking verb joins a subject with a subject complement (a noun, a pronoun, or an adjective). The subject complement renames or describes the subject.

Ms. Roberts **became** a newspaper reporter.
She **feels** proud of her work.
The author of that article **is** she.

Common linking verbs are *be, appear, become, feel, grow, look, remain, seem, smell, sound, stay, taste,* and *turn*. Some of these verbs can be transitive, intransitive, or linking verbs.

He **felt** the heat of the sun on his back. (transitive verb)
She **felt** strongly about winning the game. (intransitive)
Danny **felt** tired after the game. (linking verb)

Modal Auxiliaries

Modal auxiliaries are used to express permission, possibility, ability, necessity, obligation, and intention. They are followed by main verbs that are in the base form. The common modal auxiliaries are *may, might, can, could, must, should, will,* and *would*.

Any amateur chef **may join** the committee. (permission)
We **might assign** dishes at the meeting. (possibility)
Blanca **can bake** delicious cakes. (ability)
Everyone **must agree** on the menu. (necessity)
Cooks **should prepare** enough food for everyone. (obligation)
Marco **will act** as the contact person. (intention)

Phrasal Verbs

Some transitive and intransitive verbs are phrasal verbs. A phrasal verb is a combination of a main verb and a preposition or an adverb. The noun or pronoun that follows a phrasal verb is the direct object.

He **looks after** his little brother on weekends.
Yesterday he **set up** the croquet set.
He **wakes up** with a smile each morning.

Principal Parts

The four basic parts of all verbs are the present, or base form; the past; the past participle; and the present participle. The past and past participles of regular verbs are formed by adding *-d* or *-ed* to the base form. The present participle is formed by adding *-ing*.

Base	Past	Past Participle	Present Participle
sail	sailed	sailed	sailing

Regular Verbs

The past and the past participles of a regular verb are formed by adding *-d* or *-ed* to the base form.

Base	Past	Past Participle
walk	walked	walked
smile	smiled	smiled
try	tried	tried
hop	hopped	hopped

Transitive Verbs

A transitive verb expresses an action that passes from a doer to a receiver. Every transitive verb has a receiver of the action. That receiver is the direct object.

> Sheila **kicked** the ball into the net.

Voice

Voice shows whether the subject of a transitive verb is the doer or the receiver of the action.

Active Voice

When a transitive verb is in the active voice, the subject is the doer of the action.

> Sheila **kicked** the winning goal.

Passive Voice

When a transitive verb is in the passive voice, the subject is the receiver of the action. A verb in the passive voice is formed by combining some form of *be* with the past participle of the main verb.

> The winning goal ***was kicked*** by Sheila.

Mechanics

Capitalization and Punctuation

Apostrophes

An apostrophe is used to show possession.

the man's coat   the boys' jackets

An apostrophe is used to show the omission of letters or numbers.

can't   we'll   the flood of '98

An apostrophe is used to show the plural of lowercase letters but not of capital letters unless the plural could be mistaken for a word

a's   *u*'s   *P*s   *U*'s   *A*'s

Capital Letters

A capital letter is used for the first word in a sentence, the first word in a direct quotation, and the first word of most lines of poetry and songs.

My dad asked, "**W**ould you like to take a trip?"

My country, 'tis of thee,
Sweet land of liberty.

A capital letter is used for proper nouns and proper adjectives.

Abraham **L**incoln   the **G**ettysburg **A**ddress
the **L**incoln **M**emorial   **W**ashington, **D.C.**
American hero   **K**entucky rail-splitter

A capital letter is used for a title when it precedes a person's name.

President Lincoln

A capital letter is used for the directions *North, South, East,* and *West* when they refer to sections of the country.

We left the **S**outh and drove north toward home.

A capital letter is used for the names of deities and sacred books.

Holy **S**pirit   **B**ible   **K**oran   **O**ld **T**estament

A capital letter is used for the principal words in titles (but not the articles *a, an,* or *the;* coordinating conjunctions; or prepositions unless they are the first or last words).

To **K**ill a **M**ockingbird   "**T**he **W**illow and the **G**ingko"

Capital letters are used for abbreviations of words that are capitalized.

Mrs.   **D**r.   **J**an.   **A**ve.

Colons

A colon is used before a list when terms such as *the following* or *as follows* are used.

I'd like to visit the following cities: New Orleans, San Francisco, and Chicago.

A colon is used after the salutation of a business letter.

Dear Senator Smith:

Commas

Commas are used to separate words in a series of three or more.

My family has two dogs, a cat, and some fish.

Commas are used to separate adjectives of equal importance before a noun.

It's a little, white, fluffy kitten.

Commas are used to set off the parts of addresses, place names, and dates.

Abraham Lincoln was born on February 12, 1809, in Hardin County, Kentucky.

Commas are used to set off words in direct address and parenthetical expressions.

Did you know, Eleanor, that the ship really sank?
Titanic was, as you may know, a popular movie.

Commas are used to set off nonrestrictive phrases and clauses.

The *Titanic*, a famous ocean liner, hit an iceberg.
The ship, which everyone had thought was unsinkable, disappeared under the icy waters.

Commas are used to set off a direct quotation or the parts of a divided quotation.

"I hope," said Mrs. Litwac, "you have all finished your work."

A comma is used before a coordinating conjunction that is used to connect clauses in a sentence.

I read the directions, but Joey built the model.

A comma is used after a conjunctive adverb in a compound sentence.

I missed a step in the directions; consequently, the model fell down.

Dashes

A dash is used to indicate a sudden change of thought.

My uncle cooked the whole dinner—a surprise to us all.

A dash (or dashes) is used to set off a series of words, phrases, or clauses in apposition.

The dinner—chicken, greens, and mashed potatoes—was delicious.

Exclamation Points

An exclamation point is used after most interjections and to end an exclamatory sentence.

Help! The rope is breaking!
Wow, that was close!

Hyphens

A hyphen is used to divide words between syllables at the end of a line.

The scientists studied the bone of the Tyranno-
saurus rex.

A hyphen is used in numbers from twenty-one to ninety-nine and to separate parts of some compound words.

drive-in   mother-in-law

A hyphen is used to form some temporary adjectives.

He completed the three-year project.

Italics

Italics are used to set off the titles of books, magazines, newspapers, movies, television series, ships, and works of art. If you are handwriting, use underlining for italics.

I saw a picture of the ***Titanic*** in the ***Atlantic Monthly***.

Periods

A period is used to end a declarative or an imperative sentence.

The dog is hungry. Please feed it.

A period is used after an abbreviation and after the initials in a name.

Co.   Mrs.   mi.   R. L. Stevenson

Question Marks

A question mark is used to end an interrogative sentence.

What do you feed your dog?

Quotation Marks

Quotation marks are used before and after direct quotations and around the parts of a divided quotation.

"Why," asked my brother, "didn't you play the game?"

Quotation marks are used to set off the titles of stories, poems, songs, magazine and newspaper articles, television shows, and radio programs.

They sang "Deep River" and "Amazing Grace."

Single quotation marks are used to set off quoted material within a quotation.

"Did they sing 'America the Beautiful'?" Salma asked.

Semicolons

A semicolon is used to separate clauses in a compound sentence when they are not joined by a conjunction.

It rained all afternoon; the game was cancelled.

A semicolon is used to separate clauses in a compound sentence that are connected by a conjunctive adverb.

The water washed out the flowerbeds; furthermore, it flooded the basement.

Semicolons are used to separate phrases or clauses of the same type that include internal punctuation.

> There were also floods on July 8, 2001; October 22, 2003; and August 15, 2005.

A semicolon is used before expressions such as *for example* and *namely* when they are used to introduce examples.

> Many streets were under water; namely, Morris, Elm, Cornelia, and State.

Index

Acknowledgments

Art and Photography

When there is more than one picture on a page, credits are supplied in sequence, left to right, top to bottom. Page positions are abbreviated as follows: **(t)** top, **(c)** center, **(b)** bottom, **(l)** left, **(r)** right.

Photos and illustrations not acknowledged are either owned by Loyola Press or from royalty-free sources including but not limited to Alamy, Art Resource, Big Stock, Bridgeman, Corbis/ Veer, Dreamstime, Fotosearch, Getty Images, North Wind Images, Photoedit, Smithsonian, Wikipedia. Loyola Press has made every effort to locate the copyright holders for the cited works used in this publication and to make full acknowledgment for their use. In the case of any omissions, the Publisher will be pleased to make suitable acknowledgments in future editions.

iStockphoto, Frontmatter: iii, iv, v, vi, vii, viii **Section 1:** 2, 3, 5, 6, 7, 8, 9, 11, 16 **Section 2:** 18, 20, 22, 23, 25, 26 **Section 3:** 32, 34, 37, 38, 39, 40, 42, 43, 45, 46, 47, 48, 51, 53, 56 **Section 4:** 58, 59, 60, 61, 62, 63, 64, 66, 68, 69, 70, 71, 72, 73, 74, 77, 78, 79, 82 **Section 5:** 84, 85, 87, 88, 89, 92, 93, 94, 95, 96, 99, 102, 103, 104, 105, 108 **Section 6:** 110, 111, 112, 113, 114, 115, 116, 117, 118, 119 **Section 7:** 124, 125, 126, 127, 128, 129, 130, 131, 138 **Section 8:** 140, 141, 142, 144, 145, 146, 148, 150, 151, 152, 154, 158, 160, 161, 164 **Section 9:** 167, 168, 170, 171, 172, 173, 175, 176 **Section 10:** 183, 185, 187, 189, 191 **Section 11:** 198, 200, 204, 205, 206, 208, 215 **Chapter 1:** 222, 223, 226, 227, 228, 231, 232, 233, 234, 235, 236, 237, 238, 239, 240, 241, 242, 243, 245, 247, 250, 251, 259 **Chapter 2:** 260, 261, 263, 264, 265, 267, 268, 271, 272, 273, 274, 275, 276, 277, 278, 281, 282, 283, 285, 287, 288, 289, 296, 297 **Chapter 3:** 298, 299, 301, 302, 303, 304, 306, 308, 310, 311, 312, 313, 314, 315, 316, 317, 318, 319, 320, 321, 322, 324, 325, 326, 327, 329, 330, 331, 333, 335 **Chapter 4:** 336, 337, 339, 340, 341, 342, 343, 344, 346, 347, 349, 350, 352, 353, 354, 355, 356, 357, 358, 359, 364, 366, 367, 369, 371, 373 **Chapter 5:** 374, 375, 376, 377, 378, 379, 380, 381, 382, 384, 386, 387, 389, 390, 391, 393, 394, 395, 396, 397, 398, 400, 401, 403, 404, 406 **Chapter 6:** 412, 413, 416, 420, 421, 424, 425, 429, 435, 437, 441 **Chapter 7:** 450, 451, 462, 463, 464, 465, 471, 472 **Chapter 8:** 488, 497, 500, 505, 506, 511 **Chapter 9:** 166, 168, 169, 174, 177, 180 **Chapter 10:** 182, 183, 186, 188, 189, 190, 194 **Chapter 11:** 196, 197, 199, 200, 201, 202, 203, 205, 207, 209, 210, 213, 214, 215, 220, 204–205, 218–219

Jupiterimages Unlimited, Frontmatter: v, viii **Section 2:** 19 **Section 4:** 67, 79 **Section 5:** 87, 94, 95 **Section 7:** 135 **Section 8:** 145, 155, 156, 157 **Section 9:** 166, 168, 169, 174, 177, 180 **Section 10:** 182, 183, 186, 188, 189, 190, 194 **Section 11:** 196, 197, 199, 200, 201, 202, 203, 205, 207, 209, 210, 213, 214, 215, 220, 204–205, 218–219 **Chapter 2:** 260 **Chapter 3:** 307, 308, 328 **Chapter 4:** 341, 364 **Chapter 5:** 388, 389 **Chapter 6:** 412, 414, 415, 416, 417, 418, 420, 425, 427, 429, 431, 432, 433, 435, 436, 437, 440, 442, 443, 444, 447, 448, 449 **Chapter 7:** 450, 450–451, 451, 453, 454, 454–455, 455, 457–458, 457, 459, 465, 466, 467, 468–469, 468, 469, 470, 472–473, 473, 474, 475, 477, 478, 479, 480, 481, 483, 484, 485, 487 **Chapter 8:** 488, 489, 490, 491, 492, 492–493, 496, 499, 502, 505, 506, 507, 508, 509, 515, 516, 518, 520, 522–523, 524–525

Frontmatter: iii Clockwise from upper left (a) Stock. **(b)** iStockphoto. **(c)** iStockphoto. **(d)** iStockphoto. **(e)** iStockphoto. **(f)** iStockphoto. **(g)** Hulton Archive/Getty. **vii Clockwise from upper left (a)** iStockphoto. **(b)** iStockphoto. **(c)** Kathryn Seckman Kirsch. **(d)** iStockphoto. **(e)** Leland Bobbe/ Getty. **(f)** iStockphoto.

Section 1: 10(tl) Stinger/Getty Images. **11(t)** Antar Dayal/ Getty Images.

Section 2: 30 Bruce Laurance/Getty Images.

Section 3: 33(t) Hulton Archive/Getty Images. **35** Michael Ochs Archives/2007 Getty Images. **36** HultonArchive/2003 Getty Images. **39(b)** Girl Ray/Getty Images. **41** Michael Dwyer/Alamy. **44** Antar Dayal/Getty Images. **50** William Manning/Alamy. **51(t)** Pictorial Press Ltd/Alamy.

Section 4: 64(b) Time & Life Pictures/Getty Images. **65** Pictorial Press Ltd/Alamy. **76** PanoramicImages/Getty Images. **77(b)** Tim Wright/Corbis.

Section 5: 91(t) Kathryn Seckman Kirsch. **91(b)** Trinity Mirror/ Mirrorpix/Alamy. **96(t)** AFP/2007 Getty Images. **97** Dinodia Images/Alamy. **98(t)** North Wind Picture Archives/Alamy. **100** North Wind Picture Archives/Alamy. **101(t)** Colby McLemore/ Alamy. **101(b)** Time & Life Pictures/Carl Iwasaki/Getty Images. **102(bl)** Panoramic Images/Getty Images.

Section 6: 122 Hulton Archive/Getty Images.

Section 7: 125(c) Danita Delimont/Alamy. **131(t)** Renaud Visage. **132** North Wind Picture Archives/Alamy. **135(t)** The Print Collector/Alamy. **143(t)** North Wind Picture Archives/Alamy. **143(b)** Classic Image/Alamy. **147** North Wind Picture Archives/ Alamy. **149** Ellen Rooney/Getty Images. **153(t)** Peter Horree/ Alamy. **153(b)** North Wind Picture Archives/Alamy. **159(t)** Karen Kasmauski/Science Faction/Corbis. **159(b)** 3D4Medical.com. **172(t)** Robert Harding Picture Library Ltd/Alamy. **173(tr)** Cynthia Baldauf.

Chapter 1: 222(b) Neil Fletcher/Getty Images.

Chapter 2: 260(tl) Kathryn Seckman Kirsch. **263(t)** Susan Estelle Kwas. **269(b)** PhotoStockFile/Alamy. **273(b)** Kathryn Seckman Kirsch.

Chapter 3: 289(br) Kathryn Seckman Kirsch. **293(r)** Phil Martin Photography. **295** Phil Martin Photography. **298(bl)** Phil Martin Photography. **299(cr)** Phil Martin Photography. **301(b)** Mango Productions/Corbis. **309** Blasius Erlinger/Zefa Photography/ Corbis. **334** Motofish Images/Flirt/Veer. **335** Phil Martin Photography.

Chapter 4: 337(c) Kathryn Seckman Kirsch. **337(tr)** Kathryn Seckman Kirsch. **337(bl)** Kathryn Seckman Kirsch. **338** Susan Estelle Kwas. **349(bl)** Phil Martin Photography. **351** North Wind Picture Archives/Alamy. **353(t)** Leland Bobbe/Getty Images. **357(t)** Clive Brunskill/Getty Images. **360** Phil Martin Photography. **361(t)** Nathan Benn/Alamy. **365** Phil Martin Photography. **369(bl)** Phil Martin Photography.

Literature

Common Proofreading Marks

Use these proofreading marks to mark changes when you proofread. Remember to use a colored pencil to make your changes.

Symbol	Meaning	Example
¶	begin new paragraph	over. ¶Begin a new
⌒	close up space	close u͜p space
∧	insert	students ∧think *should*
℘	delete, omit	that the the book
/	lowercase letter	/Mathematics
∾	letters are reversed	letters are revesred
≡	capitalize	washington
⌄" ⌄"	quotation	I am, I said.
⊙	add period	Marta drank tea⊙